The Play World

THE MAX KADE RESEARCH INSTITUTE SERIES:
GERMANS BEYOND EUROPE

Series Editor *Founding Editor*
Daniel Purdy   A. Gregg Roeber

The Max Kade Research Institute Series is an outlet for scholarship that examines the history and culture of German-speaking communities in America and across the globe from the early modern period to the present. Books in this series examine the movements of the German-speaking diaspora as influenced by forces such as migration, colonization, war, research, religious missions, or trade. This series explores the historical and cultural depictions of the international networks that connect these communities, as well as linguistic relations between German and other languages within European global networks.

This series is a project of the Max Kade Research Institute located on Penn State's campus. It was founded in 1993 thanks to a grant from the Max Kade Foundation, New York.

The Play World

TOYS, TEXTS, AND THE
TRANSATLANTIC GERMAN CHILDHOOD

Patricia Anne Simpson

The Pennsylvania State University Press
University Park, Pennsylvania

Library of Congress Cataloging-in-Publication Data

Names: Simpson, Patricia Anne, 1958– author.
Title: The play world : toys, texts, and the transatlantic German childhood / Patricia Anne Simpson.
Other titles: Max Kade German-American Research Institute series.
Description: University Park, Pennsylvania : The Pennsylvania State University Press, [2020] | Series: The Max Kade Research Institute series: Germans beyond Europe | Includes bibliographical references and index.
Summary: "Examines German theories and practices of play, parenting, and pedagogy from 1631 to 1912. Explores the role of the domestic sphere and home economies in establishing transatlantic networks that influenced the emergence of gender, class, race, and religious identities for Germans beyond Europe"—Provided by publisher.
Identifiers: LCCN 2020027018 | ISBN 9780271086996 (cloth)
Subjects: LCSH: Play—Germany—History. | Play—United States—History. | Play (Philosophy)—History. | Toys—Germany—History. | Toys—United States—History.
Classification: LCC HQ782.S56 2020 | DDC 306.4/810943—dc23
LC record available at https://lccn.loc.gov/2020027018

Copyright © 2020 Patricia Anne Simpson
All rights reserved
Printed in the United States of America
Published by The Pennsylvania State University Press,
University Park, PA 16802–1003

The Pennsylvania State University Press is a member of the Association of University Presses.

It is the policy of The Pennsylvania State University Press to use acid-free paper. Publications on uncoated stock satisfy the minimum requirements of American National Standard for Information Sciences—Permanence of Paper for Printed Library Material, ANSI Z39.48–1992.

Sarah Marie Simpson (1926–2018)
In memoriam

Contents

List of Illustrations (ix)
Preface (xi)
Acknowledgments (xv)

Introduction: The Play World: Toys, Texts, and the Transatlantic German Childhood (1)

1. The Protestant Play Ethic (30)

2. Professional Parenting: Enlightened Play (59)

3. Revolutions in Play (92)

4. Colonizing Childhoods: The African Imaginary (116)

5. Ethnographic Play and the American Imaginary (149)

6. The Home and the Nation (183)

7. Empire of Toys (208)

   Conclusion: "A Very Brilliant House" (233)

   Notes (243)
   Bibliography (260)
   Index (274)

Illustrations

1. Johann Zoffany, *John, Fourteenth Lord Willoughby de Broke, and His Family*, ca. 1766 (2)
2. "Probieren geht über Studieren," from *Auerbach's Kinder-Kalender auf das Jahr 1889* (Leipzig: Fernau, 1889) (20)
3. "Morgenstunde hat Gold im Munde," from *Auerbach's Kinder-Kalender auf das Jahr 1889* (Leipzig: Fernau, 1889) (20)
4. Anna Köferlin, "Kinderhaus," Nuremberg, 1631 (41)
5. Frontispiece from Ernst Gottlieb Woltersdorf, *Kinder-Lieder* (New York: Amerikanische Traktat-Gesellschaft, 1823) (45)
6. Visitation of the Magi, from Ernst Gottlieb Woltersdorf, *Kinder-Lieder* (New York: Amerikanische Traktat-Gesellschaft, 1823) (51)
7. Daniel Nikolaus Chodowiecki, "Die Wochenstube," ca. 1770 (60)
8. Title page from *Oekonomisches Handbuch für Frauenzimmer*, vol. 2, 4th ed. (Stuttgart: Steinkopf, 1826) (64)
9. Hessian figurines, Staffordshire, ca. 1820 (93)
10. Guillotine, from *Beschreibung der Hinrichtung des Königs von Frankreich Ludwig XVI*, ca. 1793 (101)
11. Carved bone guillotine scene, 1815, from The Clive L. Lloyd collection (101)
12. Guillotine, ca. 1793, from Karl Gröber, *Children's Toys of Bygone Days: A History of Playthings of All Peoples from Prehistoric Times to the XIXth Century* (London: B. T. Blatsford, 1928), pl. 153 (101)
13. "Emigrant jouant au yoyo," ca. 1792 (107)
14. "Belle Adeline faisant aller son Emigran," ca. 1792 (107)
15. Johann Conrad Seekatz, *Die zwölf Monatsbilder: Januar*, ca. 1759–63 (118)
16. *Catalog von E. Steiger in New York* (New York: E. Steiger & Company, 1883) (122)
17. Cover illustration from *Ein Kongo-Neger* (Stuttgart: Verlag von Rob. Bardtenschlager ca. 1900) (123)
18. Gemini, from *Auerbach's Deutscher Kinder-Kalender auf das Jahr 1889* (Leipzig: Fernau Verlag, 1889) (135)
19. Cancer, from *Auerbach's Deutscher Kinder-Kalender auf das Jahr 1889* (Leipzig: Fernau Verlag, 1889) (135)
20. Leo, from *Auerbach's Deutscher Kinder-Kalender auf das Jahr 1889* (Leipzig: Fernau Verlag, 1889) (135)
21. Scorpio, from *Auerbach's Deutscher Kinder-Kalender auf das Jahr 1889* (Leipzig: Fernau Verlag, 1889) (135)

22. Libra, from *Auerbach's Deutscher Kinder-Kalender auf das Jahr 1889* (Leipzig: Fernau Verlag, 1889) (137)
23. "The nutcracker," from "Knecht Ruprecht in Kamerun," attributed to A. Bahr, *Münchener Bilderbogen*, vol. 2, 2. Auflage (Munich: Braun & Schneider, 1892) (146)
24. The sacrificial doll, from "Knecht Ruprecht in Kamerun," attributed to A. Bahr, *Münchener Bilderbogen*, vol. 2, 2. Auflage (Munich: Braun & Schneider, 1892) (147)
25. Max Loose, illustration of Caschumka and Anita for "Die kleine Urwälderin," from *Auerbach's Kinder-Kalender auf das Jahr 1902* (Leipzig: Fernau, 1902) (168)
26. Max Loose, illustration of Anita and the monkey for "Die kleine Urwälderin," from *Auerbach's Kinder-Kalender auf das Jahr 1902* (Leipzig: Fernau, 1902) (170)
27. J. H. Pehling toy store advertisement, from *Deutscher Pionier am Río de la Plata*, newspaper, 30 November 1879, no. 143, 2 Jahrgang, S. 2 (171)
28. Fritz Koch-Gotha, illustration of the three chiefs for "Eine Indianergeschichte," from *Auerbach's Kinder-Kalender auf das Jahr 1904* (Leipzig: Fernau, 1904) (179)
29. Fritz Koch-Gotha, illustration of the defeated chiefs for "Eine Indianergeschichte," from *Auerbach's Kinder-Kalender auf das Jahr 1904* (Leipzig: Fernau, 1904) (181)
30. Fritz von Uhde, *Die Kinderstube*, 1889 (186)
31. "Unterricht in Schule und Haus," from *E. Steiger in New York*, June 1883 (192)
32. "The First Gift," from *Catalogue of Steiger's Kindergarten Material*, June 1883 (192)
33. "The Third Gift," from *Catalogue of Steiger's Kindergarten Material*, June 1883 (193)
34. "The Fourth Gift," from *Catalogue of Steiger's Kindergarten Material*, June 1883 (193)
35. "For Boys and Girls," "For Girls and Boys," from *Catalogue of Steiger's Kindergarten Material*, June 1883 (194)
36. "Embroidering," from *Catalogue of Steiger's Kindergarten Material*, June 1883 (194)
37. The A. Schoenhut Company's circus bandwagon, 1910–30 (216)
38. The A. Schoenhut Company's "Teddy's Adventures in Africa" (221)
39. The A. Schoenhut Company's "Negro Dude," ca. 1907–18 (221)
40. "Sing Mama, I Play!" from The A. Schoenhut Company, *Forty Years of Toy Making, 1872–1912* (Philadelphia: A. Schoenhut, 1912) (225)
41. Christmas advertisement, "Schoenhut Toys, Made in U.S.A. Since 1872," 1918 (240)

Preface

I never intended to write a book about play, nor to stray so far from my gravitational center in the literature and philosophy of the long eighteenth century, but ultimately I could not look away from real toy stories and what they still tell us about the hegemony of a German play world. In 2007, while conducting research on violence in the contemporary Federal Republic, I sought distraction and began visiting toy museums. Wandering through the Spielzeug-Museum in Sonneberg, I encountered dioramas of aristocrats in miniature, with exquisitely wrought furnishings and accoutrements, not least among them a lavishly detailed tea set—the scene complete with African servants. Around the corner, a miniature mechanical rack, that reliable medieval instrument of torture, supported a wax doll that stretched with the turn of a wheel. I paused before a showcase with an 1845 model derived from Jonathan Swift's satirical *Gulliver's Travels or Travels into Several Remote Nations of the World* (1726). The captured gigantic Gulliver, trussed with a weave of threads by the depicted Lilliputians, made my sense of scale began to reel as I mentally flipped through my recall of Susan Stewart's analyses of the gigantic and the miniature (*On Longing*, 1984). A question began to formulate about the model of realizing a particular version of the world, drawn from the reader's imagination; about the mobility of theories, objects, and ideologies; and about the role of texts and toys in constructing and appropriating "remote nations of the world." So I embarked on a decade-long search for a narrative about the purpose of play, the intersection of material culture and cultural identities, and the past of the future-oriented study of childhood and its accessories.

Contemporary discourse is suffused with play imperatives, but defining the activity and its indispensability takes different tacks. In popular terms, working groups in institutions, from the corporation to the academy, have been rebaptized "sandboxes"; language acquisition pedagogy extols the use of play and games in the classroom; Google employees have a range of options to transform work into play. Without the freedom and stress-reduced environment that play can produce, creativity and the imagination suffer. The intervention of neuroscience, combined with philosophical, pedagogical, and practical arguments, theories, and anecdotes, respectively, insists that human existence and the play impulse are synonymous. Neurobiologist Gerald Hüther and philosopher Christoph Quarch collaborated on a trade book (2016) that sounds an alarm: the functionalizing and economic drive in modern life endanger play, effectively rendering human beings an endangered species. Nothing less than freedom and beauty in life are at stake: "Deshalb werben wir für unseren zivilisatorischen Imperativ: Rettet das Spiel!" (For this reason, we are advocating for our civilizational imperative: Save play!). In accessible prose, with cultural context provided by the usual suspects, including Friedrich Schiller and Johann Huizinga, the cross-disciplinary pair walk the reader through the effect of proper play on the brain—its ability to create, coexist, and achieve "breakthrough innovations." The authors take pains to differentiate between the conditions for real play and leisure activities that trigger stress or require supervision. That type of play has a history with a particularly German component within a sustained deliberation, lasting more than three centuries, on the nature of play.

The imperative to "save" the game and play raises ethical questions, particularly with regard to causative violence and conditioning adult behavior. A cursory Google search yields mostly questions. High-profile acts of violence or aberrance tend to usher in studies and headlines, yet there are staunch and opposing arguments over whether there exists a direct cause-effect relationship between play and criminal behavior. *New York Times* articles popularize scientific studies, fueling debates about the neuroscience of play, or the detrimental effects of overscheduling the child ("We Have Ruined Childhood," Kim Brooke, 17 August 2019, for example), or, by contrast, what works well ("What Makes Berlin a Playground Paradise," Anna Winger, 1 June 2016). The nonhovering parent who allows the child to take a risk at the playground gains the upper hand. Somehow, German play yielded happier children.

In December 2018, I followed those leads all the way from Lincoln to Hello Kitty Land (Sanrio Puroland) in Tokyo. There, I saw firsthand the hegemonic influence of the German model of childhood: "A musical that is a dream collaboration bringing together the internationally loved Hello Kitty with the classic tale of Alice. Get ready for an exciting adventure in a magical land of fantasy and fun!" Attraction number one, as listed in the "Parade and Attraction Information" guide, was performed in the "Märchen Theater." Outside the performance space, cases displayed books and films based on a distinctly German tradition of childhood, fantasy, and the dangers and dramas of attachment to playthings. The words themselves, printed in German Gothic script, unfurl atop musical symbols, such as the G-clef, on a substance that resembles the wood of half-timber houses. The material itself—or a reasonable facsimile thereof—evokes the architecture inhabited by E. T. A. Hoffmann's *The Nutcracker*, which is featured prominently under the glass. In the gift shop, just about everything is available in miniature for purchase. Several books on a range of topics, from female leadership to the rise of far-right populism in Europe and the United States, have appeared while I continued to follow leads toward answering my questions. This book is the result of that journey.

September 2019
Lincoln and Bozeman

Acknowledgments

In writing this book, as in many scholarly (ad)ventures, I accumulated debts of gratitude. With deep appreciation, I would like to acknowledge the help and support of colleagues and research institutions for their contribution to my efforts. For introducing me to the dollhouse collection at the Germanisches Nationalmuseum and for her unflagging devotion to the cultural life of Nuremberg, I thank Dorle Messer-Schmidt. Her energy and dedication sustained a group of artists while we worked on a new Orpheus opera, for which I had been commissioned to write the libretto. Wearing my more scholarly hat, I extend thanks to the colleagues who listened to a series of papers on the miniature guillotine and the Reign of Terror, on interiority and epistemologies of the playroom, on paternity and play, and on Goethe's favorite toys. Their invaluable feedback helped shape the development of this project.

The German Historical Institute, Washington, DC, provided me with the financial support needed to conduct research at the Joseph P. Horner Memorial Library, German Society of Pennsylvania, in 2011. For their incredible and enthusiastic assistance, I thank special collections librarians Violet Lutz and her successor, Bettina Hess. On more than one occasion, Victoria Gray, collections manager at the Strong National Museum of Play, came to the rescue with source material and image permissions. Inspiration came from many sources. At the Atkins Goethe Conference (State College, PA, October 2017), comments made during a discussion of my presentation on "Frankfurt School Philosophy and the Age of Goethe: Elective Aversions?" shaped my overall argument. In particular, for their interventions in the conversation, I owe thanks to Eva Geulen, who raised the notion of Goethe's eccentricity, and Simon Richter, who pointed to Herbert Marcuse as a potential alternative Frankfurt School–model of play. Walter Benjamin's essays on toys and material culture were the focus of my remarks at the roundtable. More generally, I express continued appreciation for the inspiration and support from friends and colleagues of the Goethe Society of North America (GSNA). A particularly vibrant scholarly community, the GSNA sustains a complex and inviting conversation about the *Goethezeit* and the long eighteenth century, from which I profit immensely and persistently. I am indebted to Edgar Landgraf and Elliott Schreiber, editors of *Play in the Age of Goethe* (Bucknell University Press, 2020), for their insightful reading of an earlier version of chapter 3. In addition, I thank Bucknell University Press for allowing me to reprint sections of that book chapter here.

Additionally, the German Historical Institute (GHI) commissioned me to contribute an entry to their online collaborative research project on immigrant entrepreneurship. The research that went into my article on the German American immigrant entrepreneur and toy maker Albert Schoenhut proved central to my understanding of German toys and their impact in the transatlantic world ("Albert Schoenhut," in *Immigrant Entrepreneurship: German-American Business Biographies, 1720 to the Present*, vol. 3, edited by Giles R. Hoyt, German Historical Institute, Washington, DC, published August 2015). This article, the basis of chapter 7, is to be reprinted in full in a catalogue for a toy exhibition in Schoenhut's hometown of Göppingen, Germany. I thank the GHI for permission to republish portions of that work here, and to Dr. Karl-Heinz Rueß, director of Göppingen Museums, whose research clarified the genealogy of A. Schoenhut and his immigration to the United States. The German version of my article, "Albert Schoenhut: Ein Lebensweg von Göppingen nach Philadelphia," is scheduled to appear in the catalogue *Schoenhut Toys: Wie der Göppinger Drechsler Albert Schoenhut in Philadelphia zu einem der bedeutendsten Spielzeugfabrikanten der USA wurde*, edited by Karl-Heinz Rueß (Göppingen, 2020).

I owe gratitude on personal and professional levels to Dr. Adjai Paulin Oloukpona-Yinnon and Dr. Anna Babka for their invitation to present my lecture "Beispielhafte Bekehrungen: Interkontinentale Kolonialkulturen, 1840–1932" (Exemplary conversions: Intercontinental colonial cultures) at the conference organized by the Humboldt-Stiftung and international scholars on "Germanistik als Sprach- Kultur- und Geschichtswissenschaft: Der 'neue deutsche (Kolonial)roman' in kulturwissenschaftlicher, interkultureller und postkolonialer Perspektive." It was an honor to be hosted by the Université de Lomé, Faculté des Lettres et Sciences Humaines in Lomé, Togo (April 2014). This lecture appeared later as "Transatlantische Afrikabilder (1840–1911) aus postkolonialer Sicht" (Transatlantic images of Africa, 1840–1911, from a postcolonial perspective), in *Postkolonialität denken—Spektren germanistischer Forschung in Togo*, edited by Obi Assemboni, Anna Babka, und Axel Dunker (Vienna: Praesens, 2017), 253–65, which lays the foundation for chapter 4. My debt of gratitude extends to the organizers and audience of the conference and the editors of the volume, and to Praesens Verlag for kind permission to reprint previously published material here. I had an opportunity to present an English-language version of this work, "Race, Religion, and Revolution: German-American Images of Africa, 1840–1932," at Williams College (19 February 2014). Dr. Helga Druxes made this opportunity possible, and I thank the colleagues and students at Williams for their lively contributions to the development of this work. With inexplicable enthusiasm, Dr. Druxes also provided feedback on an important chapter draft within hours—it is a privilege to work with such a colleague.

The analysis of the "jungle girl" story in chapter 5 appears under the title "Colonising the Play World: Toys, Texts and Colonial Fantasies in German Children's Stories Around 1900" in the *Jahrbuch der Gesellschaft für Kinder- und Jugendliteraturforschung*. The editors, Gabrielle von Glasenapp, Emer O'Sullivan, Caroline Roeder, Michael Staiger, and Ingrid Tomkowiak, along with two anonymous readers, gave me useful feedback that also strengthened the chapter, and I thank them. The colleagues in Lincoln of the Program in Nineteenth-Century Studies provided essential feedback on an earlier presentation of this material at our annual workshop. Christy Hyman, PhD candidate in the College of Arts and Sciences, Center for Research in Digital Humanities, earned my deepest appreciation. Her enthusiasm reignited my commitment to this project at a time when the demands of chairing distanced me from a sense of local intellectual community. The College of Arts and Sciences supported the final phase of this work with an ENHANCE grant.

Patricia Halfpenny, curator emerita of ceramics and glass, Winterthur Museum, helped in identifying and dating the Hessian figurines whose image appears in chapter 3. Independent scholar of early English earthenware and author Myrna Schkolne separately responded to my "cold call" inquiry about the same Hessian figurines (ca. 1820) while on a vast internet image search; both shared expertise, great attention to detail, and generosity. Schkolne immediately granted me permission to use her photograph of the figures, and I am deeply grateful for her assistance and expertise. Special thanks go to Stephanie Lloyd Downs, daughter of the collector and historian Clive L. Lloyd, for permission to reprint the image of a model guillotine from his work—and for sharing with me a memory about the process of collecting artifacts of war beyond the battlefield.

Colleagues, friends, coauthors, and coeditors have been generous and patient in their willingness to read drafts and abstracts; all provided insightful feedback. For their assistance, I thank James D. Le Sueur, Eve Moore, Birgit Tautz, Gail Hart, Marc Mueller, and Yvonne Toepfer. Dr. Todd Larkin, associate professor of art history at Montana State University, shared his expertise in eighteenth-century European portraiture and guided me toward crucial source information when I found myself in his field. Dr. Christoph Wingertszahn, director of the Goethe-Museum in Düsseldorf, kindly extended an invitation to speak about Goethe's favorite toys, "Goethes Lieblingsspielzeuge," at the museum (17 May 2017). I benefitted greatly from his questions and comments, along with the vibrant Q&A with the audience. Through every phase of review and production, the project gained strength and momentum only with the help of admired and appreciated colleagues at The Pennsylvania State University Press, and I thank Daniel Purdy, Kathryn Bourque Yahner, Maddie Caso, and Brian Bowles for their efforts and enthusiasm. Two anonymous readers provided amazing feedback, for which I am grateful.

This project has accompanied my own "migrations" across country and continents. At every locale, I have found the necessary Patience and Fortitude—so are the stately marble lions named at the entrance of the New York Public Library—inside welcoming research centers. The Rose Main Reading Room inspired hours of research and revising, which took place as well in numerous libraries and archives that have hosted my fierce reading and, I am assured, comical keyboarding. I thank the accommodating colleagues at the Bozeman Public Library, the Brewster Ladies Library, the Ibero-Amerikanisches Institut, Staatsbibliothek zu Berlin, the Biblioteca Nacional Mariano Moreno (Buenos Aires), the Biblioteca Nacional de Chile in Santiago, and, closer to "home," the Love Library at the University of Nebraska–Lincoln. I could not live without interlibrary loan. Nor without the quiet (or boisterous) hospitality and quality beverages at Treeline, Zocalo, Café Schneiderei, The Coffee House, and The Foundry. Never underestimate the grace of baristas.

Not least, I continue to draw strength and inspiration from the love of my family. My husband, Theo Lipfert, who accompanied me to Sanrio Puroland, has continued to encourage my ambitious research projects with the mantra "You should *so* do that." This work began when our two sons were still at home in Bozeman. Jackson and Colton are discerning critics and occasional skeptics. Upon discovering that I was writing a book about play, they observed, virtually in unison, "You can take the fun out of anything." For all the help and compassion bestowed on me, there are shortcomings, and they are my own. Finally, my parents, William J. Simpson and Sarah Marie Cardillo Simpson (1926–2018), worked three full-time jobs between them (with frequent overtime and seasonal retail) so that we could play, attend university, and choose our own paths, and I am forever grateful. This book is dedicated to my mother.

Introduction
The Play World

TOYS, TEXTS, AND THE TRANSATLANTIC GERMAN CHILDHOOD

In early modern to Enlightenment Europe, discourses about play obtain for adults as well as children, frequently in shared private spaces that are, nevertheless, for public consumption. The former engage in a range of activities associated with leisure, among them cards, gambling, and flirting, with the occasional blurring of social, class, and gender boundaries.[1] In the conversation piece (fig. 1) by German-born and -trained artist Johan Zoffany (1733–1810), the family at breakfast in their estate encapsulates the intergenerationally shared play world of the privileged. Zoffany moved to London, where he enjoyed commissions, exhibitions, and success. His conversation paintings document, with a certain naturalism, intimate family moments (albeit for public display). Zoffany captured these scenes "made up from the small pleasures of life in the family or with friends."[2] Art historian Mary Webster provides an expert voiceover to this painting of Lord Willoughby de Broke at breakfast, narrating the scene with a description of the objects in the room, from the Persian rug, the Chinese tea service, and the japanned tray to the Italian seascape poised above the mantel. The mother, Lady Louisa, holds their young daughter, Louisa (born 1765), while the younger son, George (1763–1773), "surreptitiously clutches the tray and seizes a piece of toast."[3] With more an appetite for play, their older son, John (1762–1820), enters the room with his red wooden horse on wheels. The father wags a finger at the toast thief while the mother casts an eye toward the child with his toy.

FIG. 1 Johann Zoffany, *John, Fourteenth Lord Willoughby de Broke, and His Family*, ca. 1766. Oil on canvas, 101.9 × 127.3 cm. The Paul Getty Museum, Los Angeles. 96.PA.312. Photo: The J. Paul Getty Trust. CC BY 4.0.

In its time, this painting enjoyed great popularity, admired for "its action and naturalness, seeming to catch a lively moment in the intimate life of a father and mother and their small children."[4] Beyond admiration for the artistry and apparent spontaneity, other dynamics are visible. The family hierarchy regulates pleasure and play, need and consumption. For my purposes, this conversation piece is emblematic of the conundrum at the center of the Atlantic play world. Zoffany's painting instantiates the illusive logic of play: it is simultaneously reserved for the private sphere—the breakfast room—and put on display to demonstrate the intactness of the family unit. It has purpose but must be subject to regulation. Virtually all discourses about childhood and nurturing orient themselves toward a model that insists on the child as an essential subject, integral to the construction of public identities. Play of a mimetic and emulative nature takes precedence in my analysis. Humans play: this basic truth applies across temporal and geographic boundaries. That German eighteenth-century cultures continue to teach the world to play is admittedly a bold assertion, one that I hope to justify. Perhaps more audaciously, my story reveals the ways in which a modern notion of "model" childhoods is German, with its taut dialectic of innocence and guilt, reward and punishment. My aim with this book is to increase the visibility of domestic economies in the transcultural construction of the play world.

Researchers who observe similarities between biological play drives in animal and human activities note that there is something like a play circuit in the human brain, though the scholarly community has not always been so receptive to examinations of the relationship between empirical study and the emotions, particularly with regard to the presumed innocence of the child at play.[5] While the German term *Spielwelt* (play world) can encompass not only the actual spaces of children's activities but also imaginative terrain, it more conventionally denotes the former. When ethnographer and historian Ingeborg Weber-Kellerman calls attention to the variation in meaning of the *Kinderzimmer* in the nineteenth century, for example, she describes the transformation from a *Schlafraum* (sleeping space) to a *Spielwelt*.[6] Though there are hints at more connotative usage, the term signifies a physical, architectural space. Renate Gehrke-Riedlin observes that the eighteenth-century *Kinderstube*, segregated as it was from the "real world," was transformed into the primary locus of instruction. As she argues, *Kindheit*, or childhood, became a *Schulkindheit*, or the school of childhood: the "playroom" proper manifests itself only later in the century.[7] The play room of the domicile, as I demonstrate in this study, lays the cornerstone of the play world. Though purportedly shielded from destructive, disruptive forces, the innocent imaginary of childhood is poised on the edge between entertainment and edification, between public spectacle and private space—and always between the opposing desires of the familiar and the unknown.

Philosophies of play emerged alongside considerations of real-world spaces, and canonical German thinkers exerted considerable force over this discourse. Around 1800, adult leisure activities retained the patina of play, and there was considerable interplay between the adult imagination and the child's play world.[8] The family scene of instruction and breakfast in the Zoffany painting captures the oldest child entering the room, tugging the play world with him. The intersection of social forces, the encoding of bourgeois subjectivity as ensconced in the domestic realm, and the emerging institutionalization of pedagogy attracted philosophical debate. The cultivation of play practices in the eighteenth century formed the basis of deliberations about a play imperative. Developing from sustained engagement with Immanuel Kant (1724–1804), especially his *Critique of Judgment* (1790), for example, discourses about play subsume it into the cognitive category of aesthetic judgment and the emancipatory imaginary. In 1790, Kant describes play as "an occupation that is agreeable on its own account," in contrast to labor, "which on its own account is disagreeable."[9] Friedrich Schiller (1759–1805), in his *Letters on the Aesthetic Education of Man* (1795), identifies the *Spieltrieb*, or play drive, as the expression of human freedom. This popularization of a play imperative, defined in opposition to work, forms the core of debates about play and games. Either they constitute a form of practice for labor or an oppositional diversion therefrom, or play enfolds the essence of humanity and human freedom as a right and a biological drive that manifests in the realm of the aesthetic. Both positions interest me, for historically, the former is ascribed to the segregating of childhood as a discrete phase, whereas the latter remains the provenance of the adult.

Interpreting this legacy, Herbert Marcuse crafts an argument about the aesthetic as a necessary condition for negotiating and imaginatively negating the dominance of reason, the optimization of labor, and the organization of repressed instincts, in a blended lexicon of psychoanalytic and Marxist critique. In a repressive world, he writes, "the aesthetic function is conceived as a principle of governing the entire human existence, and it can do so only if it becomes 'universal.'"[10] That universality unfolds in a dialectical relationship with the particularities of history, national narratives, economies, and intersectional identities. Marcuse's *Eros and Civilization* offers an example of this persistent philosophical inheritance. He foregrounds the second half of the eighteenth century as the period in which Kant's philosophy stabilized the definition of the aesthetic.[11] In general terms, the aesthetic—and by extension in my reading, play—is not only connected to a feeling of pleasure and a cognitive faculty but rather, Marcuse concludes, the aesthetic dimension emerges "as its *center*, the medium through which nature becomes susceptible to freedom, necessity to autonomy" (emphasis in the original).[12] Play involves freedom, aesthetics, and autonomy. These undergo pedagogical transformation when directed at the child.

Marcuse, interpreting the legacy of play without purpose in Kant, recuperated as emancipatory in Schiller, expands the syntax of play in modernity as the necessary correlative to a hyperrational regime of labor: "Play is *unproductive* and *useless* precisely because it cancels the repressive and exploitative traits of labor and leisure; it 'just plays' with the reality."[13] Whereas some aspects of Marcuse's reading of the politically liberating dialectic of play and work obtain, my approach shifts the conditions of the discourse to the theorization and practices of teaching children to play.

Jürgen Habermas's foundational *Structural Transformation of the Public Sphere* posits the capacity of social institutions to participate in the construction of modernity's collapse of the hierarchies between the private and the public, in which reason, undergirded by ideals of rational thought and critical debate, exercises dominance. Although the soundness of his historical narrative is vulnerable to criticism for its exclusionary politics, the premise of blurred boundaries as constitutive of modernity remains persuasive. Mapping these blurred lines in the play world gains importance in the examination of German cultural practices beyond Europe.

CHILDHOOD STUDIES AND PLAY

In transatlantic modernity, evidence of the German cultural iconography of play abounds. Philippe Ariès's foundational work *Centuries of Childhood* persuasively locates the "discovery of childhood" in seventeenth-century France.[14] The national, from an historical perspective, is always implicated. Ariès's study derives its considerable authority from the artifacts of power and privilege in which play sustains and trains the elect and elite in early modern France. In positing a play world, I contend that German instructional material of the eighteenth century invents play. Although theorists outline multiple types of play, the foremost category for my enterprise is performative. Children's play, according to Ariès's argument, was dominated by games of emulation; embedded in that model is the assumption that at play, children mimic adult behaviors.[15]

Johan Huizinga's *Homo Ludens: A Study of the Play Element in Culture* represents one significant scholarly contribution to the categorization of the human being not only as *homo faber*, man the maker, but also man at play.[16] The category of play pertinent to this study, situated at the nexus of imaginative and imitative, involves a profound, sometimes subliminal mimicry inspired by toys and texts—and child-directed. This performative play replicates not only behaviors but also objects. Ariès's work followed the publication of Roger Caillois's study of games and play, *Les jeux et les hommes*, in which the French sociologist elaborates on Johan Huizinga's opus on man and play. Caillois characterizes four major types of play: agôn (competitive), alea (chance), mimicry (imitative), and ilinx (induced vertigo, giddiness).[17] Neither Huizinga nor Caillois distinguishes between children's and adults' games. The childhood Ariès delineates as a separate sphere of human existence remains only a peripheral concern in theorizing play. Caillois, for example, observes the importance of play as innate, emphasizing that it is shared in the animal kingdom; he acknowledges, however, that his four categories cannot cover "the entire universe of play."[18] Caillois positions crossover (child-adult) play in an "imaginary universe."[19]

In this study, I accept the premise that childhood is "a cultural construction and not a biologically determined period of life; its existence varies depending on country, social class, time and gender."[20] Each attribute in the effort to approach childhood intersectionally factors into my analysis. There is a disjuncture between the original European practices of play and Western inventions of a modern, model childhood. With great explanatory force, the concept of "islanding" has productively framed increased attention to childhood as a discrete phase of human existence.[21] A tension reemerges when play theories and practices enter the realm of signification for national identity and the geography of the nation-state. On the one hand, the "islanding" of play sequesters the playing subject; on the other, the assumption persists that play is performative, preparatory for engagement with adult life. The play world I elaborate derives much of its performative power from its intersection with the real, for play as a pedagogical practice, as it was theorized in certain German cultural traditions, creates a compelling connection between figurative and literal spaces and lives. The purpose of this book is to examine the generative relationship between play and pedagogy that emerged concurrent with the articulation of middle-class subjectivity and the role of model childhoods in the self-identity of modern European and European American family structures. I contend that in transatlantic modernity, toys, texts, and their production and distribution through play construct a German childhood as the model.

Play, though thought to be transhistorical, demands historicization. World events—wars, revolutions, slavery, and industrialization among them—generate a historical conscious and unconscious, the attributes of which travel with transatlantic immigration. Not only does play participate in historical identity formation, but it is further shaped by the social construction of collective or "national" characteristics impacted by a relationship to a particular ethnically envisioned geography. More specific to identity politics, Henri Lefebvre's arguments about space being both historically and ideologically constructed connects the theory of natural space to that of the built environment. With great rigor, he delineates a science of space: "The fields we are concerned with are, first, the *physical*—nature, the Cosmos; second, the *mental*, including logical and formal abstractions; and, third, the *social*. In other words, we are concerned with logical-epistemological space, the space of social practice, the space occupied by sensory phenomena, including products of the imagination such as projects and projections, symbols and utopia."[22]

The utopian products of the play world and the innocent imaginary coexist with eccentric, damaged, and debilitating topoi of the child as victim. These categories compete: the innocent and the uncanny. Countering a popularized notion of childhood as sacred and sequestered, Lloyd deMause, embarking on a pioneer path to study the history of childhood in a coalition of professional historians, some with a psychoanalytic frame of reference, introduces the topic forcefully: "The history of childhood is a nightmare from which we have only recently begun to awaken. The further back in history one goes, the lower the level of child care, and the more likely children are to be killed, abandoned, beaten, terrorized, and sexually abused. It is our task here to see how much of this childhood history can be recaptured from the evidence that remains to us."[23] The multiple contributors to his edited volume cover topics that include infanticide, castration, swaddling, and breastfeeding and a time span from antiquity to the late nineteenth century. However, a less expansive approach garners insights into the existence and stakes of competing discourses about childhood innocence and the inculcation of guilt prior to the sentimentalization of the young. These debates assume a moral patina about the purpose of play and the objects that accompany or regulate it. These two major cultural forces, I argue in this book, are marked with traces of German concepts and practices of play and constructions of the play world.

The narrative arc this analysis traces acknowledges the adult-child relationship as one between a dominant and a subordinate, as eloquently argued by Joseph Zornado: "The way in which the adult invents the child—and so reproduces the dominant culture—is key to understanding the history that leads from the slingshot to the megaton bomb, for the production and reproduction of our style of human culture occur first and foremost in our style of human relationships, which is first experienced by the child at the hands of the adult."[24] Zornado's insight underscores the discrepancy in the power relationship between adult agency and the structuring of childhood play. His assertion contrasts sharply with the nostalgic and frequently romanticized "invention" of childhood, a foundation for a counternarrative to the adult experience as loss-of-innocence.

THE TRANSATLANTIC

The "transatlantic" world is historically defined by the ocean and interactions among Europe, Africa, and the Americas. And yet, as D'Maris Coffman and Adrian Leonard observe, the tripartite construction contains a bias. Their work underwrites returning to a more expansive approach: world history.[25] Departing from models of cultural production based on the organizing principle of the nation, scholars have expanded the range of spatially specific formations to include global trends aligned with trade, travel, and exploration—synonymous with exploitation. Nonetheless, the unreflected, triumphant, and celebratory nature of the transatlantic story warrants examination for its Eurocentrism. In this study, the German American domination of the play world shapes the analysis and the selection of texts and toys for further examination. As Jan Stievermann observes of Pennsylvania Germans: "The history of this minority was, in the interpretations offered from the late nineteenth century well into the second half of the twentieth century, dominated by questions about the persistence or assimilation of specific ethnic and denominational traditions. Themes such as cross-cultural contacts and conflicts in a pluralistic environment, or transnational processes of identity formation, were largely ignored."[26] The play world intersects the national, religious, and economic narratives of migration while reflecting precisely the transnational and cross-cultural contacts that Stievermann foregrounds. Moreover, the play world aggrandizes its own agency in the pedagogical mission of its construction. It functions, I argue, as a simulacrum of the specific historical and nationalist narratives emerging in a modernity dominated by the hegemonic tripartite model of the Atlantic world. In this geography of identity, play is put to work. These artifacts, too, are agents of migration.

Saskia Sassen, whose work on defining and understanding the global city, intervenes meaningfully in theorizing agents of expulsion in a phase of capitalism fueled by the mechanisms of acquisition. In the historical context of transatlantic modernity, expulsion is an extreme articulation of migration narratives about Germans outside Germany. Sassen's discussion of accumulation related to the extraction of resources prefaces insights into inequality itself as a type of expulsion and as inflected by class, for those at both the bottom and the middle: "from a life space; among those at the top, this appears to have meant exiting from the responsibilities of membership in society via self-removal, extreme concentration of the wealth available in a society, and no inclinations to redistribute that wealth."[27] The pressures that lead to migration are evident in the texts and toys that intervene about possessions in establishing the parameters of the play world. There is a contiguous relationship between play and the world; owning and pedagogy, where childhood becomes a corollary of membership, and adult supervision and intervention function, in Freudian terms, as superego to the play world of the young id.

My preliminary argument is modest: that the German definition of the *Spielwelt* must be reimagined with the movement of Germans beyond Europe. This *Welt*, both world and globe in German, repeatedly reinvents a narrative identity of whiteness and the innocent imaginary at the expense of subjugated others. The economies of toy production, marketing, and sales lie at the nexus of pedagogically inflected, transatlantic appeals to the authenticity and superiority of German manufacture; this, too, reinforces religious, ethnic, national, and racial identities to imagine a play world that replicates a compatibility between play and privilege while preserving a moral highground, projecting it from the domicile onto the world. Examined in a transatlantic context, the paradigm perists until the decade after World War I, which coincides with the rise of American toy industry giants such as Mattel and Hasbro; they "helped transform an industry that had primarily addressed the needs and values of parents into one that appealed directly to the longings and imaginations of children."[28] To make this model visible, and to reimagine it, I examine networks—including trade and economies, national affiliation, family entanglements, and cultural iconography—that develop across the Atlantic world. Such an undertaking exposes and destabilizes its Eurocentrism.

Postcolonial scholarship of past decades has paved the way, with incisive examinations of colonial discourse in the absence of colonies, analyses of the dichotomy between Enlightenment and empire, the force of radical enlightenment and transcultural critiques of European epistemologies, and the foundational historical research that illuminates the centrality of cultural identities.[29] Though issues of gender, race, ethnicity, and mobility emerge from these studies, rarely do these works engage with the domestic realm, with the invention of childhood as a national imperative, or with the migration of German ideologies through the agency of objects. Material and cultural forces construct imaginative play *with* the world. Susan Buck-Morss repositions the philosophical legacy of G. W. F. Hegel's universal notion of human freedom—equally important to the defining history of the Atlantic world—by reading the paradox of Europe's advancing autonomy and the reality of African slavery. Again, for my purposes, the following seems to distill the complex rewriting of human history, or rather, decentering it from European whiteness: "Europeans built conceptual barriers of difference in the form of spatial distinctions between nation and colonies, a racialized distinction of *Negro* slavery, and legal distinctions as to the protection of persons, in order to segregate free Europe from colonial practices." Key to her analysis in the framework of labor in industrializing Britain and Paul Gilroy's work on the Atlantic world is the concept of porosity, which characterizes "ordering boundaries" of human experience around the category of the nation-state. Further, porosity gains relevance in "exposing ungovernable connections."[30] The construction of a distinctly German play world in Atlantic modernity can best be understood by examining its porosity—between private and public, national and transnational, cultural and transcultural. The interrogatory approach to this material is informed by the need to expose the "ungovernable connections" between German identity and a desire for ascendancy. In each chapter, I compose a set of evidence from the visual arts, material culture, and literary texts to demonstrate the ways the domestic sphere rewrites the play world, which undergoes significant changes to reflect evolving demographics, emigration patterns, and the centrality of play in the construction of national and global imaginaries.

TROPES OF WORLDING

Beyond enacting a model childhood, play enables the foundational act of worlding, which confers agency on the child.[31] Play as worlding empowers the subject to marshal energies that replicate, order, and understand the national in relation to ownership, entitlement, and hierarchizing intersectional attributes of identity. Though the trope of worlding can decenter literary studies productively away from the category of the national, childhood subjectivity recapitulates it as a necessary geography of the play world, which is historically contested space, the physical and imaginative nature of which defies easy relegation to either the domestic or public spheres but necessarily implicates both. In this context, worlding in some ways repeats the colonization process for which it has been justifiably critiqued, exposed for its performative capacity to execute a politics of inclusion and exclusion.[32] My aim is to endorse this position and to examine the ways the German cultural enterprise directed at the production and exportation of childhood participates in the trope of worlding. The mapping of borders and boundaries of the play world necessarily critiques the formation of childhood agency through narrating relationships to material possessions justified through national and transcultural ideologies. The contribution of German-language texts and material artifacts about play consists of a narrative about the spatial, social, and cultural construction of the play world as a safe space for some, with inevitable risks for others. This is still underexplored in scholarship, and my intent is to illuminate the role of the domestic sphere in underwriting cultural nationalism and transnational migration discourses.

CANONICAL AND MARGINAL

The German construction of the presumably universal play world begins in the early modern period and under the influence of religious separatism and persecution. It is necessary to begin before the dichotomous questioning of Enlightenment or empire. The question of play and power is inscribed into the emergence of the Moravian Brethren, the belief in universal education, and the migration of these ideas through discourse networks and refugees seeking protection. An early promoter in this context is Johann Amos Comenius (1592–1670).[33] His affiliation with the Protestant sect is rarely the focus of analyses, but the mobility of play theories and practices transports a common commitment to education and play as compatible with theological principles from the early modern period of German-speaking Europe. Prior to the emergence of secular instruction and the regulation of play, Nikolaus Zinzendorf (1700–1760) invested heavily in the leavening of religious instruction toward mitigating the severity of Lutheran orthodoxy and its rigid discipline of children. His emphasis on the emotions extended to an embrace of childhood innocence and a reiteration of the child as foremost in the Christian flock. Zinzendorf founded the Moravian Brethren in the eastern Saxon village of Herrnhut, which became toponymical for the dissemination of the faith through proselytizing. Through immigration, the foundational texts and hymns were disseminated in the northeastern United States. With a stronghold in Bethlehem, Pennsylvania, the Moravian Brethren exerted considerable influence on the publication of childhood texts about play. Proponents of play and preserving childhood innocence, however, are frequently suffused in moral ambiguity that gets lost in migration. As Tautz points out in her observations about the Moravian Brethren, Zinzendorf proselytized proslavery positions, ascribing to the Moravian community a "legacy of early-modern Christianity that aligned whiteness with morality and justified slavery."[34] An examination of Zinzendorf's legacy of reform religious instruction intersects with the pedagogical theorists of German-speaking Europe. Religion and play teach race.

The religious influence abates in the eighteenth century with the emergence of pedagogical theorists, the Philanthropists and their investment in human betterment, and the institutionalization of education. So much European influence is mediated by the institutions of early childhood education, the design and dissemination of which are attributed to the kindergarten of Friedrich Fröbel (1782–1852). Historians, child studies scholars, and administrators have all treated Fröbel's work in compelling ways. My intention is not to wedge an opinion into those arguments but to trace out the implications of Fröbel's advocates as they define the importance of play and humanity. These advocates broadcast theories of play in the New World to great effect. One interlocutor, Berta von Marenholtz-Bülow (1810–1893), recalls her first encounter with the "old fool" in 1849: "When one of his pupils called him Mr. Froebel, I remembered once having heard of the name who wished to educate children by *play*, and that it had seemed to me a very perverted view, for I had only thought of *empty* play, without any serious purpose."[35] In his work on the "playing child" construction, sociologist Michael Wyness writes, "Play is also seen as a part of childhood in that it is a period of time when children are free from responsibilities ... it means not having to work."[36] There is a retro quality to Wyness's assertion. To place both aspects of the quotation in perspective, I cite Fröbel: "Play is the first means of development of the human mind, its first effort to make acquaintance with the outward world, to collect original experiences from things and facts, and to exercise the powers of body and mind. The child, indeed, recognizes no purpose in it."[37] Play with purpose becomes a major German export, emanating from the "old fool's" school in Thuringia. Philosophy and pedagogy entered an existential duel.

Johann Heinrich Pestalozzi (1746–1827), Joachim Heinrich Campe (1746–1818),[38] and Fröbel (1782–1852) concerned themselves with the pedagogical purposes of childhood, but Fröbel's regime of play constitutes the most important factor in the international discussion of childhood education, domestic practices, and public institutions.[39] Fröbel relaxes the religious regulation of play, focusing instead on the homology between childhood and nature and effectively secularizing the purpose of play through subliminal pedagogy.

In contemporary scholarship, much attention is devoted to innovations that enable us to process "the great unread."[40] Reframing the question of how to rank largely forgotten texts in pursuit of understanding how what we read and do not read changes knowledge, I look not toward computational analysis, the territory of Franco Moretti,[41] but to a broader cultural context. I cast a wide evidentiary net to make a case for the centrality of German material, literary, and pedagogical cultures in the construction of the "play world" as an imaginary space in which the agents of play varyingly acknowledge and incorporate historical realities. The voices of Zinzendorf, Fröbel, Campe, and Pestalozzi can be heard across temporal and geographical distances. In this book, I go beyond the canonical. The engagement of Zinzendorf's grandmother in educating women is significant; the prescriptive handbook on how mothers should teach children to play, begun by a cookbook author, takes center stage. Goethe's mother and her objection to violent play crosses the pond. Stories by once-popular authors whose reputations have receded from memory imagine the German childhood in an amalgamated American and African wilderness, for entertainment and edification. The women who brought Fröbelian fundamentals to American education are heard. Their progressive politics, however, are not guarantors of ethical practice. The play world is fraught with such contradictions.

A moment in sociological theory is an aperçu for my argument. Max Weber (1864–1920) provides a counternarrative to an industrialized Europe dominated by a Protestant work ethic. His ideas about work sublate any theory of play as a condition of practice without purpose. At the turn of the twentieth century, Weber's consideration of work is predicated on several factors that accrue significance: increasing societal secularization; the rise of an educated but disenfranchised bourgeoisie; industrialization, albeit at a slower pace than experienced elsewhere in Europe; and patterns of transatlantic immigration that model economic rationalization. In the "Protestant Ethic," he makes connections between religious practice, professional calling, and the accumulation of wealth. From Enlightenment purposelessness to work as life's purpose, the need to theorize play in context arises and develops commensurately with bourgeois subjectivity. Play, within reason and with purpose, relaxes the ironclad religious commitment to the tenet of work as a means of salvation. Weber, in psychologizing the motivation of labor in advanced capitalism, concludes that religious piety bores the white-collar worker:

> The people filled with the spirit of capitalism to-day tend to be indifferent, if not hostile, to the Church. The thought of the pious boredom of paradise has little attraction for their active natures; religion appears to them as a means of drawing people away from labour in this world. If you ask them what is the meaning of their restless activity, why they are never satisfied with what they have, thus appearing so senseless to any purely worldly view of life, they would perhaps give the answer, if they know any at all: "to provide for my children and grandchildren."[42]

Indirectly, Weber incorporates the psychology of surplus into a rejection of religion and a faux dedication to family legacy. The connections between religion, work, and play vary with historical context and objects of play. Within the Protestant discourse about a work ethic, contested sites form as litanies about the cultivating of children through regulated play. In determining the parameters of the study, I accept Sharon Brookshaw's understanding of toys, games, and some interactive books as "the material culture of childhood"—objects produced by adults for children, in contrast to the ephemeral objects children make for themselves.[43] Texts and toys both tell stories.

TEXTS

Texts function in plural ways, with the act of reading and imaginative constructions of a play world coexisting with books as material objects. With regard to literature, we can detect major commonalities. In "The Origins of Children's Literature," M. O. Grenby focuses on Lewis Carroll's *Alice's Adventures* as a pivotal text, observing that in general there are three kinds of origins: "First, there is the historical genesis of children's literature as a commercial product. Second, there is the idea that children's literature has naturally developed from a culture of adult-to-child storytelling. And third, the biographical accounts surrounding the conception of individual books."[44] This focus on the individual segues into the conclusion David Hamlin draws for the playing subjects—namely, that the telos is individualism.[45] This assertion holds true, but in transcultural play worlds, the often hidden or unarticulated networks of signification show themselves in the codes that construct class-based, ethnic, and racialized identities as the prequel to transitioning into citizenship. Therein lurks the danger.

The powerful critical tool of intersectionality—with attributes of race, gender, class, ethnicity, sexual identities, age, religion, citizenship status, and other elements of plural identity formation—has had an impact on the study of children's literature.[46] In the American cultural tradition, a trenchant and uneuphemized critique of "classics," such as *Huckleberry Finn*, as exemplifying racism and white supremacy challenges the ostensible unassailability of a national canon; others push back with a defense of reading for Mark Twain's critique of the social norms that sanctioned slavery. Even taking both seemingly irreconcilable viewpoints into consideration, a result remains: the act of reading can contribute to a naturalization of racism. The author may encode criticism but cannot control the quality of the reading. Through the refracting lens of intersectionality, the specific national, historical, geographic, and racial characteristics of literature aimed at listening, reading, and observing youth with the goal of emulating and replicating the family and class structures of the adult world become legible.

Concurrent developments to the study of images underscore the potentially subliminal—or ideologically overt—educatory elements of literature for a young reader. Noting this evolution, Teresa Colomer and colleagues write: "Research confirms that, at its best, picturebook illustration is a subtle and complex art form that can communicate on many levels and leave a deep imprint on a child's consciousness."[47] Although the interaction of reading and of viewing images in children's books can function in subversive ways, the performative force of doing so accrues increased powers of persuasion when situated in a pedagogical model that governs the leisure activities of children, from reading and indoor play to outdoor recreation and parties and holidays. Taken together, these arguments obviate any potentially exculpatory narratives about classics, canons, and the imperative to historicize their contents when representing racial, gendered, and class inequality, injustice, or violence.

Recent research into the relationship between childhood learning, images, and their connection to scientific knowledge connects visuality with the play world more explicitly in the geography of German-speaking Europe in the post-Enlightenment era. The national and linguistic cultural traditions vary across continents and oceans, and in her *Die Welt in Bildern* (The world in pictures)—a well-researched analysis of the pictorial as an epistemological category—Silvy Chakkalakal identifies a connection between Friedrich Justin Bertuch's (1747–1822) *Bilderbuch für Kinder* (Picturebook for children) and the dissemination of scientific knowledge in the considerably larger framework of visual culture in the long eighteenth century.

Published from 1790 to 1830, the *Bilderbuch für Kinder* not only popularized and disseminated scientific knowledge but also helped define childhood as a temporal, experiential, and cultural category. Chakkalakal's concern is primarily with the copperplate reproductions of nature and their ability to structure the transfer of knowledge to the German-speaking and youthful audience, though these images appeal to adults as well. However, her analysis resists any reductive notion of childhood and a visually entertaining pedagogical project.[48] Chakkalakal's study reveals the importance of unpacking the idea of images as amusement; the visual conveys knowledge, which has important implications for any understanding of early modern epistemology.[49] The centrality of sense perception for cognitive and cultural development comes to the foreground in this sustained interpretation of a homology between scientific knowledge and visual cultures. This science of seeing and knowing establishes a specifically German legacy in children's cultures within German-speaking Europe and in migration. In the European American play world, the pedagogical moment occurs in the interpreted construction of whiteness embedded in the transference between an image and an accompanying text.

MATERIALITIES OF THE PLAY WORLD

While the verbal and visual telling of stories and reading of texts elicit interpretation, explanation, and imagination, producing, purchasing, and playing with toys engages aspects of commerce, labor, family roles and finances, and often regulation and supervision.[50] Much available work on toys, from an historical perspective, is the product of collectors, yielding stunning and inviting catalogues with glossy photos of well-preserved fragments or pristine incarnations of their favorite things.

Multiple collectors and historical materialists have a voice. Walter Benjamin, the philosopher tangentially associated with Frankfurt School philosophy, drafts in his essays on toys a model of material culture; he further attends to the means of production and consumption that are adapted by sacred and secular diacritical marker. Benjamin's model further recodes the pedagogical imperatives of playing to save the soul. His filtering of play activity through a Freudian lens of repetition compulsion extends the line of thought in Weber's work ethic to a secularized play ethic. This context encompasses the "social life of things," to borrow from Arjun Appadurai's notion that objects circulate in "different *regimes of value*."[51] My focus, not exclusively economic, highlights the pedagogical, exchange value of toys that model sacrifice and gain in moral, national, and racial registers.

Historically, collectors engage in practices that intersect with natural science epistemologies. Historian Anke te Heesen defines the study of material cultures as "a subject that has increasingly penetrated the concerns of historians, has found its most important expression in the history of collecting."[52] In a less rigorous sense, cultural artifacts speak to the verve of enthusiasts and aficionados, but the ephemeral nature of toys, as material objects, can present insurmountable challenges to the historian. Toys bear witness to history, shape identity, and do the heavy lifting in mimetic play. In the words of Appadurai, "Contemporary Western common sense, building on various historical traditions in philosophy, law, and natural science, has a strong tendency to oppose 'words' and 'things.'"[53] Toys as commodities figure prominently in the contouring of model childhoods, inhabiting a space between verbal and material, intersecting the commercial creation of desire and mimetic drive to reproduce hierarchies of identity. In his study of consumerism in the age of Goethe, Daniel Purdy argues that Germany developed "a vibrant and complex consumer culture" in the eighteenth century prior to its industrialization. The act of reading, in this case, of Friedrich Bertuch's *Mode Journal*, proves to be pivotal in producing desire through "readerly imagination."[54] In the context of the play world, the materiality of texts and toys as commodities performs desire coterminously, but with transatlantic influence. Historian Leora Auslander, in her seminal essay "Beyond Words," makes the point that material objects are not only "the product of history, they are also active agents in history. In their communicative, performative, emotive, and expressive capacities, they act, have effects in the world."[55] Toys not only accrue cultural and emotional capital, they migrate along with the value systems contained in the culture of emotions. As toy historian Richard O'Brien observes, "When the Europeans arrived in the New World, toys came with them. It was only natural. Toys had been a part of European life for centuries."[56] Evidence of German toy-making skills, which straddled the line between craft and commerce, survive in products collected and displayed as folk art.[57]

Toys, as material objects and signifiers in a web of human meaning, both inhabit and construct the play world. As historian Gary Cross writes of modern children and their toys, "Only in modern times have toys become primarily objects for children, props in a play world separated from adults. In the transformation of play and toys from medieval times to the mid-nineteenth century, toys gradually became specifically children's playthings."[58]

Into this general statement about the American context, I introduce the argument that the play world structured between 1750 and 1914 was profoundly influenced by German and German American philosophers, celebrity parents, toy manufacturers, and German- and English-speaking authors; this national, historical, and linguistic cognate of modern play provides an underexamined narrative about the parameters of a model childhood that elevates the pedagogical over the pleasurable experience of play—though this theorizing and regulation do not always progress in a linear manner. The play worlds of modern, model childhoods are further contested by competing religious, ethical, and social discourses about the attributes of citizenship at home, in public, and in migratory transit.

In their work on modern childhood, Marta Gutman and Ning de Coninck-Smith emphasize the contiguities in a childhood relationship to material culture, writing "that spaces and settings made for children are pivotal to the construction of modernity in global society, and that children are social actors in their own right who use and interpret material culture on their own terms."[59] They further assert a seemingly transhistorical and transnational definition of a model childhood, based on the assumption that children differ from adults and that childhood is a discrete phase in human life warranting special circumstances: children "should have a childhood that is in at least some manner protected, nurturing, and playful; that a child's education ought to be centered on mental, emotional, and physical development; and that a specialized material culture is needed to make possible the 'good and happy childhood' as lived experience."[60] The model childhood, however, cannot be universally experienced; nor is there consensus about its qualities.

Texts and toys align in the book as a material object. The marvelous, the ungraspable contained therein evokes Susan Stewart's discussion of the book as miniature.[61] This scene of instruction enables the transmission of racialized knowledge through regions of the geographical imaginary, but in neutralized, ostensibly innocent ways. The materiality of the letter, to raise the specter of deconstruction, is the method. Late eighteenth-century letter and word games were designed to appeal to early readers. Based on the idea of ABC books, extant examples date from 1795. The *Neues Deutsches Buchstaben-Magazin* (New German letter box) takes the game of reading and writing into three dimensions. With 224 cardboard pieces of letters, numbers, and punctuation marks, the collection was available in Latin, French, and Italian.[62] Directed at a young audience, the pieces exploit the materiality of the letter, projecting the imaginative onto the lexical, the play onto and off the page. A direct descendant of such a letter game, the picture puzzle (*Bilderrätsel*) invites heterodox methods of reading in order to play. The seemingly neutral introduction of images, however, controls the narrative. In the example from 1889, words of wisdom, maxims such as "Probieren geht über Studieren" (roughly, the proof is in the pudding) (fig. 2) and "Morgenstunde hat Gold im Munde" (roughly, the early bird catches the worm) appear to deliver brain-teasing glyphs and letters. In the first instance, letters and pictographs solve the puzzle. In the second (fig. 3), the image of the *MOHR* is noteworthy for the visual and conceptual baggage it carries. The nonchalant visual rendering of the black figure confuses the literal and figurative signification of the Moor. A later reading of blackness in this volume will articulate the associations created and cemented by the deployment of this African imaginary.

In this sense, my work explores the interplay among the physical, mental, and social spaces that contribute to a German-cultural hegemony of the play world, contiguous with the playroom, the playground, and the nation. My goal is to analyze the meaning of the playroom, the playground, and the play world as locations of material culture and social conditions of childhood from an historical and transnational perspective.[63] *The Play World* provides insight into the role of children prepped to become modern subjects—as consumers and producers of play, as citizens of highly contested built environments, and as human "sites" of negotiation in a long-standing debate about education, public institutions, and national identity. The study of childhood necessarily brings together disparate and sometimes contentious disciplines. Moreover, the academic inflection of that project often focuses on the realm of literature. As the editors of *Keywords for Children's Literature* observe, "'Children's literature' itself has become a kind of umbrella term encompassing a wide range of disciplines, genres, and media."[64] The materiality of the book, however, is often overlooked in the study of texts. It is imperative, I believe, to consider the materiality of childhood in transatlantic modernity, for it is located at the nexus of play, work, and identity.

CHAPTER OVERVIEW

In this section, I take the opportunity to introduce the lesser-known writers and their work, along with the role played by more canonical figures. While digital humanities methodologies generate metadata in the "slaughterhouse

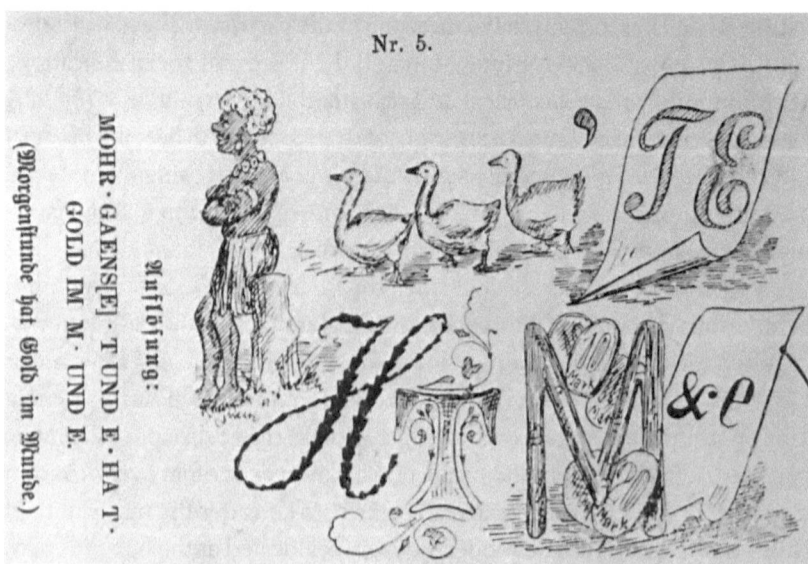

FIG. 2 "Probieren geht über Studieren." From *Auerbach's Deutscher Kinder-Kalender auf das Jahr 1889* (Leipzig: Fernau, 1889), 38. Joseph P. Horner Memorial Library, The German Society of Pennsylvania. Photo: author.

FIG. 3 "Morgenstunde hat Gold im Munde." From *Auerbach's Deutscher Kinder-Kalender auf das Jahr 1889* (Leipzig: Fernau, 1889), 38. Joseph P. Horner Memorial Library, The German Society of Pennsylvania. Photo: author.

of literature,"⁶⁵ my exploration collects evidence from the margins and connects textual and material artifacts into a darkly imagined play world. The narrative arc of my argument stretches back to the early modern period and fades with the hegemony of German influence on toy production in the early twentieth century. Each chapter lays out a network of biographical, aesthetic, and material connections that extent from Europe to the Americas. Religious regulation of pleasure and play yields to an overarching natural, secularized model of childhood in which attrtibutes of intersectional identities—from religious affilication, economic class status, and race—feature prominently. Germanness itself, the prosperity of its immigrant communities and virtues of their linguistic and technical superiority, assumes greater importance in the export of play theories and practices—and products, especially legible in the late nineteenth century and until the onset of World War I. The German literary canon, with Goethe at its pinnacle, additionally functions as a signifier of ethnic influence and accomplishment. Within this cultural narrative, economic and political mechanisms, along with the production, consumption, and distribution of toys, propel the construction of transatlantic German childhoods as exemplary and eccentric.

Chapter 1, "The Protestant Play Ethic," examines a network of writers and pedagogues who leave their mark on early modern religious discourses about play. In her work on seventeeth-century "marginal" women, Natalie Zemon Davis, in acknowledging an intellectual debt to Michel de Certeau, writes about the significane of dialogue in spiritual discovery.⁶⁶ My decision to begin with a cast of seemingly minor characters from seventeenth-century thought can be justified by their engagement in a transatlantic dialogue about the potential for spiritual—and other types—of discovery through prayer and play. The artifacts and discursive influence produces a communicative network that constitutes a model of play that casts a long shadow. Among these narrators of play is Henriette Catharina Freifrau von Gersdorff (1648–1726), a poet and patroness who expressed a desire for divinity, eschewing material possessions. Her work calibrated morality in ownership and thus planted the seed of the Protestant play ethic. Celebrated by contemporaries, the "Fürstin unter den deutschen Mädchen" (princess among German girls) called attention to the importance of educating across gender for the welfare and reputation of the nation.⁶⁷ Her influence is filtered through family connections, and foremost among these is her grandson and ward, Nikolaus Ludwig Count von Zinzendorf, who founded Hernnhut as the material and spiritual center of the Moravian Brethren.

A counterexample is her own son, who ignored her ministrations and proved prodigal. In their transatlantic dissemination, hymns participate in the network about childhood experience and the regulation of play. Gersdorff's oeuvre yields to an eighteenth-century Pietist. Another marginal figure, Ernst Gottlieb Woltersdorf (1725–1761), was a poet and pastor who studied in Halle and composed 218 spiritual hymns, sermons, and edifying texts. He is best known beyond Germany for his work at the Halle orphanage of August Francke, the project also endorsed by Freifrau von Gersdorff. Woltersdorf's work, popularized in the United States, continues a cycle of regulating joy and play in song about appropriate roles for children in a spiritual community. In twentieth-century America, these sentiments reverberate through theories of early childhood eduction. Through pedagogical theory, the Protestant play ethic impacts transatlantic secular institutions, and the chapter ends with the American reception of Zinzendorf's beliefs about childhood, community, and play. Henry H. Meyer's *Child Nature and Nurture According to Nicolaus Ludwig von Zinzendorf* captures the sense of early modern liturgical texts, the purpose of doll houses, and the didacticism of hyms, all of which he updates and collates to establish a canon of German texts that shape the construction of modern childhood. Gersdorff taught children *not* to play—not so Zinzendorf. That redemptive aspect dominated the American reception of the Protestant play ethic.

Whereas the Protestant play ethic overcomes a resistance to play, an early modern inheritance, textual and practical responses to major theories about Nature and childhood prompt the contemplation of more secular models. Zoffany's domestic scene typifies an eighteenth-century constellation of civilizing childhood and parental oversight. The second chapter, "Professional Parenting: Enlightened Play," foregrounds the gendering of supervisory roles in parental interactions with playing children. The professionalizing of parenthood in this period is evident in manuals about maternal and paternal instruction. Parental roles assume responsibility for mediating between intimate and familial spheres, on the one hand, and public and historical ones, on the other. Beginning with representations of the *Kinderstube* (children's room), this chapter identifies the host of characters in physical spaces, then moves to the analysis of a little-known manual that instructs mothers how to teach play. The fourth edition of a popular household handbook for women, the *Oekonomisches Handbuch für Frauenzimmer*, elaborates on a cookbook originally penned by Friederike Luise Löffler (1744–1805); it contains, in addition to the publication history of the volume and the previous three prefaces, an appendix with a detailed description of contemporary mothering practices. The authorship of the *Handbuch* itself poses some authentication and attribution problems. Löffler of Stuttgart authored a cookbook that gained extreme popularity such that her name became something of a franchise, variously borrowed as "Charlotte Löffler" and "A. Löfflerin."[68] Her daughter, Henriette Huttenlocher (1780–1848), carried on her mother's tradition and possibly wrote the later forewords to subsequent editions (they are unsigned). As consulting the contents of handbooks of handbooks attests, this "how to" volume enjoyed enormous popularity and wide circulation around 1800. This influential volume ultimately portrays play as central to a child's health, the provenance of the mother. In the second part of the chapter, the focus shifts to a contemporary manual model of the *Hausvater* and the anxiety driven by female-dominated spaces. An examination of Christian Friedrich Germershausen's *Die Hausmutter in allen ihren Geschäften* and *Der Hausvater in systematischer Ordnung*, as well as a story from Johann Heinrich Campe's *Kleine Kinderbibliothek* (Little children's library), substantiate the claim. Finally, to offer a contemporary contestation of the paterfamilias and showcase nuances in the debates about models of fathering, I analyze the stories of a parent-writer who crafts ideal sons through the rejection of alpha-masculine play but also endorses a play space beyond evangelical control. Advancing an alternative masculinity and model of paternity, resistant to games of violence and war toys, is the fiction of Christian Friedrich Wilhelm Jacobs (1764–1847). His readers meet a loving paternal protagonist who is deeply invested in the development of his two motherless sons. His three-volume *Allwin und Theodor* was in great demand by the middle of the nineteenth century.[69] Though noncanonical, Jacobs was both popular and read. His pedagogical interventions into masculine play enlighten parenting; their legacy is evident in the transatlantic world. One example of this model's transatlantic reach can be found in *Der deutsche Kinderfreund: Ein Lesebuch für Volksschulen* (The German children's friend: A reader for public elementary schools). Written by Friedrich Philip Wilmsen (1770–1831), the author introduces the first American edition published in 1830. Identified as a preacher at the Parochial-Kirche zu Berlin, Wilmsen, a teacher and pastor, gained further reputation and income writing a range of pedagogical books about history, the German language, and natural and earth sciences (*Natur- und Erdkunde*). The texts written for children and young readers circulated beyond German-speaking Prussia.[70] The model of the indulgent mother, wild child, and dire consequences of unrestricted play conveyed by Wilmsen's allegories survives in their migration to the New World, thus exporting the Protestant play ethic for the professionalizing, enlightened parent beyond Germany.

With sustained consideration of interactions between objects and texts, a dominant play paradigm becomes visible. Each chapter gathers threads of a transatlantic narrative that centers around the developing child-parent constellation as a subject of public discourse. Just as objects serving as agents of history accrue national significance outside the familiar play world, migrants and immigrants imbue artifacts, but also language and cultural patrimony, with special significance. Play influences the writing of history. In the third chapter, "Revolutions in Play," I bring together toys and texts related to the French and American revolutions to make this point. The spotlight shines on Johann Wolfgang von Goethe as a player, parent, and poet and on his legacy in the United States. Goethe's involvement with toys—the miniature guillotine and the yoyo—ultimately reveals a political unconscious with connections to traumatic histories and narratives of the French Revolution and Reign of Terror. Toys, I argue, provide the necessary leverage to transform destructive into creative impulses. Yet the American reception of Goethe as an exemplary cultural icon responds to the great poet's toy preferences with ambivalence, and a more eccentric figure enters the German American imaginary.

Chapter 4 explores the intersection of latent and manifest artifacts of German colonial ideology. In "Colonizing Childhoods: The African Imaginary," emulative play and engaged reading model ideal ways to think nationally and transnationally—to think "colonially." With the wide world and the cosmos encapsulated in a play room, history enters the domestic sphere. In the late nineteenth century, toys and texts awaken a desire for acquisition that maps colonizing entitlements onto the play world. Territorialization functions to map a cognitive landscape onto an emerging racial identity; it is manifest in the history of colonization, and deterritorialization certainly counts as a tool in the toolbox of postcolonial theory and the analysis of economic globalization.[71] In alignment with an ideology of the appropriative mapping of ownership onto a "wilderness," the metonymy is constructed between the wild and *Naturvölker* (conventionally translated as "primitive or indigenous peoples"). The untamed nature of the child is displaced by populations in need of subjection. As I demonstrate in this chapter and the next, children's toys, texts, and play practices replicate racializations of identity that are rehearsed in the play world and inscribed onto non-European geographies—whether official colonies or not. Entering the age of empire, German-language texts increasingly associate the child with the "wild." I examine a novella for young readers by a once canonical, now minor writer. W. O. von Horn, the second pen name of Friedrich Wilhelm Philipp Oertel (1789–1867), was an evangelical pastor who first published *Dorfgeschichten* (village stories) under the pseudonym Friedel Lips: he found writing for a young audience more lucrative. In addition to his republications of popular works, he edited a series of "Jugend- und Volksschriften" (writings for the young and the people) for the publisher Niedner & Kreidl—he himself wrote seventy-five volumes, the themes of which encompassed adventure and the prevalence of Christian values even under dire circumstances. The novella *Ein Kongo-Neger: Eine Geschichte aus Sankt Domingo* (A Congo-negro: A story from Santo Domingo) purveys a colonial fantasy of racial difference and harmony amid the atrocities of slavery and violent uprisings; it disparages revolutionary politics within Europe while extoling them in the New World. The image of Africa in the play world informs the structure of German whiteness and colonializing identity for the child. In the almanac *Auerbach's Deutscher Kinder-Kalender auf das Jahr 1889*, this is evident particularly in the calendar section itself. Founded in 1883 by August Bertold Auerbach, son of the well-known novelist, the almanac regularly featured a calendar, games, puzzles, stories, and letters directly addressing the readers. In the general context of Auerbach's calendar, the optics of race depart significantly from the representation of the more conventional fairy-tale illustrations. The fate of the *Oktoberkind* (*Negerkind*), under the sign of Scorpio, reinforces assumptions about the dangers of rhapsodizing the exotic wilderness and the validity of manipulating the world through knowledge. The caricature of Africa in children's culture is replicated in the appearance of a calendar-like pamphlet aimed at a young audience and harnessed the innocence and noblesse oblige encoded as whiteness, the expectations of Christmas, and the horror of encountering racial otherness during the colonial period. "Knecht Ruprecht in Kamerun" comprises a series of twelve frames, each with a grim caption to collate the experience of Saint Nicholas's best-known attendant in the tropics with the German-language audience. In this artifact, we see traces of the semiotic shift between children, the influence of an unbridled landscape, and race. This caricature shares the white supremacist suppositions of so many "classics," though it has received very little scholarly attention. The African imaginary yields to dystopian pressures of history. The shift in tone, after the 1904–6 Herero "uprising," also known as the Nama Herero War, provides a harsh wake-up call to the romanticizing and exoticizing impulses of the African adventure tale. By contrast, the racially harmonized Eden of Horn's novella is inscribed into the American political and aesthetic imaginary.

In chapter 5, "Ethnographic Play and the American Imaginary," I add detail to the map of the play world by projecting it across the Americas. The act of reading and the practice of play are intertwined in play manuals from the middle of the nineteenth century. One example, Julie Hirschmann's *Guckkasten-Bilder*, launches a party that revolves around simple group play—all that is needed is feather or a piece of cotton. However, these naturalized, weightless objects are embedded in a complex economic history that connects Europe and the Americas in ways that the stories and toys discussed in this chapter convey. Selected stories and images about play at home and abroad, drawn from calendars, miscellanies, and museum collections, represent the coexistence of didactic fiction and material objects. Moreover, the interactions among material objects and the narratives complicate the formation of an imperial identity—even in the absence of extensive (German) colonies. Exemplary stories of European childhood on other continents, such as "Die kleine Urwälderin" (The little jungle girl, 1902) and "Eine Indianergeschichte" (An Indian story, 1904), replicate a white-settler mentality in conflict with the Plains Indians of North America and the acquisition of indigenous cognitive and practical skills of South America. These stories, framed by a reading of travel and ethnographic literary texts, work against facile portrayals of first peoples and bring into focus other continents in the play world as viewed through the lens of German-speaking Europe. The existence of empire endorses what cultural historians have defined as the imaginary citizenship of young adult readers. The stories in this chapter instruct a particular brand of imaginary citizenship. The concept of an imaginary citizenship for children resonates with the concept of a national or imperial citizenship, redeeming possessions for the play world.

Chapter 6, "The Home and the Nation," follows the counterdiscourse about nature for constructing a play world to challenge teaching economies of possession. I reconsider the breadth and reach of Friedrich Fröbel, who laid the foundations for modern childhood education in the institution of the *Kindergarten*. In transnational debates about play, German play theory is exported to the United Kingdom and the United States. My focus is on two influential works: the first, published by Ernst Steiger (1832–1917), represents an effort to introduce Fröbel's tools into a larger discourse about the education system in the United States in the later nineteenth century. The German American author weighs in about the role of German theory in American institutions but also provides ample commentary on the efficacy of one national theory in another context. The second text, by Emily (Anne Eliza) Shirreff (1814–1897), appeared a bit later and takes up Fröbel's cause in England. Their respective reception of Fröbel shares a concern with adult supervision of child's play. The mode of that supervision becomes increasingly institutionalized through educational practices that insist on a separate sphere of play and pedagogy. My interest in Fröbel's complex reception in England and the United States highlights the play agenda of his transatlantic proponents. Throughout the nineteenth century and industrialization in Europe and the United States, multiple factors—among them demographic shifts, increasing polarization between agrarian and urban landscapes, and intensified mechanisms of capitalism, accompanied by political and philosophical responses to widening gaps in income—exerted considerable force on the lives and representations of families and children. Together, both historical documents make a case for the national signatures of play in Anglo-American institutions. Paradoxically, in an attempt to assert the international validity of play, the authors engage in advancing the dominance of national identities.

Toys, as agents of history, cross the Atlantic literally. Chapter 7, "Empire of Toys," traces the intricate network surrounding the production and consumption of toys and childhood accessories that capitalize on German origins combined with American energies. I begin with the German Albert Schoenhut (1849–1912), who began as a wood lather in Göppingen. As an immigrant in Philadelphia, Schoenhut would found the Schoenhut Piano Company in 1872. The enterprise expanded and became a family business. During the production period preceding World War I, Schoenhut and company manufactured and marketed toys that drew inspiration from the Bible, the circus, the faces of Schoenhut children, and the historical characters of American popular entertainment. With reference to insights from recent scholarship in disability studies, I examine the rise of ethnographic exhibits, human zoos, the Wild West Show, and their impact on the making of American toys with German origins. In particular, racialization is the process by which toys, themselves objects of history, confer agency on the child through ownership and repeated play practices. This yields insight into a family business that generated a binational legacy and exposes the imperial impulses evident in the making and marketing of transatlantic toys.

In concluding this study, I try to make visible some aspects of the cultural, communicative, and trade networks that comprise the German play world and enable its circulation. The inscription of Goethe as a player and cultural icon, the dismay about toys and trauma, the amassing of a sugar fortune in the Gilded Age, and the legacy of Fröbel in asserting play as a human right all factor into the narrative of global German identity until World War I. I open with an unsigned review of an 1896 Metropolitan Opera House gala night performance in which a critic describes a "brilliant house" bursting with mythical and human figures of the devil, ghosts, and lovers driven to distraction alongside soldiers and courtiers. Goethe's (perhaps misconstrued) Romanticism contributes to the construction of this image. Around 1900, with German immigration still enhancing a cultural and political profile of the immigrant communities across the United States, his iconic status is a matter of celebration—in the elaborate world of the opera stage. The German "player" is poised between the highbrow and heterodox: the discourse revolves around play and his play ethic. About a decade later, on another coast, one headline in the *San Francisco Call* (7 February 1910) reads: "Guillotine as Toy for Children in 1793: Goethe's Mother Refused to Buy Machine for Youth." The article recapitulates a discussion of Goethe, his mother's disapproval, and the appetite for toy trends. Noteworthy is the provenance. The *San Francisco Call* itself establishes a connection between the San Francisco publisher John Dietrich Spreckels (1853–1926) and the complex history of sugar production and consumption. German influence migrates across the expanse of the United States, from the toy manufacturing center of Philadelphia to the Midwestern homesteaders and synods to the rush toward prosperity in California. The Spreckels's family history participates in a genealogy of cross-cultural influences. Weimar's cultural presence in San Francisco is more than contingent; it is enabled by sugar.

PLAY AS A HUMAN RIGHT

One intended consequnce of this study is to articulate connections between the brutalities of geopolitical economic realities, such as the sugar plantation economy, and the constructon of an insulated, innocent island of childhood. This holistic narrative argument surreptitiously follows the spread of the connections across the Atlantic world and the Pacific; it tells of the play world's story. At the same time, Fröbel's idealistic international disciples tout the imperative of play as a democratizing force. One advocate, Stoyan Vasil Tsanoff, is credited with the first book published in America devoted exclusively to playgrounds. Tsanoff, the author and also the general secretary of the Culture Extension League, advocates passionately for the building of playgrounds in his *Educational Value of the Children's Playground: A Novel Plan of Character Building*. Here he stakes a claim to the playground and play as a human right. Finally, to conclude the German story, I discuss the radical change in tone of the Schoenhut company's marketing. At the onset of World War I, German-language prohibitions interrupted the cultural continuity established by immigrants across the United States. By the close of the war, the Schoenhut advertising repudiated its German origins; instead, it foregrounds the persistent need to recreate the innocent imaginary through play: "Upon the happiness of little children the shadow of war should not fall. The Christmas days of childhood are all too few. We must not let even one of them be saddened."[72]

Play, over the course of centuries, becomes a progressive force, and in its German legacy, a compensatory activity that could overcome unequal access to resources, dysfunctional family relationships, and the alienation of urban life. Play teaches mimesis; it writes adult agendas onto the hard drive of citizenship. From the built environments of early modern Nuremberg to the role of parenting, praying, and producing toys to advocating play as a human right, play becomes the master signifier for a modern childhood: spaced, gendered, and nationalized. Before World War I, Schoenhut and Company will redefine the play world in American terms: "It is our hope that the past is but a prophecy of the future and that Schoenhut Toys and Dolls—and all American-made play-products—will be an increasing element in peopling the American Children's play world."[73]

CHAPTER 1

The Protestant Play Ethic

I consider children, who must be tenderly used, who must play, and have play-things.
—JOHN LOCKE, from "Some Thoughts Concerning Education" (1693)

Ich will nicht kleine Gaben, du Gottes-Kind, von dir; dich selber will ich haben, und bitten, daß, in mir, du mögst gebohren werden; entreiß, o Heyland! Mich mir und der eitlen Erden, und zeuch mich ganz in dich.

I desire no small gifts from you, Child of God; it is you I want, and ask that you may be born in me; Wrest me, oh Savior, from myself and the vain world, and make me whole in you.
—HENRIETTE CATHARINA FREIFRAU VON GERSDORFF, from *Geistreiche Lieder und poetische Betrachtungen*

To challenge the stalwart John Locke (1632–1704)[1] with a verse from a devout hymn by a virtually unknown woman who disdains the desire for "small gifts" in a devout hymn announces the dual purpose of this chapter. Locke's legacy needs little elaboration; while he admonishes early modern parents for indulging their offspring and treating them like "play-things," he acknowledges the importance of play as constitutive of childhood. More invested in channeling acquisitive behavior in the young, the hymns and poems of Henriette Catharina Freifrau von Gersdorff (1648–1726) might seem modest, but the essential relationship between things and their stories issues from the adult actively curating the moral experience of child's play. For the former, education concerns the cultivating of moral behaviors in the young, coaxed forth with a combination of emotional carrots and often literal sticks. In contrast, von Gersdorff (also Gersdorf) raised her personal voice to express a transitive desire for human unity with the sacrificial divine and eschewed material possessions; thus she planted the seed of what I call the Protestant play ethic. Whereas Locke's major works continued to dominate various brands of political and economic theory, Gersdorff's hymns left a barely perceptible trace on the history of the Pietist play world and its export across the Atlantic. As I hope to demonstrate, there is a relationship between major trends and minor contributions to German cultural patrimony and between texts and the agency of material objects that draws and repeatedly extends the boundaries of the play world according to a German-national, European model.

I intend my formulation to evoke theories of social stratification more typically associated with sociological thought. As Anke te Heesen argues, Pietism and professionalism introduce the sacred and secular world of work, even through toys.[2] In mapping the play world, the interconnections among the human life spheres of work, faith, and economic prosperity invite a consideration of Max Weber's seminal study of religion and capitalism, *The Protestant Ethic and the Spirit of Capitalism*. The desire for modeling a life of purposeful labor and moral uprightness pervades the theory and practice of family formation, crucial to the act of play as a scene of instruction. Prior to the institutionalization of play as an integral part of early childhood development in an outgrowth of kindergarten movements inspired by the work of Fröbel, play was, both for children and adults, central to an elaborate negotiation that in turn solidified class, gender, and religious identity; that identity, I argue, accrues significance through a metonymic relationship to domestic space. The representation of the house constitutes the private sphere of early modern play and display, in which aspects of childhood indulgence, adult aberrance, and transatlantic influences unfold within the binary opposition between play, a signifier of excess, and diligence, a signifier of piety.

Inevitably, issues of gender emerge as corporeal and cognitive material in the social and cultural construction of play categories. For the timespan considered in this book, masculinity and paternity in the late eighteenth- and early nineteenth-century texts discussed in subsequent chapters establish a theme, with female interventions posing problems when the play room and play world fall under women's jurisdiction. Women's early modern voices cannot be ignored. In general, social and intellectual movements throughout Europe exclude most women; though the early modern period fluctuates across Europe, German literary history designates 1350–1700 as the timespan.[3] By contrast, scholars whose focus is England designate 1500–1700 as early modern.[4] Rhetorics and stylistics respond to "a rise of universal German as an administrative language and to the penetration of writing into all areas of daily life."[5] The advent of print media in the Gutenberg era informs the early modern discourse about objects of play that attracts my interest. In the English context, as Hilary Hinds has elaborated, women were well represented in the "seventeenth-century eruption of prophetic and polemical discourse."[6] Further, she identifies prophecy and participation in polemics as articulations of female agency in the public sphere, though confined to the 1640s and 1650s. This public empowerment of private convictions and the ensuing sociopolitical negotiation of women's voices sponsor transitions and upheavals in religious discourses that accommodate female agency through writing. In the German context, hymns gain importance. The debate about children at play and their relationship to objects, I argue, in the early modern German-speaking world emerges from hymns, which cross the Atlantic as constitutive of the Protestant play ethic.

Scholarship on women's writing in this period in England abounds; by contrast, attention to the German-speaking realm tends to target individual authors, such as Catharina von Greiffenberg (1633–1694), who is remembered primarily as an Austrian protestant writer of devotional poetry against the more expansive background of baroque German-language literature,[7] or Luise Adelgunde Victoria Gottsched ("Die Gottschedin," 1713–1762), who is best known for her satirical *Die Pietisterey im Fischbein-Rocke Oder Die Doctormäßige Frau: In einem Lust-Spiele vorgestellt* (1736).[8] In this scheme, hymns by a philanthropic woman occupy more than the margins of a Protestant play ethic. The impulse to exert lasting control over one's male offspring and subsequent generations exceeds the provenance of the father. Seen from a Protestant, capitalist perspective, the proof of continued paternal influence over the child is the degree of dedication he displays toward his work. The paternalized personality proves his moral purity through labor. Is there any space in that life world for children's play? As it unfolds in this chapter, the developing coalition of Protestant moral industriousness with an infusion of play functions as an antecedent to Weberian formulations.

The dominance of Weberian theory leaves a narrow margin for nuance in the discourse about raising children, imparting religion, and modeling good citizens. If we briefly scan European cultural artifacts about the fate of children in Protestant households, bleak, grim images register. In the eighteenth century, we have the example of Friedrich Hölderlin and his parsimonious Pietist mother after the death of his father. More prominent and popularized in more recent cultural memory, Ingmar Bergman's 1982 film *Fanny and Alexander*, for example, depicts a domineering and unforgiving inflection of the exacting paternal figure as a Lutheran bishop; he marries a bereaved and bohemian mother and becomes a cruel and controlling father figure to her children. A less known film from the same era thematizes the stern Protestant father of West German sisters in the 1960s, one of whom grows up to be a terrorist.[9] These extreme examples of Protestant fathers from late twentieth-century European film feature the culmination of a stereotype as foil to the imaginative spirit and innocent child: the severe and exacting father whose rigidity and calculated aloofness, except when delivering punishment, denies any space for pleasure and exploits a facile association between Protestant paternity and white-knuckled, self-righteous control. How deep are those roots? In her discussion of love and marriage and US religious and intellectual movements, Ann Taylor Allen writes of one leader, William Ellery Channing, who "rejected grim Calvinist beliefs in original sin and eternal damnation and affirmed that God was a benevolent creator."[10] Domestic, parental control over giving and receiving comes to be considered the provenance of the male parent. Weber observes the shift away from religion to business, recognizing a neoliberal model of paternal authority within the family. Of those who live for work (rather than for the pursuit of personal happiness, for example), he writes, "If you ask them what is the meaning of their restless activity, why they are never satisfied with what they have, thus appearing so senseless to any purely worldly view of life, they would perhaps give the answer, if they know any at all: 'to provide for my children and grandchildren.' But more often and, since that motive is not peculiar to them, but was just as effective for the traditionalist, more correctly, simply: that business with its continuous work has become a necessary part of their lives."[11] As I noted in the introduction, this unusually emotional account of the driving spirit that motivates the type recognizable as the modern workaholic gives us a glimpse into the economy of work and play within the family. The justification of restless activity through family bonds gives my argument a hook into the domestic sphere from the public realm. Within that family economy—the material attributes of play as it relates to work within a political economy—the play ethic is formulated.

Seldom is the legacy of matrilineal commentary on play and prayer considered in interactions between the domestic sphere and institutions, such as religion and labor. In the slender excerpt of her extensive and popular songs, Catharina von Gersdorff sets a tone for primary relationships between the devout and the divine. This tone regulates family business as well. Her works, which became a staple in Protestant services, enjoyed wide circulation and considerable influence over human behavior. Gersdorff, of noble birth and advantageous marriage, embraced Pietism; she wielded her considerable talents, social status, and writings to extend her influence into the political sphere.[12] The *Deutsches Literatur-Lexikon* has no entry under her name, whereas Ulrich Maché concisely summarizes her life and work with emphasis on her status as a learned woman, as a devout Pietist influenced by Philipp Jakob Spener during his stint as *Oberhofprediger* in Dresden (1686–1691), and as a contributor to the canon of the baroque church song, though her hymns are stamped by the profound emotion associated with Pietism.[13] This value system governs play for centuries, though each era reinvents the discourse to reflect historical context. More conventionally, Gersdorff projected the force of her convictions onto the domicile and her family life, but in doing so, she modeled piety for public practice. As a patroness, she advocated for education across class boundaries. Her marriage to Nicol Gersdorff, whose political career as privy council and other positions made his wife "hoffähig" or socially acceptable,[14] brought four children into her care; she bore thirteen, seven of whom survived.[15] An early modern multitasker, Gersdorff led a life worthy of more than virtual obscurity beyond local acknowledgment. As a mother, wife, patron, caregiver, benefactor, poet, and political protector of religious refugees, Henriette Catharina von Gersdorff left a legacy occluded by modernity's skepticism toward religious devotion, wherein lies the early modern nexus of pedagogy and play.

Throughout her life, education played a major role in an advocacy of Pietism, which emphasized literacy as fundamental to religious practice. She supported the goals of the Moravian Brethren who were fleeing religious persecution, and here her significance as a maternal patroness in the private and public spheres accrues greater importance.[16] Her contribution to the transatlantic dissemination of the Protestant play ethic is comprised of Gersdorff's hymns about human relationships to objects. Her verse, quoted above, sheds light on an aspect of early modern subjectivity in religious discourse predicated on the desire for *Gaben*, gifts, which, according to

Grimms' dictionary, connote both literal and figurative objects.[17] The history of exchanged objects, as Arjun Appadurai reminds us, undoes any religious definition of material and spiritual. He critiques this model: "Gifts, and the spirit of reciprocity, sociability, and spontaneity in which they are typically exchanged, usually are starkly opposed to the profit-oriented, self-centered, and calculated spirit that fires the circulation of commodities."[18] Appadurai continues: "Further, where gifts link things to persons and embed the flow of things in the flow of social relations, commodities are held to represent the drive—largely free of moral or cultural constraints—of goods for one another, a drive mediated by money and not by sociality."[19] The groundbreaking study of this type of connectivity provides a new light in which to read the *Gaben* of early modern religious instruction and the economy of sacrifice and gain. In this regard, the Pietist scaffolding in the context of teaching early modern children and her rejection of small gifts in favor of less tangible rewards reaped through religious devotion are emblematic of the interchange between the religious imaginary and the ability to teach a desire for worldly goods. With Fröbel, as Allen writes of the later theorist and practitioner, the *Gaben* qualify as playthings.[20] In early modern German-speaking Europe, however, Gersdorff teaches children the reasons *not* to play.

Gersdorff is exemplary in ways beyond her reputation for piety, cosmopolitan politics, and education delivered across gender and socioeconomic boundaries. Embedded in the local, she understood the web of community relations required for social and moral exemplarity—synonymous with edification. After the death of her husband in 1702, Gersdorff effectively managed three manors, Großhennersdorf, Berthelsdorf, and Heuscheune, until the heir, the youngest son Nicol III, came of age. In 1722, she sold the only manor she owned outright, Berthelsdorf, to her grandson and ward, Nikolaus Ludwig Count von Zinzendorf, who founded Hernnhut as the material and spiritual center of the Moravian Brethren. Meanwhile, Nicol led a life worthy of his mother's disapproval; he drank excessively, gambled, and owed significant sums. As his mother, Gersdorff knew well the value of objects and the burden of debt. Robert Langer relates one particularly poignant incident involving a shoemaker who had provided her son with a new pair of shoes on a monthly schedule between 1722 and 1724. Nicol, in deteriorating health, owed the worker a substantial sum. Facing financial challenges—in addition to his labor, the man had paid for the leather—and the birth of his fifteenth child, the artisan turned to Catharina von Gersdorff, "Weil mir Dehro Hoch Christliebende Gnade von

Jugend auff bekand, bey Zeiden des Hoch Seeligen Herrn Doctor Speners (,) von welchen ich auch durch Gottes Gnade seinen heilsamen Kinderlehren, den grund meines Christenthums richtig erhalten habe" (Because your Highness's Christ-loving grace has been known to me since my youth, and in time also that of the blessed Dr. Spener (,) from whose edifying children's instruction through God's grace I have preserved with uprightness the foundation of my Christianity).[21] Nicol died in 1724. Langer speculates that the sale of her property to Zinzendorf served a strategy of insulating the mother from her son's debts. Described as Europe's "damals gelehrteste Frau" (most educated woman of the time),[22] her private life as the mother of a profligate implicates her public persona as a generous benefactor. Apparently, it takes more than a village and a Pietist mother to teach a noble son the value of objects. Nicol rejected the object lessons, which were a constitutive element of his upbringing. Anyone, it seems, even Catharina von Gersdorff, can produce a wild child.

As Colin Heywood reminds us, childhood "is a social construct, which changes over time and, no less importantly, varies within social and ethnic groups within any society."[23] Gersdorff assumed responsibility for the upbringing and education of Count von Zinzendorf, and it illuminates her relationship to Nicol, the wayward son. She welcomed into her home religious refugees from Bohemia and Moravia, perhaps compensating for the lack of control over her youngest. Most significant for my purposes, she leverages the image of adults as children of the divine and connects this definition to the renunciation of material gifts, read alongside the cautionary tale of her son's excesses. Gersdorff's emphasis on nonmaterial possessions and extended influence on the dissemination of a particular Protestant upbringing cast her in a leading role in the pedagogical world of early modern European childhood. Her ward Zinzendorf, however, will vary the theme of her exemplarity and incorporate a sense of play and joy into the community experience in the "chorus" of childhood. A radical and gendered shift ensues, from preaching piety to teaching play.

Early modern childhood, as retrofitted through historical, cultural, and anthropological research, reveals the formation of childhood subjectivity that prefaces the equivalence between play and pedagogy. That definition is predicated on a metonymic relationship between the family and the dwelling space and extends the metaphor of the body as spiritual architecture of embodying Christ. That said, in the generation between Gersdorff and Zinzendorf, a rift opened. Whereas she espoused the continuities of childhood to adulthood, minimizing the difference, Zinzendorf, whose work was carried across oceans, sought religious reform through modeling the child, situating childhood in a redemptive play world.

Increasingly, the rhetoric of ownership comes to dominate the place of children within the family, also reflected in the pedagogies of play, which inculcated the young with a sense not only of their situational and economic selves but also an ethos of behavior toward other subjects and objects. Play participates in the sacred, secular, and entrepreneurial aspects of childhood in transatlantic modernity, emanating beyond the borders of German-speaking Europe. Verbal and visual lessons model best behaviors both for adults and growing children. Teaching children to play morally is voiced as a concern in the early modern world of doll homes and toy making. In his "Familie—Kindheit—Jugend," Klaus Arnold includes the performative aspects of play in a brief discussion of Nuremberg as a toy-exporting center, but he emphasizes homemade authenticity as well. His vocabulary echoes Kantian attributes of aesthetic experience: "So nahmen die Eltern als Aufsicht über das Spiel wie als Produzenten des meisten Spielzeugs ihrer Kinder am Kinderspielzeug teil. Es war demnach nicht völlig zweckfrei; sein Ziel war auch Sozialisation, die erlernte Einordnung in die Gesellschaft" (Thus the parents took part in the supervision of play and as the producers of the majority of toys. It was accordingly not without purpose; its goal was also socialization, the process of learning position).[24] Even this description fast-forwards to an Enlightenment-era prospectus of play that connects its objects to family and socialization. Significant, I maintain, is the religious influence of early modern pieties of play.

These pieties cast a long shadow. Andrew O'Malley, in a retrospective about his study of children's literature in England, begins from "the premise that the training and management of children was the focal point for a number of middle-class ideological concerns in late eighteenth-century England."[25] While Ariès and others acknowledge temporal boundaries and shifts from the study of aristocratic, early modern childhood to the emergence of a middle-class subjectivity in post-Enlightenment European societies, objects of play create a narrative of continuity—perhaps more accurately, of expanding concentric circles, radiating outward from the nucleus of the family. The focus of O'Malley's study is the construction of class identity, primarily through pedagogical and medical models transmitted through imaginative literature. Material and visual cultures contribute significantly to that construction in a more literal sense. The blurring of lines between play and acquiring the attributes of citizenship constitutes the pedagogical unconscious that connects intersectional aspects of white, European, upwardly mobile bourgeois identity. In German-speaking Europe and through immigration narratives and practices, it is possible to discern the connective threads among seventeenth-century childhood, Protestant practices, and community.

The playing child in this period, and transhistorically, invokes a sense of Susan Stewart's elaboration of the miniature. Her observations highlight the architecture of the play world: "Transcendence and the interiority of history and narrative are the dominant characteristics of the most consummate of miniatures—the dollhouse."[26] The dollhouse, its owners and residents, in turn configure the spaces of containment and responsible ownership that rely on pliable boundaries between history and narrative, between home and society, and between childhood and citizenship. In *On Longing*, Stewart also writes about the book as one of the "metaphors of containment."[27] The longing and desire she theorizes as the objects that mediate between language and experience are visible in dollhouses and in books, toys, and texts. For the former, alongside desire, anxiety about difference in scale abides. The miniature house becomes an object of instruction and didactic play to offset any uneasiness about scale. According to Stewart, the flip side of the miniature—the gigantic—also inspires ambivalence, but my focus here is the miniature. Further, to include particularities in Stewart's universal, dollhouses undergo renovations that reveal changes in the relationship between subjective play and object lessons. In the examples of seventeenth-century Nuremberg dollhouses, the materiality of the objects themselves are built and decorated with the ideological accessories designed to impart moral lessons.

Ariès's *Centuries of Childhood* does locate the emergence of the "child" as a human being different from adults in the seventeenth century. Though some have critiqued the selection and relevance of his evidence, the arc of his argument about the absence of a childhood in the medieval period and the historical emergence of the child in the upper classes of early modern Europe is corroborated by the examples from visual and material culture of the time. A stunning collection of seventeenth-century dollhouses displayed in Nuremberg provides a mimetic miniature of domestic interiors in early modern Europe, at least for the prosperous classes. The extant dollhouses (and "apartments") replicate to some extent the contemporary architecture of patrician homes and the residences of well-heeled businessmen. Though not exact copies, these simulacra nonetheless represent domestic life and the architectural taste from the region. As such, they pay dividends for many areas of inquiry, but details of decoration and renovation shine a bright light on a shift in the practice of play from early modern childhood to modernity.

THE DOLLHOUSE

The Nuremberg dollhouse collection is a cornerstone for the study of play. Karl Gröber asserts that they are not intended to be exact replicas of real houses, though they aspire to accuracy, with great attention to lavish interiors: "The child for whom after all these houses were primarily made would have quickly rejected any error in the familiar picture of its home, and the more exact and complete the likeness, the greater would be its joy."[28] Subsequent research leads to different conclusions. Heidi A. Müller uses contemporary literary and other sources, such as examples from the visual arts, to underwrite assertions about the realistic rendering of the dollhouses. In his preface to Müller's work, G. Ulrich Großmann emphasizes that the dollhouses were, rather than "toys," "vielmehr Anschauungsstück und Lehrstück über die Einrichtung eines Nürnberger Bürgerhauses und die Hauswirtschaft" (much more objects for admiration and pedagogical pieces about the furnishing of a Nuremberg bourgeois home and the household).[29] The dollhouses, appointed with both real and ideal moments of bourgeois living, embody a premodern notion of "play" that relies on display. This difference proves crucial to an understanding of modern childhood and the place of active, imaginative, and mimetic play in the development of enlightened pedagogy.

The houses transitioned from privately owned play objects to museum pieces in the late nineteenth century. The most prominent object in the collection is the Stromer house, named for the family that owned it last.[30] Built in 1639, the dollhouse boasts an inventory of more than one thousand individual pieces. Other houses possess varying degrees of detail, but all point to a collective household life that includes parents, children, and domestic servants, as well as animals. The household also embodies "die Einheit von Familie und Haus" (the unity of family and home),[31] which further functions as a foundation for social organization. The degree of detail in these artifacts is stunning. This inventory includes kitchen canisters with the names of spices—from cinnamon and cloves to nutmeg, the ingredients invoke the famed Nuremberg spice cookie *Lebkuchen* and the city's role in the spice trade—that contributed so much to the municipality's economic prosperity. Among the furnishings is a desk with accounting ledgers. In this sense, the structures and their contents function as realistic replicas of a household in a larger society. To appear realistic in miniature is not their sole purpose. These houses also represent the physical space in which to lead ideal lives; they are both mimetic and imagined.

In another example, Müller describes a *Kinderhaus* (house of children) designed by Anna Köferlin, a woman from another city (Neustadt) who married a prosperous Nuremberger; he was the son of a reputable accountant. The house design is printed on a woodcut engraving; it advertises the public display of the house model, which plays a poignant role in Köferlin's life. According to records Müller cites, Köferlin gave birth to two children: both died, and Köferlin remained childless.[32] The 1631 flyer displays a noble four-story structure in the baroque style (fig. 4). A father and son in the lower left foreground gaze up admiringly; in the lower right, a mother accompanied by a boy and a girl gestures instructively at the house and directs the siblings' gaze. The house, architecturally accurate, also illustrates an idealization on several levels. Köferlin intended the design to serve as a "Beitrag zur praktischen Unterrichtung der Jugend" (contribution to the practical instruction of the young).[33]

The original dollhouse is no longer extant, but the purpose of its design and display, extrapolated from the flyer, can be construed as pedagogical because the structure and the family gaze it depicts are both idealized and exemplary: the purpose is to shape the vision of the young—announced in the idiom of the *Wunderkammer* (*nie gesehen noch gemacht*; never seen nor made). The learning is implicit in the mimesis of domesticity in miniature. We can speculate as well about the role this house played as a sublimation of Köferlin's own maternal feelings; perhaps its creation performed the labor of mourning. Speculation and imagination aside (for the moment), the Latin inscription quotes the *Five Solae* of the Protestant reform doctrine. "Principio respice finem / Soli deo Gloria" (Beginning to end / Glory to God alone).

Modeling, both literally and figuratively, served as a form of pedagogical play in the seventeenth century. The houses—and other objects, such as mechanical toys—mimic the life world, occupy the play world, and mediate between childhood and adulthood. Over time and changes in "home" ownership, play practices, conventions, and instructive (though largely passive) observing segued into the act of play in a play world where active manipulation of objects is both permitted and encouraged. Play changed. In the same Stromer house mentioned above, there is an indication that the lower floors are accessible, possibly for "hands-on" activity.[34] Müller notes that the figure of the stable boy is the only movable element, again, possibly available to a child's touch. There are small-scale toys in the *Kinderstube*, and a *Laufwagen* or walker that had an authentic counterpart in the seventeenth century as well, though its use was controversial.[35] Müller suggests that the

THE PROTESTANT PLAY ETHIC   41

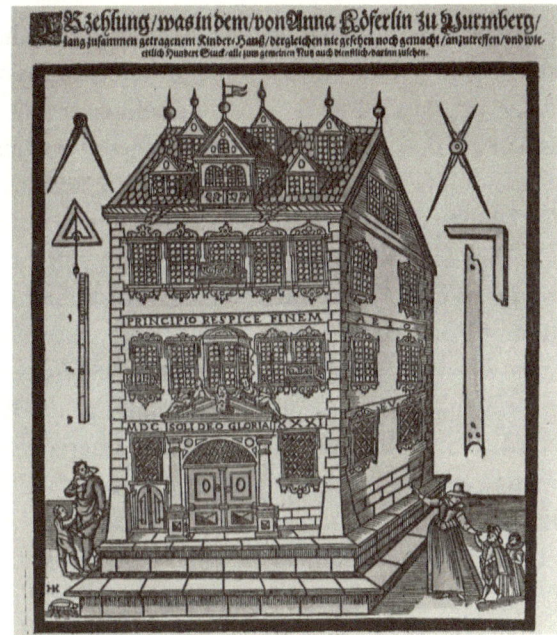

FIG. 4 Anna Köferlin, "Kinderhaus," Nuremberg, 1631. 42.6 × 48 cm. Photo: INTERFOTO / Alamy Stock Photo.

objects in the household in miniature served as talking points to instruct the young observers in the ways of furnishing and running a large house for the family and staff.[36] Of interest here is the use of the "toy" to ground a relationship between children and adults—not necessarily parents. Learning was interactive and intergenerational. Understanding the class, gender, and generational roles in the family was the point of the lesson. The object lesson deduced from these examples can be summarized in the following: to teach work, teach play. In the dollhouses, the wall murals also functioned in a regulatory way. The material object—the doll house—and its interior décor connect life stories, moral lessons, and the pious undertone of song.

THE TRANSATLANTIC PLAY ETHIC

Pietism and its adherents contributed fiercely to a transatlantic play ethic. In his work on the interconnections between Hernnhut and America, Valdis Mezerers highlights the legacy of Zinzendorf and his influence over the Baltic region. With a sweeping, broad-stroke historical survey of religion in the Baltic, Mezerers foregrounds the receptivity of the people to

Pietism, based on the hostility cultivated by other faiths. He attributes strength to a robust identity and its ability to resist preaching and orthodoxy that extolled serving masters before serving God. With reference to Isaiah 40:28–31, Mezerers writes, "When the Church gave so little of the Bread of Life and the Living Water, where was one to find the presence of God and to renew and increase his strength in order to walk and not faint? . . . They found it in the fellowship of the Herrnhuterian Brotherhood."[37] Mezerers elaborates on the particular history associated with this inflection of Protestantism and ethnic identity, also noting the importance of 1722, when the Brethren made their way to "Zinzendorf's open and receiving heart and hands in his large county property."[38] The significance of spiritual and physical space occupies Mezerers and his praise of disseminating literacy and religious conviction across the Atlantic. One major milestone reaches back to 1739 with the building of a large hall for worship and, most meaningful for my purposes, the publication of the first hymn book. Song features prominently in the celebration of spirit and community; it allows for the coincidence of praise and prayer in choruses that reflect the divisions of labor within the congregation. The hymns echo in song across the sea. In the eighteenth century and beyond, the artifacts of hymnody provide elements of continuity in the state of European American migration among German-speaking Protestants. Historian Thomas S. Kidd writes in his exploration of the far-reaching influence of evangelicalism on the culture of colonial America that "Pietism contributed an intense focus on the heart, often in conflict with the decayed state of formal, established religion."[39] In the context I wish to establish, I claim a relationship between the ameliorating influence of song, its uplifting construction of community, and its inclusion of humanizing views toward children; that conviction correlates with a changing attitude toward play. Hymns function as a prelude to the mother-child play projects in the nursery songs later composed and translated in the Fröbel toy chest.[40] Hymns—their content and performative capacity—preface the acceptance of children at play as a legitimate outcome of religious education. In another example, children's hymns and songs underscore the element of beauty in worship. It is significant that these hymns echo across the Atlantic. Ernst Gottlieb Woltersdorf (1725–1761), a Pietist poet and pastor who studied in Halle, composed 218 spiritual hymns, sermons, and edifying texts and is best known beyond Germany for his work at the Halle orphanage of August Francke (1663–1727), the project also endorsed by Freifrau von Gersdorff. Woltersdorf's psalms and songs exerted extensive influence, with the "Fliegender Brief evangelischer Worte an die Jugend" described as the most popular; it was reprinted into the twentieth century.[41] In 1754, he became director of the orphanage in Bunzlau; his affiliation with Halle most probably emerged during his theological studies, as Woltersdorf served additionally as a teaching assistant. Decades after his death, Woltersdorf's *Sämtliche Neue Lieder oder Evangelische-Psalmen* enjoyed its first American publication, in German, in 1823. While there are striking differences among the various Protestant sects that took root in nineteenth-century America, the legacy of the Moravian Brethren, with its intimate connection to Pietism and Pietists, is salient for my analysis of play and pedagogy.

To manage the extensive material, I focus in this section first on the religious hymnal canon that foregrounds the innocence of childhood and the emphasis on joy in play. This prefaces a sustained examination of an influential work about the eighteenth-century hero of the Moravian Brethren, Zinzendorf, whose relative and patron I discussed above. The legacy of hymns, attention to transitive (material) and intransitive (spiritual) desire, and education practices extend from seventeenth-century Saxony to the twentieth-century Ivy League. In Henry H. Meyer's *Child Nature and Nurture According to Nicolaus Ludwig von Zinzendorf*, the Yale PhD reaches into the religious past to contribute to the history of childhood and childhood development.[42] In considering Zinzendorf's intervention into the discourse about child development, one thing stands out: for the eighteenth century, the opposite of play is prayer; later, work occupies the role of antinomy. For this reason, the intersection of religion and childhood play theory is paramount. In his preface, Meyer writes, "Recent developments in religious education have focused attention upon the child as the all-important factor in human progress."[43] His perspective on childhood is motivated by an interest in religious education. He locates his subject, Zinzendorf, at the "beginning of the modern pedagogical movement,"[44] insisting on Zinzendorf's timeliness in 1920s America. Meyer attributes insights to Zinzendorf about religious instruction that should serve as general pedagogical models. Moreover, Zinzendorf's restructuring of the family into subcommunities, based on age, gender, and marital status, provides insight into the mid-eighteenth-century reformer's acknowledgment of human stages of life and crafting of childhood through the practice of play.

The transatlantic migration narrative of Zinzendorf's preaching and practices prioritizes the importance of religious community and divinized family over stories that frequently feature absent or distracted mothers. The allegorical mother willingly abdicates the well-being of the child to the community and its savior. Family and the practice of play continuously reflect socioeconomic shifts; in the realm of German toy stories, the tenets of religious instruction segue into the secularity of the domicile and thus mirror evolving professionalizations of parenthood. Migration and class stratification disseminate this professionalization in the United States through individual and institutional approaches to education. Concurrent with the evangelical approach to child's play as a thread of the curriculum in a model transatlantic childhood, a secular method to motherhood and maternal agency developed along with an equally urgent debate about a mother's role in child's play through the role of the female teacher. The eighteenth-century counterpart to the liberalization of play reverberates through Protestant children's songs.

The hymn as an agent of pedagogy is one of Germany's exports across the Atlantic, though not normally recognized for the scope of its influence. The model of song based on devotionals is transmitted by Johann Heinrich Campe in his two-volume *Robinson der Jüngere*, which was inspired by Daniel Defoe's *Robinson Crusoe*, first published in 1719 and translated into German the next year. The description of Campe's novel in the Library of Congress's World Digital Library indicates its robustness: "The book, published in 1779 (volume one) and 1780 (volume two), was aimed at children between the ages of six and ten. Campe's *Robinson* subsequently reappeared in numerous new printings and editions until the middle of the 20th century, and to this day it counts among the most successful children's books ever written in German."[45] The interchange between the canonical and popular and the rituals of everyday life construct the play world through a subliminal pedagogy. In Campe's novel, the father narrates for a small audience; the narrator incorporates hymns into the entertainment narrative. For example, in the story of young Robinson's awakening on a beautiful day, the father embeds a *Morgenlied* (morning song) based on a hymn by Christian E. Gellert (1715–1769), which appeared in his 1757 volume. "Dein erstes Werk sei Preis und Dank," with minor variations from the original, is well received, so much so that the son Gottlieb asks for a written version to recite before he arises, and Nikolas is thrilled that a friend can teach them the song, for he finds it beautiful.[46] In other words, the model of a hymn, embedded in an adventure narrative about the young protagonist shipwrecked presumably in the East Indies and surviving in fear of the wild people and surrounding, manages to embrace the day with praise of God through a hymn, not identified as such. This is a scene of reading and a scene of

FIG. 5 Frontispiece from Ernst Gottlieb Woltersdorf, *Kinder-Lieder* (New York: Amerikanische Traktat-Gesellschaft, 1823). Joseph P. Horner Memorial Library, The German Society of Pennsylvania. Photo: author.

instruction that implicates the hymnody of the Protestant canon, in which we find both orthodox and heterodox lessons.

The arguments put forward here regarding the unconventional and unorthodox approach in Zinzendorf's teachings to religious doctrines of childhood may benefit from comparison with other influential and contemporary examples. For contrast, I turn to Woltersdorf's *Kinder-Lieder* (children's songs). He indeed wrote the book of Calvinist hymns, though his songs do leave a margin for transfiguration and redemption. Woltersdorf, the son of a devout preacher, was born in Halle, where he also studied. At twenty-three, he became a preacher in Silesia (Lutheran congregation in Bunzlau). In addition, he founded an orphanage, which was an especially important institution during the war years of 1757 and 1758. Among his other duties and activities, Woltersdorf organized prayer hours for boys and girls on Sundays. He died suddenly at the age of thirty-six, but his hymns were widely popularized, with the first US edition published under the auspices of the American Tract Society (fig. 5).[47]

In the introduction to this edition, as well as in the songs, we can detect a narrative of transformation—of drifting toward evil only to (re)discover Jesus through word and song, and eventually returning to the good. This pattern is evident in his own life. The editor writes:

> Bei unserm Ernst Gottlieb dauerte es fast anderthalb Jahre, ehe er vom Suchen zum Finden der Gnade Christi gelangte. Das kam daher: er meinte immer, sein Herz müsse erst besser geworden seyn, um Jesum als seinen Heiland ansehn zu können; und es wollte ihm doch nicht gelingen, besser zu werden. Endlich sagte ihm ein erfahrener Freund, er müsse zu Jesu kommen, so wie er sey; er könne nicht durch sein Thun selig werden, sondern nur durch den Glauben an Jesum. Dies fasste er und fing nun an, den Frieden mit Gott zu schmecken durch den Glauben an Christum. Die Liebe Gottes wurde reichlich ausgegossen in sein Herz durch den heil. Geist, und strömte wieder aus ihm hervor in seinen Werken, Worten und Liedern.
>
> In the case of our Ernst Gottlieb, it took him nearly one and a half years before he came to the search to find the grace of Christ. It happened in this way: he always thought his heart would have to be better first before he could see Jesus as his Savior. Finally, an experienced friend told him he would have to come to Jesus just as he was; he could not become blessed through his actions, rather through his faith in Jesus. He understood this and thus began to taste the peace with God through faith in Christ. The love of God was amply poured into his heart through the Holy Spirit, and it flowed again from him in his works, his words, and his songs.[48]

This is a typical trajectory, though Woltersdorf's path is not as radical as some. He faltered, then found his way. Generally characterized as evangelical, he appreciated the tenets of Pietism and its practitioners, embracing a personal relationship to the Savior and devoting himself to a life of good deeds. His expressed relief at the early conversion motivated his writing of children's songs in particular: "Sein Herz blutete, wenn er sah, wie die Jugend von Jesu nichts wusste und in Sünden dahin lebte. Von ganzer Seele wünschte er, sie recht frühzeitig mit dem Herrn Jesu bekannt zu machen, der sowohl der kleinen, wie der grossen Sünder Freund und Heiland ist" (His heart bled whenever he saw youths who knew nothing of Jesus and lived in sin. With his whole soul, he wanted to make them acquainted with the Savior as early as possible, as He is the friend and Redeemer of both small and great sinners).[49] We learn from the preface as well that Woltersdorf placed emphasis on teaching children in formal settings but also instituted prayer hours for boys and girls at his home during the week, in addition to the general prayer for children on Sundays. He met with them individually but also consulted their parents; he avoided any *Heuchelei* (hypocrisy) and insisted the children fulfill their household duties as well.

The songs themselves integrate the stages of Christ's life as a model for real-life works. Woltersdorf devotes one hymn to the life of Christ as a twelve-year-old boy. He addresses himself to "Euch Kinder, die ihr zwölf Jahr alt seyd" (you children who are twelve years old) (19), then recounts the New Testament story from Luke about Christ at the Temple (Luke 2:40). Christ may be doing his father's work, but his terrestrial parents search for him with great concern. Christ speaks of his duty to his heavenly father but follows his parents' directives. From the verses we learn of his obedience and deference. In stanza 12, the narrative voice speaks directly to the children: "O Kinder, lasst euch so zubereiten, / Wie Jesus war!" (O children, allow yourselves to behave the way Jesus did! [21]). The final two stanzas speak in the voices of the children:

> 14. Du heil'ger Knabe, wir bitten Dich:
> Fass uns an und zeuch uns gnädiglich
> Von den Kindereien, von wilden Lüften,
> Die uns verderben und sehr verwüsten;
> Ach lass uns nicht!
> 15. Gib heil'ge Freude! gib uns Verstand!
> Mach' uns deinen Namen recht bekannt,
> Dass wir ihn mit Worten und Werken preisen,
> Und Gott und Menschen zur Luft beweisen,
> Wir seyn (seien), wie Du! (21)

> 14. You holy child, we ask of you:
> Embrace us and nurture us in grace
> Ah, do not forsake us
> To childishness and wild winds
> That debase and corrupt us!
> 15. Give us holy joy! Give us understanding!
> Make us know your name
> that we may praise it in words and deeds,
> And prove to God and to mankind
> That we are like you.

The deployment of the Christ figure as a model for children is common to different inflections of Protestantism and is transdoctrinal. What Woltersdorf renders subject to criticism in this song is childish behavior, the *Kindereien* cited above. While he, as an early convert, harbors a deep desire to make that transformative experience available to children at as young an age as possible, he also fosters a reciprocal maturity. In other words, childhood is not the discreet phase of life represented in Zinzendorf, although some of the same instructional tools can be found in the Protestant-lite toolbox.

In another example, the point of difference becomes acute. "Dringende Reizung, die Jugend Jesu aufzuopfern" (Urgent need, youth makes sacrifices to Jesus [29]) praises the stimulated need for the young to devote themselves to Christ. The second stanza, for example, laments the wasted hours of faithlessness. Those who experience the fullness of Christ are blessed (*selig*), and the appeal is intergenerational, but the happiest are the young. The implicit joy in community, present in Zinzendorf, eludes this song. In the fifth stanza of Woltersdorf, the older believer is suffused in feelings of loss and regret for not having converted to Christ earlier:

> 5. Doch wirft er den Blick
> Zur Jugend zurück,
> Darin er geträumt,
> So schmerzt es ihn, dass er so Vieles versäumt. (31)

> But if he glances back
> to his youth
> in which he spent so much time dreaming,
> it pains him, to have missed so much.

In a further elaboration on this retrospective regret, the song exults in the potential happiness of the young:

> 6. Wer aber noch klein,
> Kann glücklicher seyn;
> Je früher man sucht,
> Je reichlicher schmeckt man die herrliche Frucht. (31)

> Who, however, is still young
> can be happier;

the earlier one seeks,
the more richly does one taste of the divine fruit.

The rhetoric of these songs conveys a sense of opportunity to live longer, more peacefully, and more fulfilled, provided the affirmation of belief in Christ takes place as early as possible. Maturity and adult understanding of loss and belatedness shape the individual stanzas, though childhood in itself is not disparaged. This restraint changes in the song:

9. Hat Jugend ihr Spiel
Und sündiget viel
Auf mancherlei Art,
So wird ein Kind Jesu vor Allem bewahrt. (31)

If the young have their play
and sin a lot
in many ways,
yet a child of Jesus is protected from all.

In this poem, the author posits an equivalent relationship between play and sin. Not only do the words constitute an impure rhyme, they state a causal relationship between play and exclusion from the protected field of belief. This position is affirmed in another song, adapted from Luke 19:42–33:

6. Weg Leichtsinn, Spiel und Schlaf,
Hinweg mit euren Ketten!
Soll ein verlornes Schaf
Nicht seine Seele retten?
Ach Jesu, Flügel her!
Ich eil' in's Gnadenmeer. (34)

Away with frivolity, play, and sleep,
away with your chains!
Should not a lost sheep
try to save its soul?
Oh, Jesus, spread your wings,
I rush into the sea of grace.

Pastimes, sleep, and especially play constitute nearly demonic dangers to the Protestant child. Conversely, obedience, subservience, and industry (*Fleiss*) earn accolades: "Den Fleiss auf Wucher lenke; wer täglich mehr gewinnt, / Der ist dein liebstes Kind" (Steering industry toward usury; Whoever profits more each day / He is your favorite child [35]). In the moderate persuasions of these songs, the Protestant work ethic raises its voice and asks the children's choir to harmonize.

Religious education for children aspires to transform and sometimes reform the youngest members of the congregation. The redemptive metamorphosis mirrors the rites and narratives about conversion but also achieves another level of religious inspiration. In Woltersdorf's model, children emulate adult maturity and devotion. They renounce frivolous activities, such as play, in favor of belief and prayer. Either they follow Christ's exemplary lead, or they avoid the egregious errors of sinners whose remorse and regret cast a pall over the hymns. The primary Protestant directive, the work ethic, echoes in these mid-eighteenth-century songs. One paints a picture of salvation only after laziness dies (Wenn nun der Faule stirbt [36]). More radically articulated and perhaps more challenging to understand in terms of childhood experience is the moment of darkness before the moment of decision. In one stanza of the song of remorse ("Von der Reue"), Woltersdorf writes:

> 10. Fühlt ihr euch nur recht verloren,
> Dass ihr Höllenkinder seyd,
> O so wird der Trieb geboren,
> Der nach nichts als Gnade schreit. (42)

> 10. If you feel completely lost,
> That you are the children of hell,
> Oh, thus is born the drive,
> To cry out for nothing but grace.

Even the Calvinist Woltersdorf holds out the possibility of redemption. In the resolution to this long hymn, the *Höllenkinder* (children of hell) transfigure into *Gnadenkinder* (children of grace [43]). While reform is possible, children are not role models.[50]

The hymnal, with its exemplary and admonitory moments, does not eschew celebration. In particular the Christmas holiday as a holy day provides an occasion for joy. In the accompanying illustration, the narrative

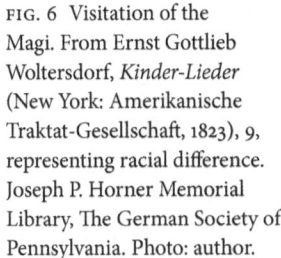

FIG. 6 Visitation of the Magi. From Ernst Gottlieb Woltersdorf, *Kinder-Lieder* (New York: Amerikanische Traktat-Gesellschaft, 1823), 9, representing racial difference. Joseph P. Horner Memorial Library, The German Society of Pennsylvania. Photo: author.

of Christ's birth also displays racial difference. The adoration of the Magi, kings of the east bearing gifts, creates a placeholder in the Protestant hymnal for a hierarchy that depicts whiteness in the light of the divine but does not exclude the "orient," though its attributes are subsumed into a model of ecumenical worship (fig. 6). Beyond the portrayal of Christianized racial difference, the image illustrates the ethical parameters of gifts, the commercialization of which in later centuries (around 1900) would become a class issue with the potential to derail the holiday—and redirect the religious zeal and joy of nativity. In the context of German holiday play worlds, children's texts often tilt toward an emphasis on nature; toys, however, prevail.

THE GOSPEL ACCORDING TO ZINZENDORF

In regulating the reception of play, Zinzendorf's influence is significant and transatlantic. Some biographical information is needed. Zinzendorf was born into a noble and Protestant (Pietist) family and was raised under Gersdorff's influence. He attended school in Halle and studied at the University of Wittenberg in preparation for a diplomatic career. Zinzendorf's marriage plans were thwarted, and he embarked on a religious path, firm in his belief in personal devotion and compassion. He, along with a small circle of friends, explored alternatives to Lutheran orthodoxy. Eventually he came into contact with members of the persecuted Moravian Brethren and gave them asylum in Herrnhut, the settlement on his property. While he was still on commission to the court in Dresden, Herrnhut became known as a place of religious freedom, though strife among members was inevitable. Zinzendorf returned to his estate, reestablished harmony, and wrote a covenant for living together. The doctrine of love in the daily life of the community became integral to the Moravian church. A renewed commitment to love and community, fostered by group prayer and organized in *Banden*, led to a communion that came to be known as the Moravian Pentecost, marked on 13 August 1727. He restructured the community according to age, gender, and marital status, converting the *Banden* into "choirs." Zinzendorf's encounter with a former slave from the West Indies inspired missionary work. Eventually the Moravian Brethren would proselytize in North and South America, Greenland, India, and Africa. Zinzendorf himself traveled to North America with the intention of doing missionary work among the Iroquois, among others, and there is evidence of an intense impact on different peoples prior to the American Revolution.[51] In 1741, he visited Pennsylvania, among other destinations, and paved the way for a settlement there in Bethlehem.

The brief overview of Zinzendorf's life prefaces a more sustained discussion of his pedagogical innovations. One reason for his success as an orator exceeds religious fervor. In Meyer's terms, "How well he succeeded in adapting his language to the village populace and to cultured society, to learned scholars and to little children, is evident to anyone who compares his gospel sermons, preached to the Moravian congregations, with his theological defense of the Augsburg Confession; or his addresses to the children with those delivered to the Lutheran and Reformed churches in Philadelphia" (14).[52] Meyer describes Zinzendorf's relationship to the Moravian congregations as "paternal," and other scholars have commented on the bishop's restructuring of the family in the religious community. Also noteworthy is Meyer's description of Zinzendorf's death and its timing: "He died in 1760, twenty-five years before the birth of Froebel, when Pestalozzi was still a boy of fifteen" (17). Zinzendorf appealed to the educated and to children, addressed the latter in a particular idiom, and did so well in advance of those pedagogical giants who set the standard for subsequent educational theories. In an era of increasing secularization such as the late eighteenth century, Zinzendorf's religious bent would be too close to divinity for comfort, or not orthodox enough for others more invested in public institutions for education. Meyer, with the benefit of lapsed time, can read retrospectively for the nuggets of educational wisdom in the praise.

Meyer characterizes Zinzendorf by his resistance to dogma and discipline. His *Lautere Milch* (Pure milk) comprises Zinzendorf's teachings, "intended to be a text for the use of parents in teaching their little children" (22). With this, Zinzendorf departs from models of catechetical instruction, "all of which regarded children as miniature adults capable of comprehending the whole system of theology if only this be simplified and condensed sufficiently for their consumption." The lessons begin with the most real and immediate—the body—and this starting point is familiar from other writers' efforts to move from the concrete to the abstract. Meyer highlights the use of the Garden of Eden story, which Zinzendorf interprets literally, "but the simple language and familiar pictures employed in this text did convey to little children a very vivid sense of greedy disobedience and its dire and perfectly natural results" (32). Meyer lauds Zinzendorf's concern with his target audience, especially when compared to the catechisms of Watts and of the Wesleyans. Meyer writes:

> [Zinzendorf's *Lautere Milch*] is better adapted to the interests and capacities of children in several particulars. . . . [It] is less theological and more pedagogical. The approach to each new idea or concept is inductive, from the known to the unknown. . . . The appeal throughout is more to the motive of love than to that of fear, the thought of the whole text moves in the realm and creates an atmosphere of trust and devotion rather than of commands and rewards. In these respects the catechism of Zinzendorf's reflects the author's psychological insight and his understanding both of the limitations and the possibilities of religious experience for a child. (30)

Meyer here recapitulates Zinzendorf's sentiment, the same one expressed later, for example, in Jacobs's stories—that authority should be inspired by feelings of love. While Jacobs posits a bond between fathers and sons, Zinzendorf ties an emotional knot between a text and an audience of children. His unorthodox way of teaching children religion mimics the family structure to some extent, but he insists on generalizing the feeling of kinship to a community of the faithful. He achieves this through example.

PLAYING WITH SALVATION

Zinzendorf's writings had lasting influence, and in his own opinion, his *Enchiridion*, which he intended as a Bible extract or summary for children, was the most important among them. It is an abridged version of the Bible for children, and along with sermons, hymns, and litanies for this age group, these texts were crafted to appeal to children through making the exemplarity of Jesus accessible in narrative. The means of communication and worship accommodate the needs of each audience. Meyer reminds his readers of two important factors: "(1) the Moravian habit of worshipping and teaching through song, and (2) the use of daily Scripture mottoes with subjoined antiphonal responses consisting mostly of individual hymn phrases" (60–61). The talks to children are comprised of eighty-six addresses from the daily talks (from the three-year period of May 1755 to May 1758). The last one focuses on Jesus as "Our Example," and the children's addresses exhort the audience to model behavior on that of Christ. Meyer here quotes Zinzendorf: "Dear children who believe on Him: Here are some of the talks which I have given to your little play-fellows in our German congregations" (quoted on 62). Though it is not Meyer's primary concern, the casting of worship as a community of children at play is mine. In forming German communities of Moravian Brethren, the appeal to children, through reference to the life of Christ, solidifies a sense of shared pleasure more than communal restrictions and punishments for sin. The talks are infused with emotional appeals, though always in the context of friendship and play, but also in song. The hymns are used to leverage concrete or the "sinnlich" into the abstract and divine: "This method of instruction by means of hymns employed over a period of many years led Zinzendorf in 1759 to declare, 'It is an established and well-known fact that our hymns provide the best method for inculcating divine truths and for conserving these in the heart' (J. H. D. Dec. 9, 1759)" (quoted on 76). Ritual song functions as a scene of instruction, but children can be inducted into a pleasurable play world with the proper models.

In Zinzendorf's introduction to the 1773 edition to the litanies, he describes the Savior as "the best friend of children" and writes, "May he give you the grace to benefit, even in the years of your childhood, by what he has earned for you by his holy childhood, his life, his suffering and death. . . . And may you never forget how much it cost him that you might be saved, that you might in good time become seed which should serve him, and proclaim the Lord to men from generation to generation" (quoted on 76). The content of his religious zeal aside, the persuasive force of Zinzendorf's words to children relies on his ability to forge imaginative identification between the children themselves and the Savior's childhood. Christ becomes a playmate. This approach crystallizes another means of instilling and replicating the "divine truths" precisely by defining childhood as discrete and religion not as inborn, predetermined, or hereditary but rather as a matter of choice. In Zinzendorf's litanies, we can observe a shift in religious practice: his rhetorical strategies presuppose the decision-making agency of children.

Meyer's analysis proceeds quite differently; he remarks on Zinzendorf's innovations, but he also notes that these drew opposition from orthodox Lutherans. More specifically, Zinzendorf's unconventional approach to teaching children, in my view, prompted the criticism. In his third chapter, "Child Nature and Nurture," Meyer acknowledges that Zinzendorf did not draft or publish any systematic treatment of child-rearing, but instead dwelled on a "personal relationship to children" (93). He identifies the breach between Zinzendorf and Lutheran orthodoxy: "Zinzendorf breaks away from this conception [of children as miniature adults] and from the simplified doctrinal catechisms for children, offering instead a more childlike presentation of what he conceives to be the essence of religion. This for him consists in an understanding of the love of God revealed in Jesus, and in the case of the individual child, in love for, and simple-hearted obedience to the Saviour" (90–91). Meyer's concern with the finer points of Zinzendorf's perceived and punished heterodoxy informs his study, whereas I am primarily interested in the reasons these teachings to and about children and childhood were so controversial—clearly Zinzendorf did not intend them to be.[53] Some of his language is erotic, some ecstatic. Some condemned various activities at Herrnhaag, the community established by Zinzendorf and shepherded—or led astray—under the tutelage of his son, Christian Renatus von Zinzendorf (1727–1752), whose elaboration on the belief in the feminine nature of the soul and blending of physical and metaphysical love influenced ritual practice in the Single Brethren's Choir.[54] Zinzendorf the elder intervened, and scandal ensued after one celebration, though the homoerotic nature of the hymns and visual and verbal adoration of Christ is widespread in Christianity. The insular nature of the Moravian communities and celebration of the spiritual and ecstatic in the body contributed immensely to the controversies swirling around the sect. Historian Paul Peucker has documented two eighteenth-century sources in which Moravians are accused of sodomy.[55] Instructions to choir helpers explicitly document admonitions against sexual contact, including with children.[56] In Christian Renatus Zinzendorf's hymns, references to children and childhood are limited to a metaphorical imperative for simplicity: "Mache uns in Allem gründlich / Aber auch in Allen kindlich" (Make us sound in all things / And in all things make us childlike).[57] Embedded in these practices and guilty by association is the play principle at work in religious instruction.

In Zinzendorf's *Kinder Reden* (1755–1758), he writes in general terms about gendered work in the household: boys learn writing and math, girls darn stockings, and these activities follow the model of Jesus's exemplarity. Zinzendorf tries to follow the example of Christ's work with children and also use his life as exemplary, as noted above. Children are taught to pray but also to play. In the *Kinder Rede* of 12 March 1755, Zinzendorf articulates education and play as part of the child world:

> There is in your heart still another school in addition to the one which we conduct with you . . . . The Saviour, who is near to us grown folks and to you who are already able to use your understanding, and who is near to the little children who can play and sing just a little, he is also near to the tiny ones, even much nearer than one can express in words. . . .
>
> This school I recommend to you. It must continue in you. The Saviour's presence which these little ones have had—who cannot yet either sit, or stand, or walk, who are still wrapped in babies' clothes—must remain and develop from year to year. (Quoted on 101)

Even the youngest children play, and older ones should participate in the cultivation of this tendency.

The next critical departure from the prevailing religious approach to childhood consists of Zinzendorf's principle of free development. Meyer describes it in the following way: "It is this principle which demands freetime activities for children as well as for adults" (102), and this is not only allowed but actually "enjoyed" in adult life. "So likewise does one permit children to engage in all kinds of free play, not only gladly permitting them to play, but encouraging them in so doing" (quoted on 102). Meyer quotes Zinzendorf's words, beveling the edginess of his claim, to explain that harm results only "when 'play becomes to the child an occasion for willfulness and stubbornness,' in which case it 'ceases to be free play and great harm instead of good may result therefrom.'"[58] Zinzendorf, who believes that happiness is the natural state of a child, insists on free-play as an asset to the natural development of children: "Spontaneous self-expression in free-time activities, including play, are essential to normal growth" (105). Espousing play is the heterodoxy of Zinzendorf's theory.[59]

The child's instruction forms the core of community. In his teachings, Zinzendorf portrays the family as a recapitulation of the congregation and also posits a larger alignment between the religious community and society. If, as I have interpreted it, his work indicates that religion, while itself not optional, is plural and subject to human agency and cognitive choice, then his rhetorical practices become performative; they have to persuade to be believed, to be lived. If children are the foundation of the religion, they must be included in the conversation. Skeptical readers would emphasize the evangelizing, perhaps even actuarial value in treating children, with their imaginative impulses, their play practices, and their openness, as clients for religious instruction. The clichéd phrase "preaching to the choir" comes immediately to mind. Zinzendorf displays adaptive talents, which, in contemporary terms, would qualify him for his own programming as a televangelist. In addition to his producing hymns, litanies, and addresses or talks aimed at children, he established and implemented festivals of renewal in which children play a major or even central role, and his practices were inclusive of all generations and economic brackets. For example, Meyer observes that in 1723 Zinzendorf founded a day school for poor children (143).[60] There are also "children's love feasts, which were sometimes held by classes and sometimes by the choir as a whole" (168). The festivals included rites of passage, celebrated by the community or in gender-specific subsets. In these celebrations, different stages of maturity are honored. There were rites of passage from the children's choir to the girls' or boys' choir and older girls' choir, the choir for young women. These were special events, and Meyer describes the practice at a chastely enacted "love feast": "All the girls, clad in white, sat in a circle in the center of the hall, immediately in front of the choir officers . . . with the partaking of bread and water with song and prayer. Then followed the promotion ceremony" (173).

The correlation between family and religious community begins at home. Zinzendorf wrote for all members of the tribe, and many have touted his attention both to the importance of motherhood as well as to the need for girls' education. In the address to the choir of married persons, dated 11 September 1756, he writes:

> For the success of home training, special responsibility will devolve upon the mother: "As long as a child remains in the mother's hands

> she must watch over it more than over a costly treasure." Such a mother, however, will find great comfort of heart, if, when her child is turned over to the congregation, she is able to say: "Thus far I have safeguarded this child. I know that he belongs to the Saviour. His heart has received grace. Until now I have faithfully kept the covenant. Now I give him to you, that you also may prove faithful to the trust." (Quoted on 138)

The purpose of motherhood is to cultivate the child as a future citizen of the Moravian community, only to remand him or her into religious custody at an appointed time. Meyer calls attention to Zinzendorf's "conviction that parental training is the natural method as compared with institutional training which is artificial," but he does not comment on the institutional nature of the religion. From his perspective in the early years of the twentieth century, Meyer probably is referring to early childhood public education, but this was also Zinzendorf's purpose—to "adopt a program of institutionalized nurture and training even for little children" (142). The historical and figurative construction of institutionalizing that training unfolds in professional parenting in the eighteenth and early nineteenth century. The play world falls under maternal jurisdiction.

CHAPTER 2

Professional Parenting
Enlightened Play

Whereas religious practices and praise songs transmitted through Protestant hymnody relegate playthings to the toy chest as tools of potential evildoing and waywardness, and the transatlantic commentary on *Gaben* (gifts) extends the renunciation of untoward material possessions, secular texts, and plural pedagogical theories, illustrated in children's literature that falls outside the canonical, nonetheless evolve models of maternity, paternal masculinity, and playful childhoods. The professionalizing of parenthood in the eighteenth century unfolds alongside regulating practices of play, usually confined to the domestic sphere. Theories of maternal and paternal instruction and supervision assume responsibility for mediating between intimate, familial spheres and public, historical ones. The space of play accrues gendered attributes with eighteenth-century German origins. In this chapter, I examine the gendering of protected play space through maternal hearts and paternal minds. Beginning with representations of the *Kinderstube*, I define the cast of characters in this discourse before moving to a little-known manual that instructs mothers how to teach play, thereby establishing a matrilineal legacy. In the second part, I shift the focus to a contemporary manual model of the *Hausvater* and the anxiety driven by female-dominated spaces. Finally, to offer a contemporary contestation of the paterfamilias and showcase nuances in the debates, I analyze the stories of a parent-writer who crafts ideal sons through the rejection of alpha-masculine play but also endorses a play space beyond evangelical control.

FIG. 7 Daniel Nikolaus Chodowiecki, "Die Wochenstube," ca. 1770. Oil on pinewood, 30 × 25 cm. Gemäldegalerie, Staatliche Museen zu Berlin. Photo: Wikimedia / The Yorck Project (2002) *10.000 Meisterwerke der Malerei.*

By the mid-eighteenth century, vernacular architecture merged the sleeping room with the functional space for children's play activity. The segregation of children into feminine space generates anxiety about their upbringing and play practices. Language usage provides evidence of the newly, doubly purposed room. Zedler's lexicon from 1742 defines the *Kinderstube* as such, and the room was usually heated, which was indicative of sustained occupation.[1] The gendering of such spaces prompted angry response, and we find one prominent example in a medical discourse. A popular essay by William Cadogan (1711–1797) leads the charge; he extols the intervention of rational men into the presumptions of women's wisdom in the raising of children. Cadogan's advocacy of natural treatment, including breastfeeding, was to exert considerable influence over child-rearing practices, and he often criticizes not only women in general but female servants in particular.[2] This challenge to a female private sphere, the triangulation of child, mother, and maidservant, is reflected in the visual arts of the time. One iconic image, "Die Wochenstube" (1770) (fig. 7), is the work of artist Daniel Nikolaus Chodowiecki (1726–1801).

It depicts the corner, curtained bed used for giving birth; a woman gazes at her nursing newborn while two servants observe the scene. Beds were located until well into the eighteenth century off the main family room;[3] privacy emerged with the growth of the urban bourgeois lifestyle and a concomitant notion of the "intimate" sphere. In the painting, the sentimentalized harmony of the nursery belies the contested space that was subject to controversy. In Cadogan, once the medical issue of natural feeding is settled, the mother surrogate can reenter the equation: "Thus far Nature, if she be not interrupted, will do the whole business perfectly well, and there seems to be nothing left for a Nurse to do, but to keep the Child clean and sweet, and to tumble and toss it about a good deal, play with it, and keep it in good humour."[4] The mother surrogate role played by servants evolved throughout the eighteenth century; expanded duties softened the hard maternal heart. Purposeful play and its supervision shifted to the professional mother. To chart this transformation of caregiving roles, I examine examples from the literature that instructed mothers and fathers to indicate their responsibility toward servants and children.

MATERNAL HEARTS AND ENLIGHTENED PLAY

Although the topic of "mother love" and "mother heart" is often associated with nineteenth-century sentiment,[5] late medieval and early modern occurrences of the term attest to its place in the history of the emotions. According to an entry on "Mutterherz," Hans Sachs (1495–1576), the poet and *Meistersänger*, uses it to describe a mourning mother. Paul Gerhard (1607–1676) also wields the term to designate lament. Friedrich von Hagedorn (1708–1754), too, employs the term as anguish expressed at the death of a child.[6] The composite substantive reveals a history of emotional loss. The relationship between adults and children is perennially problematized by issues of class, race, and kinship that can function as an index of morals and stories. In particular, the discursive construction of a "mother's heart" becomes polyvalent: the agency of articulated grief and loss is channeled into a repudiation of the hired help and the new responsibility of teaching a child how to play.

These instructions and their rationales abound in the fourth edition of the extremely popular household handbook for women, *Oekonomisches Handbuch für Frauenzimmer*. This edition contains, as noted in the introduction, an appendix with an elaborate description of contemporary mothering practices that for the first time include structuring play in a healthy manner. Though a marginal text, this handbook proved influential in the domestic sphere as evidenced by its republication. D. Friedrich Benedict Weber, for example, a professor of economics and cameralistics, compiled a handbook of handbooks, with twenty-seven entries listed under "Allgemeine Schriften über die weiblichen Hauswirthschaftsgeschäfte überhaupt" (General writings about female household duties).[7] Pertinent is the section on play and the furnishing of an ideal *Kinderstube*. The fourth edition provides crucial evidence that the theories of play and childhood at the level of philosophical and political discourses were also topics for the social construction of childhood at the very practical level. These obscured sources define the child's place in the maternal realm: *Küche* and *Kinderstube*, kitchen and play room.

Many scholars and historians point to the spread of Enlightenment thought, the rise of an educated middle-class, and demographic and democratizing shifts in attitudes toward the permeability of class boundaries as indicators of adjustments in attitudes toward women's roles. In his work on German attitudes toward women's education, Peter Petschauer foregrounds the exceptions—the women who, in the 1730s and 1740s, varied from the theme of preparing women for household duties, ever ancillary to the inevitable husband. The theme of women's education, he writes, "can be traced through the entire literature pertaining to household management, the so-called Hausväterliteratur, and practically all the literature dealing with educational reform, particularly the writings of the philanthropists."[8] Petschauer points out that around 1750, the term *Beruf*, profession, signified secular employment, distinguished from activities confined to the domicile.[9] He concludes that the dissociation, while not absolute, assured men of their professional status because it in turn enabled women to be seen as "laboring professionals inside [the household]." Leaders in pedagogical thought vary this theme and temper their reactions to professionalized households and women's work—some sources begin to empower women as mothers.

OEKONOMISCHES HANDBUCH FÜR FRAUENZIMMER: THE OWNER'S MANUAL OF MODERN MOTHERS

This guide for mothers epitomizes the anxiety about maternity while assuaging it in a series of practical and philosophical chapters, ranging from what to eat while pregnant to proper ventilation of a playroom. The inaugural cookbook led to a series of print editions within a few years; the volumes attest to the manual's success and widespread popularity. The first edition appeared in 1791. The second edition was "gänzlich vergriffen" (completely sold-out); a third appeared in 1810 and also sold quickly, and by 1826, the fourth edition was in wide circulation. The preface to the final edition boasts a new section, "Ueber die Erziehung der Kinder in den ersten Lebens-Jahren" (on raising children in their first years). This appendix was added for a specific reason: "hinten beygefügt, in der Ueberzeugung, dass diese Abhandlung eine Stelle in diesem Buch verdiene, und dass uns das schöne Geschlecht für deren Einrückung gewiss Dank wissen werde" (added at the end in the conviction that this treatment has earned a place in this book, and that the fair sex will certainly be grateful to us for including it) (vii–viii).[10] The full title, however, points to a much more ambitious project. A compendium of a housewife and mother's general knowledge, the manual leans toward practicality. Additionally, the text demonstrates class-consciousness and comfortingly modifies recommendations and guidelines for income levels. The nature of the advice and its applicability in the household encompass a wide range of activities, from personal hygiene and maintenance to diet and remedies for common ailments (fig. 8).

The appendix of the book begins with recommendations for diet and nutrition during pregnancy. The table of contents follows the developing child from infancy through the acquisition of teeth and through the joy and jeopardy of play. The advice ranges from the predictable to the speculative. Mothers are discouraged from the use of wet-nurses and surrogates, and fathers are advised to be actively engaged. To make the point, the author elevates maternity to a calling in the service of humanity: "Die Mütter, denen die erste Erziehung vorzüglich obliegt, haben grosse und wichtige Pflichten, aber auch grosse, lange nicht genug erkannte Verdienste um die Menschheit" (the mothers, who are primarily responsible for early nurturing, have great and important duties but also great and insufficiently acknowledged services to humankind) (781). In this context, the *Miethlinge* (hirelings), nurses and wet-nurses, are disparaged as not in possession of a *Mutterherz* (mother's heart). Once the responsible parties/parents are appointed, the plan for raising children must be moderate, following the model of nature ("dem Gange der Natur folgen") (781). Accordingly, the mother must encourage the self-development of her children by nurturing them without indulging them emotionally ("ohne sie zu verzärteln") (782). A similar sense of moderation applies to all aspects of child-rearing:

FIG. 8 Title page from *Oekonomisches Handbuch für Frauenzimmer*, vol. 2, 4th ed. (Stuttgart: Steinkopf, 1826). With an appendix on raising children in their early years. Joseph P. Horner Memorial Library, The German Society of Pennsylvania. Photo: author.

body and spirit must be in balance (783); the physical environment should not expose young ones to excessive heat or cold (784); extreme impressions should be avoided: "Alle heftigen Eindrücke auf Sinne und Körper der Kinder müssen im ersten Alter sorgfältig verhütet werden" (all powerful impressions on the senses and bodies of children must be carefully avoided in the first years) (785). Nursing is part of the process: "Die Mutter erleichtert sich die Erziehung des Kindes in dem ersten Jahre ungemein, wenn sie es selbst stillt. Sie hat für ihren Liebling das beste Nahrungs- und Heilungs-Mittel immer bey der Hand" (the mother makes raising the child much easier in the first years if she nurses the child herself. She has the best nourishment and healing remedy for her little dear always at hand) (803–4). As the tone of the manual indicates, the bond between mother and child should be both emotional and rational.

The topics covered include proper feeding and nourishment before and after the appearance of teeth, appropriate sleeping arrangements (not more than one child per bed), and adequate clothing. Beyond the practical advice, the manual augments its influence, especially when discussing the role of physical activity and play in early childhood. All activities are measured by degrees of "natural" identity: "Bewegung ist Kindern so natuerlich als Essen und Trinken" (movement is as natural to a child as eating and drinking) (823). Further, the urge toward movement is naturalized.

> Der Triebe zur Bewegung ist den Kindern eingepflanzt; man überlass sie sich selbst, und man wird mit Vergnügen sehen, wie geschäftig sie sind, wie sie ihre Glieder zu brauchen wissen; je mehr sie Bewegung haben, desto besser gedeihen sie. (823)
>
> The drive to move is innate to children; if they are left to their own devices, one can observe with pleasure how active they are, how they understand the movement of their limbs; the more movement they have, the better they thrive.

As long as the rules of moderation are familiar and upheld, ample movement, appropriate clothing, and children's physical autonomy serve everything and everyone well. The mother's role in supervising free play in the open air involves restraint: she must not overreact to spills and falls (843).

For reasons of health and happiness, fresh air demands free play. The challenge to mothers involves allowing the child to develop and learn without her intervention. According to this manual, nature and play constitute important parts of primary education: "Man lasse sie, ihr Spiel im Freyen treiben; in freyer Luft müssen sie den ersten Unterricht geniessen, unmittelbar aus der sie umgebenden Natur geschöpft" (One must let them play outdoors; in fresh air they must enjoy the first lesson, immediately in the environment of nature created around them) (854). Boys can in fact play without hats—this note begins a distinction between boys' and girls' play: "Man lasse die Knaben in Wind und Sonne ohne Hut ihr Spiel treiben" (One allows the boys to play in the wind and sun without their hats) (856). Other contemporary sources, such as the religious stories from children's books, caution against overheating or allowing children to drink cold water or other beverages directly after play, as does this manual (856). The shift, however, from religious discourses about the purity of the soul to a secular concern with the health of the child placed under maternal jurisdiction, extends the pedagogy of play into the realm of parenting.

The focus shifts also from outdoor to indoor activity, and in this appendix we have a detailed description of the ideal children's room, with a nod at class difference and mobility. In the section "Von der Beschaffenheit der

Kinderstube" (on the physical condition of the children's room), the author stresses cleanliness and order, qualities independent of income:

> Die Kinder bringen in ihren ersten Jahren den grössten Theil ihres Lebens in der Stube zu. Es kommt daher, in Hinsicht der Sorge für ihre Gesundheit, sehr viel darauf an, wie die Stube beschaffen ist. Freylich vermögen gewöhnlich nur vermögliche Leute in diesem Betracht für ihre Kinder zu sorgen. Aber auch minder Wohlhabende können sich wenigstens in manchen Punkten die gegebenen Vorschriften zu Nutzen machen. (865)

> In their first years of life, children spend most of their time in the room. Therefore, with regard to caring for their health, the physical condition of the room is extremely important. It is, of course, more often the case that prosperous people can better provide for their children in this manner. But even less wealthy people can at least in some respects make use of many points of the prescribed guidelines.

The manual proceeds with a call for ample space, relative dryness, and positioning above the first floor. In prescribing the attributes and location of the room, the author editorializes on the tendency to disparage the *Kinderstube*.

> Die Kinderstube sollte aber geräumig seyn, damit sich die Kinder darin ausbreiten, und wenn sie nicht in die freye Luft kommen können, doch im Zimmer Raum genug haben, herumzuspringen, und ihre Spiele zu treiben. (865–66)

> The children's room, however, should be spacious so that the children can spread out, and if they cannot play outside in the fresh air, they still have enough space in their room to jump around and play their games.

The commentary chastises those who skimp on children's space. Crucial here is the transition from a children's room, reserved primarily for sleeping and lessons, to one that serves the purpose of play.

The prose is rigorous about the physical condition of the room, which should not be too bright. Red curtains are to be avoided, and rich people should definitely reserve two rooms for a child—one for daytime activity, one for sleeping. Further, it must be clean, airy, and dust free. The prohibitions speak volumes about contemporary households: the children's room should not be used for preparing animal feed, washing, drying, or ironing clothes (866). There should not be soot from coal or wood, and temperature extremes as well as drafts should be avoided (869). The placement of the bed, vis-à-vis oil-burning lamps, must be monitored. No animals should be allowed in the room, and it is best to leave a child on the floor, rather than on a table, if he or she is to be unsupervised, but they should really not be left alone. These common sense dos and don'ts fall into the category of safety and mutual convenience, but they are noteworthy for that reason. The detailed descriptions of everyday activities of a household indicate those that mark the presence of children and encode it as under the supervision of the maternal eye and hand, which acquire agency. Maternal agency, more importantly, is achieved through making the *Kinderstube* child-centric.

By contrast, earlier guides directed at young and inexperienced brides inculcated the readers with the virtues of cleanliness and purity, but as civic virtues. The 1812 edition of *Die Hausmutter in allen ihren Geschäften* cultivates the image of the woman presiding over an immaculate household as a dutiful citizen. The middle-class woman who models cleanliness for the *Gesinde* or servants instills in them finer customs. Gericke writes, "Ich glaube, unser Vaterland hat schon viel dadurch gewonnen" (I believe our fatherland has already benefitted immensely from this).[11] In other words, the punctilious lady of the house, with her love of cleanliness, advances the interests of the entire people: "Jene reinliche Hausmutter ist daher eine Patriotin, indem sie in ihrem Zirkel die Volksmenge befördert" (For this reason, every tidy matron is a patriot because she promotes the people within her circle).[12] It is worth remembering that this substantial volume is essentially a cookbook. The author editorializes about patriotic value in the occupation of the middle-class matron. This editorializing reflects the spirit of the times—elevating the mother to patriot. By contrast, the shift in tone we detect in the later *Handbuch* deemphasizes the role of woman as citizen; the guidelines about daily practices indicate instead a growing trend toward the professionalization of parenting, directed exclusively at the mother as reader and consumer. In this context, a discussion of play as mandatory and imperative professionalizes the maternal role, and it redistributes a mother's duties to include the supervision of the child and children's play.

THE PLAY DRIVE: *BESCHÄFTIGUNG*

The concluding sections of this nine-hundred-page volume focus on activity and play. The drive toward activity is naturalized; it is part of childhood, and nature serves as the measure of all things. This guide encourages the earliest possible encouragement of activity: "Der Trieb zur Thätigkeit kann in den Kindern nicht früh genug erweckt und befördert werden.—Man gebe ihnen daher die Gelegenheit, sich zu beschäftigen" (The drive to be active cannot be awakened and encouraged early enough in children—if one gives them the opportunity to be active) (872).[13] In this excerpt, activity assumes nearly moral overtones: active lives are the ones worth living. Children as young as three or four should undertake tasks and games that develop their hands and feet; they can pick up dropped things, and

> Man lässt sie dieses und jenes von der Erde aufheben, was heruntergefallen ist, um es den Aeltern zu bringen, gebe ihnen Fleckchen zu zupfen, Federn zu schleussen, lässt sie ganz Bogen voll kritzeln, auf der Schiefertafel mahlen; und wenn sie älter werden, stricken, spinnen, nähen; sie verrichten allerley ihren Kräften gemässe Arbeiten im Garten und in der Wirthschaft; sie fahren mit einem kleinen Wagen oder Schiebkarren Steine oder Erde im Hofe oder im Garten. (872)

> One allows them to retrieve from the ground this or that fallen object, and to bring it to the parents, or can give them a little patch of garden to weed, or pluck feathers, let them scribble all over a page, paint on the slate and when they are older, they can knit, weave, sew; they can accomplish all kinds of tasks that are appropriate to their abilities in the garden or the house; they can remove stones or earth in the yard or in the garden with a little cart or wagon.

Indoor and outdoor activities and chores are enumerated with some caveats: a parent should combine a task with a particular goal so that the activity seems sensible and purposeful. The tasks or games should encourage physical activity and not involve sitting for extended periods of time, nor should they go on for hours without interruption, and children should get accustomed very early to order and a schedule, but not with excessive pedantry (873). Within the same parameters, children should learn to do things for themselves, such as picking up their own toys, dressing themselves, and ordering their belongings.

These prescribed activities are supplemented by early childhood learning. Excessive learning is considered unnatural: "Gelehrte Kinder erziehen wollen, ist ein wahres Verbrechen gegen die Natur" (To want to raise erudite children is a true crime against nature) (874). The foundation for future learning takes place in early childhood, so the manual freely admits, but it advocates play over school:

> Man muß bedenken, daß Kinder in dem ersten Alter bey ihren Spielen weit mehr Nützliches lernen, als zu den Füßen eines Lehrers.—Ein Kind lernt da von dem andern, ein Begriff wird aus dem andern entwickelt; es versteht sich, daß ein solches Kind in keiner verdorbenen Gesellschaft ist. Nur nicht zur Schule geeilt, so lange die Kinder noch nicht wichtigere Dinge für ihr Alter zu lernen haben als das ABC und Vokablen. (876)

> One should keep in mind that children in their earliest years learn far more useful things while at play than they do at the feet of a teacher. At play, a child learns from another, a concept evolves from another, provided that the child is not in bad company. Just do not rush to school, provided the children continue to have nothing more age-appropriate to learn than their ABCs and vocabulary.

Even mental exercises should be performed outdoors, if possible, rather than in the confines of a schoolroom. Further, toys can make a child proud for the wrong reasons. Nothing outshines the school of nature during this time period: "Die Natur ist des Menschen sicherste Lehrerin; von ihr müssen wir zuerst lernen" (Nature is the most reliable teacher of people; we must learn from her first) (876). This may strike us as a version of Rousseau-lite; significantly, the dissemination of this paradigm—Nature as benevolent pedagogue—attests to the "trickle-down" of the model, from the literati to the domestic sphere, from philosophers to mothers. The collective agency of children at play instructs, with Nature as the appropriate teacher presiding over the play world.

In the section, "Von den Kinderspielen in Rücksicht auf die Gesundheit" (Of children's games with regard to health) (890), the authors attempt to steer parents away from the exigencies of prevailing taste. Parents must intervene in the games children play, without abandoning decisions to trends:

> Es ist nicht einerley, welche Spiele die Kinder treiben, oder welche Werkzeuge und Spielsachen wir ihnen geben. Man sollte hierbey nicht alles dem Zufalle, der Mode, dem herrschenden Gebrauche und den Einfällen der Kinder überlassen. Bey Allem, was der Mensch thut, muß, wenn es mit der Vernunft übereinstimmend seyn soll, ein gewisser Zweck zum Grunde liegen, und dieß ist auch der Fall bey der Behandlung und Erziehung der Kinder. (890–91)

> The games children play, or the tools and toys we give them, are not insignificant. Here one must not leave anything to chance, fashion, prevailing custom, and the whims of children. With everything a human being does, if it is to accord with reason, there must be a certain purpose underlying it, and this is also the case with the treatment and the raising of children.

This text, so full of practical advice and grounded in raising children in incremental steps, alters in tone when it comes to the discussion of play. The practical transitions into the philosophical realm of purpose.

The figurative language of the manual asks the reading parent to be judicious about the selection of toys so as not to endanger or jeopardize the health of a child: "Wir sind sorgfältig in der Wahl der Speisen, die wir unsern Kindern geben, warum nicht auch in Rücksicht ihrer Spielwerke?" (We are careful about the choice of food we give our children, why not with regard to their toys as well?). The same philosophical idiom about purpose is repeated: "Bey den gewöhnlichen Spielen und Spielzeugen liegt gar kein Zweck zum Grunde" (The usual games and toys have no purpose) (891). There is all the more reason to regret any frivolous choices that lead to harm or cause injury:

> Die wenigsten Aeltern denken darüber nach, ob dieses oder jenes Spiel nicht etwa der Gesundheit ihrer Kinder nachtheilig seyn könne? Und doch ist so manches Elend in Kinderstuben, ja selbst der Tod eines solchen Kindes nicht selten die Folge einer solchen Unaufmerksamkeit. Es ist daher Pflicht, Aeltern und Erzieher auf die Wichtigkeit dieses Gegenstandes aufmerksam zu machen. Fast alle Spiele können der Gesundheit nachtheilig werden durch die unzweckmäßige Art, wie man sie spielt. (891)

Very few parents think about whether this or that toy could possibly be detrimental to the health of their children? And yet there is so much misery in children's rooms, indeed, even the death of a such a child is not seldom the result of such inattention. It is therefore a duty to make parents and caregivers aware of the importance of this object. Nearly all games can be dangerous to health if they are not played in the appropriate way.

The manual indicts any game that uses the human body in a way that could cause injury, either through falling or inadvertent strain. What one child can do and enjoy may cause the death of another. And the location of these tragic injuries is the *Kinderstube*. Those addressed—parents and other supervising adults—will be culpable. In the next section, I examine a counternarrative—that of fathers and of paternal roles in the domestic sphere.

PATERNAL MINDS: FATHERS AT PLAY

Eighteenth-century debates about maternal roles in children's play reveal some anxieties about the masculine provenance: paternal roles remain somewhat circumscribed. Yet a desire for enlightened play, accompanied by the gendered division of labor, still exerts the regulatory impact of rational thought over theories of play and the importance of shaping the child's desire for toys. Male-authored cautionary tales from manuals and marginal literature elaborate the model of the middle-class father and his responsibilities toward child's play. Briefly, I consider J. H. Campe's influence, then Germershausen's *Der Hausvater in systematischer Ordnung* (1783), advancing this chapter with an analysis of stories by a writer who posits ideal paternity through perfectly imagined sons. In its conclusion, I observe the transatlantic influence.

In one example from the *Hausväterliteratur* genre of the eighteenth century, the empathetic child exemplifies middle-class piety and resistance to self-indulgent privilege in contrast to her narrative foil, the pampered and unrestrained daughter of the house. In Christian Friedrich Germershausen's *Der Hausvater in systematischer Ordnung*, the author devotes a chapter to the regulation of gendered *Gesinde* (servants). In a spoiler title, he clearly condemns abusive behavior from the youngest citizens of the household: "Den Kindern muss nicht gestattet werden, das Gesinde mit Schimpfen und

Schlagen übel zu behandeln" (The children cannot be allowed to abuse the servants with ranting and beating).[14] In a series of examples, Germershausen sketches the petulant, insulting, and sometimes violent way children act out against male and female household help. The degree to which the culprits are culpable, however, remains a question; attributing responsibility for the behavior is a close second, since children are presumed to mimic the behavior their parents model. Moreover, play itself takes the blame: "Manche Aeltern denken, wenn sie von ihren Kindern sehen, wie sie dem Gesinde mit spielen, sie seyn noch klein, es könne eben den Leuten nicht sonderlich schmerzen; was ihnen von den Kleinen wiederfahre, müssen die Dienstboten zum Spaß gleichsam erdulden" (Many parents, when they see their children playing with the servants, think that they are still small, they really cannot hurt people very much; whatever the little ones do to them, the servants must endure for fun).[15] Instructive manuals strike a chord that seeks to harmonize domestic relationships involving play, for the domicile constitutes the play world.

The parental thought process embarks on a slippery slope, resulting in the unchecked child. In one story, one guest at a festive dinner, a close relative of the hosting family, having observed the unrestrained and offensive behavior of six-year-old Friederike, whispers about her own daughter, Armgard. Friederike's abuse empowers her mother to criticize the servant and scold her outside the dining room. The servant reenters, calmed, but a second servant is sent to stand sentinel behind Friederike. The anxious back-up fears a repeat performance. Like a commenting chorus, the whispering guest, described as a related *Dame*, assures her listener that her own slightly older daughter Armgard is quietly crying tears of sympathy with the abused servant; the girl is hiding her sensitive response behind her napkin: "Sie hält sie vor Gott und ihrem Gewissen, wie alle Menschen, für ihre Nächstinn, ob sie schon nicht unsers äusserlichen Standes ist" (Before God and her conscience, she considers all people to be her neighbor, regardless of their social status).[16] Armgard excuses herself to seek out and comfort the chambermaid. She consoles the young woman with the promise that her own mother will hire her away from her aunt's house and all will be well. In the exemplum, servants are not to be "played with" by abusive children, as noted by the virtuous and god-fearing. The identification between the good daughter and the abused servant, mediated through a religious lens, models the ability to empathize across socioeconomic stations to the history of the emotions. Same-sex gender identification aligns with gentler worldviews: children's behavior could be measured in relationship to their treatment of the household staff—and a humanitarian reaction to maltreatment. The story is embedded in a manual, combining instruction and instructional narrative. In defining household spaces and subsequent instruction, child's play becomes the provenance of bourgeois motherhood.

J. H. Campe's importance is enhanced not only by his insistence on the feminine regulation of the *Küche* (kitchen) and *Kinderstube* (children's room) (from *Väterlicher Rath für meine Tochter*, 1788; 1796), but also by his agency as an author and editor of children's literature. His stature as public pedagogue is predicated on patriarchal privileges of the private sphere. His popular pedagogical follow-up to the Robinson tale and the discovery of America's adventure/travel narrative took the form of the *Kleine Kinderbibliothek* (Little children's library). These volumes, full of exempla and illustrations, collect stories of growing children who learn the dangers of disobedient play and the joys of undergoing a steep moral learning curve through benevolent supervision. One piece for my argument about toys, girls, and servants, "Das Kind und die Hofmeisterin" (The child and the governess), depicts a familiar triad: the misbehaving child, a mediating doll, and a household servant, albeit an educated and educating one, who shepherds the child to moral high ground.

In Campe's *Kleine Kinderbibliothek*, the stories portray a range of gendered models to emulate, among them strict fathers and mother surrogates. Beyond kitchen duty, females supervise the upbringing of children, with attention to gender divides. In the stories represented in the first of Campe's edited volumes, a father enforces strict obedience from his sons, for example, while a governess or *Hofmeisterin* (private female tutor) administers more than orders. In "Das Kind und die Hofmeisterin," the young reader encounters a girl playing the scold and engaged in a monologue with her doll:

> So, Mamsell? Sie wollen mich nicht hören? Sie wollen den Kopf immer schief halten? Warten Sie nur, ich werde böse werden: noch viel böser, als meine Hofmeisterin gestern war, als ich den Hund schlug.
>
> So, Mademoiselle? You will not listen to me? You will not hold your head up? You just wait, I will get angry: even more angry than my governess was yesterday when I hit the dog.[17]

The petulant girl upbraids and threatens her doll, projecting onto her behavior that can have no agency or intentionality; in so doing, she reveals a mean streak a mile wide and invokes the justifiable anger of an authority figure, the governess. The latter overhears the one-sided conversation and engages the girl in a Socratic dialogue meant to bring the child to self-knowledge and impart a moral lesson. With gentle words and terms of endearment ("meine Liebe"), the governess informs the child that she was not angry but rather saddened by the behavior: that the child hurt the dog, and that, had it continued, the dog could have bitten her. There is a brief, reconciling embrace preceding the pedagogical conversation.

Care forms the emotional basis of the bond between the child and her private tutor. This benevolence in itself marks a shift away from a more corporal relationship between the young and their adult supervisors. The tale of the child, her doll, and the relatively caring governess signals a benevolence in the scenes of instruction that achieves learning and moral development not through physical brutalizing but through guided dialogue. The educational, healing embrace that prefaces reconciliation between the tutor and her pupil forms the basis of trust and support; these guarantee continuous compliance. The brief exemplum concludes with a fast-forward into a future of good behavior achieved with a single governing glance. Lesson learned. The pedagogical relationship progresses from enforcement-through-beating to a nonverbal reminder; the act of mimicking adult behavior through role-play with a doll sets the wheels of instruction in motion. The text models gentle interventions into the child's play world.

Much of the regulatory literature about controlling sons' behaviors occupies a moral high ground; it derives from religious training and doctrine, but this circumstance makes the exceptions to these genres all the more interesting and compelling. In the fiction of Christian Friedrich Wilhelm Jacobs (1764–1847), we meet a loving paternal protagonist who is deeply invested in the development of his two motherless sons. Jacobs did have one son, though information about any family is sparse. Thin biographical evidence notwithstanding, we do know that Jacobs published stories in addition to his substantial and influential work on Greek grammars and edited editions, with his perhaps most significant scholarly contribution being a thirteen-volume Greek anthology. The *Deutsches Literatur-Lexikon* entry relays information about his philological work. Susanne Barth, by contrast, includes the texts aimed at a younger reader. The three-volume *Allwin und Theodor*, she writes, "erfreute sich bis zur Mitte des 19. Jh. Großen Zuspruchs" (enjoyed immense popularity until the middle of the nineteenth century).[18] Further, she observes that one work, written to help process the death of his wife, was recommended for girls, and, like many of his peers, he took interest in the education of women. But my interest lies in his pedagogical interventions into masculine play. A trained classical philologist, the author-scholar incorporates an appreciation for nature and society into his children's stories. His Leipzig publisher circulated books on topics such as archaeology from a Christian perspective, but Jacobs's stories maintain a moderately religious, yet civic-minded, sense of balance and perspective—he himself suffered discrimination from Catholic priests, and after a brief period in Bavaria he returned to the Northern German city of Gotha where he worked as a library administrator for the remainder of his life. His children's stories do acknowledge sectarian differences, but his young protagonists maintain their sense of reason and moderation, modeling an ecumenical heterodoxy that advances ethical behavior in children into a human universal. These stories, the subject of this chapter, provide ample evidence of gentle paternal guidance as the beacon of ethical play, predicated on a healthy appreciation of human community, natural beauty, and a skepticism about the material world of toys.

In *Allwin und Theodor: Ein Lesebuch für Kinder*, Jacobs introduces the third edition of his stories with an address to adult readers. In a second prefatory section, he dedicates the stories to his son. This imaginative work invokes masculinity in ways that complicate the prevailing militarized hegemony of Napoleonic-era soldiers by insisting on paternity and education in beauty—in Nature. The stories rebuke militarized masculinity as a model for sons; instead, Jacobs, in the introductory prose, unfolds a theory of paternity that reveals skepticism about current methods of educating boys. His aim is to cultivate masculine traits:

> Um Kinder zu Männern zu bilden, um sie der Geistesträgheit zu entreissen, die schon darum erniedrigt, weil sie nicht erhebt, muss man mit ihnen männlich sprechen. Man muss ihre Einbildungskraft zu beleben, man muss die Selbstthätigkeit ihres Gemüthes zu erwecken suchen, und, indem man ihnen die Natur und den Menschen in heitern und gefälligen Gestalten zeigt, oder indem man in ihnen die Ahnung des Unendlichen erweckt, worauf die ganze Menschheit ruht, muss man die reinen Quellen eröffnen, aus denen Religion und Andacht, Achtung gegen das Große und Schöne, Hass des Schlechten und Verachtung des Gemeinen entspringt. (iv)

> In order to form children into men, to rip them from their intellectual torpidity, which debases them because it does not elevate them, one must speak with them in a masculine way. One must seek to activate their imaginative abilities, to awaken the independence of their character, and, in showing them Nature and human beings in diverting and pleasing figures, or in stirring a sense of the eternal in them on which all humankind is based, one must open the pure sources from which religion and devotion, reverence for the great and beautiful, hatred for the base and disdain for the common originate.[19]

In the spirit of masculinizing children by animating their imaginative abilities, which are innate, Jacobs elaborates a paradigm for human cultivation in Nature. Though committed to personal development, Jacobs provides noninstitutional models to achieve these goals in his protagonists and invests his stories with the belief that masculinity plays well with others. Trendy pedagogical methods can stifle any sense of the great and beautiful. He criticizes pedagogues for missing the point (iv–v).

Jacobs advocates granting freedom to the child's developing character ("dem kindlichen Gemüth nur Freyheit gönnte") (iv–v). In an undialectical sense, Jacobs attributes his brand of freedom to the child's nature and character. However, this attribution implies the power hierarchies of intersectional identities. In the *Allwin und Theodor* narratives, the young protagonists become aware of their own privilege, leveraged by the ministrations of a benevolent father, and eschew their own power plays in order to model universal, masculine maturity acquired through the practice of ethical play. The overly and overtly practical training of the imagination robs the child of aspirations to abstractions, such as greatness, lofty thoughts, and beauty. In his opinion, the philosophical and the practical have joined forces to induct children into the human condition.

Jacobs's introduction speaks the idioms of education and play from Campe and Fröbel. He finds fault with constant instruction and supervision. The persistence of some adult presence becomes an instrument of surveillance that inhibits real growth, which, Jacobs explains, requires self-reflection and interiority:

> Aber in seinen ernsten Beschäftigungen, wie in seinen Spielen, geleitet, von der Einsamkeit, als der gefährlichen Feindinn, gehütet, wird das Kind selten oder nie Bedürfnis fühlen, in sich selbst

hinabzusteigen, und sich durch eignes freyes Denken, Träumen und Dichten über die engen Schranken zu erheben, mit denen die Ängstlichkeit seiner oft allzu beschränkten Erzieher die frischen, jugendlichen Kräfte umschlossen hält. (v)

But supervised in his serious activities as in his play, protected from loneliness as from a dangerous enemy, the child will rarely or never experience the need to look inward, and to lift himself, through his own free thinking, dreaming, and poetic thought, above narrow boundaries surrounding his fresh, young abilities and policed by the anxiety instilled by his often all-too limited teachers.

Here it is useful to recall the attention to *Beschäftigung* in the *Handbuch*, in which activity of a certain, supervised kind serves as the desired outcome. Though this author aims at persuading the young to emulate appropriate masculine traits, he does not specifically gender the supervisor.

In this assault on relentless adult guidance, Jacobs names supervised play as one weapon in the pedagogical arsenal of stifling a child. Instead, he wants children to strive—*streben*—for citizenship in an invisible world (*unsichtbarer Welt*) (vi), and this is not attained through prevailing methods of teaching. Time and the conditions for introspection must be accommodated. Again, play is part of the problem:

Um der Menschheit dieses Besitzthum zu sichern, muss sich jeder bemühen, den ökonomischen Geist aus der Erziehung zu verbannen, und die *Humanität* in dieselbe zurückzuführen. Diese aber besteht nicht in der Entfernung körperlicher Züchtigugnen, nicht in der Anwendung von Belohnungen und Ehrenzeichen, nicht in spielenden Erleichterungsmitteln des Unterrichts, sondern in dem unablässigen, frommen Bestreben, das Gemüth auf alle Weise zu reinigen und zu läutern, indem es mit einem *uneigennützigen* und begeisternden Wohlgefallen an dem Großen, Guten und Schönen erfüllt und über den Dunstkreis des gemeinen Lebens erhoben wird. (vi–vii)

To guarantee this possession for human kind, everyone must take pains to banish the economic spirit from childrearing and to return *humanity* to it. This, however, does not consist of removing physical punishment, nor in the use of rewards and badges of honor,

nor in the use of playing devices to simplify teaching, but rather in the relentless, devout striving to purify the spirit in all ways and to reform it so that it will be filled with an *unselfish* and inspiring pleasure experienced with the great, good, and beautiful and lifted above the foggy circle of common existence.

Jacobs intends his book for private use, not public instruction, but the target audience is presumed to be familiar with methods of teaching through the use of play in instruction. The intangible "possession" (*Besitzthum*) of identity established by citizenship or belonging to an invisible world directly counters the acquisition of material objects, displacing them through advocacy of decency and proximity to the ministry of Nature. While the author supports mobilizing children's imaginative capabilities, he disparages the type of self-esteem-building strategies we take for granted today. In closing his appeal to parents, he draws attention to and places his faith in the "miraculous economy of the human intellect" (viii). The Greek original *oikos* here best renders the German "Ökonomie," with its polyvalent embrace of the home, family, and domestic ecology. There, in the quiet and secluded recesses of human existence, children discover their own humanity. Thus he appropriates the figurative meaning of ownership derived from any literal acquisition of wealth and property.

The remarks from the 1802 edition preface a heart-felt dedication to Jacobs's son, which takes on the tone of an almanac. A contented heart is compared to a summer day, whereas discontent forecasts dark, stormy winter weather. The comparison creates tension with the remonstration to inspire and cultivate an ability for abstract thought. The dedication contains advice meant to outlive the natural life span of Jacobs Senior:

> Dieß kann dir noch nützlich und ermunternd seyn, wenn ich längst gestorben bin. Der fleißige Landmann pflanzt Bäume, von denen seine Enkel und Urenkel die Früchte brechen; und eben so legt ein Vater den Saamen des Guten in die Herzen seiner Kinder, und dieser geht auf und erfreut die Welt, wenn er längst von ihnen geschieden ist. (x)

> This can be of use and comfort to you long after I have died. The industrious farmer plants trees, the fruits of which can be plucked by his children and grandchildren, and just in this way a father

sows the seeds of good in the hearts of his children, and he ascends and gladdens the world, long after he has been separated from them.

The use of the planting metaphor to illustrate a parallel between literal fruits and figurative harvests of goodness may distract from the poignant concern of all parents of all generations who attempt to answer the question of what will happen to children after the parent's death. The seeds of goodness fuse with the emotional muscle of the heart in the promise of future yields. The inclusion of emotional territory on the paternal map destabilizes the presumed duality of parental roles in which the mother nurtures and the father distances. The single-parent Jacobs embraces moral and emotional well-being as the provenance of paternity.

LEARNING PATERNAL LOVE

Paternal love is taught and learned in the outdoor play world. The stories often involve long walks through lovely natural surroundings, interspersed with dialogue leading to insight about family life and the world. Individual stories provide narrative models for the abstract values espoused in the introduction. Other stories exemplify paternity in the animal world. In "Das Nest," the three characters observe the activity of a model aviary father building a nest for his babies. The father interprets this as an act of love—and highlights the power of the paternal mind:

> "Diese Liebe," sagte der Vater bey einer solchen Gelegenheit, "ist ein unschätzbarer Trieb, den die Natur in das Herz der Thiere gelegt hat. Ohne ihn würde die thierische Welt zu Grunde gehen. Selbst der nachdenkende Mensch würde ohne ihn die Mühe kaum ertragen, welcher die Besorgung und Erziehung kleiner hülfloser Kinder ihm auferlegt." (10)

> "This love," said the father on this occasion, "is an inestimable drive that Nature has instilled in the hearts of animals. Without it the animal world would not survive. Even the thoughtful human, without this drive, would hardly be able to tolerate the trouble required for the care and raising of small, helpless children."

The father notes that the care of young in the animal world lasts only while the babies are helpless. By contrast, human love exceeds the period of complete dependence and is mutual. Both boys end up embracing their father; they are thinking of the life of the children after the death of the parents. The story concludes with the imprimatur: the sons attest to the legacy of paternal love:

> Der Vater schwieg bey diesen Worten; sein Herz war gerührt. Theodor hing sich an seinen Hals und sagte: "Ich werde dich nie vergessen, lieber Vater, und dich nie betrüben, und wenn du tod bist, will ich dennoch so denken und handeln, als ob du noch lebtest." (11–12)

> The father was silent at these words; his heart was moved. Theodor hugged him around the neck and said: "I will never forget you, dear father, and never disappoint you, and when you are dead, I will still think and act as if you were still alive."

The primary bond between father and son, strengthened by a shared commitment to an idea of morality, also grounds the fraternal relationship. Jacobs's protagonist makes a promise, verbally assuring his future masculinity. We read: "Allwin umarmete seinen Vater, ohne etwas zu sagen; aber in seinem Herzen dachte er so wie sein Bruder" (Allwin embraced his father without saying anything, but in his heart, he thought just like his brother did) (13). The paternal legacy in these exemplary tales leads not to rivalry but to alliances between brothers.

To conclude this section on paternal absence, I turn to a narrative example of an absent father in Jacobs's short story "Der Krieg," the tale of a twelve-year-old flute player who has lost his father to war. Many young protagonists of the more orthodox religious genres age in direct relationship to the life of Christ; twelve is standard, but Jacobs inflects the standard, suggesting his intent to foreground the secular and civic nature of upstanding behavior, not in opposition to, but extending from, the directives of organized religions. The narrative can be also situated among soldier stories produced in the first two decades of the century, among them Clemens Brentano's "Die Geschichte vom braven Kasperl und dem schönen Annerl" (1817), first published in the *Gaben der Milde*. Achim von Arnim, in his novella *Der tolle Invalide auf dem Fort Ratonneau* (1818), displaces the bellicosity of the present, from the Seven Years'

War (1756–63) to Napoleonic aggression and the so-called *Befreiungskriege* (Wars of Liberation, 1813–15). Portraying the consequences of war on the constitution of family destabilizes and reconstructs the image of masculinity, disseminating a nonhegemonic model of masculinity through the act of reading. Similar challenges to male models can be found in the Grimms' soldier tales. While the genre of the "fairy" tale dominates their reception, the original designation of the "Kinder- und Hausmärchen" encompasses folk tales that met a range of reading and narrating needs. In the soldier tales, as I have argued elsewhere, an alliance forms between the reader and the ex-soldier, the foot soldier, and even the deserter, in direct challenge to the rhetoric of elevated bellicosity and ultimate sacrifice for the emerging nation. In "Bearskin," for example, the former soldier, remaindered in times of peace, makes a deal with the devil, and yet he prevails. A populist support for nonhegemonic soldiering, despite its subversive potential, prevails.[20] These stories dismantle the projection of elevated, militarized masculinity and cultivate an allegiance with the displaced, the remaindered, and the dispossessed. In his war story, Jacobs enlists a character displaced from the Palatinate, a reference to the War of the Second Coalition (1798–1802), who with dignity and his music follows his deceased father's moral compass under duress. The area, occupied by French revolutionary forces from 1794, was annexed by the First French Republic in 1797 and saw its sovereignty negotiated with the Congress of Vienna in 1815.

"Der Krieg" opens with descriptive prose about the beauty of the natural surroundings. The setting in this story contrasts the pleasures of a walk and a garden in early May with the privation and isolation of the young piper. On a Sunday, the boys and their father succumb understandably to the lure of music and pleasures to be found in the public garden. Jacobs further opposes the labors of the week with the earned amusements of the day associated with worship and rest: "Es war Sonntag, und eine Menge vergnügter Menschen vergaß hier die Arbeiten und Mühen der vergangenen Tage" (It was Sunday, and a crowd of satisfied people were here to forget the work and cares of the last few days) (16). Before the protagonists and reader encounter the source of some music, the author embeds the adjective "friedlich" or peaceful to describe the setting: "Alle schienen von einem Geiste friedlicher Eintracht und ruhigen Genießens beseelt" (Everyone seemed to be inspired with a spirit of peaceful harmony and quiet enjoyment) (17). While the crowd disperses to follow another distraction, the boys stay behind, intrigued by a boy playing and singing a song in praise of peace. As so many young characters in Protestant stories, the boy is about twelve, invoking parallels to the life of Christ. He is poor but his clothes are clean; he treats a gray dog kindly: "Sein Anzug war ärmlich, aber rein, und seine Bewegungen hatten eine gewisse natürliche Anmuth, die jedermann wohlgefiel" (His suit was poor but clean, and his movements had a certain natural grace that was pleasing to everyone) (19). In indirect speech (subjunctive I), he is asked who he is, where he comes from, and to whom he belongs. His answer is a war story.

The pedigree of the young musician includes an upstanding and sorely missed father and a desperate need to support his destabilized and distant mother. The story's ambiguous and almost allegorical title invokes a universal experience of war. The particularities of this tale, though, strengthen the resolve of the young reader to honor absent parents. The plight of the residents in the Palatinate, which fell under the jurisdiction of France and became a violently disputed borderland, was compounded by their vulnerability to both warring sides; hungry soldiers, either advancing or retreating, trampled noncombatants. The boy, complying with requests to share his story, describes his father's agricultural enterprises in wine country, their modest house near the river, and the few domestic animals that helped meet their needs: "Denn wir sind zufrieden mit dem, was uns Gott bescheert, und begehren nicht mehr, als wir haben" (For we are content with what God bestows on us and do not desire more than we have). These conditions change with war and the spread of evil acts, which spare no one, "weder alt noch jung" (neither old nor young) (20). First, refugees came from the other bank of the river; next came the soldiers, "bald Freunde, bald Feinde" (now friends, now enemies) (20–21). When they hear canon fire and word of the enemy's defeat and retreat, the father keeps watch in the night. Politely, he answers the door to find a group of soldiers demanding money with drawn sabers and pointed pistols. The boy recounts his actions, running to his father and begging him to give them all he had. The "wild riders" hold him and his mother hostage while his father retrieves all they have. Approaching canon fire disperses the riders for a temporary reprieve. Three riders approach, demanding money. The narrator inventories the weapons: "In dem Augenblick schwang ein Reiter den Säbel über ihn, und nannte ihn einen Hund, und ein anderer drückte sein Gewehr gegen ihn ab; und wir sahen meinen Vater in seinem Blute fallen" (In that moment, one rider swung his saber over him and called him a dog, and another aimed his pistol at him and unloaded, and we saw my father falling in his own blood) (23). The narrator concludes the paragraph with the observation that tears cover the boy's face and his audience is moved.

The young, indirect protagonist of this story is also a refugee from warzones, however humble his fate. Common to bellicosity, the soldiers on both sides behave "wildly." Jacobs pens a pacifist story in opposition to the market for war play. The failure to take sides and trumpet victory or lament defeat points to a more important antiwar message. We see none of the glory nor male agency at play. In contemporary toys, for example, we witness a shift from antiquity to historical and contemporary figures.

The toy soldiers express differently the mediation between acts of war and acts of play through material objects and their military history. The distant history of Roman soldiers designates a more allegorical conversation with antiquity. Increasingly, however, in response to France's imperialist aggressions, German intellectuals identified themselves with Greece, attributing the narrative of a failing empire to its bellicose (and yet victorious) neighbor. In early nineteenth-century plays, for example, Kleist's *Die Hermannsschlacht* (1808),[21] Arminius's victory over Rome's forces leverages local patriotism and emerging national sentiment—though in an act of potential misreading. At the Battle of Leipzig (1813), the turban-like decoration on contemporary toys was evident in the Kürassiers' helmets.[22] Some soldiers resemble historical figures. Invocations of Frederick and greatness, incarnated in convenient toy form, multiply after the routing of Prussian forces at the Battle of Jena (1806), attested to by calls for military reform in contemporary journals for officers.[23] Other toy warriors, however, represent infantry in contemporary uniform; they are potentially recognizable from the child's experience of war. Still other toys replicate artillery.[24] This temporal realism enables identification between the playing child and the object, between the boy and the enterprise of defending the "nation." In one historically specific colorized etching of German origin and dating to circa 1809, we see a celebrated bond between Major von Schill providing breakfast for his hussars. Paintings and engravings of the time document the original for the toys. The accompanying text emphasizes the camaraderie and purpose of the major and the hussars, noting their "unauslöslich Band" (insoluble bond).

Later toy reception renders boys synonymous with war games and attributes to their devotion and collecting drive the specificity of the objects themselves. In Paul Hildebrandt's work on toys and games, published around 1900, he writes:

> Und es gibt in der Tat kaum eine bessere historischer und kriegerischer Ereignisse, als die getreue Reproduktion von Soldaten,

Feldherren und Schlachten, ob es sich nun um Griechen und Trojaner oder um Russen und Japaner handelt, und deshalb haben auch die Nürnberger Bleifigurfabrikanten seit dem Vorgehen Hilperts im 18. Jahrhundert den Grundsatz befolgt, in Ausrüstung und Ausführung ihrer kleinen Bleigeschöpfe so gewissenhaft wie möglich vorzugehen, zumal Kinder oft viel schärfer sehen und beobachten als Erwachsene.

And in fact there is hardly a better historical and military event than the faithful reproduction of soldiers, generals, and battles, whether they are Greeks and Trojans or Russians and Japanese, and that is why the Nuremberg manufacturers of lead figures, ever since Hilpert's process in the eighteenth century, have been adhering to the principle of being as conscientious as possible in equipping and executing their little lead creatures, especially as children often see and observe much sharper than do adults.[25]

Hildebrandt alludes to the tinsmith Johann Gottfried Hilpert (1748–1832), who worked in pewter and tin, presumably from the rich mines around Nuremberg, to recreate with accuracy and colorful paint the soldiers of the Seven Years' War, among others, and also Frederick the Great. In his emphasis on the realism and fidelity to detail, Hildebrandt forges a further connection, not only between play and art but between toys and history. He segues into a discussion that offers an example of play transcending national rivalries: "Spielen unsere Kinder mit den kleinen Soldaten Krieg, dann verliert meist die unbeliebtere Nation, aber trotzdem soll das Heer der verlierenden Partei kampftüchtig sein, sonst wäre es ja kein Gegner, den es sich belohnte zu bekämpfen" (If our children are playing war with the little soldiers, then most often the less-popular nation loses, but in spite of that the army of the losing party must be battle-ready, otherwise it would not be an opponent worthy of the battle).[26] The reception of toys and playing war, when Hildebrandt takes a long view, opens the possibility for rivalry between worthy opponents. Toys allow for the repetition of battles won or lost, but Jacobs upsets the equanimity and equipoise of this interpretation of officers' masculinity.

Jacobs's story works against the grain of gendered war play. By depicting the personal experience of a model protagonist through the age-appropriate eyes of Allwin and Theodor, Jacobs intends an act of peace to displace any glory or victory from the blight of war. In his tale, the surviving boy witnesses not only his father's death but the burning of their home to the ground, followed by the collapse of his mother. In some ways, the soldier tales I allude to above depict protagonists who suffer from PTSD—Bearskin comes alive in the heat of battle, he cannot survive peace without a pact with the devil, he deteriorates physically (though by agreement), and yet he prevails. Jacobs portrays the decline of the maternal figure who falls ill, a decline that is compounded by the guilt of burdening the poor widow who, though she has next-to-nothing herself, takes them in because the murdered father had shown her kindness. The boy chooses his father as a model. Describing his experience alone at the grave, the young survivor recounts that he "rief meinen Vater mit Namen; und dann betete ich, und nahm mir vor, auch so gut zu werden, wie er" (called my father's name, and then I prayed, and I vowed to become as good as he). The boy alleviates his mother's fears and tries to lift her spirits through his own determination, self-reliance, and fortitude: "Aber seyd nur getrost! Kann ich nicht Doppelpfeife spielen und allerley Lieder singen? Ich will mich auf die Reise begeben, und Musik machen" (But take comfort! Can I not play the double flute and sing all kinds of songs? I will travel and make music) (26).

The gathering is moved and impressed by the young man, whose piety and decency and humility earn him high moral marks. One listener adopts him and assumes care for his mother as well. A father surrogate is secured, facilitated by the child who honors his absent father through his deeds.

In the introduction to adult readers, Jacobs declares that toys can make a child proud. In the narratives, he illustrates different aspects of his convictions. The importance of paternal love as a contributing force in the emotional development of children is uncontested and enacted in the stories I discuss above. What does Jacobs tell us about play, and perhaps more importantly, how do his young protagonists behave in the play world? At first glance, the answer must be—they play very little. Instead, activities in the play world evoke an earlier standard of learning through a structured gaze, as in the seventeenth-century dollhouses. Allwin and Theodor are immersed in thoughtful observation of Nature and dialogue about it. Some later stories in the volume concentrate on travels or relate other narrators' experiences within a reconfigured textual framework in which the father, Allwin, and Theodor are themselves characters. One story, however, speaks to the issue of toys and play and resonates with the introductory remarks on toys as potential contributors to a child's sense of economic pride. At play, Allwin and Theodor demonstrate that they are their father's sons.

In "Das Krankenbett" (The sick bed), the reader meets one of the boys' friends, Karl. The nine-year-old character lives in a country house and visits often when his parents are in residence. The boys are friends, and "sie liebten sich gegenseitig von ganzem Herzen. Denn sie waren alle drey gut geartet, und selten störte ein Zwist die Fröhlichkeit ihrer kleinen Spiele" (they loved each other with all their hearts. For all three of them were good-natured, and seldom did strife disturb the happiness of their little games) (35). The friendship is based on their similar good characters and dispositions. The narrator does not shy away from describing their friendship in terms of love and innocence. As the story unfolds, we learn that the friend falls ill with fever; he asks to see Allwin and Theodor, but at that point in the story, they were still in the city. When they return to the country, the boys hear their friend is ill, and plan to visit:

> Und jeder wählte von seinem Speilzeuge aus, was er für das schönste hielt. Ach, er hat Blumen so gern, sagte Theodor. Ich hole ihm von meinen Hyacinthen, sagte Allwin; und nun liefen sie noch in den Garten, und pflückten ihre schönsten Blumen, und jeder band einen Strauß. Mit diesen Gaben gingen sie nun in das Haus des tödtlich Erkrankten. (36)

> And each selected a toy he felt was the nicest. Oh, he really likes flowers, said Theodor. I am going to bring him some of my hyacinths, said Allwin. And so they hurried into the garden, and picked their most beautiful flowers, and each prepared a bouquet. With these offerings they departed for the home of the fatally ill boy.

The boys' first unselfish impulse is to choose their best toys to give to their sick friend but also to think about what pleases him. So they bring flowers because they are beautiful, but also, and perhaps more tellingly, they know Karl likes them. During the visit, the destiny of the two types of gift differs: "Das Spielzeug nahm er nicht in die Hand, aber die Blumen erfreuten ihn. Mehrmals griff er nach ihnen, nahm sie in die Höhe, betrachtete sie mit innigem Wohlgefallen, legte sie hin, und nahm sie wieder" (He did not pick up the toy, but the flowers brought him joy. Several times he reached for them, lifted them high, admired them with profound pleasure, put them down, and picked them up again) (37). Karl obviously prefers the beauty of the flowers to the unobserved attributes of the generic "toy." The boys respect and act on their friend Karl's wish to see the trees again; with these in view, he confides to the Allwin and Theodor that he believes he will die that very day with the sun, but he asks them not to tell his parents in order to shield them from the news as long as possible. He dies; the boys come home with a terrible image of death, but also with a sense that life is precious, too precious for toys when flowers are at hand.

In Jacobs's collection, the stories obliquely refute popularized notions of pedagogy and play, instead casting them as contributing factors to the moral turpitude of youth. Toys lead to pride in possessions and economic self-definition, forerunners to a dangerous identity that valorizes ownership and consumer power over interior development and a well-calibrated moral compass. Nature models beauty and goodness, and the father's task is to provide the silence and space for his sons to attain that realization on their own. While some of Jacobs's critique is deft, some, as in the story about the dying Karl, seems heavy handed. The flowers take precedence over the toys, and the father's words to heed the aesthetic guidelines of the natural world effectively repurpose the bond between brothers and their friend. In sickness and death, play is portrayed as an afterthought, a distraction from life and death that even a child can recognize for its lack of real purpose.

The purpose of paternity for Jacobs combines unabated love with cultivating independence, but not through supervised play. Instead he teaches interiority: discipline, dialogue, and diary writing. A lengthy excerpt from Allwin's diary comprises one section of the collection. Allwin writes about being in the garden, and his autumnal thoughts (in October) turn to winter and his upcoming birthday. Jacobs portrays him recalling his fictional father's words: "Du hast mir oft Freude gemacht. Fahre auf diesem Wege fort; sey fromm; thue, was recht ist; widerstehe deinen Begierden; so wirst du zufrieden und glücklich werden" (So often you have brought me joy. Continue on this path; be devout; do what is right; resist your desires; in this way, you will be content and happy). In the scene, father and son embrace. Allwin cries: "Als ich dann wieder allein auf meiner Stube war, erinnerte ich mich alles des Guten, daß ich meinem Vater verdankte'" (When I was alone in my room again, I remembered all the good things for which I was grateful to my father) (62). This intensely recollected scene furthers the twelve-year-old boy's resolve to be a good person—to fight the "Hang zur Zerstreuung" (tendency to seek diversion), to pay more attention to his work, and to stop procrastinating. The fictional son imaginatively inscribes the lessons of paternity into the larger lesson of the narratives. Jacobs's examples ultimately offer a secular path through the garden of free Nature and male childhood. The protagonists' sense of freedom in the natural world, their play world, exceeds any social network bound by regulation and restriction rather than by the garden of children, a play world planted and cultivated not by toy soldiers or military masculinity but rather by paternity.

TRANSATLANTIC MODEL

The tendencies of roughly contemporary literature to portray absent or inadequate mothers[27] contextualize this reading of the self-help approach to parenthood in the long eighteenth century. Significant is the message of German pedagogy and parenting beyond Europe. What content, in the models analyzed above about enlightened parenting and play, takes hold of the transatlantic world? One example from a volume that was published just a few years after the fourth edition of the *Handbuch* serves to illustrate the contrast between its approach and the religious mission to shape a faithful flock. In *Der deutsche Kinderfreund: Ein Lesebuch fuer Volksschulen*, Friedrich Philip Wilmsen (1770–1831) introduces the first American edition published in 1830. F. P. Wilmsen attended school in Berlin; he studied theology and pedagogy in Frankfurt an der Oder, then in Halle. He became a teacher and was eventually ordained, later assuming the post of his deceased father at the parochial church and taking on the position of inspector of an orphanage. Married with six children, he wrote about a range of subjects. The texts written for children and young readers circulated widely, reaching American shores.[28] The publication information includes reference to sixty European editions—that is, with a wider reach presumably than the advice to women—and these combine didactic stories, geographical information, and also, in this particular volume, a German-language supplement for the American school audience. The *Volksschule*, the target audience for this edition, includes German-speaking Americans being educated outside the public system, most likely in the German language. This extracurricular setting emphasizes religious as well as linguistic training but also gives a particular slant to parenting through telling a cycle of cautionary tales. The impact of his writing is impressive: the first volume of the *Kinderfreund* underwent 226 editions before 1888.

Wilmsen's stories and supplements offer a striking example of how the exact same childhood behavior is regulated with religious authority, one that crossed the pond with impunity. The manual advocates balance, whereas the stories exemplify the absence of balance and its consequences. I highlight one story because the maternal role is exposed as weak and failing. In story 39, "Traurige Folgen der Wildheit" (Sad consequences of wildness), the wayward protagonist is fifteen-year-old Ferdinand. He has recently lost his father; his mother is described in sentimental terms:

> Die Mutter war zu weichherzig, als das sie sich hätte entschliessen können, den wilden Ferdinand zu züchtigen, wenn er ungehorsam gewesen war; sie wollte ihn so gern durch liebreiche Ermahnungen und Warnungen ziehen. Aber darauf achtete der Wildfang nicht. (95–96)

> The mother was too soft-hearted, such that she could have been able to decide on cultivating or taming wild Ferdinand when he had been disobedient; she so wanted to raise him with loving remonstrations and warnings. But the wild thing paid no attention to that.[29]

Through his own unimpeded movements, "gefährliche Sprünge" (dangerous leaps), and "Klettern" (climbing), he sustains a serious injury. The story is directed as much at impulsive young male readers as it is at their soft-hearted (and possibly widowed) mothers.

Attention to moderation and temperature control, an important topic in the manual, also works its way into the minister's narratives. In another cautionary tale, children want to swim. For one boy, the quick change from too hot to excessive cold has tragic consequences: he drowns. The minister appeals directly to young readers:

> O vergeßet es doch nicht lieben Kinder, daß Vorsichtigkeit bei jedem Unternehmen nothwendig ist, vorzüglich aber da, wo nahe Gefahr des Lebens droht!—Sollten nicht endlich so viele Beispiele durch ihre eigene Schuld Ertrunkener, Vorsicht und Behutsamkeit lehren! (175)

> O please do not forget, dear children, that caution is necessary in every undertaking, especially where there is immediate danger that can be life-threatening!—If only there were not so many examples of those who drowned through their own faults to teach others to be careful and vigilant!

Wilmsen also deals with issues of physical activity, as important for children as it is for adults. In part seven, "Von der Bewegung und Ruhe" (Of movement and rest) (182), he writes:

> Die körperliche Bewegung, besonders in freier Luft, hat mannigfaltigen Nutzen für den Menschen; sie bewirkt Hunger und Durst, hilft Essen und Trinken verdauen, und macht dass es gedeiht . . . sie giebt Ruhe und einen sanften Schlaf. Die körperliche Arbeit besonders ist dem Menschen überaus heilsam; sie verschafft ihm eine blühende Gesundheit und ein langes Leben, schenkt ihm Heiterkeit und Wohlstand, und bewahrt ihn vor vielen Uebeln. Ohne viele körperliche Arbeit kann der Mensch unmöglich gesund sein. (182)

> Physical movement, especially in fresh air, has many uses for people; it impacts hunger and thirst, helps digest food and drink, and makes one thrive. . . . It gives rest and a gentle sleep. Physical labor is completely beneficial for people; it enables one to enjoy blooming health and a long life, gives one happiness and well-being, and protects one from many evils. Without much physical labor it is impossible for a human being to be healthy.

Wilmsen ends the praise of physical activity and work by identifying its importance for children: "Den Kindern ist Bewegung eben so nöthig, als Erwachsenen" (For children, movement is as important as it is for adults) (183), but with the caveat that "wild" is bad, as in the example of wild Ferdinand.

Wilmsen offers prescriptive advice without hesitation. For example, he insists that children should have their own beds unless prohibited by extreme need (186). He covers other practical topics, forging a connection between the activities of the housewife and mother and the conditions of faith. In the section "Von den Wohnungen" (On apartments), he writes, "Stuben und Kammern müssen alle Tage gekehrt und gereinigt, und wo möglich alle Jahre zwei bis dreimal geweißt werden. Dieß ist gesund und auch löblich, denn es ist ein Zeichen der Liebe zur Ordnung und Reinlichkeit" (Rooms and chambers must be ordered and cleaned every day, and where possible, bleached two or three times a year. This is healthy and also praiseworthy, for it is also a sign of love of orderliness and cleanliness) (187). The implied readers and pupils of Wilmsen's prescriptive narratives are mothers and growing children. While some of his protagonists have clearly taken the wrong path, they become exempla, allegories of wayward behavior, excessive activity, unhygienic lifestyles, and sentimental mothers.

Unlike these and other cautionary tales of the time, the *Handbuch für Frauenzimmer* resists the religious economy of infraction and punishment that dominates so much of the literature directed at women about their children, and at child readers themselves. Not a single paragraph in this tome is devoted to verbal scolding or punishment. The prevailing secularity of the *Handbuch* locates it firmly within a domestic sphere in which motherhood is an active and ongoing vocation and evolving profession, and maternality is supported by research and reason. With such mothers, play is repurposed to align with a more generalized concept of a healthy individual, a development that moves play away from moral institutions and installs it in the proper play rooms of the domicile while encouraging a healthy relationship to games and toys. Jacobs, in comparison, imbues his figurative sons with a portable sense of appreciation for the objects not of toy manufacturers but of the natural world. Jacobs's eschewing of material possessions, albeit from a secularized perspective, provides a counterpoint to privation and war—a play world in which Nature accommodates and heals. The model of the indulgent mother, the wild child, and the dire consequences of unrestricted play conveyed by Wilmsen's allegories survives in its migration to the New World, thus reviving and exporting the Protestant play ethic for the professionalizing, enlightened parent.

CHAPTER 3

Revolutions in Play

The domestic guides about parenting as a supervision of play assume a timeless tone; children behave badly or well depending on the author and audience. The balanced approach, grounded in the cycles of the natural world and domestic economy, comes to characterize enlightened and principled parenting for both genders. Frequently, the domestic sphere is portrayed as ahistorical, while history is inscribed onto the public sphere. In the transatlantic play world, Nature accrues attributes of an unchanging refuge from the malaise of modern life, as a history-free zone, which is challenged by transnational, transatlantic tropes of war. Jacobs posits a masculinity in contrast to bellicosity, but his model is more exception than rule. The portrayal of perennially wild children who meet harsh but justified ends constitutes one thread in the connective German network between Europe and the Americas. In the revolutionary century, German-speaking lands fail to make history. Yet transnational fantasies of German interventions in the spirit of resistance to tyranny are articulated in unexpected ways. War toys, as I demonstrate in this chapter, do not always invite the direct connection between toy soldiers, miniature weapons, historically accurate uniforms, and real wars. Some upset the balance of enlightened parenthood. The noncanonical figures I have discussed, such as Löffler, Jacobs, and Wilmsen, may have exerted considerable influence among their contemporaries and successive generations. In this chapter, I shift

FIG. 9 Hessian figurines, Stafforshire, ca. 1820. Photo: Myrna Schkolne.

my focus to a canonized, major author and his less-than-legendary parenting skills. Goethe's approach to play, the role of toys in his family romance, and select aspects of his literary texts inscribe him and his iconic status into the transatlantic grid.

Cultural politics in German-speaking Europe around 1800 grappled with the trauma of revolutions. Miniaturization references wars with toys and other objects from the decorative arts. In the image below (fig. 9), the Hessian musicians allude to a German presence in the American revolutionary story, possibly regaining some type of status or acceptance in miniature form. Absent a (German) revolution against tyrannical princes, Friedrich Schiller broaches the subject of Hessian conscripts in the second act of *Kabale und Liebe*; the play laments the abuse of German subjects for foreign wars.[1] The realm of miniatures, of toys and porcelain, allows entry of ambiguous historical references into the play world. A revolutionary ethos dominates the play world around 1800 with a transatlantic impact. My case studies of two objects in Goethe's purview tease out some of the ambiguities.

The scope of the Seven Years' War (1756–63) encompassed all major European powers, redistributing power and redrawing intricate affiliations. Waged across continents, diplomatic alliances ultimately situated Prussia in a position of shared victory with the British. Persistent bellicosity between France and German lands permeated national histories and perforated the domestic sphere. Though not all Germans experienced New World revolutions directly, the medial transmission through texts, material objects, and, not least, toys constructed a play world with an intoxicating dose of the dangerous and fantastic. Around 1800, writers, philosophers, and toy makers inscribe contemporary and historical traumas into the German national imaginary; this construct culminates in a transatlantic trope of childhood around ideals of freedom, power, and war. In addition to the involvement of prominent poets and diplomats in battle, integrity in war extends a web of meaning over the politics of literature and play. Near and distant battles search for German hooks. Causes and casualties, near and distant, influence the formation of the play world. The fraught, sometimes competing receptions of revolution and revolutionary politics featured in this chapter aligns with the German cultural heritage in the transatlantic world. Goethe's celebrity is exceeded by its heterogeneity. Two objects of his play world connect Goethe's legacy to a debate about toys and play trends and eventually confirm his heterodoxy in his American reception.

While toy producers around 1800 supplied consumers with a range of uniformed soldiers, mostly in tin, uniforms indicated historical and contemporary warriors alike. The practice of eighteenth-century warfare shifted in the three major revolutions of the transatlantic world—the American Revolution (1776), the French Revolution (1789), and the Haitian Revolution (1792). Even in the absence of direct German "national" battle, German identity transmitted to the young through play fabricated connections and inspired investment in world events. American wars infiltrated the German national imaginary in ways that invite us to examine Goethe's reputation as a parent, political figure, and player, attributable to his commentary on American acquaintances and events. In the Americas, as evident in Schiller's *Kabale und Liebe* previously mentioned, German lives matter in the battle against tyranny. Whether the Hessian figures cited above indicate a recuperation of realigned allegiances between European powers against the new American nation, or the appeal to the legacy of the Hessians who deserted and fought with revolutionary forces, the cultural inheritance inscribes German identity as beleaguered, sometimes persecuted, and central to transatlantic progress. Goethe's Lothario, from the *Lehrjahre*

(1795), is credentialed as a fighter on the side of America in the wars of liberation.[2] The legacy of revolution toward building a utopian society segues into colonial impulses.[3]

Connections between Goethean legacies and the English-speaking world have been the focus of scholarship, though primarily through the lens of canonical texts. Justifiably, questions of intertextuality between Goethe and English literature prevail.[4] German American scholars in the early twentieth century, prior to World War I, devote considerable attention to the proper translation and reception of Goethe's oeuvre and biography.[5] Beyond literature and biography, Goethe's life and legacy have had an impact on national—and transnational—narratives about toys, play, and the human condition. Often elevated as an exemplary figure, Goethe takes center stage in a range of studies that honor his contributions to transatlantic cultural legacies, to education, and to the development of genius. In many ways, transnational portrayals of Goethe as a cultural icon established his exemplarity—yet there are many Goethes, instrumentalized for as many purposes. Alongside his poetic production, Goethe's relationship to play attracted attention in his contemporary context and in the transatlantic world, especially in the early twentieth century. His relationship to play via parenting also reorients Goethe's legacy, creating tension between his purported exemplarity and potential eccentricity.[6] Goethe plays darkly; in his parenting, poetics, and politics, he relies on the repetitive temporalities that perform and destroy in the same gesture. Goethe's complex relationship to toys reveals the darker side to play, one that departs from prevailing notions of play in terms of purpose, pedagogy, and innocent experience; it differs markedly from that of Schiller as elaborated in his aesthetic letters. Finally, gendered behaviors and the agency of parental regulation of play connect this analysis with Goethe's family romance. Reliance on material culture and reference to pedagogical theory frame my case-study approach to "favorite toys"—not necessarily the puppet theater of his youth, nor the broken crockery of his autobiography—that ultimately reveal the historical unconscious, embedded in traumatic histories and narratives, of Goethe's favorite (play) things. His ambivalence about imaginative play, especially in connection to war and revolution, migrates with his legacy across the Atlantic.

Goethe's relationship to play reorients his legacy, creating tension between his seemingly irreconcilable attributes. In different ways, these biographical and textual properties of Goethe and his legacy further inscribe stories about the relationship between generations and geographies, between material culture and migration stories. Two objects relate to the migration of war cultures and Goethe's dissemination of play: the miniature guillotine and the yoyo. In the former, it behooves us to recall that Goethe himself had a role in deciding executions.[7] Additionally, he chose to experience the battlefield and induce cannon fever, yet, through the approbation of playing with particular toys, he proves capable of dissociating from these memories as traumatic—and these decisions impact parenting. The yoyo, in contrast, embodies the heart of the poet and partner in a love poem that turns out to reiterate, rather than eschew, bourgeois masculine subjectivity and desire—for the stable domestic existence of family. The metonymic relationships between toys and their historical antecedents, mediated by Goethe's biography as a parent, poet, sexual and conversation partner, and diplomat, ground the argument of this chapter. These "toys" represent significant historical links among trauma, migration, and toys in the *Goethezeit*.

During Goethe's age, toys and games clearly referenced and represented historical events, such as the French Revolution and contemporaneous events. Thomas Stauss's monumental study of two major toy and game catalogues from the late eighteenth century pays forward a continental treasure trove of historical trauma. He draws one example from the pricelist of Georg Hieronimus Bestelmeier (1764–1829): "Ein Revolutions- oder Dreieck-Spiel" (A revolution or triangle game).[8] In this challenge, a copperplate reproduction of the Bastille is represented on paper, folded and cut into thirty-two triangles that must be assembled. The 1803 issue advertises the directions in German and French. Stauss includes the dates of the first and subsequent appearance of this object in documents: the earliest stems from 1796, seven years after the Storming of the Bastille that triggered the French Revolution, followed by 1803, 1807, 1812, and 1838. A parlor game dating from 1814 provides the German patriot with a more victorious and vicarious moment: "Der Marsch nach Paris" (The battle of Paris) was designed by Wilhelm Burucker, a third-generation Nuremberg artisan and mechanical draftsman. This *Belagerungsspiel* (siege game) involves a maximum of four players.[9] On a board with Paris in the center, three hostile armies follow different routes; the fourth player, the "Pariser Gouverneur," defends the city. While the players could adapt to identify with neutral or unallied armies, the timing and design evoke the 1814 Battle of Paris in which the Sixth Coalition of Prussian, Russian, and Austrian forces faced the French Empire and routed Napoleon's depleted forces, which resulted in his abdication. The games footnote historical events; they appeal more to adults, with geographical puzzles and "homeland" games catering to a younger, more impressionable and educable audience: these are the toys and games of historical consciousness. The guillotine and the yoyo, by contrast, derive their significance for Goethe in ways that invite closer examination. Games of war bring traumatic history into the domicile. In the case of Goethe, his childhood favorite, the puppet theater, interacts with the theater of war and the experience of fatherhood and domestic partnerships. To connect these complex relationships, I first outline theories of play that foreground the proximity of pleasure and regulatory responses to performative play, a mode that posits a causal logic between childhood practice and adult behavior. Goethe's multilayered responses to play as performance invite closer examination, for the tensions revealed in his various roles as poet, political operative, son, parent, and, not least, cultural icon are central to his transnational legacy, poised between exemplarity and eccentricity.

Play has been overlooked as a litmus test for situating Goethe's aesthetic theory among his contemporaries. Friedrich Schiller, who in part popularized Kant's philosophies, devotes significant attention to the human aspect of play in his *Die ästhetische Erziehung der Menschen, in einer Reihe von Briefen* (*The Aesthetic Education of Man in a Series of Letters*). In 1794, Schiller engages further with Kant's aesthetics and the French Revolution and its aftermath in his attempt to understand the concept of the play drive in terms of affect/sensuousness and rationality as a totality. In aesthetic play, human beings become human. He writes:

> Der Spieltrieb also, als in welchem beide verbunden wirken, wird das Gemüth zugleich moralisch und physisch nöthigen; er wird also, weil er alle Zufälligkeit aufhebt, auch alle Nöthigung aufheben und den Menschen sowohl physisch als moralisch in Freiheit setzen. Wenn wir Jemand mit Leidenschaft umfassen, der unsrer Verachtung würdig ist, so empfinden wir peinlich die *Nöthigung der Natur*. Wenn wir gegen einen Andern feindlich gesinnt sind, der uns Achtung abnöthigt, so empfinden wir peinlich die *Nöthigung der Vernunft*. So bald er aber zugleich unsre Neigung interessiert und unsre Achtung sich erworben, so verschwindet sowohl der Zwang der Empfindung als der Zwang der Vernunft, und wir fangen an, ihn zu lieben, d. h., zugleich mit unsrer Neigung und mit unsrer Achtung zu spielen.

So the play impulse, in which both combine to function, will compel the mind at once morally and physically; it will therefore, since it annuls all mere chance, annul all compulsion also, and set man free both physically and morally. When we embrace with passion someone who deserves our contempt, we feel painfully the compulsion of Nature. When we are unfriendly disposed toward another who commands our respect, we feel painfully the compulsion of Reason. But as soon as a man has at once enlisted our affection and gained our respect, both the constraint of feeling and the constraint of Nature disappear, and we begin to love him— that is, to play at once with our affection and with our respect.[10]

Between the sensuous and the formal drives, Schiller's play impulse originates. Yet the drive and its reception develop away from actual play. In the Fifteenth Letter, Schiller qualifies the sphere of the play drive's influence:

Freilich dürfen wir uns hier nicht an die Spiele erinnern, die in dem wirklichen Leben im Gang sind und die sich gewöhnlich nur auf sehr materielle Gegenstände richten; aber in dem wirklichen Leben würden wir auch die Schönheit vergebens suchen, von der hier die Rede ist. Die wirklich vorhandene Schönheit ist des Spieltriebes aufgegeben, das der Mensch in allen seinen Spielen vor Augen haben soll.

Certainly we must not here call to mind those games that are in vogue in actual life, and which are commonly concerned only with very material objects, but in actual life we should also seek in vain for the Beauty of which we are now speaking. The Beauty we actually meet with is worthy of play-impulse we actually meet with, but with the ideal of Beauty that Reason sets up, an ideal of the play-impulse is also presented which Man should have before him in all his games.[11]

Here, Schiller's explicit and Goethe's implicit theory of human play and games diverge: connections between the aesthetic realm and the lightness of play are at stake. The former artist is unconcerned with games currently in vogue; Goethe, as I demonstrate, participates directly and indirectly in toy trends, especially when real and material objects are a factor.

Yet Goethe, in the example of his life and work, parents and plays toward different ends. A selective yet holistic model of Goethe at play offers an alternative to Schiller's dominant connection between the aesthetic and the beautiful. Goethe's investment in history and leisure activities makes legible their embeddedness in the darker side of imaginative, repetitive, and imitative play. The darker side further informs the dissemination of a nationalized reception of an exemplary Goethe at the expense of his playful eccentricity.

THE GUILLOTINE

Few challenges prove more vexing in contemporary childhood studies than generating reliable data about the correlation among children's toys, play practices, and predispositions to violence. While many acknowledge the connection among play, cognitive and social development, and learned/performed gender traits, there is little consensus on the issue of childhood development and a causality factor of toy weapons. Contemporary social psychologists have conducted extensive studies and concluded that expectations in play supervisors and gender-typed toys can influence children's development in ways different than gender-neutral objects.[12] When we ask a different question about toys, mimetic play, and learned behavior, we get a different answer, one that suggests causality. Even if there is no demonstrable cause-effect relationship among the material objects of mimetic and imaginative play and learned behavior, discourses and controversy persist about the ability of play and its accessories to shape adult agency and identity. Nor are these discourses confined to the present.

Goethe's toy preferences, some more obvious than others, suggest cognitive and contemporary connections that establish networks of meaning beyond his intention. A particular toy and his memory of it constructs his relationship to Italy, for example. In his travel writing that encompasses a journal entry, letters to Charlotte von Stein, and the published *Italienische Reise*, Goethe reports his encounter with a gondola and its triggering effect:

> Wie die erste Gondel an das Schiff anfuhr, fiel mir mein erstes Kinderspielzeug ein, an das ich vielleicht in zwanzig Jahren nicht mehr gedacht hatte. Mein Vater hatte ein schönes Gondelmodell

von Venedig mitgebracht, er hielt es sehr sehr werth und es wurde mir hoch angerechnet wenn ich damit spielen durfte.

As the first gondola approached the ship, I remembered the first toy I had as a child. I had not thought of it in perhaps twenty years. My father brought me a beautiful model gondola from Venice that he considered to be quite valuable, and it was carefully calculated when I was allowed to play with it.[13]

The memory structures familiarity with his unfamiliar surroundings; the toy and his childhood recollection preface his experiences in Venice. The miniature gondola encoded a precious, warm memory, but points to a immediacy between the toy and the historial truth that proves disconcerting with instruments of execution.

The image of the guillotine was certainly familiar from the print press as an instrument of execution and horror (fig. 10); French prisoners held captive in English prisons carved "models" from bone and other material (fig. 11).[14] The toy trended in 1793 and 1794, which inspired contempt and dismay in Goethe's mother (fig. 12), an issue with repercussions for the legacy of Goethe in the world. The materiality of the mechanical toy, its macabre associations, and its ability to elicit repulsion to this day will be treated more extensively below. Moreover, the intergenerational relationships and tensions in Goethe's prominent family reveal much about the role of paternity in late eighteenth-century German-speaking Europe. Benjamin's contemplation of toys, play, and their political, material, and historic associations, though not sustained, nonetheless sheds light on the darker side of play and its connections to a reading of Goethe. In his 1928 essay "Zur Spielzeugausstellung des Märkischen Museums" ("Toy Exhibition at the Märkisches Museum"), Benjamin acknowledges not only the complexity of the play psychology of the child but also the therapeutic moments of repetition for adults: "To be sure, play is always liberating. Surrounded by a world of giants, children use play to create a world appropriate to their size. But the adult, who finds himself threatened by the real world and can find no escape, removes its sting by playing with its image in reduced form."[15] In the combined context of Marxist and psychoanalytic interpretations, the toy guillotine's connections to history warrant further exploration, also with the consideration of intersectional identities.

Gender and emerging senses of national identity come to the forefront of the family romance when war and violence are involved. Goethe's

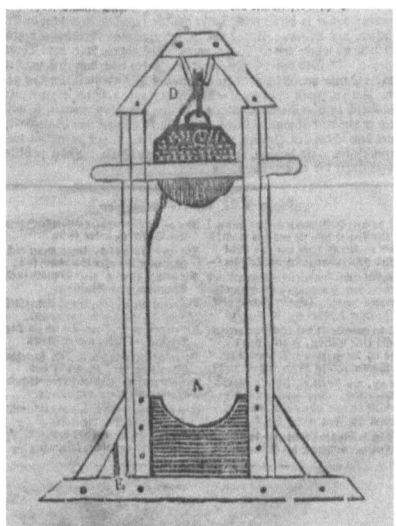

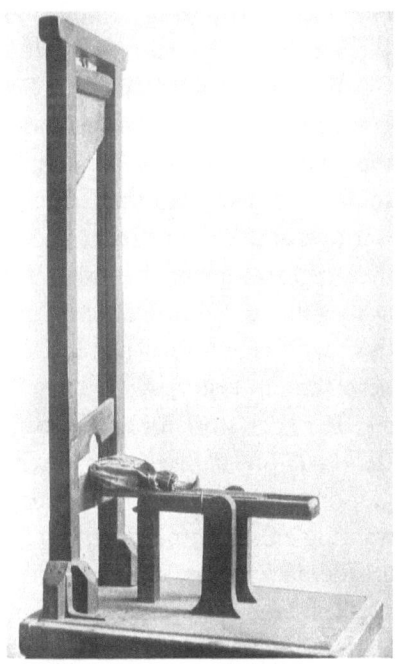

Clockwise from top left
FIG. 10 Guillotine. From *Beschreibung der Hinrichtung des Königs von Frankreich Ludwig XVI* (Description of the execution of the king of France Louis XVI), ca. 1793. Staatsbibliothek zu Berlin. Preußischer Kulturbesitz, 50 MA 47195. Photo: SBB-PK.

FIG. 11 Carved bone guillotine scene, 1815. The Clive L. Lloyd collection. From Clive L. Lloyd, *The Arts and Crafts of Napoleonic and American Prisoners of War, 1756–1816* (Woodbridge: Antique Collectors' Club, 2007), 165. Reproduced with kind permission by Stephanie Lloyd Downs and the author's estate.

FIG. 12 Guillotine, ca. 1793. From Karl Gröber, *Children's Toys of Bygone Days: A History of Playthings of All Peoples from Prehistoric Times to the XIXth Century* (London: B. T. Blatsford, 1928), pl. 153.

mother remained adamant about not supplying war toys in general. As Dagmar von Gersdorff writes in her book about Goethe's grandchildren, the family celebrated Christmas with ritual and fanfare. Frau Aja sent gifts and food from Frankfurt, not available in Weimar—and did much of the baking herself:

> Unbekannt waren in Weimar auch die Frankfurter Brenten, die Frau Aja zusammen mit Maronen und Pfeffernüssen pünktlich zu jedem Weihnachtsfest für den kleinen August geschickt hatte, wobei sie sich weigerte, die von Goethe bestellten Kanonen mitzuliefern: Für Kriegsspielzeug sei sie nicht zu haben.
>
> The Frankfurt Brenten, which every Christmas Frau Aja had sent promptly to little August along with chestnuts and peppermint cookies, were also unknown in Weimar, though she refused to deliver the cannons Goethe ordered: for war toys, she was unavailable.[16]

The cannon, more generically associated with war and bellicosity, held specific meaning for Goethe. He writes about cannon fever in the *Campaign in France* (1792), using his body to slake his curiosity about the battlefield experience.[17] He would not spare August the toy cannon nor guillotine. Gersdorff further explains that Goethe's love for his son extended to the grandchildren; instead of his mother, Marianne von Willemer provided the pastries and playthings for Walther and Wolfgang, including toy soldiers, though not of tin but of wood with painted cardboard.[18] While war toys and weapons seem to occupy a universal category in male play, their regional/national, historical, and technical attributes reveal particularities that invite closer consideration. The mechanical toy guillotine, in this case, inspires revulsion in Goethe's mother that was shared by twentieth-century historians.

The art historian Karl Gröber articulated the sentiment in his work, *Children's Toys of Bygone Days*, echoing the admonitory words of August's grandmother: "Monstrosities, such as every art can show, have not been wanting either; witness the outrageous toy guillotine for beheading doll aristocrats which cropped up fairly often in the French Revolution."[19]

The late eighteenth- and early nineteenth-century European discourse about childhood inscribed a professionalizing household and the roles of its protagonists into a larger social narrative about constructing and cultivating good human beings. Careful selection of toys and their regulation constituted one element of parenting and grandparental practice. The general antipathy toward instruments of war and their potential to model bellicose behavior and inculcate the young and impressionable with detached callousness toward execution indexes a dangerous insensitivity toward human life and historical upheaval, specifically, the violent and existential-political trauma of the French Revolution and Reign of Terror. The paternal desire to amuse the son with a mechanical toy provides evidence that Goethe himself was capable of dissociative play. In some ways, the trivializing of mechanical beheading and capacity for repetition, enabled through wax and the imagination, along with transferring the agency of execution to the playing hand and eye, could function as a distancing and displacing mechanism—a diversion that processes one's own experiences of proximity to death on the battlefield, perhaps, or mourning for lost lives and lifestyles. Goethe and his contemporaries shared varying degrees of knowledge of the Revolution and Terror; he himself thematized capital punishment and was involved in decisions regarding executions;[20] and, not least, the general public displayed a fascination with the act of beheading.[21] Repetition—and the ability to reattach a wax figure's head, only to repeat the execution indefinitely—incarnates one form of mimesis. The yoyo, also implicated in the historical trauma of the late eighteenth century, provides a less macabre example.

THE YOYO

In a significantly different semiotic and behavioral register, the yoyo informs Goethe's play theory and practice with greater investment in the dynamic of physical and emotional relations between adult interlocutors. Insights into games, play, and Goethe's poetic practice precede my consideration of the yoyo in the *Venetian Epigrams*. Pierre Bertaux, in his suggestive analysis of Goethe's play drive, devotes a chapter to erotic games. Alighting on the biographical attractions and their motivating, sublimating impulse into literature, Bertaux situates Goethe's loves from Weimar to Milan. Christiane Vulpius's appearance in the narrative is a game-changer. The family constellation recenters Goethe's play drive and interactions with toys and games. In his classic study of ambiguity in the definitional language of theorizing the "play sphere," Brian Sutton-Smith writes in a generously inclusive way about practices that breach boundaries between the childhood play world and adult enterprises: "Sexual intimates are said to play with each other in innumerable ways, painting each other's bodies, [eating food off of each other, playing hide the thimble in bodily crevices] and, in general, testing each other with playful impropriety."[22] Sutton-Smith, a play theorist who devoted his work to understanding the cultural significance of play in human life, describes body play in a way that encompasses the intimacies embedded in Goethe's *Roman Elegies* and *Venetian Epigrams*. Immediately, however, the nexus of generative language and erotic pleasure in Goethe's sexualized poetics is invoked: the creative moment gives a purpose to play that exceeds Sutton-Smith's theoretical and tactile framework. That moment is recapitulated in Goethe's celebrated verse from the seventh elegy: "Oftmals hab ich auch schon in ihren Armen gedichtet / Und des Hexameters Maß leise mit fingernder Hand/Ihr auf den Rücken gezählt" ("Often I even compose my poetry in her embraces, / Counting hexameter beats, tapping them out on her back").[23] Goethe poetically publicizes the moment of creative and erotic proximity, captured in the "fingering hand." In this image, the body of the poet becomes an instrument of play, metaphorically transforming the bodies into toys. The hand—the noun occurs four times in twenty lines, lightly inflected: "busily thumb" or "mit geschäftiger Hand" (with a busy hand), "die Hand leite die Hüften hinab" (and down over her hip slide my adventuring hand), "mit sehender Hand" (with fingers that see), and again tapping the rhythms out "mit fingernder Hand" (with one hand's fingers)[24]—assumes agency of its own in this process of transfiguration into the nightly play world. In some ways, the poems of the *Elegies* and *Epigrams* cast Italy and the Italian journey and sojourn in general as a type of sex tourism.

Goethe, in *Venetian Epigram* 37, continues his erotic itinerary, introducing the trendy toy that replicates his exploratory sexual adventures. In Benjamin's attention to toys, Goethean wisdom lends authority to solemn words about play. Benjamin quotes Goethe in "Randbemerkungen" ("Marginal Notes"):

> In der Tat: jedwede tiefste Erfahrung will unersättlich, will bis ans Ende aller Dinge Wiederholung und Wiederkehr, Wiederherstellung einer Ursituation, von der sie den Ausgang nahm. "Es ließe sich alles trefflich schlichten, / Könnte man die Sachen zweimal verrichten," nach diesem Goetheschen Sprüchlein handelt das Kind.[25]

> And in fact, every profound experience longs to be insatiable, longs for return and repetition until the end of time, and for the reinstatement of an original condition from which it sprang. "All things would be resolved in a trice / If we could only do them twice." Children act on this proverb of Goethe's.[26]

The impulse to repeat, however, dissolves in the invocation of yoyos in one epigram. In brief lines about longing, nocturnal loneliness, and the religion of the Nazarene, Goethe alludes to the yoyo as an accessory of love:

> Welch ein lustiges Spiel! Es windet am Faden die Scheibe,
>   Die von der Hand entfloh, eilig sich wieder herauf!
> Seht, so schein ich mein Herz bald dieser Schönen, bald jener
>   Zuzuwerfen; doch gleich kehrt es im Fluge zurück.[27]

> What an agreeable toy (amusing game)! A disc on a string, I unwind it,
>   Casting it out of my hand, and it rewinds in a trice.
> That's how I seem to be casting my heart at this and that beauty:
>   But it is never long gone, bounces straight back, as you see.[28]

Browne and Davis identified the object of the epigram and Goethe's probable knowledge of it: "But even as early as 1790, before the full strength of the fad hit Europe generally, Goethe must have been aware of its existence and popularity. The conjugation of Goethe's general propensity for keeping well-informed and the wide-spreadness of the cult of the yo-yo, plus the various literary comments the phenomenon elicited, lead to the inevitable conclusion that Goethe must have known the yo-yo."[29] The yoyo as a fickle heart that is cast and comes back has been interpreted in various ways, with some scholars suggesting the presence of Goethe's attachment to Christiane Vulpius (1765–1816) and their son as the ultimate destination.

Scholars have, however, identified the central role of Christiane's presence in the poems, perhaps the point of return and core of his desire.[30] More generally, critics have responded varyingly to the *Epigrams*, their reception often situated at the nexus of the biographical, the erotic, and the classical.[31] The playful hand, however, that engages in an affectionate game of "fort/da" with the yoyo, may be performing an erotic legerdemain, but the object itself also recapitulates a momentous historical narrative. The allusion is to Sigmund Freud's game of fetch, in which his toddler grandson tosses an object from his bed, meant for his mother to retrieve, thus asserting control over maternal presence.[32] While Goethe's epigram suggests dalliances of a poetic and sexual nature, the yoyo arrests the string of fickle and capricious signifiers. Bertaux insists that Christiane plays a different role in the poet's life: she is the only female "with whom Goethe did not play."[33] With this family constellation, for Goethe, play stops.

Benjamin understands the relationship between the child, play, and a dialogue with the nation. His visit to the toy exhibition prompts deep insights into the nature of playful repetition; he connects Goethe's words consciously with play theory and catharsis. Yet there are more sinister connections that exceed the model of Marxist analysis. In his essay on "Die Kulturgeschichte des Spielzeuges" ("The Cultural History of Toys"), Benjamin observes that children constitute "ein Teil des Volkes und der Klasse, aus der sie kommen. So gibt denn auch ihr Spielzeug nicht von einem autonomen Sonderleben Zeugnis, sondern ist stummer Zeichendialog zwischen ihm und dem Volk" (a part of the nation and the class they come from. This means that their toys cannot bear witness to any autonomous separate existence, but rather are a silent signifying dialogue between them and their nation).[34] In the adult world as well, the yoyo also accrues sinister and satirical significance. Here, my focus is extremely narrow; my aim is to probe the real toy story of the yoyo and its late eighteenth-century representation.

In these images (figs. 13 and 14), we see a representations of the yoyo in everyday life: the historical context is the aftermath of the French Revolution and its emigrants, some of whom ended up on the wrong side of revolutionary politics and practices. According to Chris Goto-Jones, the history of the name varies:

> In fact, the notion that a yo-yo should immediately return to the hand pre-dates the use of the term "yo-yo" in the West. Before Pedro Flores introduced the Filipino practice of looping the string (rather than tying it or otherwise fixing it) around the axel, the yo-yo had been known by a variety of different names: the *bandalore* in France, the *quiz* in England, the *chucki* (an Indian name) during an 18th-century popularity boom in Europe. Historians assume that the yo-yo was known as a *yo-yo* in Asian history, reaching back at least as far as 1000 B.C. in China. In Europe, archaeologists have found twin discs with fixed axels and images that seem to depict people playing with yo-yos as early as 500 B.C. in Greece. This ancient pedigree fuels the myth that the yo-yo is the second oldest toy in history.[35]

Other sources indicate that playing with a yoyo was a popular pastime, not only among the aristocracy of the late eighteenth and early nineteenth centuries: yoyos "became the favorite toys of famous European conquerors,

FIG. 13 "Emigrant jouant au yoyo" (Emigrant playing with a yo-yo), ca. 1792. Access courtesy of Stanford University Libraries. Reprinted with permission from the Bibliothèque nationale de France.

FIG. 14 "Belle Adeline faisant aller son Emigran" (Beautiful Adeline playing with her Emigran), ca. 1792. Access courtesy of Stanford University Libraries. Reprinted with permission from the Bibliothèque nationale de France.

such as Great Britain's Duke of Wellington and the French Emperor Napoleon Bonaparte."[36]

The nomenclature has a more sinister side. As popular-culture scholar and historian of the yoyo Valerie Oliver observes, the alternate eighteenth-century name of the yoyo is *l'emigrette* (the emigrant). Aristocrats fleeing the perils of French soil took their yoyos, made of glass and ivory, along with them. The alternate name, *de Coblenz*, embeds the historical narrative into the lives of émigré aristocrats who congregated on the safer side of the Rhine. Noting the yoyo's role as a stress-reliever, Oliver writes, "While being a fashionable toy for the French nobility, those less fortunate are said to have played with their emigrettes to reduce the understandable tension on their one-way trip to the guillotine."[37] In his comments, Benjamin acknowledged the links between toys and truths: in these dwell "Verwandlung der erschütterndesten Erfahrung in Gewohnheit, das ist das Wesen des Spielens" ("the transformation of a shattering experience into habit—that is the essence of play").[38] The migration of the toy across contested European borders—geographical, political, philosophical, and economic—follows a history of privilege, trauma, and seismic shifts in the balance of power.

GOETHE'S EXEMPLARITY

Goethe and his works did not always enjoy a privileged place in the German cultural pantheon. Curiously, around the turn of the century, his transatlantic reception had an elevating effect on his stature—in certain spheres. His international reception celebrated his genius and exemplarity—particularly with regard to early childhood—but at the expense of his play-oriented parenting, his willingness to engage in dissociative aesthetic games with violent outcomes, and his more Mephistophelian sensibility, as well as his positional power. Ellen Key's highly influential *The Century of the Child* inspired a generation of parents and educators on an international scale. A Swedish teacher, suffragist, and writer, Key advocated state support in raising children, instilling moral uprightness through equality in the household, and approaching children as creative and intelligent beings who benefit from disease-free homes and balanced outlooks. In other words, she rejected the practice of raising children in a childhood separate or, in contemporary terms, "islanded" from the adult world. With great explanatory force, the concept of "islanding" has productively framed increased attention to childhood as a discrete phase of human existence.[39] By contrast, Key attacked the idea. Homes that produce the best "men and women with the strongest morality" treat children as human beings. She wrote, "In a home like this nothing is especially arranged for children; they are regarded not as belonging to one kind of being while parents represent another, but parents gain the respect of their children by being true and natural; they live and conduct themselves in such a way that the children gain an insight into their work, their efforts and, as far as possible into their joys and pains, their mistakes and failures."[40] Throughout her treatise, Key referred liberally to works of literature and philosophy that dominated the German-European tradition, from Goethe to Nietzsche, among a host of others.[41] Her rhetoric is suffused in the canonical teachings of Protestantism and is nuanced when it comes to feminism. Like many of her contemporaries, she espoused cringeworthy views about hygiene, heredity, and race that leave subsequent generations of readers in a state of profound moral ambivalence vis-à-vis her ostensibly progressive politics on gender equality.

The responsibility of preparing children as individuals for the future is predicated on recognizing the insights of the cultural past. In her chapter on education, for example, she extols Goethe's literary representations of the child: "Goethe showed long ago in his *Werther* a clear understanding of the significance of individualistic and psychological training, an appreciation which will mark the century of the child. In this work he shows how the future power of will lies hidden in the characteristics of the child, and how along with every fault of the child an uncorrupted germ capable of producing good is enclosed."[42] Key then quotes a passage from *Werther* in which the protagonist vocalizes a secularized version of Christian belief in the innate goodness of children, and she crystalizes all contemporary education by paraphrasing Goethe's notion "that almost every fault is but a hard shell enclosing a germ of virtue." Countering the practices of fighting evil with evil, she instead avows allowing nature "quietly and slowly to help itself, taking care only that the surrounding conditions help the work of nature." Succinctly, she concludes: "This is education."[43]

Extending the model of the homology between childhood and nature, Key naturalized education. Goethe, again, is central to her investigation. In a subsequent discussion of pedagogy and psychology in the Swiss and German traditions, she eschews any sustained consideration of Johann Heinrich Pestalozzi, Johann Bernhard Basedow, and Friedrich Fröbel. Instead, she writes, "I will only mention that the greatest men of Germany, Lessing, Herder, Goethe, Kant and others, took the side of natural training."[44] The expansiveness of Goethe's life and literary productivity enable anyone to find just about anything in his example, a construct to which Key contributes, exploiting the supposition that greatness and natural training are coterminous.

Werther is rarely the model for Goethe on education. Goethe's theories of education, at least as encoded in fiction, have received considerable scholarly and pedagogical attention. In her discussions with Friedrich Fröbel—they met in 1850—Bertha von Marenholtz-Bülow likewise relies on Goethe's greatness and exemplarity and bends him to her purpose. In their discussion of Goethe's *Pädagogische Provinzen* (School regions) from the second book of *Wilhelm Meister's Journeyman Years*, Marenholtz-Bülow and Fröbel note the similarities between the views expressed in fiction and Fröbel's own pedagogical practice: "Goethe, truly, with his seer's glance into the future human development, could not but concur in Froebel's view, which also embraced humanity in its past, present, and future."[45] This "province" of pedagogy bears resemblance to the actual institution sponsored by Goethe's contemporary, the Pestalozzian reformer Immanuel von Fellenberg, whose son, Wilhelm, was received by the great writer in Weimar.[46] The idea of graduated work and progressive identificatory codes, such as uniform color, define the method of educating boys to men. In the novel, Wilhelm delivers his son, Felix, to the school. This education involves work. The pedagogical model, which Goethe penned in the early 1820s, represents a moderate yet regulatory approach to shaping masculinity. Many have noted the words inscribed on Pestalozzi's grave: "Man, Christian, and Citizen. All for others, nothing for himself."[47]

Elsewhere, Goethe reveals a more cutthroat approach to childhood activity. Here one thinks immediately of the hard lessons learned at play in "Der neue Paris. Knabenmärchen" ("The New Paris: A Boyhood Fairy Tale") in the second book of *Dichtung und Wahrheit* (*From My Life: Poetry and Truth*): the original reads "Gewalt ist eher mit Gewalt zu vertreiben" (Violence is more likely to be banished with violence, *or* Force can usually be repelled by force).[48] While boys at the Fellenberg-influenced school learn through work, in the second example, boys are the presumed players who meet violence with violence, though, importantly, the sentence continues: "aber ein gut gesinntes, zur Liebe und Teilnahme geneigtes Kind weiß dem Hohn und dem bösen Willen wenig entgegenzusetzen" (but a kindly child, one inclined to love and sympathy, is poorly prepared to defend himself against derision and ill will).[49] Goethe gives us a glimmer of justifying aggression in his childhood incarnation; moreover, in retrospect, he may be speculating on better ways to prepare the well-meaning for encounters with evil and violence in the world. In the realm of play, presumably Christian principles of turning the other cheek, especially to local bullies, simply pale. This countermodel undermines the Christian principles Key mines in Goethe's work.

In particular, Key elevates Goethe as a specimen of holistic education, citing his pedagogical experiences as "ideal, considered apart from some pedantry due to his father's influence." She elaborates:

> At his mother's work-table, he learnt to know the Bible; French he learnt from a theatrical company; English from a language master, in company with his father; Italian, because he heard his sister being taught the language; mathematics from a friend in the household, a study which Goethe applied immediately, first in cardboard

diagrams, later in architectural drawings. His essays he prepared in the form of a correspondence in different languages between different relatives, scattered in various parts of the world. Geography he eagerly studied in books of travel in order to be able to give his narrative local colour. He knocked about with his father, learnt to observe different kinds of handwork, and also to try himself small experiments of his own skill.[50]

Her inventory of Goethe's cognitive skills and artisanal abilities acquired and practiced *in situ* stops short of any acknowledgment of formal training in the visual arts, university legal studies, trips to Italy, and the practice of a profession at court, but Key's point pertains to the cultivation of originality and genius: her Goethe is a paragon.

This version of Goethe the man as exemplary and as a benevolent educational theorist is highly selective and equally assailable. For example, the favorite imaginative activity of his youth, performed with his *Puppentheater*, receives no attention, but this critique distorts Key's project, which involved elevating Goethe as pedagogical model for raising generations to greatness. Goethe provides posterity with moments of equal and greater importance, evidence of churlish behavior or less natural training. One immediately recalls the early passage in *Dichtung und Wahrheit* (*From My Life*), also known as *Poetry and Truth*, in which he reconstructs his childhood performance for himself and his neighbors, the three brothers von Ochsenstein, the gleeful breaking of crockery that celebrates the unleashed creative and destructive forces of play. The command "Noch mehr!" (Still more!), to which he responded by enthusiastically fetching additional breakable implements, parallels the repetition compulsion in play; in Goethe's performance, destruction releases creative energy.[51] This indulgence in nihilistic play warrants no mention in Key's citations of Goethean greatness, founded on a belief in his proximity to nature, but, as Hamlin notes, "toys are not products of nature."[52] But the simultaneous act of creation and destruction shines a light on the construction of Goethe's other favorite toys.

GOETHE'S ECCENTRICITY

Goethe takes play seriously, however, not only as a poet, but also as a parent. The legacy of his exemplarity coexists uncomfortably with his eccentricity. We see this in his approaches to play and the acquisition of toys. The legacy of his mother's lament echoes across time and oceans, but in 1793, Frau Rath Goethe's chief consideration remains an ethical and maternal objection to the objects of war for play.

Goethe himself does not always set the best example. In some ways, he passes on his dedication to fantasy and imaginative play. He encourages, for example, August's interest in the *Puppentheater* he loved so much as a child and an adult. August's occasional letters dutifully document his activity, and he describes a birthday party in a letter dated 2 October 1797:

> Auf dem Abend spielten wir ein Schattenspiel, das uns viel Vergnügen machte: da kamen ein Hanswurst mit seiner Columbine, ein Nachtwächter, ein Teufel, der Doctor Faust, ein Höllendrache, Bäume, Häuser, Blitze, ein Zauberer, eine Einsiedlergrotte und zuletzt eine lebendige Katze vor, welche das Licht auslöschte. Ehe uns aber die Katze diesen Streich machte, nahm der Teufel den Hanswurst, die Columbine und den Doctor Faust mit sich fort in die Luft. Leben Sie wohl und behalten Sie mich lieb. August Göthe.

> In the evening, we performed a shadow play that gave us great pleasure: Hanswurst appeared with his Columbine, a night watchman, a devil, Dr. Faustus, a dragon from Hell, trees, houses, lightening, a magician, a hermit's grove, and finally, a lively cat that put out the light. But before the cat played this trick on us, the devil took Hanswurst, Columbine, and Doctor Faust with him into the air. Be well and continue to love me. August Göthe.[53]

Play, theatrics, and magic culminate in the Faust material. The interest in magic will skip a generation for Goethe, who invests quite of bit of energy into outfitting his grandchildren with state-of-the-art "Taschenspielerkasten" (magic kits).[54] He allowed the grandchildren to take magic lessons from a visiting magician and encouraged their performance before an audience. Goethe defended his actions with reference to the pedagogical aspect of play to Eckermann: "Es ist, besonders in Gegenwart eines kleinen Publikums, ein herrliches Mittel zur Übung in freier Rede und Erlangung einiger körperlichen und geistigen Gewandtheit" (It is, especially in the presence of a small audience, a wonderful way to practice speaking and gaining physical and mental agility).[55] Behind the puppet theater and imaginative play associated with performance lurks bellicosity: with the possibility of the opening of "an extension of the theater of war into our area," the puppet theater that Goethe recollects in his autobiography was produced to keep the children at home and engaged in indoor amusements.[56]

The context of Frau Rath Goethe's original letter provides some further information about her convictions when writing to her son. Beyond the toy-specific diatribe, Elisabeth Goethe forges stronger connections between the mechanical guillotine, historical events, and national identity. In the remainder of the letter, dated 23 December 1793, she provides an account of the local men who inspire feelings of pride in Frankfurt citizenship; they are good Germans with German blood in their veins and uniforms on their backs, prepared "ihrer Vaterstadt im fall der Noth beyzustehn" (to defend their city in an emergency).[57] She further describes the sacrifices made by locals, the support for the injured, and the voluntary spirit of generosity, winding down with the exclamation: "nun verwunder mann sich noch daß Franckfurth reich wird" (and you wonder why Frankfurt is becoming so rich).[58] Perhaps most significantly, she signs the letter "deine treue deusche Mutter Goethe" (your faithful German mother Goethe). Of the 414 letters Frau Aja wrote to various interlocutors, this is the only instance of a patriotic variation on a formulaic signature. In fact, in an addendum, she refers to her previous commentary: "Kaum hatte ich meinem Vaterländlischen pradiodißmuß Luft gemacht, als dein Lieber Brief ankam, auf den ich mit ein paar Worte noch antworten will" (I had hardly finished airing my patriotism for the fatherland when your dear letter arrived, and I would like to answer with a few words).[59] For Goethe's mother, though in a teasing tone, patriotism is constitutive of parenting.

Both exceptional and exemplary, Goethe represents an emerging model of European masculinity that includes hands-on paternity: the engaged father serves as liaison between the child and the play world. While most of the evidence points to a more focused relationship between fathers and sons, the intervention of male exemplarity in the play sphere effectively inculcates masculinity's attributes into playing children, but it also concurrently enables a range of masculinities to become legible in the public sphere. As a corollary, the texts and toys that target the cultivation of masculine traits through imaginative and imitative play prepare the boy reader/player for the seamless transition from imagined to adult citizenship; play embeds political consciousness and historical events into the practices and accessories of play.

The two objects of play examined in this chapter function separately but with shared significance. While play and certain accessories of play assume universal characteristics, their particularities reveal a political unconscious in the social life of material objects. The yoyo, an object that facilitates an adult and childhood pastime, is present at the site of execution, the last distraction of the condemned, however hygienic and rational and humane the death-delivery-device, the guillotine, was purported to be. The mechanical, miniature, "toy" guillotine and the yoyo admittedly perform different tasks in Goethe's life and work, respectively, but ultimately they share a certain historical semantics of trauma and migration. Each in its way is representative of the political id that erupted in the aftermath of the French Revolution.

In Goethe's parental life, the guillotine becomes a generational bone of contention, embodying a territorial struggle between himself and his mother, one that recapitulates the attributes of European bourgeois masculinity and its replication through mimetic play. With the repetition of the yoyo in the realm of the erotic, Goethe as a poetic subject himself segues into a conventional European masculinity, predicated on monogamy, eschewing the to-and-fro of the diverting disc and its pendular movement. Through repetitive play with real objects, Goethe parents toward militarized maleness and partners in respectability. Both objects of play connect and mature the masculine emotional range—always with the possibility of recidivism prompted by the play drive.

With its different back story, the yoyo is eroticized; its movements mimic the arc of affection (and desire) that ultimately returns to the owner, at least as a literary incarnation. In contemporary visual culture and everyday practice, however, the yoyo is an accessory of distracted play, a pendulous pastime for the politically inconsequential and the uprooted aristocracy waiting for death. Play becomes a metric for gauging Goethe's plural responses to historical trauma and its impact on creativity. For Goethe, the creative impulses of poetry, the repetition of wandering desire, and the bourgeois masculinity of partnership transfigure the underlying connections to trauma into erotic play. The violence implied and denied in the repeated swipe of the guillotine's blade rehearses a militarized masculinity that depends on dissociative capacities. Goethe's draft of European parental masculinity encompasses both his exemplary and eccentric impulses: to entertain and educate with games of life and death.

Beyond a thwarted attempt to play at revolution and terror with August, Goethe prevented his son's conscription in 1813.[60] His desire to engage in the violent, repeatable mime, however, showcases Goethean desire for acting out in play. Tropes of brutalizing, harsh punishment in play come to signify the German play world. To put my reading of what is, admittedly, privileged play into the context of more popularly disseminated texts and discourses, the eccentric impulses indulged in Goethe's desire for the killing machine align with the dire outcomes for evil stepsisters in the Grimms' fairy and folk tales and, in that mode, in the unrepentant children in the tales of Heinrich Hoffmann (1809–1894), *Struwwelpeter* (1845). The cautionary tales of misbehaving, disobedient children illustrate extreme consequences. The figures are familiar: the girl who plays with fire self-immolates; the boy keeps sucking his thumb until both are cut off with scissors. Hoffmann's impetus for writing—a supplement to the moralizing narratives about good behavior—serves as a pendant not only to Jacobs's stories, but to Goethe's transatlantic appeal. The resistance to Romanticism present in the mature Goethe's work is recapitulated in his view of the United States. An article about Goethe in America from 1909 is in essence a bibliography, critical of British Goethe reception. By 1949, German American efforts to recuperate a cultural legacy grounded in an American imaginary gain acceptance. Ch. F. Melz references Goethe's poem about America and the caution to avoid excessive imagination. Goethe becomes not only Emerson's "The Poet" but also the subject of criticism for his excess and indulgence.[61] More recently, Nicholas Saul has drawn out comparisons between the *Wanderjahre* and James Fennimore Cooper's Leatherstocking novels, which Goethe read intensively.[62] In American romanticism, German figures enter the imagination as the emissaries of the dark side. From the perspective of enlightened German texts and toys, the victims of tyranny, such as the Hessian conscripts, enter the transatlantic world not as heroes or victims but as ghosts. The relationship is reciprocal. In 1806, Washington Irving embarked on a visit to Germany and sailed the Rhine. His *Tales of Sleepy Hollow* (1809) introduce the Headless Horseman—the poltergeist of a Hessian soldier who lost his head to cannon fire. A descendant of the German legend, the *Kopfloser Reiter*, the Hessian specter recalls his legendary ancestry. The vengeful spirit punishes with a transatlantic reach. Competing signifiers of moral and misbehaving children, of exemplary and eccentric toys, characterize German play in the transatlantic world. The connection between the "wild" and the "child," however, can be disrupted by racial hierarchies that are intrinsic to the play world. These usher in revolutions in play. In the next chapters the projection of an African and American imaginary onto the act of reading and scenes of instruction engender colonial subjectivity in child's play.

CHAPTER 4

Colonizing Childhoods
The African Imaginary

He mutilates his dog, his horse, and his slave.
—Jean-Jacques Rousseau, *Emile* (1762)

Enlightenment educational principles elevate the innate innocence of childhood, fostered under the ministry of Nature. The presumed homology between the nature of childhood and "Nature," constructed as the aesthetic and benevolent agent for the nurturing of children, traces its history to Rousseau's influential novel *Emile*. The widespread reception of his fictional work as a treatise on education aligns with its first publication; its German translation appeared a year before the English version (1763), and Rousseau reception shaped the growth of "radical Enlightenment" in German-speaking lands.[1] The Philanthropists, among them J. H. Campe, endorsed Rousseau's paradigm, though often with more didactic messages. Campe's *Robinson der Jüngere* exemplifies the narrative within a narrative about family structure, the natural world, and the childhood experience of adventure. Manuals, markets, and pedagogical stories, such as those discussed in "Professional Parenting," had the effect of mediating, not bridging, the gulf between abstract ideals about the proper principles of educating humanity in conversation with "Nature" and corresponding ideas about the naturalness of the play world as a hygienic habitat for the young. How that habitat intervenes in the play world must be contemplated in conjunction with Lefebvre's physical and mental space, the nexus of which forms the dominant model of late nineteenth-century discourses about and representations of children, play, and, with escalating intensity, their relationship to territory beyond the borders of a nation. While toys of terror and war fascinate Goethe, and Hessian musician miniatures occlude the violent brutalizing of those who tried to desert or fell captive to the ruling British, objects of colonialism generate tales of adventure in which German-speaking figures identify with European racialized thought and acts of victory and violence. Aspects of this regime of identity between the child and the natural world draw considerable force from literary legacies across Europe and the United States.

Presumed wild in its expression, nature features prominently in the formation of the imaginary spaces. In German thought about play beyond Europe, objects and texts project national rather than natural characteristics onto the landscape. In emulative play and engaged reading, the theoretical child learns to think nationally and transnationally. With the wide world, the cosmos, and the entirety of human history encapsulated in a play room, history enters the domestic sphere. In the late nineteenth century, toys and texts awaken a desire for acquisition that maps colonizing entitlements onto the play world.

The literal and historical desire for domination manifests in colonial expansion and the presumably justifiable cultivation of unmapped land. In the United States, the appropriation of "wilderness" territories, though symptomatic of similarly compulsive acquisitiveness, presents as a symptom in the mythologizing of immigration destinies. On both shores of the Atlantic, the use of literature to reimagine Nature in the service of countering mechanisms of industrialization additionally fosters close associations between the Europeanized child and undamaged life. For example, in the wall paintings of Johann Conrad Seekatz (1719–1768), whose work was familiar to the young Goethe, the organic, holistic, and cosmic representation of the astrological signs, myth, and children engaged in outdoor work and play illustrate modern European imaginary of divine, human, and natural harmony (fig. 15).[2] Seekatz's series of paintings now hang in the garden room of the Goethe Museum in Frankfurt am Main. They depict zodiac signs with children, portrayed conventionally as small adults, frolicking and working in the natural world, appropriate to the season. This image frames all levels of Lefebvre's science of space: the Cosmos, the natural realm, and the symbolic. The upper and lower frames contain heavenly and earthly images to represent the respective sign. Here, in January (Aquarius),

FIG. 15 Johann Conrad Seekatz, *Die zwölf Monatsbilder: Januar*, ca. 1759–63. Oil on canvas, 251.2 × 48.1 cm. Freies Deutsches Hochstift / Frankfurter Goethe-Museum, inv. no. IV-01070. © Freies Deutsches Hochstift / Frankfurter Goethe-Museum. Photo: David Hall / Wasserman / Artothek.

amicable sliding and skating set the chilly tone of leisure—disrupted in modernity. The play world, constituted by natural cycles, seasons, and landscapes, transforms with a fantasy of conquerable territory where the model child can play in relation to the local and global.

This model requires a particular calibrating of any relationship to different natural worlds across multiple national imaginaries. As Collin Haywood writes, "Indeed, the association of childhood with innocence became deeply embedded within Western culture, particularly after Romantics had made their mark in the nineteenth century."[3] As "Nature" undergoes a European process of mythologizing, it becomes subject to nostalgia and thus deterritorialized, rendered a mobile signifier that is transferable across cognitive, geographical, and political boundaries. The obverse process, enhanced by European convictions about ownership and entitlement, concurrently manifests itself in literal appropriations of territory. Territorialization, as I adapt the use of the term from Deleuze and Guattari, functions to map a cognitive landscape onto an emerging racial identity; it is manifest in the history of colonization, and deterritorialization certainly counts as a tool in the toolbox of postcolonial theory and analysis of economic globalization.[4] In alignment with an ideology of appropriative mapping of ownership onto a "wilderness," the metonymy is constructed between the wild and *Naturvölker*. The untamed nature of the child is displaced by populations in need of subjection. As I demonstrate in this chapter and the next, children's toys, texts, and play practices replicate racializations of identity, rehearsed in the play world and inscribed on non-European geographies. In contrast to the colonial literature by and about German women in the protectorates who signify the civilizing forces of fragile whiteness,[5] the cultural artifacts that focus on children at play merge historical conflict into a natural imaginary encompassing Africa and the Americas. Indeed, the signifiers of a wild, threatening, and adventurous non-European world compose a grammar of colonial pedagogy derivative of Fröbel's pedagogical theories of childhood gardens. These, while gaining ground in formal educational institutions, prepare for imaginative play and the act of reading as constitutive of citizenship in the German play world.

The acquisition of knowledge represents a crucial first step to enable child-citizens to insert themselves into the national imaginary. In his work, Bowersox analyzes the attributes of educational reform in the disciplines of natural science in the imperial age, but especially in geography. He writes that "school geography reformers folded a broadly acceptable patriotic and colonial worldview into efforts driven chiefly by professional and pedagogical imperatives."[6] Bowersox further observes that there was an increase, beginning in the 1860s, of publisher interest in appealing to a large youth audience; the marketability of colonial themes increased decisively. At the time, North American and African settings represented "an untamed space filled with wild beasts and strange noble, or savage natives."[7] Entering the age of empire, German-language texts increasingly associate the child with the "wild." In her work on the historical characteristics of doll play, Insa Fooken discusses scholarship about the objects and activities as a microcosm; further, she underscores the evolving conceptualization of the young as "junge Wilde" (young wild ones).[8]

In the 1880s and 1890s, youth interest in colonial adventure rose to make it the most popular entertainment genre.[9] In his argument, Bowersox notes that some entertaining literature was perceived to be low-brow, even trashy, and needed to be hidden from parents and enjoyed as forbidden fruit.[10] His focus remains on the educational experience. By contrast, the material in this chapter belongs in the category of play and pleasure—though edification, and with that the acquisition of racializing knowledge, comes into focus. German colonizing subjects acquire and rehearse agency in the play world, related both by metonymy and synecdoche to the learning and living environments. Products of colonialist ideology, the material artifacts that replicate the world, including the cosmos, have a long history—as does colonialist ideology. The history of the globe as an instrument of instruction intersects with the spaces of childhood and has done so for centuries. Thomas Stauss calls attention to the play world as a "lustvolle Konstruktion aus Wissenschaft, Magie und physikalischem Amüsement" (pleasurable construction from science, magic, and physical amusement).[11] His characterization of objects originating around 1800 encompasses an impressive range, from magic mirrors and magnetic puzzle boxes to a children's microscope and hydraulic fountains.[12] Coaxing time and space onto a human scale represents a fifteenth-century effort, marked by the commissioning of the globe by Martin Behaim in 1492.[13] Late eighteenth-century models replicate the earth and heavens (*Erd- und Himmels-Globen*), smaller versions of which (*Erd- und Himmels-Kugeln*), dating from around 1800, were intended to provide children with knowledge of geography and astronomy.[14] By 1823, a new species of world miniature became available: a foldable cardboard globe. With nineteenth-century exploration, this information and composition were updated to reflect, for example, Sir William Edward Parry's "Entdeckungen am Nordpol" (discoveries in the North Pole).[15] Parry (1790–1855) joined the search for a northwest passage in 1819; material objects of pedagogical play prepared the way for the scientific justification of German colonial expansion. This ostensibly playful, adventurous engagement in the acquisition of noncontinguous land occurs beyond overtly imperial games, such as "Deutschland's Kolonien-Spiel," a boardgame in circulation ca. 1890.[16] Texts and toys about the young German-speaking reader/player establish subject identity in an imaginary geography that crosses the Atlantic.

EIN KONGO-NEGER AND THE REVOLUTIONARY IMAGINARY

The adventure narrative for children and young readers referenced otherness beyond stereotypical portrayals of the American Indian. In the stories that targeted a young audience, the tales of adventure and exploration blended with the genre of the village story (*Dorfgeschichte*), popularized by Bertold Auerbach (1812–1882). Born Moyses Baruch and trained for the rabbinate, Auerbach changed direction after his reading of Spinoza and turned to literature. The moral stories were widely imitated; we see evidence of Auerbach's influence on one story here under consideration. W. O. von Horn, the second pen name of Friedrich Wilhelm Philipp Oertel (1789–1867), was an evangelical pastor who first published *Dorfgeschichten* (Village stories) under the pseudonym Friedel Lips. He studied theology in Heidelberg and, in 1835, became superintendent in Sobernheim as well as the district school inspector.[17] After 1845, he changed his pseudonym to W. O. von Horn and focused on writing narratives for young and young adult audiences. He was prolific in this genre, and his themes encompassed adventure and the prevalence of Christian values even under dire circumstances.[18]

A cursory glance at Horn's titles reveals that the author left few parts of the globe uninhabited by his prose: "Der Orkan auf Cuba" (The hurricane in Cuba), "Auf dem Mississippi" (On the Mississippi), "Der letzte Ghazwah oder Sklavenjagd im Sudan unter der Regierung Mehemed Ali's von Egypten" (The last ghazwah or slave hunt in the Sudan during the rule of Mehemed Ali's of Egypt), and "Die Eroberung von Konstantinopel durch die Türken im Jahre 1453" (The conquest of Constantinople by the Turks in the year 1453). His stories frequently thematize race and racial difference, and several stories deal explicitly with slavery within the larger framework of European history, Christian values, and the triumph of reason and decency, such as "Simon: Die Lebensgeschichte eines Negersklaven in

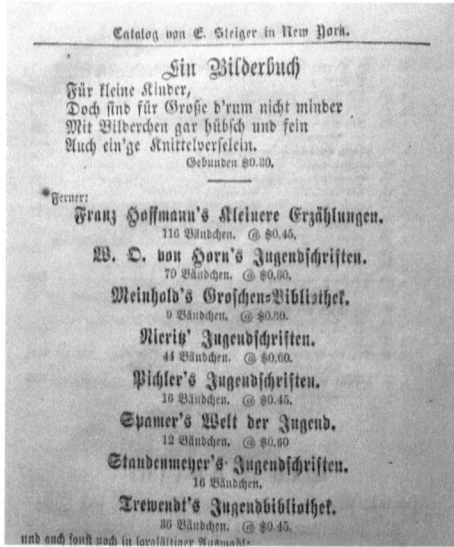

FIG. 16 *Catalog von E. Steiger in New York* (New York: E. Steiger & Company, 1883). Joseph P. Horner Memorial Library, The German Society of Pennsylvania. Photo: author.

Brasilien" (Simon: The life story of a negro slave in Brazil).[19] The novella *Ein Kongo-Neger: Eine Geschichte aus Sankt Domingo* (A Congo-Negro: A story from Santo Domingo) interests me in this context because it not only purveys a colonial fantasy of racial difference and harmony amid the atrocities of slavery and violent uprisings but also disparages revolutionary politics within Europe while extoling them in the New World. Assessing the influence of his stories presents challenges, but it clearly reached a transatlantic audience as well. In the 1868 *Catalog von E. Steiger in New York*, a bilingual medium for books in and about the German language and Germans in America, seventy volumes of W. O. von Horn's *Jugendschriften* appear on the last page under the category of "Steiger's Jugendbibliothek" (10–12) (fig. 16).

The legacy of blackness in European structures of servitude has deep roots, nurtured by the visual and vernacular arts, but also evident in texts and migration. The legacy is voiced in the genre of children's and young adult entertainment literature with a transatlantic audience. In *Ein Kongo-Neger*, the European protagonist embodies the reformed version of an absentee plantation owner; its resolution exculpates, for a German-speaking audience, the logic of racism.[20]

The power disparity between races, mediated by ownership, reifies a political and social order that Horn reaffirms. In approximately the midpoint of his story, the narrator inserts a description of the revolution in France and expresses sympathy for the nobility, "mit ihnen starben zahllos

FIG. 17 Cover illustration from *Ein Kongo-Neger* (Stuttgart: Verlag von Rob. Bardtenschlager, ca. 1900).

viele der edelsten, achtungswertesten Menschen" (with them countless numbers of the most noble, respectable people died).[21] Racial difference and Christian values inflect revolutionary politics on Santo Domingo. The story instructs a nineteenth-century youthful audience about universal and immutable ethical standards through historical narrative. Once again, a benevolent uncle is the figure of the storyteller, and the author himself occupies that role on the level of the metanarrative.

In a further attempt to elucidate the title this chapter, I select Horn's story because its historical subject matter, the Haitian Revolution and slave rebellion on the French colonial island of Santo Domingo in the late eighteenth century, occupies a transitional space between play and prose, between the original publication date of 1854 and the reincarnation of the volume around 1900. This story demonstrates not how to play but how to own. The cover illustration from that time (fig. 17) locates the white plantation and slave owners in the foreground; they engage with a mixed-race overseer, the middleman who, in Horn's story, embodies the evils of racism and cruelty; the African slaves, shackled and subjugated, are grouped in the upper background. The composition does not reflect population to demographic scale.

It is noteworthy that the illustrator does not eschew depicting the instruments of torture or the racial hierarchy. The story and its illustration occupy a pedagogical space: a site of instruction for racial relationships that ultimately define whiteness. When Bowersox discusses public interest in German-specific spaces post-1904 and after the uprisings in German protectorates, he writes that "German men put their disorderly spaces back in order, to the ultimate benefit of all concerned."[22] In the incarnations of this text and its introductory illustrations, a German-language text imposes moral order on a French colonial failure.

The interaction between text and image has the ability to produce racialized knowledge in the young consumer. Recent scholarship on the relationship between stories and illustrations in children's culture moves past the supplemental or compensatory relationship outlined in Auslander's work on material culture. Describing the historian's practice and their reliance on words, "everything else is merely illustrative or supplementary."[23] Material culture constitutes extralinguistic territory; while the dynamic between the cover illustrations and the same text is illuminating, the reinforcement of the aesthetic and ethical modes of communication in the production of contemporary toys can add another dimension of understanding. Toys, which can subvert racializing hierarchies, also frequently reiterate them. The incorporation of blackness into toy production at the end of the nineteenth and early twentieth century generally tends to corroborate ideas of hierarchy.

Horn emphasizes the age spectrum in his audience with the directive: "der deutschen Jugend und dem Volke erzählt" (told to German youth and the people). The production of the story, with its subsequent reincarnations at critical moments in German history and colonization processes, raise the stakes of the genre blending between the village narrative and the adventure tale. Horn inserts moral and ethical principles to regulate race relations into a revolutionary history that interprets politics idiosyncratically. Consistent with the journalistic narratives from South America around 1900 about German identity and colonial facts and fictions, and united in theme and tone by consistent criticism of competing colonial powers such as Britain, Horn's story savors the taste of moral superiority over the brutality of French imperialism. At the same time, the narrator disparages the emancipatory impulses of the French Revolution even while extoling the protagonist's empathy with enslaved Africans and supporting their freedom. This contradiction serves as an index to read the moral lesson of defining and defending white privilege.

Horn intends his narrative works to model good behavior under the direst of circumstances. His historical settings tend to favor the eighteenth century and demonstrate enlightened principles, though even a cursory glance at the reception history indicates that his popularity bewilders contemporary literary critics, who hold up the exquisite and ironic novellas of Heinrich von Kleist. Horn pales by comparison. Quoting Horn's expressed desire "von den romanhaften Gebilden der sonstigen Jugendschriften zur Auffasshung wirklicher Lebensverhältnisse hinüberzuleiten" (to guide [the readers] from the novelistic images of most writing for young people over to the understanding of real living conditions),[24] Wolgast is uncompromising in his negative assessment of Horn's stories, from their weak and unconvincing composition to their insipid politics and a distinct lack of experience with real living conditions. Another accuses him of banality and kitsch.[25] Several stories feature sets of nephews; good and bad behavior are measured by how each treats an uncle.

The historical framework of *Ein Kongo-Neger* organizes a transatlantic *Dorfgeschichte*, generously borrowing from the Robinsonade tropes of adventure and survival—in an ethical and existential sense. Focused on the noble family Malpays and their extensive holdings on the banks of the Seine, the opening paragraph lingers on the literal meaning of the name and holdings, but the productivity and beauty of the land contradict the connotation of "bad country." Here the reader also encounters the Oheim or uncle of the two young counts Malpays; the moral backbone of the story, the Oheim is described as learned, the canon of the Notre Dame cathedral. The family also has colonial holdings on the island of Santo Domingo; the parallel possessions create the expectation of productive, cultivated, and profitable land. The story commences in the mid-1780s with the death of both parents and the quiet and studious guardianship and stewardship of the uncle. Count Robert, the older son, is twenty at the time; Count Sulpiz, the canon's godson and favorite, is nineteen. The narrator lauds the careful parenting of the two sons while disparaging the absenteeism of the father, who attended to his home at the castle only during hunting season. The Oheim implicitly redeems and redirects the male lineage of his generation and shepherds the neglected sons with good tutors and an appropriate education. With reason and compassion, the canon decides that the older nephew, Robert, should administer the Santo Domingo property, while Sulpiz assumes responsibility for the French holdings. The manager of the former, Fonton, "war ein schlauer, eigennütziger und habsüchtiger Mensch" (was a sly, self-serving, and avaricious human being) (6).[26] Under his mismanagement, the mortality rate of the Malpays's African slaves was high, and though the overseer lived opulently, the land remained peculiarly unprofitable. Economy and ethics intersect in this exemplum.

The avuncular narrative, embedded in the framework of the colonial tale and delivered prior to Robert's embarkation for the French West Indies, recapitulates the relationship among tropes of adventure, fantasies of colonial aggrandizement, and European moral zealotry. The narrator articulates the canon's intention: to instruct his nephew in the history of Santo Domingo. Beginning with the biography of Christopher Columbus, the Oheim's lecturelike narrative balances the excesses of adventure tales with historical facts and ethical regulators: "Alle Köpfe waren voll abenteuerlicher Märlein und Erzählungen von unbekannten Meeren, Inseln, Ländern, und je wunderbarer die Erzählungen weitgereister Leute klangen, desto gläubiger nahm man sie an und haute darauf fort" (All heads were full of adventurous tales and stories of unknown seas, islands, lands, and the more marvelous the stories of people who had traveled great distances, the more faithfully one heard them and set off to find them) (7). Immediately the Oheim catalogues extant signs from the distant shores; included among this exotic inventory is the corpse with "eine kupferrote Haut" (a copper-red skin) (7), tossed by the sea. The body, like a macabre compass, signified land to the west of the Canary Islands.

The Oheim's compressed history of discovery follows the arc of an adventure narrative, displaying conventional descriptions: "die wilden Einwohner" (the wild inhabitants), "das Paradies der ersten Menschen" (the paradise of the first people), and further references to the peace-loving nature of the natives (8–9). Productive land and the phenotype of the natives, described in anthropological detail, create an organic relationship between field and folk, culminating in the description of the local customs as "mild und sanft" (mild and meek) (9). The corrupting and devastating impact of Spanish colonial rule bursts the narrative bubble. This narrating uncle, embedded within the framework of the story, mediates the reception of the adventurous tales through an ethical lens to balance fantasy with the reality of colonial brutality and transatlantic slavery.

The Oheim's account reaches a turning point with the inevitable decimation of the Amerindian population. With his intention to spare the delicate sensibilities of his nephews and the author's to protect those of his young readers, the canon delivers the grim facts: in 1514, only fourteen thousand of the several million original inhabitants remained, and they were forced into brutalizing slavery. The narrative sets in motion a syntax of racism and racial hierarchy: African slaves replace Amerindian victims, the former inserted into the grammar of Spanish colonialism. The narrative filters history through an ethical and textual sieve. Citing the arrival of a man with a "Herz voll Liebe für die unglücklichen Wilden" (heart full of love for the unfortunate wild ones) (12), the canon names Bartolomé de las Casas (1484–1566), a Dominican friar and bishop of Chiapas who did advocate for the humanity and rights of Indians. The canon relays the disturbing information that las Casas suggested importing black Africans as slaves to cultivate the land. The statement, prefaced by "Leider" or unfortunately, is corroborated by las Casas's *Memorial de Remedios par alas Indias* (1516), though he later retracted it. *Ein Kongo-Neger*, however, marks this as the inaugural moment of the transatlantic slave trade, piracy, unscrupulous buccaneers, and the French colonization that sets the stage for the revolution on Santo Domingo.

The transformation of the adventure tale into an ethical and economic quest occurs within a pedagogical framework that contains and conveys colonial epistemologies. In lexical terms, the author defines and translates possibly unfamiliar colonial concepts. The word "Kolonien," for example, is followed by "(Pflanzstädte)," an archaic usage literally meaning "plant cities." While the framework narrative stresses ethical and ethically evolving but economically sound treatment of slaves and the land itself, the overarching theme remains the struggle of European nations for hegemony in the New World. The use of parenthetical explanations inculcates the young reader with the zeal of German-language discourses about colonial acquisitions—though in fact these were modest and in the German motherland there was less than consensus about them—around the time of the work's first publication.

The instructive tone of the Oheim's story connects the dots between Malpays's family history and three centuries of imperial geographies. Embedded in the pedagogical content are exculpatory rationalizations about individual ethical responsibility and moral courage—or the lack of it—against the historical canvas of human slavery. In the episodes that relate the struggle for European hegemony in the Americas, the Oheim notes that the French also had "Schwarze" as slaves, qualifying this fact as "eine durch den Gebrauch ungeführte Sache, bei der man sich wohl befand" (through custom, an unquestioned thing about which there was general agreement) (13). The Oheim inscribes in this context the story of Malpays, who acquired the plantation in Santo Domingo. Robert must go forth and assume responsibility for the property and the family inheritance.

He demonstrates his character before departure by expressing his desire to reveal his true identity only to the governor, a family friend, and to seek employment from the sly and suspect Fronton.

Robert's character and Christian stalwartness become the focal point of the narrative, accompanied by a belief in an unwavering moral compass even when navigating the shifting dynamics of race, economics, and ethics on the mid-eighteenth-century's major sugar-producing island.[27] On the sea voyage, the ship's captain converses openly with Robert about their destination. He cautions the young man about "das Sklavenwesen" (17) and, prompted by Robert's desire to enter into Fonton's service and a question about what a "Farbiger" is, shares information about racial categories on the island. He explains that "Farbige" are mixed-race natives with white or European parentage, or the father was "ein rothäutiger Eingeborener" with a white mother. He characterizes their skin color as variably yellow, but concludes: "Der Weiße ist nur allein ein Mensch, der Farbige ein halber und der Schwarze gar keiner! Er wird als Tier, ja noch schlimmer behandelt" (Only the white man is a human being, the colored man half and the black not at all! He is treated like an animal, indeed, even worse) (20). Robert reacts with horror at the idea that skin color determines a man's worth, not his disposition and *Herz* or heart. The sage captain counters with a question about whether things are better in Europe, conceding that things are measured differently in Santo Domingo. With graphic detail, he describes the escalating punishments and torture of slaves, repeating the advice that Robert will have to adjust.

Once immersed in the ethically hostile climate of Santo Domingo, Robert enacts his plan. Among his first encounters is a slave auction. The *Sklavenvogt* (overseer) is a man of mixed race who describes the slaves as *Ebenholzblöcke* (blocks of ebony)(28). The Africans' facial expressions range from mournful to barely contained rage. This is followed by a precisely worded, ethnographic description of the "Neger," and attention turns to "der wildeste Bursche" (the wildest one) (29): Biassou, the son of a chief, is destined to become Robert's friend, for the latter expresses concern "und strich ihm besänftigend über die Wangen" (and stroked his cheeks soothingly) (30). Fonton notes the behavior and influence of the human rights advocates in France and wonders aloud if Robert will be of any use to him in service. Closely intertwined with the characterizations, even caricatures, of the island tale are threads of historical discourses about the eighteenth-century revolutions with long legacies. Circa 1900, the reimagining of the postrevolutionary, post-Enlightenment model of human rights functions alongside the contemporary discourse about colonial proprieties. Defining universal entitlements figures prominently in this process. The capacity for cruel, race-appropriate behavior, along the lines of the master-slave dialectic, is central to the overseer's job description. Hired despite the lapse in required qualifications, Robert ventures to Fonton's estate—his own—and is served by an older slave who calls him "Massa (was 'Herr' heißt)" (Massa, which means 'master'), and also the long-suffering and angelic Agnes, Fonton's ward who is described as a white slave. The narrative posits a symmetry between African and female servitude, belying historical accuracy. Agnes, however, sanitized of any erotic connotations familiar from the visual arts—such as one might see in Jean Lecomte du Noüy's 1888 *L'esclave blanche*, for example—redeems the Orientalizing fantasy of the enslaved white woman, portrayed naked, smoking, and languishing in a harem. In the novella *Ein Kongo-Neger*, however, ethical sameness attracts. When Biassou is beaten and imprisoned, Robert reveals himself to be the true owner of the plantation. Fonton leaves the island; Biassou is made the *Sklavenvogt* and all inhumane treatment forbidden.

The improvements in treatment include the ability to buy freedom, but for several chapters, the story insists on the possible harmony between economics and ethics. Slaves who are able to earn the purchase money choose to work for Robert and trust the funds to him. When neighboring owners condemn his practices and the disruptive influence on their plantations, Robert delivers the platitude: "Die Liebe tut mehr als die Peitsche" (Love can do more than a whip) (49).

Masterly love forms one pillar of the narrative, but a love story is destined to unfold. Against the background of Maroon colonies of escaped slaves and an angry attack during which Robert sustains a severe head injury, Agnes appears as an angel clothed in white to nurse the unconscious nobleman. With a deteriorating political situation on the island, Agnes disappears; even Robert's slaves flee to join the rebellion, and Biassou admits he can no longer protect "Massa," because "auch der beste Weiße ist unser natürlicher Unterdrücker" (even the best white man is our natural oppressor) (64). Parallel love stories, between Biassou and Natoli and eventually Robert and Agnes, sentimentalize Kleist's literary antecedent, "Betrothal in Santo Domingo." In Horn's considerably less accomplished tale, the two couples enjoy a respite in the refuge provided by Jamaica. In the relative repose of a small farm, Biassou laments the history of slavery, exploitation, and bellicosity brought by white rule. From Senegal (presumably) he speaks as "der Sohn Afrikas" (the son of Africa) (77). Threads of racialized discourses interweave Biassou's saga of his people: "Aber sie waren nicht zu Menschen erzogen, gehetzt wie die wilden Tiere ihrer Heimat, wurden sie zu blutgierigen Hyänen und zu reißenden Tigern. Konnte es anders kommen?" (But they were not raised to be human beings, hunted like the wild animals of their homeland, they became blood-thirsty hyenas and vicious tigers. Could things have been different?) (77). The biracial harmony contrasts sharply with the brutalizing tragedy of Biassou's commentary.

The avuncular narrative cedes to the immigrant nephew's New World order. And Urika, the elderly servant who accompanied them with her homespun wisdom and native cognition, stands in for the surrogate aunt. As the story approaches its conclusion, Robert journeys to Freetown in order to read a newspaper, available in a café. There he coincidentally meets a French neighbor who updates him on the events at home, including the family tragedy: both Count Sulpiz and the canon were condemned to death. Geopolitical allegiances figure prominently in the conclusion. Alarmed and frightened aristocrats seek refuge in Germany and Switzerland. Robert decides against acquiring a plantation on Jamaica because he has witnessed the horrors of slavery; instead, he resolves to build a life in the forests of the United States, acquire some land, "und lebe dann als ein Freier unter freien Menschen, esse das Brot, an dem kein Fluch der Sklaverei klebt, und sterbe einst in dem Herrn ruhig und friedlich" (and then live as a free man among free human beings, eat the bread to which the curse of slavery does not stick, and at some time die in the Lord calmly and peacefully) (85). The winds in their favor, they sail to New York. Virtue prevails; Robert ultimately receives his inheritance through the family friend in Santo Domingo. Agnes, with Biassou's help, sells a diamond-encrusted crucifix, and Robert is able to purchase an ideal farm and realize the vision he failed to achieve in Santo Domingo, "nämlich des trauten Einklangs der Weißen mit dem Schwarzen" (namely the trusted harmony of the whites with the blacks) (88). Urika teaches Agnes how to run a farm, Natoli sells at the market, and Robert and Biassou work the land. The story ends with two ideal farmhouses, each accommodating a family.

> Aber sie waren und blieben ein Herz und eine Seele, erlebten ein hohes Alter und sahen ein blühendes Geschlecht, das sie segnete, als sie alt und lebenssatt hinübergingen zu den Herrn, der seine schwarzen und weißen Kinder an sein Herz nimmt, und bei dem allein gilt ungefärbter Glaube und ungeschminkte Liebe. (96)

But they were and remained one heart and one soul, lived to an advanced age and witnessed a blossoming race, that they blessed when, old and satisfied with life, they passed over to the Lord, who takes his black and white children to his heart, and who values only uncolored/unstained faith and unadorned love.

The fictional mapping of a "color-blind" utopia, in which divine and human agency transcend the brutal horrors of African slavery in the Americas of the late eighteenth century, replicates the colonizing trope of European cultivation of a wilderness. The nineteenth-century author additionally projects the possibility of a spatial freedom onto the past. He locates the fiction in the immediate aftermath of political revolutions and reevaluations of power hierarchies that succeeded in liberating whiteness while denying emancipation to black slaves. With contempt for the French Revolution and ambivalence toward the Haitian Revolution, Horn valorizes the American by positing an Eden in agrarian New York, blessed by divine benevolence in a reading gesture that renders a young reader complicit in romanticizing the brute force of historical truth. The novella recapitulates the intrigue of adventure narratives and incorporates a fictionalized German colonial subjectivity predicated on the purportedly morally defensible treatment of slaves and the migration of racial harmony to a distant colonial fantasy.

ZODIACS AND RACE

As evident in one German-language children's almanac, the authoritative yet avuncular voice of a benevolent, omniscient, and instructive narrator pervades the edifying entertainments. *Auerbach's Deutscher Kinder-Kalender auf das Jahr 1889* occupies an authorial perspective that assumes a counseling persona and cooperative tone. He addresses children directly, providing them with a series of activities appropriate for all occasions, including different seasons. Founded in 1883 by August Bertold Auerbach, son of the well-known novelist discussed above, the almanac regularly featured a calendar, games, puzzles, stories, and letters directly addressing the readers. The *Kalender* was first housed in Berlin; after 1887, Fernau Verlag in Leipzig became the publisher.[28] Under the direction of its fourth editor, Georg Bötticher (1848–1918), and his successors, the almanac gained widespread circulation and popularity. Later incarnations of the volumes display open allegiances with Nazi ideology.[29] Routinely, calendars' plates were reprinted in multiple editions with the same poems but different dates for corresponding years. The contents also contain narratives with young protagonists who serve as examples for the young-adult audience. The play activities described above accrue additional value as preparation for the adult work world, but an additional form of subliminal education is engaged in the interaction between the words and the images of Africa. German intellectual prowess spells success; the play ethic, without knowledge of colonial subjectivity and imperial identity, devolves into indolence. "Africa" presents the thrill of physical threat to the young reader.

In the voice of Onkel Auerbach, the omniscient narrator wryly infuses the description of an amorphous African nature with a moral panic about European childhood boredom. In the 1889 volume, his introduction comments on one particular set of activities recommended to alleviate this condition during the school vacation:

> Selbst recht fleissige Schüler und Schülerinnen—und dazu darf ich Euch doch alle, alle zählen—freuen sich auf die Zeit der Erholung, wo sie frei von allem Schulzwang luftig durch Feld und Wald schweisen und ungehindert sich fröhlichem Spiel hingeben dürfen.
>
> Even very industrious pupils (boys and girls)—and I may count you all among them—look forward to the time of recovery, in which they can, free from all school pressures, frolic in the field and forest and can devote themselves unhindered to joyful play.

The authorial voice acknowledges the legitimacy of entertainment, such as that provided by the calendar, at the appropriate time, describing the freedom any student feels at the onset of a well-earned holiday. These golden days, however, can grow tarnished. The risk of excessive imagination enters the discourse. Silvy Chakkalakal, in *Die Welt in Bildern*, observes: "Im Nichtstun entwickelt die Einbildungskraft ihre unheimliche Macht" (In indolence the imaginative capacity develops its uncanny power).[30] Her observation about eighteenth-century picture books persists into the miscellany of the German colonial era. In direct address to his audience, Onkel Auerbach asks each reader about a certain monotony that ensues, when even the best soldiers or dolls lose their appeal. He diagnoses the problem:

Ihr habt Langeweile; es fehlt Euch an Thätigkeit und Beschäftigung und das Spiel hat seinen Reiz verloren, weil es nicht mit der Arbeit wechselt. "Aber sollen wir denn auch in den Ferien arbeiten?" fragen vielleicht manche von Euch verwundert. Gewiss, Kinder, denn Ihr wollt Euch doch zufrieden, froh und glücklich fühlen; Arbeit aber macht das Leben süss, darum müsst Ihr Euch auch in den Ferien, die zwar eine Zeit der Erholung, aber nicht des Müssiggangs sind, zu beschäftigen wissen.

You are bored: you are lacking activity and occupation and play has lost its charm because it is not altering with work. "But are we supposed to work during the vacation as well?" perhaps some of you are asking with astonishment. Certainly, children, because you want to feel content, happy, and joyful, but work makes life sweet, and for that reason, even during vacations, which is indeed a time of recovery, but not of laziness, you should be able to keep yourselves occupied.

Auerbach recommends reviewing schoolbooks but also activities that are less important than his argument that play is justified by work and that boredom is caused by an imbalance between the two. Even school children on holiday must absorb the duality of the play and work ethic for their own good. Entertainment culture should be edifying as well. These artifacts purport not to be the "flights of fantasy"[31] disparaged by reform-minded administrators, but rather serve as diverting cautionary tales that propose correctives to the purely diverting. In this regard, the calendar itself—structured by connections to the zodiac—and its representation of Africa introduce racializing elements into the discourse of education.

In the general context of Auerbach's calendar, the optics of race depart significantly from the representation of the more conventional fairy-tale illustrations, such as the one we find on the inside cover, a visual derivative of animated crockery and cutlery from *Beauty and the Beast*. Inside the cover, the representation of children, both fortunate and afflicted, reserves a particular visual style for a victimized *Negerkind* from the calendar month of October. The miscellany, with practical, early "interactive" abilities (children could write important notes and events in the book), avails itself of the astrological signs to inflect the process of edification with entertainment. In the representation of the twins (Gemini, May-June) (fig. 18), undistorted and unperturbed boys harmlessly hunt for butterflies while frolicking.

Even the crab-bitten Cancer allegory (June-July) (fig. 19) suffers, but the visual proportions remain consistent. In the poem, we learn that the lad himself is at fault: "Ein Fürchten und Zaudern bring häufig Gefahr" (It is dangerous to fear and to hesitate). The boy's faltering agency in the hunt is the source of his pain, in other words.

In the next image, we even catch a dignified glimpse of Africa, embodied in the majestic lion (Leo, July-August) (fig. 20). The poem that accompanies the sign anthropomorphizes the lion into a head-of-household who commands his wife to prepare for a trip to the shore, away from the intense summer heat: "Er brüllt zur Löwin: Mach dich fertig / Wir reisen über Land! (He roars at the lioness: Get ready / We are traveling across country).

Into this visual and astrological syntax, the caricature of a child and the seemingly laughing snake-frame inserts a striking punctuation mark. In this image, the overarching snakes create a frame, not unlike the use of bestiaries in illuminated manuscripts from various European and non-European traditions. But the snakes are not the greatest threat in this topography of pain and *Schadenfreude*: the placement of the scorpion (lower right) (fig. 21) aligns in an almost skeletal way with the elongated shadow of the stung child. The illustrator explicitly references race in the visual vocabulary of the human form.

In his stunning work, *Advertising Empire: Race and Visual Culture in Imperial Germany*, historian David Ciarlo rivets our attention onto the "intertwined phenomena" of "modern advertising culture and the subjugation of colonized peoples."[32] He further identifies German colonialism's political themes: "overseas exoticism, obsession with British imperialism, a fascination with primitives, and delineations of racial difference."[33] Ciarlo notes that the "racial imagery saturated the advertising of the United States" at this time.[34] He cites, for example, the appearance of racial motifs in postcards and trading cards but emphasizes that "racial and racist imagery took center stage beginning in the 1880s," and Aunt Jemima dates from 1889—the year this calendar was published.[35] Aligning with that visual culture, this image serves the purpose of "clownishness or ridicule" for a white audience.[36] Returning to the Leo image, the reader/viewer perceives that Africa is not named but implied. In the Scorpio image, by contrast, the accompanying poem explicitly locates the act of reading, mapping the catastrophe onto a hostile nature: "In Afrika, da giebt es Schlangen, / Die giftig sind, / Und übel ist es hier ergangen / Dem Negerkind" (In Africa, there, there are snakes / That are poisonous, / And here it went badly / For the Negro child). I translate awkwardly with intention. The author underscores the

COLONIZING CHILDHOODS   135

FIG. 18 Gemini. From
*Auerbach's Deutscher
Kinder-Kalender auf
das Jahr 1889* (Leipzig:
Fernau, 1889). Joseph P.
Horner Memorial Library,
The German Society of
Pennsylvania. Photo:
author.

FIG. 19 Cancer. From
*Auerbach's Deutscher
Kinder-Kalender auf
das Jahr 1889* (Leipzig:
Fernau, 1889). Joseph P.
Horner Memorial Library,
The German Society of
Pennsylvania. Photo:
author.

FIG. 20 Leo. From
*Auerbach's Deutscher
Kinder-Kalender auf
das Jahr 1889* (Leipzig:
Fernau, 1889). Joseph P.
Horner Memorial Library,
The German Society of
Pennsylvania. Photo:
author.

FIG. 21 Scorpio. From
*Auerbach's Deutscher
Kinder-Kalender auf
das Jahr 1889* (Leipzig:
Fernau, 1889). Joseph P.
Horner Memorial Library,
The German Society of
Pennsylvania. Photo:
author.

importance of place: "there" and "here" point respectively to the distant danger and to the present image, this example. Helpfully, the narrator informs us that a scorpion stung the child: "Nun schreit es sehr" (Now it/he is screaming a lot). The open-jawed image of the child, the invocation of poisonous reptiles, and the menacing canopy of the uncoiled snakes contribute to an indelible sense of menace. The concluding stanza posits an opposition between this topography of vulnerability and the place of the reader: "In schönen Ländern ist doch schädlich / Gar manches Tier. / Drum bleib' im Land und nähr' Dich redlich, / Das rat' ich Dir!" (In beautiful countries there are also many a harmful animal. / For that reason stay in the country and feed yourself honestly, / That is my advice to you!). The "there" of Africa contrasts sharply with the "here" of the *Heimat*, where honest work and good nutrition save the young German readers from the devouring sting of scorpions and the bite of snakes. The dangerous and insatiable fauna of Africa, characterized nonetheless as "lovely," serve to dissuade the young readers from indulging in colonial fantasies, a perhaps ironic reference to the warm climate and adventure stories that permeate so much of contemporary young adult literature. The interaction between the text and image function as a cautionary tale against romanticizing the colonial enterprise and its intimate association with exoticized landscapes. Auerbach counters fantasies with a middle-class imaginary of islanded childhood and corporeal security based on a rooted relationship to the homeland, far from the cacophony of snakes, the stung child, and the humiliating, one-legged, unhinged distortions of caricature.[37]

Into the visual mix, the "m" glyph that represents Scorpio presides over the overwhelmingly menacing African landscape. Centuries of speculation about its origin (possibly "m" for Mars, for example) shed little light on its significance; the whip-like flourish that adds a serif to the letter, protruding into the frame, sharpens the threat. In this frame, the interaction between the glyph and the victim recapitulates the performative nature of the miscellany itself. The implacable construction of racial hierarchies relies on their replication in the play world. The act of reading, combined with the act of manipulating the text itself—owning it, writing into it, tearing its pages and folding along indicated lines—creates a scene of instruction that engages the child-reader in performative play.

To corroborate my claim more substantially, I would like to subtotal my points in the commentary on the next image. Here, the September child (Libra, or *Waage* in German, which means "scales") (fig. 22) is charged with doing his work, with the scales precariously balanced between "reward" and

FIG. 22 Libra. From *Auerbach's Deutscher Kinder-Kalender auf das Jahr 1889* (Leipzig: Fernau, 1889). Joseph P. Horner Memorial Library, The German Society of Pennsylvania. Photo: author.

"grades." His study is reminiscent of the frontispiece of the general description of the earth and its inhabitants, but here we also find toys, signifiers of the upper-middle-class, late nineteenth-century childhood both targeted and produced by this document. The world can be mapped in a playroom, a synecdoche for the child as citizen of the world. Scholars of children's literature have analyzed the role of mapping in a range of imperialist projects. In her work on the Progressive era children's series *Bookland*, Margot Stafford foregrounds the importance of geography. The series, she writes, "emerges at a time when geography and cartography were being used as part of the imperialist project on the belief that to map and represent the globe offered the ability to know and master it."[38] Knowledge of the "globe" as an imaginable and realistic space connect to national mapping. European mappings of the "Old World" reference fifteenth-century terrestrial globes attributed to Martin Behaim in 1492. Toy capitals and commerce capitals can intersect. The fast-forward of this image involves color-coded images of Africa at 1900.

In his treatment of colonial literature for young readers, Bowersox shares a persuasive insight into the textual appeal of such stories, which portray "the imagined unruliness of the colonial world to create an adventurous realm very different from the present-day, civilized metropole."[39] The ultimately moral stories in the miscellany here under consideration have a different impact on the playing child. The interaction between the images and the poetic interventions creates a learning experience through a construction of racially charged optics in which the safety of "home" must be earned and the lure of exoticized adventure must be resisted. The puckish violation of the bond forged culturally between the child and nature overshadows the reading experience, however ensconced it may seem in the European sublime and the aesthetic recollected in the safety of protected distance from the source of violence. That experience itself—of fear in the familiar—is the inverse of colonizing flights into the foreign and fantastic.

In short, play coerces the child into exercising restraint and imposing order on desire. Into the particular play world of Auerbach's calendar, the ethics of work is inserted, reinforced through the representation of toys and instruments of learning. The presence of the globe in his study, which multitasks as playroom and office, creates a homology between the regime of knowledge and the interior of the September child's "self," maintaining the delicate balance between reward and academic performance. The image, in the context of the astrological cycle and with its extoling of temperate European climates and caution about African extremes, underwrites the construction of whiteness as the cornerstone of German imperial identity that constitutes a model childhood.

The interpretive force exerted over the young reader in these images and their intertextual relationship to the instructive poetry counteract the fantasy literature directed at children and settled in the African imaginary. The last example comes from a collection of colonial poetry and songs edited by Emil Sembritzki. Most of the content published in the colonial poem and song book, which appeared in Berlin in 1911, had already been made available to a German-speaking audience in the periodical *Kolonie and Heimat*, but the explicit aim of the volume was to reach a larger audience. Like many other contemporary works, the journal functioned as the organ of a German colonial society, in this case the Women's Association of the German Colonial Society. The magazine was published between 1907 and 1919, and in 1911 Sembritzki included the poem "Fritzchens Herzenswunsch" in the anthology because it tells a cautionary tale about Africa, making audible the voice of youthful bad behavior and threatening consequences. The pedagogical impulse forms the common thread connecting these texts of colonial racial ideology at a time of American emigration and German conquests in Africa. The literary rubrics employed to measure German colonial literature, since Amadou Booker Sadji, do not completely cover children's literature and the entertainment genres that also comprise the image of Africa. Global German studies has benefitted from the scholarly contributions and extended perspective from proponents of African German studies. This literature, as well as the intention to explain colonial and postcolonial issues about Africa in Togo, the so-called *Musterkolonie*, should create a larger framework in which polyphonic voices can be heard. Without the publication *Unter Deutschen Palmen*, for example, by Adjaï Paulin Oloukpona-Yinnon, work on colonial belles-lettres would be unthinkable. German colonial novels, he writes, "erfüllten die Träume des Lesers" (fulfilled the readers' dreams).[40] What are the colonial dreams of young Germans?

The poem I introduce here inscribes an African fantasy from an adult perspective. The imagined, endless vacation from school, inconceivable in a continental European climate, allies African nature with a fiction of childhood freedom:

> O, schickte mich doch mein Papa
> Nach Afrika, nach Afrika!
> Die Schüler weniger dort tun
> In Kamerun, in Kamerun.
> Die Sonne wärmt dort wunderbar.
> Hitzferien gibt's dreiviertel Jahr.
> O, schickte mich doch mein Papa
> Nach Afrika, nach Afrika!

> Oh, if only my Papa would send me
> To Africa, to Africa!
> The school children do less there
> In Cameroon, in Cameroon.
> The sun warms there wonderfully.
> There are heat holidays nine months a year.
> Oh, if only my Papa would send me
> To Africa, to Africa![41]

This short poem articulates a colonizing fantasy in the voice of a schoolchild; it recalls the warning from Uncle Auerbach to the young reader and cautions against a fantasy about adventurous holiday landscapes. This poem also creates a twisted pedagogy. The child expresses the desire to be sent to Africa, precisely because the oppressive heat there overcomes the equally crushing burden of compulsory education—from the point-of-view of the adult reader. The colonial literature served the purpose of awakening interest in the extended horizons of a German colonial project. This poetry book is one example of that effort. The book divides the content into colonies and protected areas: Togo, Cameroon, Southwest, East Africa, and the South Seas. The editor and former imperial governor of Victoria in Cameroon, Sembritzki, writes in the foreword from Charlottenburg: "Nun tritt in vorliegendem Büchlein ein neues Bemühen auf den Plan, dahingehend, die Schutzgebiete dem Volke mit Hilfe der Dichtkunst näher zu bringen" (Now, in this little book, a new effort is put into action to bring the protectorates closer to the people with the help of poetry).[42]

COLONIAL EXPANSION OF THE PLAY WORLD

The project of educating young readers about the geographies of whiteness accompanies the colonial project of a post-1871 unified German nation. With the demographic shifts that drove a transition in self-identification from emigrants to Germans *im Auslande*, Germans abroad, parallels in the publishing practices directed at youth audiences also become legible and visible. As Susanne Zantop argued in her classic *Colonial Fantasies*, the absence of colonies for centuries generated a literature about Germans' staking claim to a moral high ground. In the introduction to a volume dedicated to her work, Marcia Klotz summarizes the process of establishing a German colonial imaginary: "Unsullied by any colonial practice on the ground, Germans were free to imagine that they would be better, kinder, gentler colonizers than the Spanish or the Portuguese, the British or the French."[43] In the literature and illustrations directed at children and young consumers, colonial fantasies and projections create a fictional realm in which the themes of conquest narratives coincide with the ethical imperatives and moral economies of religious educational testaments that feature the innocent child as the core of racial goodness and its dissemination. This model shifts and adjusts during the colonial period itself. While German emigrants to South America occupied "Kolonien," they did not automatically or consistently affiliate themselves with the homeland, depending on the exigencies of local and regional politics. That said, as the editors of *Heimat Abroad* write, "Legally and ideologically, then, Germans abroad have always been Germans first and foremost to the homeland."[44] These inflections of German national identity inform the production of children's toys and literature literally and figuratively. German children living abroad must learn how to play; conversely, German children in the homeland, by reading about the experiences of German children abroad, learn from the representations of life in the "wilderness"—but what exactly is the content of the lesson? The inclusive tone and thrust of the stories in the miscellanies model colonial children and construct white settler and colonial fantasies about the global south and the American West that function as racial primers for the aspiring imperial citizen. Not all the lessons are sanguine.

In 1890, the first appearance of the calendarlike pamphlet "Knecht Ruprecht in Kamarun" attests to interest in Camaroon, claimed as a German protectorate in 1884. The *Bilderbogen* must have struck a chord, as it was reissued the following year.[45] In it, we see traces of the semiotic shift between children, the influence of an unbridled landscape, and race. The satirical, pictorial cartoons about the generous white legend driven to distraction and a quick exit by the uncivilized Cameroonian children powerfully undermines the sanctimony of the Christmas holiday. In her study of image and pedagogy in the eighteenth-century journal of Bertuch, Chakkalakal remarks on the construction of a homology between the child and the wild. She writes, "Der 'Naturmensch,' oft eingesetzt als Begriff für die 'wilden Völker,' wurde in anthropologischen Abhandlungen als Kind der Natur konzeptualisirt. Analog dazu entwarf man das Kind in der eigenen Gesellschaft als Wilden" (The natural human, often deployed as a concept for 'wild peoples,' was conceptualized in anthropological treatises as a child of nature. Analogous to this, one constructed the child in one's own society as wild).[46] The *Bilderbogen* portrays Knecht Ruprecht not as the sinister helper with a cane to whack misbehaving children at Christmastime, as in Theodor Storm's 1862 poem, but as the white interlocutor among the ungrateful colonized on their home turf.

Parallel to the fundamental shift Susan Buck-Morss exposes in the whitening of human, presumably universal human "freedom" in response to the reality of African slavery, European thinkers introduce race to reconcile the reality of subjugation while using "freedom" as a metaphor, with "conceptual barriers" inscribed on the national landscape.[47] The construction of that national landscape as "civilization" displaces the "wilderness" beyond borders. Aligned with that displacement, the constraints on behavior associated with the national and the colonial shift. Hannah Arendt, in "Imperialism," outlines the process by which "Africa" became "wild." During Germany's colonial period (1884–1918), equations between wild African adults and "children" surface, not without dispute. One example of this challenge occurs in Grete Ziemann's book *Mola Koko! Grüße aus Kamerun*, which she published after a sojourn in Cameroon in 1907. In negating the arithmetic that equates blackness and childhood, she writes:

> Der Neger ist kein Kind, der Neger ist eben Neger. (. . .) Laßt uns den Neger an die Hand nehmen und ihm zeigen, daß wir für ihn sorgen, und nicht bloß ausbeuten wollen, dann werden eine Anzahl bildungsfähiger Keime auch eher zur Entwicklung

kommen. Möge in dieser Beziehung das Titelbild des Buches eine Art Symbol darstellen. Man kann nur immer wiederholen, Erziehung zur Arbeit durch Europäer, die selber erzogen sind, tut not.

The negro is not a child; the negro is in fact a negro. . . . Let us take the negro by the hand and show him that we will care for him; that we do not want simply to exploit him, from this will emerge many educable seeds that will be more likely to develop. In this relation, the cover image of the book represents a kind of symbol. One can only just repeat, training to work through Europeans who themselves are thus trained is essential.[48]

The image that adorns the cover of the book reverts to the presumed innocence of the young. The cover depicts two children with stereotypically racialized attributes. The African boy with earring, modest covering, and slightly downward, forward gaze, carries a squash in one hand, while the other holds the leading hand of a young white girl, fully clothed and coiffed, with a simple ruffled dress and complete with stockings and shoes. From Columbus's fifteenth-century diary onward, the sartorial divisions between the savage and civilized prevail with astonishing tenacity, which results in the hegemony of covered flesh. In severing the need for warmth and protection from the elements, sartorial practices transform from quotidian necessities to signifiers of status and race. Their transferability further necessitates regulation.

In a pedagogical register, the persistence of complete clothing and skin covering characterizes the European child and childhood; signifiers of the worn become visible credentials of cultivation and exploration, climate notwithstanding, and imply the ability to lead the way. In this image, the perennial relationship between subjects effectively naturalizes the extension of tutelage into adulthood. The metonymic relationship between the child and the servant, as depicted in the eighteenth-century household literatures and self-help guides, is projected onto the regulatory relationship between the races, which governs in the realm of signification as well as colonial authority.

The late nineteenth century witnessed a growing appetite for children's adventure stories, the cultural and literary heirs of Campe's Robinsonade and similar tales. With the rise of Karl May's popularity, derivative writers plied their wares to a younger audience and prepared to structure geographic exploration with both edification and entertainment. In most cases, these stories appeal to a male audience. The modeling of colonizing childhoods extends beyond gender difference. As Bowersox has so keenly observed, German toy makers during the Age of Empire were obliged "to negotiate the dual imperatives to entertain and educate as they considered how to present the colonial world to young Germans."[49] Material cultural references link the nineteenth-century stories and objects of play to a larger colonial complex. In the next section, I look more closely at connections between satire, whiteness, and toys from the late nineteenth century and extending through the colonial period, especially when Knecht Ruprecht is upended in the "wilderness" of German colonial Africa.

KNECHT RUPRECHT IN KAMARUN

The uncanny attributes of mimetic toys, such as dolls, are predicated on the capacity of the human subject to animate the object. In E. T. A. Hoffmann's sand man story, Nathaniel espies the face of Olimpia through a telescope and projects his desire for her through the animating gaze. Dolls' eyes by 1900 were designed and produced to approximate humans'; they play a significant role in achieving a degree of realism that was imagined by Hoffmann's Nathaniel. In actual manufacturing, Sonneberg around 1900 became known for supplying toys with a more female appeal, while Nuremberg geared production to a male market. In the English-language version of the German Empire's catalogue for the 1904 St. Louis exposition, the section on toys calls attention to the use of glass in producing Christmas tree decorations and meeting increased demand: "The above branch of the industry which has existed many hundreds of years is very closely allied to the doll industry in Thuringia, as all the necessary eyes required for the millions of dolls' heads every year are manufactured in it."[50] The trope of the doll to tame and be tamed, to domesticate and be domesticated, extends with bizarrely racialized features into the German colonial period. Again, the central event of Christmas grounds a visual narrative of gift-giving gone wrong.

The tradition of the printed *Bilderbogen* or sheet pictures reaches back to the fifteenth century and into the baroque in German-speaking Europe, but they were first circulated in the eighteenth century and, with the development of lithograph printing, were more widely available in the nineteenth century in editions sometimes colored by hand on inexpensive paper. Often accompanied by moralizing or uplifting poems, they depicted types of flowers, a small village, mountain views, and pedagogical material. One Munich publisher, Braun & Schneider, which operated from 1848 to 1898, produced fourteen-sheet prints daily and twelve hundred *Bilderbogen*, along with approximately two hundred annual volumes. Again, the Christmas holiday in 1891 provided the occasion for the Knecht Ruprecht adventure, under the rubric "Afrika Geschenke Nikolaus." Knecht Ruprecht in Afrika, number 1039, is a visual and verbal account of Saint Nicholas's assistant Ruprecht, who is sometimes depicted as surly and recalcitrant, in contrast to the later jollification of Santa Claus. This caricature shares the white supremacist suppositions of so many "classics," though it has received very little scholarly attention.[51]

Knecht Ruprecht is himself an ambivalent figure. As the lesser companion of Saint Nicholas, Ruprecht first appears in written sources in the seventeenth century. From the realm of folklore, Knecht Ruprecht is a manservant with traits of unpredictability in his pedigree. Alternately benevolent and punishing, he brings gifts or ashes. Knecht Ruprecht and, more generally, German Christmas practices were known in the United States. As Stephen Nissenbaum observes in *The Battle for Christmas*, German American midcentury celebrations attracted headlines for their rowdiness, contributing to the move from the public to private, from the street to the parlor.[52] As the holiday was tamed into domesticity and revised as child-centric, the German Belsnickle or Pelznickle, with his punitive and disciplinary tendencies, was subsumed into the figure of Santa Claus in the 1820s.[53] By the late nineteenth century, Ruprecht's job description had been largely subsumed into the characteristics of Santa Claus, primarily beneficent but only toward the morally superior and well-behaved child. In this *Bilderbogen* Knecht Ruprecht undergoes a reversal of fortune in Cameroon that ridicules the spirit of generosity and casual enactment of Euro-white supremacist charity—dismantling the treacly sentimentality of the Christmas holiday with brutal satire.

The images, accompanied by two-line, sixteen-syllable iambic verse, illustrate the fate of the "Kinderfreund" in Cameroon. Disembarking from a ship, a trim Ruprecht, clad in red, fur-trimmed robe and hat, bends slightly with the burden of three sacks, bursting at the seams with *Gaben* or gifts. Absent is the careful planning and cultivated anticipation that usually accompanies Advent. Instead, Knecht Ruprecht travels on a whim: "Der hatte einmal nichts zu thun und dacht: 'Ich geh' nach Kamarun!'" (For once, he had nothing to do and thought, "I will go to Camaroon"). In the next image, reading from left to right, then down, the viewer witnesses

Ruprecht in a Christmas-colonial contact zone. The composition situates him centrally. Randomly dressed children gaze at and point to him; an intrepid yet curious child in the lower-right foreground pokes his back with a finger. The graphic styling makes little effort to differentiate the features of the adult, a woman holding a baby, and the children, legible as such by their size to scale. Ruprecht smiles with the clichéd satisfaction of his own benevolence.

At the end of the top row of images, boys and girls snatch eagerly at the toys he distributes. Surrounded by the young ones, he raises a *Hampelmann* (jumping jack) in his right hand; his mittened left hand is raised in a gesture that signifies the somewhat smug joy of giving and surrender to their enthusiasm. One child leaves the frame, with a doll dragged behind him. Until now, the narrative follows the perspective of the European child. Underprivileged and deprived Cameroonian counterparts want toys as much as they themselves do. Ruprecht gives beneficently and enjoys the passionate reception of his gifts. This version of the colonial myth corroborates much of the political propaganda of the era, reiterating the need for white gifts to elevate and distract the "wild ones."

The shift in narrative expectations occurs and escalates in the images of the second row. Ruprecht, hands on hips in consternation, watches as the children misuse the toys. Still, the treatment of the *Spenden* (donations) seems to stem from a lack of familiarity. In the next frame, Ruprecht assumes a more self-protecting and observant pose as he watches the children sink their teeth into the rocking horse, its tail, and a stuffed lamb. In the final frame in this transition, Ruprecht recedes into the background, shrinking away in horror, as the boys hurl spears and shoot arrows at the nutcracker, riddled with blades (fig. 23). Ruprecht's anxiety indexes a shocked Eurocentrism over the violent and celebratory seizing of power and forced recognition of the Cameroon children's agency. The decorative, ritual function of the nutcracker, sacred to the Christmas tradition, celebrated in story, song, and dance, is undone in the colony, where the colonized crack their own nuts.

The next image raises the stakes of this gift-giving expedition even higher, with the iambic lines interpreting the act of "devouring" a picture book—not figuratively, but literally. Increasingly, Ruprecht's worst fears are confirmed. Further in the background, his hands raised above his head, he watches as the youths drive their spears into the soldierly representation of a nutcracker, described as a victim. In this visual and verbal narrative, the male and female toys—the nutcracker and the doll—are dislodged from

Nußknacker mit dem bunten Rock dient ihnen gleich als Sündenbock.
Sie werfen mit den Speeren drauf — dort knackt man selbst die Nüsse auf.

FIG. 23 "The nutcracker in colorful clothes serves as their scapegoat. They throw spears at him—they crack their own nuts there." From "Knecht Ruprecht in Kamerun," attributed to A. Bahr, *Münchener Bilderbogen*, vol. 2, 2. Auflage (Munich: Braun & Schneider, 1892). Photo: author.

European realms of signification. With that rupture, the mimetic function of play inadvertently confers agency onto the children of Cameroon, who recode the toys to reveal their own quotidian practices.

The German literary and cultural tradition hosts a family story about the giddiness of destructive play. In Goethe's *Dichtung und Wahrheit*, the poet recalls a tale, firmly inscribed in family and national lore, about his playing with crockery at the window while the Ochsenstein brothers observe the spectacle. As noted in chapter 3, from boredom with the domestic toys he begins a process of smashing the breakables to escalating approbation from the audience of his peers. Cruelty toward and abuse of inanimate objects or ostracized children is often at the core of critiques involving play. Middle-class practices advocate creative, not destructive, impulses in pedagogical play. In the depiction of Cameroonian cannibals, the spectacle repudiates any sense of glee in the inappropriate disposal of European toys. In the *Bilderbogen*, the nutcracker resembles the persecuted and executed Catholic iconography of Saint Sebastian. The cloying rhymes of the text characterize the object's demise as a martyrdom. The religious impulse of benevolence, echoed in the language of "gifts" and "donations," is itself cannibalized. The next sacrifice cinches the threads of catastrophe: "Den Menschenfressern scheint's geraten, die Puppen erst am Spieß zu braten" (The cannibals, it appears, have first decided to roast the dolls on a skewer) (fig. 24).

FIG. 24 "It is advisable for the cannibals first to roast the dolls on a skewer." From "Knecht Ruprecht in Kamerun," attributed to A. Bahr, *Münchener Bilderbogen*, vol. 2, 2. Auflage (Munich: Braun & Schneider, 1892). Photo: author.

Den Menschenfressern scheint's geraten, die Puppen erst am Spieß zu braten —
Mit Schrecken nimmt's Knecht Ruprecht wahr, es sträubet sich entsetzt sein Haar.

A shift in Knecht Ruprecht's identification with the toys, from objects to a Nutcracker and Hampelmann, escalates in the roasting of the female doll. With each frame, Ruprecht's responses are paced through an exasperated resentment for misused gifts—from lament at the recoding of the toy animals from playthings to groceries to a hagiography of these citizens of the play world. The male toys suffer soldierly execution and martyrdom; the rotisserie doll image conveys a complex narrative of failed masculinity, fractured colonial self-image, and the disarticulation of European identities of benevolent obligation. The poem marks this escalation lexically; the final exclamation points to punctuate Ruprecht's surprise are replaced by a hyphen, a placeholder for the unthinkable. The African perpetrators look on with glee as the doll, arms outstretched in a gesture of crucifixion, rotates into the center of the composition. The doll face seems animated: eyes open, mouth pursed in a heart-shaped countenance, eyebrows expressively raised. The scene of giving has slid down the slope of no return. The next frame inventories the greatest hits of German toy manufacturing: building blocks, toy instrument (organ), the doll house. The hyphen recurs: "O Gott! wie sieht das alles aus" (Oh, God! what a mess). Ruprecht is pursued and escapes with his life, rowed to the ship by a grim-faced sailor.

The unsubtle depiction of the Cameroonian characters as primitive, violence-prone, uncivilized, barbaric cannibals inculcates the viewer, through macabre identification with the noblesse oblige of Knecht Ruprecht, however "humorously" the events are represented, with the visual vocabulary of soldierly death at the hands of the colonized and victimization of the white female. The naïve impulse to aid the poor children of Africa with European toys is exposed as misguided and sanctimonious. The expectation of gratitude only heightens the horror of the miniatures' fate at the hands of the other. In the Age of Empire, it was imperative for the children to see themselves in their toys. The African imaginary yields to dystopian pressures of history. The shift in tone, after the 1904–1906 Herero "uprising," also known as the Nama Herero War, provides a harsh wake-up call to the romanticizing and exoticizing impulses of the African adventure tale.

By contrast, the racially harmonized Eden of Horn's novella is inscribed into the American political and aesthetic imaginary. The preservation of a vanishing nature, on which industrialization encroached, turned attention to expansion westward. The juggernaut of Manifest Destiny and the myth of European American entitlement to the "wilderness" inspired centuries and generations of mobility and migration in the name of prosperity. Through the fictional creation of a world in which German-language characters repudiate slavery, are displaced by revolution, and map their migration onto the African experience in the sugar islands of the Caribbean, colonizing children can imagine themselves into shared victimhood and moral entitlement to the new American wilderness as settlers and conquerors—without sharing the historical guilt of France, England, and Spain. Texts about toys travel along the same channels as the images do, mapping a righteous colonialism into a play world in which African agency defers to the reader, even on the territory of German moral high ground. Through German children's culture, colonial subjectivity is projected onto a new American utopia.

CHAPTER 5

Ethnographic Play and the American Imaginary

The ahistorical racial utopia of Horn's fiction, upstate New York, does create a triangulated relationship among the young German reader, the African slave trade, and the search for harmony in the Americas; this imaginary space in *Ein Kongo-Neger* is projected onto the allegedly unspoiled wild of the northeastern region of America. In the process of their inscription in the play world, geographical spaces, Africa and the Americas, are conflated. In his analysis of Carl Schmitt on sovereignty, Giorgio Agamben writes, "In the classical epoch of the *ius publicum Europeaum*, this zone corresponded to the New World, which was identified with the state of nature in which everything was possible." In parenthesis he quotes John Locke's seeming refrain from the *Second Treatise of Civil Government* of 1690: "In the beginning, all the world was America."[1] Locke's early modern meme stands in for mapping new boundaries, from the Atlantic coast to the Amazon to the construction of the American West as America; the latter is a reference to the title of a controversial Smithsonian exhibit and affiliated catalogue from the early 1990s.[2] The quest to explore, define/measure by scientific knowledge, organize, and own space accrues national attributes in the process of transcribing the world for the purpose of play. The agency of colonization dissolves in what amounts to an emptying of space except as non-European; thus the preparation for ownership through cultivation of nature and subjugation through violence against any and all resistance finds a formulaic justification. National arguments about preserving the natural world for human health derive from a transatlantic competitive drive with the Old World.

The American imaginary is formed at the intersection of German national history and the practice of disseminating science, in this instance anthropology and ethnography, through the play world. The illustrations that fill picture books originate in ethnographic drawings. Travel literature was frequently adapted as narrative directed at the young reader. Toys themselves were designed to keep pace with the introduction of zoos, ethnographic displays, fiction, and commercial developments. Verbally, visually, and materially, the model German child consumes and controls the world. In the overlap of the Venn diagram of what Susanne Zantop refers to as latent and manifest colonialism,[3] studies of play in the age of imperialism focus on the emerging mass market, national identity, and gender.[4] In the late nineteenth century, intersectional identities in the newly united German nation (1871) increasingly seek compensatory models to corroborate the national as a stable category for spatial and ideological organization through strengthening its access to the transnational identity—one signifier of which is the possession of land. From the Protestant play ethic's regulation of material objects and interaction with subordinates, manifest imperialism extends to the acquisition of noncontiguous land as public and private property—colonies in the national imaginary. One example of this exercise is evident in the impulse to acquire material cultural artifacts from beyond the borders.

In *Objects of Culture*, Glenn Penny writes that at the time of unification, Germany's ethnographic collections were "scattered," a circumstance that would change significantly by the first decade of the twentieth century, at which time German cities can boast "internationally acclaimed ethnographic institutions."[5] While these collections' growth coincides with the establishing of the German Empire, Penny attributes the expansion to city-building rather than to nationalism. The impulse to collect and control, however, manifests in the play world of this era, exposing tensions between municipal and national imaginaries and can, I believe, when examined from a transatlantic perspective, implicate nationalism and empire-building strategies with which acts of play and reading are imbued. As David Hamlin argues, toys are a "tool to access the growing influence of consumerism in late nineteenth-century Germany."[6] His vertical analysis of toy production and consumer-oriented systems in Germany before World War I provides insights into the relationship between modernity and the emergence of "an ideal of the individual" acquiring agency.[7] My concerns overlap with issues of gendered play, but the texts about the acquisition of objects and identities in the German language beyond the *Kaiserreich* aspire to a different outcome. Through ethnographic, immersive play and reading, the colonizing play world supplants and incorporates indigenous knowledge.

In this chapter, I examine the objects in circulation across the Atlantic that create connectivity in less obvious ways than the domestication of the African "wilderness," slavery, or revolutionary politics. To create an American imaginary in the German colonial play world, implicit and invisible economic mechanisms still seep into the domestic sphere. In making this claim, I base the argument on select stories, material objects, and images about how to extend the borders of the German play world, drawn to define the textual realm in which a child reads him- or herself into the colonial experience. I base my argument on texts extracted from calendars, miscellanies, and collections that represent the coexistence of didactic fiction and material objects. The interactions among accessories and toys, such as globes and racialized dolls, and accompanying narratives, such as those depicting the child at play or work with "native informants," complicate the formation of an imperial identity—even in the absence of an extensive colonial empire.

The play world around 1900 offers adventure, extending the uncharted territory of the African imaginary to the American wilderness. In exemplary stories of European childhood on other continents, or other continents viewed through the lens of German-speaking Europe, the possibility of empire exemplifies what Courtney Weikle-Mills has defined as the "imaginary citizenship" of young adult readers. The stories under consideration in this chapter instruct a particular brand of imaginary citizenship, the privileges and priorities of which are corroborated by acts of play with material objects. Weikle-Mills formulates "the profound notion that children can ratify national narratives";[8] toys, too, testify to the truth of national narratives, while disrupting, varying, or even subverting it. The textual positing of imaginary citizenship, for which the national story functions as its proof, is countered by the introduction of toys as integral to the transnational experience. Although her work focuses on Anglo-American literary and pedagogical production prior to the 1890s, the concept of an imaginary citizenship for children that Weikle-Mills elaborates resonates with the extended model of national to imperial citizenship my reading of texts and material objects identifies.

With this transitional moment in mind, in Weikle-Mills's model, though convincing, play is ancillary to the act of reading. Specific to young readers, she writes, "While children no doubt used ideas related to citizenship to structure their play, reading often allowed individuals not just to pretend that they were citizens but to understand themselves as citizens: to see the social control as an expression of their own consent even where it could not be given, to understand the law as an expression of their own sense of justice even where they had not participated in the making of it, to view the nation and the state as representing their own interests even when they had not direct political voice."[9] We have less access to the ideas children expressed historically through play than to printed and popularized readers, calendars, and miscellanies. We do have some objects. Weikle-Mills's arguments about the connections between reading and cultivating republican citizenship nonetheless can inform a reading of children's play and stories about play from the latter half of the nineteenth century in German. With national unity and swelling pan-Germanism a relatively recent phenomenon, the prospect of empire was variously incorporated into the self-image of citizenship. In some German-language stories about play and its proper practice, however, the ideas about citizenship, predicated on whiteness, become visible through the performative model of play and storytelling. In one case, the idea is expressed as a weightless object without worth.

The construction of racial identity—specifically, that of German whiteness in a new "homeland" abroad—participates in a narrative about work, play, and upwardly mobile global citizenship. With attention to Germans outside Germany, identity acquires an imperial passport despite modest colonial possessions at the turn of the twentieth century. In this chapter, I follow migrating feathers to trace the development and dissemination of an American imaginary, created through ethnographic play, that becomes integral to the transatlantic play world.

ECONOMIES OF PLAY

> Wir Kinder, wir schmecken der Freuden recht viel,
> Wir schäkern und necken, versteht sich im Spiel.
>
> We children have ever so much fun,
> We joke around and tease, that is all part of play.[10]

The Protestant play ethic encompasses a practice of play that simultaneously celebrates playing as a free act of childhood and also lays a foundation for a life of productive work. The above quotation, repurposed to instruct children how to moderate play in the late nineteenth century, originates in a poem by Christian Adolph Overbeck (1755–1821) entitled "Das Kinderspiel" (Children's games), famously set to music in 1791 by Wolfgang Amadeus Mozart (KV 598). Julie Hirschmann (1812–1894)[11] incorporates the ritual song into the celebration of a birthday party. This chapter begins with a story that models games without toys but relies on the circulation of objects in surprising ways. If we recall Friedrich Jacobs's young fictional protagonists Allwin and Theodor and the gift of a favorite toy and a garden bouquet, we may also remember that their gravely ill friend Karl preferred the flowers. The unspecified toy was implicitly disparaged. The modeling in this cycle shows good behavior, a narrative interruption that casually invokes the "exotic" as absurd and creates what I call ethnographic toys. These hybrid objects advance a relationship between the playing child and the supervisor—an updated "servant" nonetheless.

A genre of just and appropriate amusement for the young develops alongside the popularity of mischievous children's texts, which gained great notoriety. To dwell for a moment in the German context, we can observe an historical arc in the nineteenth century: playing with objects and the perceived or constructed value of the latter serves as an index of childhood identity, establishing a point on a social moral compass. By contrast, Wilhelm Busch (1832–1908) celebrates in satirical modes the antics of the misbehaving scamps Max and Moritz, who survive seven nihilistic pranks before the ignominious end in a miller's grinder. In a round of universal justice, poultry eat the grain—the first trick resulted in their feasting on Widow Bolte's chickens.[12] The boys, who made their first appearance in 1865, occupy the play world at the same time Hirschmann forwards tamer games. With an increasing intensity, games and toys socialized children at play, with entertaining and regulatory texts proliferating to accompany and inspire the games. Though the domestic setting determines the value of play objects, all are enmeshed in transatlantic economies.

Specific games and the successfully socialized male and female protagonists as players and leaders must be taught. In a story cycle published in the early 1860s, *Guckkasten-Bilder*, Hirschmann launches the collection with a birthday party scene. A woman who lost her father at an early age, married, had four children, and then became a widow, Hirschmann explored first teaching then writing as a career. She began publishing in the 1850s, authoring books directed primarily at a female audience.[13] In the text here under examination, the child protagonists model good or moderately disruptive behavior while practicing their personalities or asserting alpha characteristics to direct the shared events and experiences. A birthday party sanctions play as an exceptional moment of celebratory parabasis, an interruption in the continuum of everyday duties and rationed play. Her audience consists of children between eight and twelve (see inside cover).[14] Toys are not invited, conspicuously absent from the social event. Group play, revealing the characteristics of the children, is paramount, and in the context of the volume it is balanced and limited by storytelling. The introduction to the birthday party catalogues possible games to play indoors on a winter day, with both boys and girls of different ages. The narrator grabs the readers' interest with the debated suggestions for play, but also through referencing the cake and hot chocolate, then describing the character traits of the children and their relationship to each other. The fictional children reveal their character traits in identification with the games they recommend.

For the younger ones, the *Ringlein* (little ring) game is top choice. This low-stakes activity keeps all guests at the table; it requires little effort in terms of physical skill or strength: "Ach nein, das Ringspiel! bitte, bitte! das ist so hübsche: Alle, die das Ringlein lieben, nehmen sich gar wohl in Acht, daß sie's fleißig weiter schieben, oder sind auf Pfand bedacht—'singt eine kleine Stimme'" (Oh, no, the ring game, please, please! It is so fun: All who love the little ring, careful you must be, that you keep it moving fast, or you pay the penalty—"a little voice sings") (1–2). For this game, the children form a ring around the person who is "it," and they pass a ring behind their backs while singing a song. If the center child guesses the ring holder's identity correctly, the two exchange places. The suggestion, though, meets with general disapproval. Another guest proposes *Feuer, Wasser, Kohle* (fire, water, coal), a game that revolves around seeking a hidden "treasure," the equivalent of hinting whether a seeker is cold, warm, or hot, depending on degrees of proximity to the desired object. The introduction explains the games and the children who play them. It not only makes practical suggestions for group activities at parties but also provides the reader with characters who inhabit archetypal roles; these become the young dramatis personae of party animals, ranging from the alpha and beta males and females to inclusive play among age groups.

At the textually modeled party, age affects and informs the levels of play desire; gender, too, determines incremental activities and responsibilities. Fritz, the oldest, and a twin brother of the more moderate Georg, is described as the most impatient: "Was sollen wir nun spielen? Es scheint etwas Quecksilber im Blute zu haben, denn: still sitzen! steht gar nicht in seinem Lexikon" (What should we play now? There seems to be quicksilver in his blood, because "sit still!" does not enter into his vocabulary) (4). The author integrates the imperative "sit still!" into the description. The narrator elaborates on Fritz's desire to become a soldier like his grandfather, despite his father's wish that he use his restless limbs to become a tailor—his personality shaped by familial professions. The constitutional inability to obey a command bodes ill for the military life, however. (No toy soldiers are invited to this party.) By contrast, the oldest girl, Emma, functions as a surrogate supervisor: she shepherds the younger ones and polices the cleanliness of their clothing. Gendered play at a coed party proves problematic: the ring game is too lame for the boys, who crave more action. Elder Emma takes charge: "Ihr hatte die Mutter auch aufgetragen, darüber zu wachen, daß kein Streit den schönen Frieden des Festes störe, und daß die Freude nicht auf Kosten der sauberen Geburtstagskleider vergrößert werde" (Their mother had assigned her the responsibility of insuring that no fights [among the children] would disturb the peace of the party and that the joy was not greatly augmented at the cost of the clean party clothes) (10). Emma is not alone in playing a parental surrogacy role; along with another boy, she directs the game "Watte pusten" (cotton blowing). This game, purportedly still popular, involves blowing a weightless object, such as a piece of cotton or, according to historical sources (not named in the text), a feather away from your opponent and off the table. Laughter serves as an audible indicator of joy in the game, and the primary challenge involves puffing through suppressed laughter. The play invokes Freudian *Schadenfreude* in its combination of abandon and constraint, albeit with low stakes—there is little risk of self-inflicted or other injury. The narrator points out how greatly it compounds the fun. You cannot laugh out loud and blow "ein leichtes Flöckchen Watte" (a light little puff of cotton) competitively at the same time: "wer das nicht mitgemacht hat, kann sich die aufgeblasenen Backen, die leuchtenden Augen, die abwehrenden Hände, die lachenden Stimmen nicht denken, welche dies unbedeutende Spiel beleben" (whoever has not played will be unable to imagine the air-filled cheeks, the bright eyes, the deflecting hands, the laughing voices that make this silly game come alive) (9–10). Emma and a well-behaved Franz insure the gaiety of the game and the safeness of the cake and clothes.

My interest in this story, however, gives weight to the gravity-defying objects at hand—a puff of cotton, or a feather. The relationship of German-playing childhood to the origin of feathers occasions a deeper analysis of the mindset of ethnographic play, German play practices, and objects. As Roland Barthes wrote of plastic, its alchemical and transformative nature, and its place in the evolution of mythic materials, a "miracle is always a sudden transformation of nature."[15] In the play world, the piece of cotton or a feather can function as the vehicle for transformations of nature into the alchemy of transnational identities.

In this late nineteenth-century volume, modern play incorporates a spectrum of desires about generational, national, professional, and gendered identities. The occasion for play serves a regulatory purpose: games must be appropriate to the celebration. The end of the century brought increasing concerns about class difference and upward mobility, particularly in immigrant communities. Games and play had the potential to instruct in the replication of hierarchies that take genealogy into consideration. The text, with its essentially interactive instructions for hosting a perfect party, models proper play for celebrations. However, left to their own devices, the children cannot keep up with their own demand for entertainment. The ethnographic and economic networks across the Atlantic enter the games and play surreptitiously. The lightness of a piece of cotton or a feather provides a connective through the narratives, toys, and games.

Economic and colonial histories belie the apparent insignificance of the two objects named for the huffing and puffing game, cotton and feathers. The connections among industrialization, plantation economies, the African slave trade, and single-commodity colonialism form the nexus of the culturally produced play world. This may be a bold claim; stories, games, and borderline obsession with the whiteness of objects, including toys, meant to replicate human skin provide corroborating evidence of a homology between materiality and racial ideologies. In the German-language stories in which cotton, leather, and feathers accrue ideological significance, the hidden histories of economic exchange and exploitation are embedded in the ostensible harmlessness and innocence of the European epistemologies projected onto the American imaginary. The imaginary, produced in the realm of fictionalization, however, is saturated with economic histories and unconscious processes of globalizing commodities. Sven Beckert, in his crucial contribution *Empire of Cotton*, succeeds in an effort to connect the multiple national and industrial histories by viewing them from a global perspective.[16] By the twelfth century, non-Islamic European cotton production flourished in northern Italy, which supplied Germany with exports, though in the fifteenth century, southern Germany drew cotton from the Levant and availed itself of cheap local labor for production.[17] The extensive research on transatlantic African slave trades and single-commodity economies connects the history of cotton with colonialism, and industrialization and capitalist hegemony motored the pursuit of profit. Beckert counts German lands and Switzerland among those who would follow the "rapacious cycle of war capitalism."[18] In those locales, cottage industries segued into workshop labor; mechanized methods and spinning factories used local workers to produce cotton yarn, following a British model, in their own areas with a history of textile production.[19] Buck-Morss calls attention to the transformation of Manchester by factories, referring to them as "an extension of the colonial system."[20] By the early 1860s, when Hirschmann's collection was published, cotton "had become central to the prosperity of the Atlantic world."[21] With the onset of the American Civil War in 1861, a global cotton crisis ensued. The German states, with more modest cotton centers, experienced symptoms of the industrial paroxysms: reduced imports of raw cotton, less work, and increased unemployment.[22] Memories of the severed supply chain in the early 1860s would later inform German cotton industrialists' and their political advocates' colonial ambitions in a search for answers to the "cotton question" and superior strategies in the global "*Baumwollkulturkampf.*"[23] The given translation of the term, "cotton-growing struggle," while accurate, swallows the word *Kultur*, for my purposes the critical concept of cotton as a signifier of cultural identity. The glee of the game in Hirschmann's story presupposes a worthlessness and gravity-defying esprit undone by the economic, political, and existential battle over cotton in the transatlantic world of the 1860s. The presumed absence of value, in other words, comes at a high price. The objects of the game, in contrast to the putative value of toys, engage the players in the practice of unthinking consumption. The children perform according to the mechanisms of the global market, predicated on the conviction that an inexpensive supply of raw cotton constitutes an entitlement. Disruptions in the chain of supply and production—wars, for example—call attention to the consumption culture that relies on a continuum for a sense of security. While the Civil War had an immediate impact, its urgency seemed diminished by distance. After World War I, German economists examined the lugubrious state of cotton: the decrease in exports, the embargo on imports, and the loss of Alsace-Lorraine, calculated as "nearly two million spindles and forty-five thousand looms," along with the workers and consumers. In short, the "textile wares produced have become too dear."[24]

Further embedded narratives introduce global signifiers of distant economies and exotic power structures through a range of experienced voices. Adult intervention and supervision regulate where children engage in the performativity of childhood in order to shape not only who they are but also who they will be. Benevolent adults also regulate attention spans, retaking control after delegating responsibility for propriety to older children, enlisting them in the containment of play. These tendencies and truths, however, are accessorized. In Hirschmann's volume, a storytelling uncle enters the scene in the nick of time; he diverts them with the *Guckkasten*, and then, while they consume *Butterbrote*, which are elsewhere defined as the wholesome alternative to sugar, narrates the source of the accompanying images.[25] It is time for stories.

Garnering rapt attention with the teaser that his dog provided the images, Onkel Baumann tells a story on the condition that the children themselves take up pen and paper and write about one of the images (15); adults can assist, and the plan is to host a storytelling event every two weeks, with play and narrative entering into a sustaining cycle of merriment and entertainment. The child protagonists systematically overcome adversity; thus they balance the party scene with distant markers of privation and pluckiness. Fables and allegories about the less privileged may create a sense of gleeful yet respectful equipoise among the partygoers, but there are no toys; a feather or a simple piece of cotton suffices to provide energized entertainment. At first, however, the interaction among the images, the narrating uncle, and the allegedly real-life artist take the young audience into the territory of national stereotype.

Onkel Baumann encounters the artist's family when Diana the dog has a mishap, with contributory negligence the cause. An overzealous older brother protects his sister and threatens the pet. Onkel Baumann tells the story of the boy's demeanor:

> Das war ein Wetterjunge! der sprach wie ein Mann, und hatte das Ansehen, als sei er höchstens zwölf bis dreizehn Jahre alt, ich ärgerte mich über seine Keckheit und dennoch zog er mich an. Das war wirklich Stolz in Lumpen, denn seine Kleidung, obgleich weder schmutzig noch zerrissen, ließ doch überall die größte Dürftigkeit erkennen. (20–21)

> He was a hot head! He talked like a man and appeared to be twelve or thirteen years old at the most, I was irritated by his impertinence, and yet he also interested me. This was really pride in rags, for his clothes, though they were neither dirty nor torn, still spoke of utmost deprivation.

Nobility speaks through the child's overreaching pride. The narrator within the narration learns the family lives in a somewhat impoverished neighborhood; the father is a painter and sickly, and the mother is not strong. "Und doch sind sie so stolz, dass sie mit unsereins kaum sprechen mögen. Und nun der Junge, der meint gar, der Kaiser von Marocco sei sein Pathe!" (And yet they are so proud that they barely speak to people like us. And the boy acts as though the emperor of Morocco is his godfather!) (25). The uppity child, Justus, eventually benefits from the uncle's patronage. Baumann enables the boy to study art, and the father and dark-eyed sister Malvine express gratitude with a gift of the images that set the stories and games in motion.

The boy-protagonist, through benevolent instruction, is able to channel the quicksilver in his veins; this character proves complex, fortunately open to ameliorating adult influence. The "exotic" emperor, invoked for the sake of hyperbole, displaces local arrogance of birth to the north of Africa in a gesture of excess and ludicrous aristocratic lineage. While art is sanctioned, creativity funded, and imagination extolled, absurd aspirations to power are displaced. The children in the framework audience finally begin to crave the stories and arrive at a consensus that they are *ausgespielt* or played out. The story demonstrates antidotes to play; playing children as portrayed in this exemplary volume learn to be self-regulating. Simultaneously, their reading and associated activities participate in a pedagogical model that reinforces prevailing socially and historically constructed identities. During the Age of Empire, as Bowersox observes, the acceleration of transportation and communication infrastructures beckoned the young to organize the world, its inhabitants, and their spaces according to "vague but nonetheless commonly understood hierarchies of relative civilization."[26] Those hierarchies intersect with micro- and macroeconomies based on exchange, cultural appropriation, and international relations. The understanding of those hierarchies of civilization and barbarism are replicated in the act of reading and modeling play. Stories accompany the children into their adult roles, but in the course of the late nineteenth and early twentieth centuries, the apparently worthless and weightless objects, commodified in play, coexist with mass toy production while the latter creates not a room nor even a house, but rather an empire of its own.

Hirschmann's volume, comprised of modeled games and play, images, and the moderating influence of narrative, simultaneously functions as an epistolary event. She inserts herself into the family structure of playing and narrative celebration with a personal valediction. First, the authorial voice advises her young readers to seek out a storytelling aunt or beloved grandfather but adds in closing:

> Oder wißt Ihr ganz was Schönes? Schreibt es mir, da will ich Euch helfen, und was auf der Welt Schönes geschieht, soll uns zum Bilde werden, von dem wir hübsche Geschichten erzählen wollen. Das soll eine Lust sein, auf die sich schon im Geiste freut.
> Eure Tante
> Julie

> Or do you know something even better? Write to me about it, and I can help you, and all the wonderful things that happen in this world should become a picture for us. From the picture, we want to tell lovely stories. That should be an eagerly anticipated delight in spirit.
> Your aunt,
> Julie[27]

The interaction between Hirschmann, the signing aunt, and her audience becomes performative and productive with the author as signatory and honorary family member. She valorizes the potential of reading to prompt writing, thus capturing the pedagogical moment in the communicative act. Reading models writing; images produce stories. The model of replicated ethics avails itself of the narrative relationship between the putative aunt and her audience. The role of using narration as a scene of play and instruction assumes a different complexion with a masculinized narrator. Hirschmann introduces the narrating uncle who intervenes in the play world to tell moral stories that rival activity and inspire the children to sit still.

The figure of the storytelling uncle is frequently reincarnated in European cultures. In the German-language children's activity book discussed in the previous chapter, Auerbach's *Deutscher Kinder-Kalender auf das Jahr 1889*, the author, who assumes an avuncular persona and tone, addresses children directly and provides a series of activities appropriate to different seasons. The longevity of the games Hirschmann describes in some ways transcends the geography of the play world, moved indoors for the season. In the beginning of the twentieth century, the stories and illustrations in Auerbach's interactive volumes assume more historically nuanced characteristics that reflect the ideologies of the global marketplace. Here, the nature of play, the origin of play objects, and processes of hybridization and transatlantic and transnational appropriations are the focus. In Thomas More's "Childhood" poem, for example, Childhood is personified, and "in play is all my mind." However, the voice projects: "But would to god these hateful books all, / Were in a fire burnt to powder small."[28] In Auerbach's calendar, play and learning purport to coincide, especially with the attribution of boredom to excessive leisure time. In that leisure time, play and work collude with subliminal lessons about race and commodities. In transatlantic modernity, filtered through the Protestant play ethic, recreational reading enjoins play to transnationalize German children.

Literary theorists, many associated with the work of Paul de Man, expound on scenes of reading as scenes of instruction. Indeed, prior to the emergence of deconstruction from the scrutiny of continental philosophical texts in the twentieth century, the structuralist foundations of historical linguistics paved the way for J. L. Austin's concept of performative language, in which spoken words and acts coincide—taking marriage vows, for example, or naming a baby.[29] In *Gender Trouble*, Judith Butler amplifies the performativity through her analysis of performance on the construction of transmutable gender identities.[30] That uncanny power of performativity drives acts of reading in the play world, moving toward normative or naturalized behavior; the text, through the presumption of inactivity, engages the imagination and composes the scene of instruction when translated into the rules of the game to be played. Play unfolds within a national canon, but also, when historicized, weaves transnational connections. With the introduction of a coercive alignment between play and personhood, particularly in the compressed age of German imperialism, the project of educating young readers about the geographies of whiteness accompanies the colonial project of a post-1871 unified German nation. The association of reading and play with golden days of leisure transmogrifies through colonial fantasies into a German transnational childhood, where Brazilian jungles and American prairies hybridize play and the work of survival and weaponize the civilized imagination into racial superiority. The stories, images, and toys discussed below provide evidence of a paradigm shift from the eighteenth to the late nineteenth centuries, leveraged by transnational infiltrations of a new, American and African "wilderness" subject to colonial strategies of entertainment. Inserted into the acculturation and socialization processes of edifying young audiences and consumers, we encounter increasingly racialized foes; the European child, thus educated subliminally and bold-facedly through entertainment and play, learns to eschew the "wild" streak within and instead identify with white settler mentalities, shepherded by representations of satirized "savages."

HYBRID DOLLS

The association between children and the "developmental" stage of non-European peoples factors into the understanding of play and the construction of adult identity that ostensibly motivates it. In particular, as Chakkalakal observes, the *Wilden* (wild ones) of other continents were characterized as children; they constellate a chiasmus between the wild and the child.[31] Beyond the eighteenth century, the nexus of this relationship provides the compass point for orienting civilizational and pedagogical processes. In particular, texts about toys offer intentional instruction about the interaction with objects and caregivers. Dolls, as simulacra of the human, necessitate a specifically European implementation of toys in compensatory and vicariously consumed domestic and colonial landscapes in order to regulate ownership. In "Die kleine Urwälderin" ("The little jungle girl"), the reader accompanies an industrious though occasionally petulant protagonist, Anita Villinger, on her adventures in the *Urwald* or primal jungle of Brazil.[32] Under the direction of its fourth editor, Georg Bötticher (1848–1918), the *Kalender* of 1902 published a six-page story by W. Helmar (Maria Hellemeyer), accompanied by two of Leipzig artist Max Loose's illustrations. Bötticher, too, earned a reputation as an author of children's and entertainment literature. Reinhard Tenberg characterizes some of Bötticher's efforts as parody and humor; in his later years, as evident in his poetry, he embraced conservatism and the spirit of German nationalism.[33] The relationship between the nation and the play world of the global south surfaces in the Helmar story.

"Die kleine Urwälderin" narrates a day in the life of a young German protagonist, Anita Villinger, who lives in what is construed as the Amazon on a plantation with her father and the domestic servant, Caschumka. Anita must earn the right to play with her beloved doll, Liesl, who accompanies the child on a ride through the jungle. Liesl is attacked by a monkey, which was initially docile and treated to a lump of sugar. With the intervention of Caschumka, Liesl is repaired with the help of locally available material—bird skin with colorful feathers. This story shares elements and characters with Helmar's first-person narrative, *Vom Urwald zur Kultur: Erlebniss eines Mädchens* (1898), a two-volume *Bildungsroman* rife with tantalizing details about "Anni" as a young woman, sufficiently grown to marry an engineer and return to "civilization" with him in Germany. Caschumka, too, travels with her mistress "Zur Kultur," the title of the second part, second volume. In the novel, the narrator describes Caschumka's origins: her grandparents hailed from some small Spanish village; they emigrated to Brazil; their daughter eventually married a "Cariboca (Mischling)" (person of mixed race). Anni identifies them both as products of a jungle upbringing.[34] She hates and fears the Indians, and she does so in a register that evokes the settlers' reports of conflict with the Great Plains Indians. In the almanac, though, Caschumka's character is streamlined into that of domestic servant; the images portray her with sufficient ambiguity to collapse the African and American wildernesses as a homogeneous "exotic." Bracketing harsh realities of history—from the decimation of Amerindians and centuries of African slavery in the Americas to European exploitation of the Amazon and its resources—the story comprises a cautionary adventure about the consequences suffered by a doll of European material and manufacture in the wild. Her hybrid nature evokes Homi Bahbha's sense of creating a new transcultural form, but in the story, hybridity retains its ambivalent meaning, diluting potentially subversive outcomes—except that the Helmar returns the doll, presumably as a stand-in for the protagonist, to Germany. In this section, I follow textual and material details—the fate of feathers across different cultural contexts—to trace the development and dissemination of an American imaginary that becomes integral to a model of German childhood.

The descriptions in the story are neither thick nor site-specific. Helmar depicts a distant land with an exoticized version of the classical German fairytale forest. The jungle is "wunderbar schön und seltsam" (wonderfully beautiful and strange), then immediately compared to a "Feengarten" (fairy garden),[35] which creates a tone of ambivalence. Yet the project of cultivating the land corresponds with the civilizing task of parenting the child. The descriptive passages invoke a compelling though challenging life on a "hacienda" run by Anita's father. The use of the word "hacienda" (Portuguese *fazenda*) collapses Spanish with Portuguese, homogenizing any linguistic or historical accuracy, but it is nonetheless helpfully glossed: "So nennt man dort ein Gut" (That is what an estate is called there).[36] Bowersox calls attention to such disregard for accuracy and describes the "confusion of colonial markers" endemic to colonial literature aimed at a youth audience.[37] Yet in this instance, the lapse remains puzzling despite the dominant image of South America as colonized by Spain and given the availability of sources in German that targeted candidates for migration.

Consulting another source, we find Georg Anton (Ritter) von Schäffer, a major in the Brazilian Honor Guard, as well as an adventurer, entrepreneur, and author who published a recruitment volume to attract Germans to Brazil. In his *Brasilien als unabhängiges Reich in historischer, mercantilischer und politischer Beziehung* (Brazil as independent empire in historical, mercantile, and political context), he recounts the working relationships in a plantation economy, using the Portuguese *fazenda* (adapted to German orthography as *Facendas*).[38] Schäffer's audience, however, was comprised of adult readers; his purpose was to portray an attractive, politically, economically, and topographically hospitable alternative to overcrowding and underemployment in Europe. While the publication of this story intersects with the German colonial period, its inaccuracies and homogenizations of lands beyond Europe reveal a voracious colonial imaginary in the absence of actual colonies. By the early twentieth century, Portugal's colonial power was severely reduced. Brazilian independence in 1820 did not coincide with the end of African slavery, which was pronounced only in 1888 and persisted as discrimination against Afro-Brazilian practices, such as the prohibition against cooking with palm oil or drumming. The story of Caschumka and her ward, however, makes pedagogical points in the language of empire.

Fantasy landscapes inhabited by characters of color populate adult and children's literature alike. Authors of popular novels, Karl May foremost among them, created fantasy worlds about faraway places that had little basis in historical reality. They reveal more about the reading appetites of German-language Europeans at the time than about contemporary African or American realities. The truth is not portrayed but imagined, and history is recast and projected onto the page and the screen of a national imaginary. This bendable standard applies as well to authors of children's literature. In the introduction to his game-changing book, Penny writes, "By 1900, Germany's leading ethnographic museums had descended into chaos. A wild array of artifacts from all over the world pushed these museums well beyond their material limits."[39] He enumerates a seemingly random list of collected and displayed material objects indicative of cultures and peoples both local and far-flung, among them Polynesian canoes, Inuit clothing, and Benin bronzes. With empirical methodologies to tame the relentless collecting, Germany's consumption of the cosmopolitan resists the descent into chaos through precisely the pedagogical epistemology at work in the narrative. The unfamiliar is rendered familiar, even in the realm of fantasy. In this way, the imagination is undergirded by the colonial project. In the story "Die kleine Urwälderin," the transposition of a forest fairytale onto a colonial fantasy elides historical facts, not least amont them the long-term social inequality that ensued from a plantation-driven economy, and instead inserts imperial signifiers into an established German syntax of the forest adventure, with a doll as the direct object. This national grammar of the German tale imposes order on the jungle world.

Just as toys were gendered and racialized, so too were stories about toys. In Bowersox's analysis of colonial games, he writes that "girls were not actively encouraged to engage in colonial play in the same way as boys."[40] In this story, however, the young European, through the assistance and guidance of indigenous and subordinate cognition, experiences the exoticized jungle as well as the domesticating miming of mothering her favorite doll. Quickly we learn that the young protagonist, Anita, dwells in Brazil with her father; her mother, Frau Villinger, is deceased. Caschumka plays the role of mother surrogate. Bowersox, in discussing entertainment literature, further observes that "media aimed at girls, by contrast, turned the colonial world into something much less adventurous and disorderly."[41] In this story, aimed at a younger audience, the spaces of the colonial imaginary retain a vague sense of adventure and risk but provide accommodation between the "European" and the "Brazilian." Paternal authority, once textually established, recedes from the short story, except to oversee Anita's regimen of book learning. Just as this narrative attempts to establish a matrilineal epistemology, it resets the complexion of citizenship. This story, however concise, elaborates on the surface of skin tone in revealing and disturbing ways. Though not a colonial experience per se, the mapping of maternal knowledge onto a fictionalized Brazilian forest reiterates the process of constructing whiteness and appropriating "native" knowledge.

The author emphasizes the trials and realities imposed by the global South, "Weit von hier, jenseits des großen Weltmeeres" (Far from here, beyond the great ocean),[42] on the surfaces of European bodies. Of interest in Helmar's formulation and her mapping of the story onto a Pan-American imaginary is the use of "Weltmeer," literally, a world sea. The body of water, the Atlantic, dominates the concept of a Europeanized world and worldview. The geography of the watery world builds the boundary for the play world. In this hybrid space, white skin is at risk. The narrator creates a comparative framework to normalize unfamiliar contrasts: "Es sah ganz seltsam aus, wenn das weiße Kind zwischen all den braunen und schwarzen Gestalten der Dienerschaft umherlief" (It was completely strange to see the white child running among all the brown and black figures of the servants).[43]

After accounting for the presence of two white German immigrants, Anita and her father, in the Brazilian primal forest, the narrator dispenses with Frau Villinger and describes Caschumka as "eine bronzefarbene herzensgute Dienerin" (a bronze-colored, good-hearted servant)[44] who oversees Anita's behavior. Here again, the narrative embeds the relationship between Caschumka and Anita in a familiar and quasifamilial setting; in doing so, the historical reality of slavery and the fact that Teuto-Brazilians in fact owned slaves are elided.[45] The myth of German moral superiority, in which the violence and brutality of other European powers contrasts with good albeit less-powerful Germans, was rampant in literature for young readers. The representation of Brazil around 1900 in children's literature modifies the definition of worlding. In his study of literature from and about Brazil aimed at young readers and children, Franz Obermeier characterizes much of the work as an attempt to process "die soziale Realität des Landes" (the social reality of the country),[46] though he leaves a wide margin for the unspecific scenarios of youth stories. We can speculate about authorial intention to make Brazil palatable for emigration around 1900; after 1888 and the abolition of slavery, a conscious effort to "whiten" the population prompted Brazilian politicians and diplomats to commit their efforts and resources to recruiting European families. The German settlements, however, eventually thrived in the south (Rio Grande do Sul). Obermeier further observes that travel literature was rewritten for younger readers and sometimes reworked as fiction.[47] Though he treats Helmar's 1898 *Vom Urwald zur Kultur: Erlebnisse eines Mädchens* (From the jungle to civilization: Experiences of a young girl) elsewhere, he does so dismissively, attributing the inadequate understanding of cultural difference in Brazil to the shortcomings of the writer.[48] Speculating on her gender, Obermeier does not identify Maria Hellemeyer as the author. Indeed, little is known about her life. While she did not achieve critical acclaim or even notice, her work reproduces a paradigm about ethnographic play and practicing whiteness that had considerable purchase on the development of European notions of culture and civilization. Obermeier notes that Brazil functions for her as a "Versatzstück einer exotischen Prägung einer Normabweichung" (a set piece for the exotic impression of a deviation from the norm).[49] I do not disagree, but the nature of those impressions interests me nonetheless. That her work appears in a miscellany for young readers indicates that her work reached the target audience. That the "exotic" involves the protection and preservation of white skin and an amalgamation of African and American tropes of the wilderness compels me to include the young jungle girl in the play world.

Adventure stories about play around 1900 unfold with the nation as a recent phenomenon and German colonization of Africa a contemporary reality. Following the unification of the German states in 1871, Germany enhanced its national narrative with colonial ambitions. The Congress of Berlin (1884–86) effectively carved up and apportioned the territory that remained of Africa. Germany established four colonies (Togo, Cameroon, German Southwest Africa, and German East Africa), encompassing approximately one million square miles and with about twelve million inhabitants.[50] Germany also acquired a series of islands in the Pacific and established a colony in Tsingtao, China. However, as historian David Ciarlo cogently observes, the majority of Germans evinced little interest in the colonies: "Despite a brief surge of interest (buoyed largely by the press), the German public seemed, at least to the die-hard colonial 'enthusiasts,' to largely ignore Germany's colonies."[51] At the same time, Germans abroad in North and South America identified with the imperial desires of the homeland, self-defining as colonists and pioneers. As I argue based on a reading of Helmar's story, the colonial adventure for the German child abroad becomes accessible through the act of reading and play. The construction of racial identity, of German whiteness in a new "homeland" abroad, generates the narrative about work, play, and global identity. With attention to Germans outside Germany, such as the fictional Anita and her father, that identity acquires an imperial passport, despite modest colonial possessions at the turn of the twentieth century. Details about migrating feathers, signifiers of the colonial experience, trace the inscription of an American imaginary that becomes integral to the transnational portrayal of German childhood.

In "Die kleine Urwälderin," the pedagogical benefits of ethnography or geography are not present. The inaccuracies do, however, perpetuate misconceptions about the topography of South America. Obermeier's work does not take this story or its author and illustrator into consideration. Indeed, he writes, "Das gefährliche Abenteuer präsentierende Land bot sich einfach mehr für die Selbstbewährung Jugendlicher oder junger Erwachsener an, als für Reisen von Kindern" (The country and associated presentation of a dangerous adventure simply appealed more to the self-examination of adolescent or young adult readers than for children's travel).[52] In the story's ethos, the reframing of aberrant behavior constitutes part of the civilizing process. A brief summary might be in order: Anita and Caschumka go about their daily activities, which include a hunt in the forest for dinner. On the ride, Anita hears a monkey in the trees and makes a small sound to attract

FIG. 25 Max Loose, "Die kleine Urwälderin." From *Auerbach's Deutscher Kinder-Kalender auf das Jahr 1902* (Leipzig: Fernau, 1902). Joseph P. Horner Memorial Library, The German Society of Pennsylvania. Photo: author.

it. At first, the monkey comes to her, compliant, and is given sugar. Upon seeing the doll strapped to Anita's back, the monkey attacks it, ripping off an arm. Anita wants Caschumka to shoot the beast, but she reasons Anita beyond that response, repairs the doll, and in its new form, at some unappointed time, Liesl returns to the homeland. The inciting incident occurs when Anita has a childlike lapse in obedience at the beginning of her day; she refuses the ministrations of Caschumka, essentially her servant, and throws a tantrum to resist the daily application of an oily substance that functions as an insect repellent. This occurs after Caschumka pulls back the mosquito netting from Anita's bed. The "rote Masse" (red mass) is a reasonable ministration with which the child must comply. The red mass metaphorically stains; revulsion ensues. The narrative invests considerable energy into the protection of white skin. Anita must comply with her guide and perform her duties. Helmar reveals the servant's appeasement strategy: to console, reward, and regulate her recalcitrant ward, Caschumka promises to give her a precious doll, access to which is carefully rationed. Better behavior is rewarded with an object of play.

Curious is the interplay between the representation of Anita and the description of the doll, especially when examined in the context of the visual images. Above (fig. 25), we see the sharp contrast between Caschumka, whose feet seem to continue the lines of the animal-skin rug, and Anita, who presents more contiguity with the unlined bed sheet. In the frame, Loose alludes to tiger stripes—there are no tigers in Brazil, which underscores the conflation of South American and African signifiers. This associative visual logic strengthens connective tissues between animal and human skins. In defining the doll, Helmar writes, "Es hatte einen weißen Porzellankopf mit roten Bangen und Lippen und blauen Augen und porzellanene gelbe Locken. Seine Arme und Beine, Hände und Füße waren aus weißem Leder gefertigt" (It had a white porcelain head with red cheeks and lips and blue eyes and porcelain yellow curls. Its arms and legs, hands and feet were made of white leather).[53] Helmar, however, does not produce the doll's features from reality alone. The child's colonial fantasy brings together the materiality of toy production, destructive encounters in the jungle, and the help of indigenous skills and resources. Around 1900, dolls' upper arms were usually made of leather and stitched to porcelain forearms. The multiple textures attest to the individual doll's hybridity prior to the jungle adventure, but the story demonstrates a further hybridizing of European and indigenous resources. Further, the doll, made precious through European origins, must be rationed, along with the leisure to play.

In the presumed progression from the jungle to civilization, the life of a German-European child in the wild of Brazil made many demands on the young protagonist; Anita bears a double burden commensurate to her dual "citizenship." She must be an industrious learner about survival, about "was man so in der Wildnis braucht, das ist Reiten und Schießen, Fallen stellen, Schwimmen und Turnen, und dann mußte sie geduldig beim Vater sitzen und Schreiben, Lesen und später Rechnen lernen" (what you need to know in the wilderness, that is riding and shooting, setting traps, swimming and doing gymnastic exercises, and then she had to sit patiently at her father's side and learn writing, reading, and later arithmetic).[54] In short, Anita has the equivalent of a day job, involving an imperial pedagogy, learning to live and play her part as a German child of the jungle; she inherits an investment in its domination and cultivation. Her progress, with some predictable childish resistance, requires the ministrations of Caschumka. With the brief mention of the daughter's duty to learn European skills at the behest of her father, the patriarchal presence makes no impression in the narrative. The dyad of indigenous cognition, represented by Caschumka, and the pluck of her ward proves sufficiently capable of writing an autonomous adventure story that blends associations between the wild of Africa and the Americas.

In this almanac, the stories, poems, puzzles, and illustrations cover a wide range of natural and supernatural landscapes, from giant mushrooms and undersea adventures to more sobering stories of mining coal and a grandfather's narration of his war stories. Helmar contributes another tale about a misbehaving child, "Die Giraffe" (The giraffe). In this *Märchen* (fairy

FIG. 26 Max Loose, "Die kleine Urwälderin." From *Auerbach's Deutscher Kinder-Kalender auf das Jahr 1902* (Leipzig: Fernau, 1902). Joseph P. Horner Memorial Library, The German Society of Pennsylvania. Photo: author.

tale), little Else spits at her nanny and her mother when called home from play. Her fate: an earth spirit appears and transforms her into a giraffe. Else's mother dies of despair, and the giraffe ends up in a cage, displayed in a zoo.[55] Wild animals populate Helmar's respective stories to different ends. In "Die kleine Urwälderin," Caschumka mediates between the child and the wild, embodied in an attacking monkey.

Loose indicates a rapprochement of sorts in his illustration (fig. 26). For the protagonist, the absence of any European peers makes mimetic play impossible—and Else would not be a paragon of good behavior in any case. Anita has no other models, so her actions conform to the environment of the jungle. She has never seen "wie europäische Kinder ihre Puppen spazieren führen" (how European children take their dolls out for a walk), so instead she slings it over her shoulder "wie man ein Gewehr trägt" (as one would carry a weapon), though she manages to tuck the doll's feet into a belt to accommodate the toy while riding a horse.[56] The author calls attention to the absence of European playthings, which were readily available in some South American cities. In the *Deutscher Pionier am Río de la Plata*, for example, advertisements for dolls and toys broadcast the import with aplomb. For example (fig. 27), in 1879, J. H. Pehling's toy store in Buenos Aires announces: "Alles, was in diesem Fache bis jetzt erfunden ist beziehe ich direkt aus Europa" (Everything that has until now been invented in this field I acquire directly from Europe).[57]

FIG. 27 J. H. Pehling's toy store advertisement. From *Deutscher Pionier am Río de la Plata*, newspaper, 30 November 1879, no. 143, 2 Jahrgang, S. 2. Biblioteca Nacional Mariano Moreno, Buenos Aires.

> 143 CORRIENTES 143
>
> Grosses
>
> ## Spielwaaren-Geschäft
>
> von
>
> ### J. H. PEHLING
>
> 47 — CALLE PERU — 47
>
> Meinen geehrten Kunden diene zur Nachricht dass ich ein grosses Sortiment der feinsten Spielwaaren erhalten habe.
>
> Die allerneuesten Sachen, von den billigsten bis zu den teuersten sind stets in grosser Auswahl bei mir vorräthig. Alles was in diesem Fache bis jetzt erfunden ist beziehe ich direckt aus Europa. Kinderwagen, Schaukelpferde, ganze Kücheneinrichtungen, aller Arten Spiele und viele andere Sachen, die des Raumes halber nicht benannt werden können.
>
> 47 CALLE PERU 47
> Gegenüber der „Ciudad de Londres"

It is important to note that the ad copy lists strollers, rocking horses, complete kitchen sets, all types of games, and so much more, the inventory of which cannot be rehearsed owing to space constrictions. The little primal forest girl's story, driven by the tension between survival and the quotidian as represented by the need for skin protection and incorporating wilderness skills into everyday existence, must eschew the acquisition of European toys. The availability of imports would distract from the authorial project of hybridization to capture the German child-reader's imagination. The story does not aspire to represent the experience of the colonial child with any realism; rather, the details mobilize the American imaginary with sufficient basis in a European epistemology to make the distant locale part of the German play world. Further, the distance between urban consumerism and the postulated "jungle" of the displaced German child is precisely placed in order to be overcome. Anita naturally and unselfconsciously practices her jungle skills. Clearly, the requisite baby carriage, a toy transport popular at the time, was not in Anita's possession nor in Caschumka's toolkit; nor would such a contrivance navigate the jungle well. Anita's play opens up multidirectional ways to model and to mime behavior and optics between Germany and a fictional Brazil. The narrative description of the natural environment creates a correspondence between play and reality, skin and porcelain. The omniscient narrator describes orchids: "Es sind dies sonderbare Blumen, die aussehen wie Spielzeug" (They are these peculiar flowers that look like toys). The natural world becomes in itself and through simile a plaything, the jungle a play world.

By the 1890s, German manufacturers engaged in widespread production of dolls with porcelain or biscuit heads and cloth or leather bodies. Especially important are the Simon & Halbig and Kämmer & Reinhardt manufacturers, both located in Sonneberg, Thuringia. Yet at the time, if these dolls were among the more popular character dolls, they would have mohair or some hairlike substitute and not the porcelain locks the narrator describes. The unusual use of the adjective *porzellanen* suggests that the author is describing the quality of the hair, not the actual substance. The material and metaphor engage in an unstable and transferable relationship. Metonymically, the doll's composition and complexion are constructed. In his review of Karl Gröber's book about the history of toys, Walter Benjamin drew a compelling comparison between literary textuality and the toy's materiality. In his discussion of the stuff toys are made of, Benjamin writes, "The alabaster bosom that seventeenth-century poets celebrated in their poems was to be found only in dolls, whose fragility often cost them their existence."[58] This short story reveals more about mimesis, transference, and citizenship than its simplicity belies.

The doll, the reader learns when she is introduced, also emits a peculiar sound, again, not an uncommon trait in contemporary toy manufacturing. Communication between Anita and the jungle environment is a point of contention. The few sounds she makes to attract the monkey elicit a response; it too makes sounds understood in a European epistemological framework: "In Europa hört sich das Piepen ganz junger Spatzen fast ebenso an" (In Europe, the peeps of very young finches almost sound the same).[59] The frame of reference needs constant comparing and contrasting to keep the inventory of European and Brazilian habitats from aligning. At this point, Anita gives the monkey some brown sugar, not white, which the narrator glosses as European.[60] Ultimately, though, "Die kleine Urwälderin" is a story about remigration and the ability of material objects, such as the doll, to acquire historical agency, demonstrating in this instance that "objects are active agents in history."[61] The toy, hybrid to begin, then in need of repair, exceeds the means of European production, with a skin graft from the tropical forest. In Liesl's posttraumatic incarnation, this doll embodies a history of servitude, immigration, and remigration in the material transformation of the toy.

This story, with its occasional Pygmalion moments, relies on the transference between young subjects and both animate and inanimate objects.

Once it consumed the treat, the monkey searches for more and encounters Liesl; it changes its behavior from "childlike" and attacks the precious object, ripping off an arm: "Eilig sprang es auf einen Baum und zerbiß und zerriß den Arm, daß die Zeug- und Lederstücke nur so herumflogen" (Quickly it sprang onto a tree and bit and tore the arm so that pieces of clothing and leather were just flying around).⁶² Incensed by the attack, Anita, in a fit of pique, wants her guardian to shoot the monkey, but Caschumka uses reason to dissuade the child from killing the irrational animal. Caschumka prevails; she describes the monkey as an "unvernünftiges Tier" (irrational animal) and convinces Anita by admonishing her about being human: "aber Du bist ein Mensch und darfst nicht böse handeln" (but you are a human being and may not behave badly).⁶³ The domestic servant and enlightened mother surrogate repairs Liesl with whatever material she has at local disposal; the repair includes bird feathers. The colorful feathers supplement the torn white leather; the doll returns to the homeland with visible traces of its adventure in the fairytale forest of an imaginary Brazil. The conclusion infers Anita's return but remains ambiguous.⁶⁴

The mother surrogate, Caschumka, plays a pivotal role in the remigration narrative—all the while, her homeland and path to Brazil, via the Atlantic slave trade, do not warrant mention, though they are the necessary prerequisites for the moral of the story. Moreover, the early modern European integration of Brazilian featherwork for ocular pleasure and display—as used in the *Kunstkammer*, for example, for costume or decoration—fully obscures the network of indigenous signification. Most associated in Europe with the coastal Tupi, their featherwork, though mobile through colonial economies, was embedded in Amerindian cosmologies. Additionally, Helmar's narrative works both with and against Loose's illustrations to homogenize any distinction between Amerindian cognition and an African slave's artisanal doll repair. Though the craft is indigenous, the labor is clearly marked as African. The amalgamated doll is the product, uncannily, of the amalgamated history that is ultimately the privilege of power and dominance. In her essay on Brazilian featherwork, Mariana Françozo writes, "A central element in early modern *kunstkammers*, feathers and featherwork arrived in European collections first and foremost as global networks of commerce and politics."⁶⁵ The use of featherwork, intentionally not plucked from the bird skin Caschumka employs to repair and export the beloved porcelain-faced doll, invokes an optics of decorative natural materials traded directly between indigenous peoples of Brazil and Europeans dating to the mid-sixteenth century, according to Françozo.⁶⁶

Further, Françozo traces the European associative thought process between Amerindians and feather dress back to the early modern period. This visual stereotype, albeit diluted and lacking in any granular detail, nonetheless populates the story of the hybrid doll.

The European child Anita, through a native informant, learns to control irrational impulses she experiences in the jungle from her bronze-skinned guardian and protector who also is invested with the balance of reason and surrogate parental power to instruct.[67] The color of skin figures in the European construction of Native Americans, as seen in the press coverage of the Wild West Shows—with abundant associations between "noble savages" and "impressive red-brick faces."[68] Like the depiction of Caschumka in the story, the description of color purports to be adulatory. Her skin tone is a repository of the necessary pedagogy for instructing young whiteness. Unlike the message conveyed by the circa-1905 periodical *The Faithful Comrade* in which the dangers of the Brazilian jungle are depicted,[69] this story relies on a surrogate to achieve the accommodation of a transnational German childhood. Caschumka combines local knowledge, which the narrative inscribes as indigenous cognition, with common sense and enlightened guardianship. Her bird-skin-and-feather repair of Liesl's torn and bitten doll body creates a hybrid toy that displays the colors of subaltern artisanship, which sutures the feathery signifiers of the tropics along the already hybrid materials of porcelain and leather, derivations from the European lineage: "So ist Liesl später auch mit einem Vogelfederarm nach Deutschland gekommen" (This is how Liesl later came to Germany with a bird feather arm).[70] These lessons and the material objects, mangled and repaired with ethnographic play and indigenous knowledge, transmit the pedagogy of colonial play that nurtures the American imaginary in a way that communicates through comparisons to European objects.

The projection of a facile hybridity onto the material object, the doll, relieves colonial anxiety. Liesl's return to the homeland, with the colonial markers of the Brazilian jungle, signifies an easy creolization of her identity. This story and its interaction with imagery succeeds not in enhancing the experience of play nor modeling European childhood as such, but rather in infusing the reading experience itself with the diverting potential of the play experience while redirecting and taming the desire for ungendered adventure through the safety net of distant inoculation. With native feathers healing the doll's wounds that were sustained at the hands and teeth of the wild jungle denizen, Liesl teaches the German-speaking reader how to play, effectively ordering the world, with a hint of color, in the unruly space of the American imaginary.

GERMANS AND INDIANS

Considerable scholarly attention has focused on the sometimes perplexing fascination Germans have historically exhibited for all things Native American, in part as a result of a need to account for what may appear to be an uncanny and unilateral elective affinity. Glenn Penny explores this dynamic in *Kindred by Choice*, with a primary focus on the long nineteenth century. While many quote the popularity of Karl May (1842–1912) and his Winnetou tales, others attribute the fascination of Germans with warrior cultures and sculptural masculinity. However, in the middle of the nineteenth century, other images of Native Americans were in circulation that effectively undergirded other myths, including that of the stoic Indian, intimately bound to the natural world and savage on the battlefield. The stories that emerge around 1900 challenge the legacy of the fearless warrior and inflect the stereotype to reassert white settler identity.

The myth of the stoic Indian originates in European interpretations of Indian behavior based on empirical observation, connecting the image to the genres of adventure writing and ethnography. Aspects of this popularized belief, as damaging as it is reifying, are challenged by liberal writing—and at least the facial design of one German doll. An example of the ethnographic reporting genre is "Ein Besuch bei Indianern in Nordamerika" (A visit with the Indians in North America) by Franz Löher (1818–1892).[71] The work of this democratic German historian and jurist appeared in the highly respected *Deutsches Museum, Zeitschrift für Literatur, Kunst und öffentliches Leben* (German museum, journal for literature, art, and public life) from 1858. It recounts his extensive travels in the United States, with a focus on Ohio, where he spent seven months. His three-volume publication from 1857 and 1858, *Land und Leute in der alten und neuen Welt* (Lands and people of the old and new worlds), was excerpted in a popular journal, but Löher's observations and reports were based on his earlier travels in 1846/47—roughly contemporary to the first iteration of the idea of America's Manifest Destiny. Of particular interest here is his extended stay with the Winnebago.

Löher spent months in the encampment of the Winnebago near a fort; he provides detailed and vivid descriptions of their *Hütten* (huts) and way of life. He writes extensively about their jests, family life, and also interactions with government agents:

> Es herrschte in diesen Tagen eitel Lust und Fröhlichkeit in den Hütten der Winebagos. Es waren die goldenen Tage, wo ihnen die Agenten der Regierung Geld, Mehl, Fleisch, Waffen und Kleidungsstücke aushändigten. Da wurde gezecht, geschmaust, gelacht, gejubelt, bis sie abends vor Müdigkeit umfielen. An die Zukunft, an die bald kommende Noth dachte aus dem ganzen Schwarme kein Einziger.

> In these days an atmosphere of pleasure and happiness reigned supreme in the huts of the Winnebago. It was the golden days when the agents of the government handed out money, flour, meat, weapons, and clothing. There was drinking, feasting, laughter, celebration, until night came and they collapsed with exhaustion. Not a single one of the swarm thought yet about the coming privation of the immediate future.[72]

The time of his visit was also a time of treaties, broken and renegotiated. Despite his well-meant explorations, Löher nonetheless inaugurates stereotypical descriptions of the people's life in the village. He is invited to smoke *Kinkenik*, the form of tobacco that slightly narcotizes; he then draws conclusions about any number of associated practices:

> So werden die Wilden schon früh gewöhnt, Leiden und Qualen schweigend zu ertragen, bis sie lautlos verenden wie der verwundete Hirsch im Dickicht. Wenn der Indianer Hunger hat oder wenn ihn sonst etwas quält, so greift er zur Pfeife. Ihre narkotische Wirkung unterbricht den Gedankengang seines Geistes wie den Stoffwechsel seines Körpers. Das ist es, was er will: vergessen. Weil sein Geist ihn nicht höher trägt, weil er über Ursache und Wirkung nicht nachdenkt, noch weniger beides begreift, so ist sein Fatalismus natürlich. Der Knabe weicht dem Schlage aus, den er kommen sieht: ist er aber getroffen oder überfällt ihn sonst ein Weh, dessen Ursache er nicht begreift, so weiß er nichts anderes zu thun als still zu leiden, die Natur unterwirft ihn dem Leiden, nicht thut es sein Heldenmuth.

Thus the wild ones are early on accustomed to bear pain and suffering in silence, until they expire without a sound, like the wounded stag in the thicket. Whenever the Indian is hungry or if something is hurting him, then he reaches for the pipe. Its narcotic effects interrupt the thought process of his spirit like the metabolism of his body. That is what he desires: to forget. Because his mind does not carry him higher, because he does not think about cause and effect, even less can he comprehend either, thus is his fatalism natural. The boy avoids the blow he can see coming: but if he is struck, or if some other misery afflicts him whose cause he does not grasp, then he knows no other option but to suffer in silence; Nature subjects him to such suffering, it does not affect his heroic courage.[73]

The conclusions Löher draws from this behavior reiterate a centuries-old European belief in the childlike nature of Indians, but he goes further in formulating intimate connections between stoicism, resignation of a nearly spiritual nature, and the impulse to reach for a narcotizing pipe. Not his focal point, the inculcation—or instruction—of children and young adults in the tribe parallels adult socialization through exposure to narcotic substances. Still, Löher rationalizes this inflicted loss of innocence through a legerdemain of European reasoning. He can only be equivocal in his limited understanding of why a young Winnebago man can accept fate; his suffering does not diminish his self-esteem or courage because it is the way of Nature. As demonstrated previously in the analysis of Auerbach's calendar images, reading and studiousness model the capacity for self-improvement and the rejection of fate in young Europeans. In Löher's observations, however problematic, he is among the earliest European writers to forge causal links between the dictates of Nature, Indian stoicism, and ritual addiction among those closely connected to the natural world with which European audiences remained captivated throughout the century and beyond.

Children's toys and books around the turn of the century reflect this fascination and demonstrate that it was not reserved for the world of adults, of German men who identified with fearless warriors and wanted to recover a sense of prowess through emulation, or of German women whose open admiration of, for example, the American Indians who traveled and performed with the Wild West Show became the subject of parody. The identification with First Nations also invokes the German love of Karl May but also the mythos of the "vanishing race" and alignment with warrior cultures. Penny observes the differential anger expressed in German positions, noting that "they tended to attribute that demise to a set of admirable characteristics rather than essential limitations inherent in these people."[74] The arrival of William F. Cody's Wild West Show introduced a dynamic and new dimension into the representation and reception of Native Americans throughout Europe. Journalists who reported on the show still subscribed to myths of the "noble savage" and the "vanishing race," but, as Daniele Florentino writes, "they were also affected by the negative stereotypes generated by colonists' narratives and by the then flourishing doctrines of racial superiority."[75] One prevailing identity construct in the 1890s in Europe stemmed from a Nietzschean critique of an ever more effete European man. In images of Indians disseminated in Europe, white masculinity is often the target of critique. It is possible to see in the German reception not only of the Native Americans (wanting them to be more "authentic") but also of the "Rough Riders" a desire for an essentially American warrior that crossed the Atlantic as the signifier of modern masculinity as "American." Julia Stetler's compelling study of Buffalo Bill in Germany offers a range of insights into the transnational history of the "America's National Entertainment," known popularly (if not altogether accurately) as the Wild West Show. With its location at the nexus of authenticity and performance, frontier and empire, and entertainment and edification, the show represented the West to America and the West as America to a host of international audiences. Stetler's analysis of the German audiences' and news reports' admiration of—and even identification with—the "Noble Savages," represented by the Native American performers, draws in illuminating ways from German identity formation, which included Teutonic tribes' victories over Rome, German romanticism, and the contemporary colonial project in which a recently united nation (1871), albeit somewhat aspirationally, identified itself as an empire. Stetler writes, "American society was equated with youth and sturdiness and infused with masculine virtues and vigor. Europe, in contrast, looked effeminate, soft, and overcultured."[76] In other words, the edge of cultural superiority claimed by Europe and wielded by so many to disparage American culture as derivative and unoriginal, was ultimately damaging to a sense of historical masculinity.

The depiction of American Indians in literature and picture books targeting a young audience lacks the fierce and awe-inspiring model of masculinity conveyed perhaps in adult popular entertainment. In the world

FIG. 28 Fritz Koch-Gotha, illustration of the three chiefs from "Eine Indianergeschichte." From *Auerbach's Deutscher Kinder-Kalender auf das Jahr 1904* (Leipzig: Fernau, 1904). Photo: author.

of toys, however, we see a unique example of a Native American child with a decidedly grim expression, and I return to this object below. Consistent with Auerbach's portrayal of the "Oktoberkind," which I discussed in the previous chapter, as racially and geographically challenged, the 1904 miscellany tells the story of three Sioux chiefs who suffer a humiliating and laughably deceptive defeat at the hands of a white settler and his wife—and their little dog, Bello.[77] In "Eine Indianergeschichte" (An Indian story), illustrated by Fritz Koch-Gotha (1877–1956), a frequent contributor to the *Kinder-Kalender*, the narrative transports the reader to the endless prairies of North America in the year 1820. Visual images of indigenous peoples of the Americas proliferated in the second half of the nineteenth century. Fueled by ethnographic collections and "exhibits," world fairs, and, not least, the popular and ostensibly edifying entertainments, typical features and dress were familiar. The popular, standard *Brockhaus-Konversationslexicon*, which began publication in 1796, contained ample, instructive illustrations; in addition, such tomes provided anthropologically influenced charts of Amerindians in encyclopedic style. A cosmopolitan-minded illustrator, even untraveled, could consult such a reference for accuracy of depiction. By 1900, the myth of Indians as the "vanishing race," underwritten by a history of genocide and forced displacement, had captured the American political imaginary and also inspired the quasi-anthropological artistic efforts to document life on reservations. In the context of a children's story, it is noteworthy that the author would revert to a time period prior to the presumptive achievement of (North) American "Manifest Destiny." Even though the Indian chiefs should inspire fear, their caricature and defeat invite ridicule as they cede the prairie to the clever, victorious "Pale Face" white settler, with whom the young reader identifies.

With assistance from the Koch-Gotha illustrations—which cast the three Sioux chiefs, Long Finger, Green Wolf, and Limping Rattlesnake, not with conventionalized phenotypes but rather with caricatured features (fig. 28)—the characters succumb to caricatures that undo the stereotype of the Indian as indefatigable warrior of fearsome masculinity. The German fascination with Plains Indians unfolds from the anthropological to the farcical. Though clad in war bonnets of eagle feathers, buffalo skin coats, and frighteningly painted faces, the three chiefs fail to inspire awe. Their ceremonial attire gestures at, while obscuring, any indigenous network of significance. The "chieflings" resolve to take the scalp, "die Kopfhaut"[78] of the "Pale Face," identified as a farmer who has settled a part of the prairie with his wife. While the narrative continues to describe the three as "fearsome" (*gefürchteten*) as they embark on the warpath, the visuals border on cartoon, thus undermining any real sense of readerly dread. Even the post that bears the sign "War Path," in German, is portrayed as a street sign with the colors of the American flag.

When the farmer, wearing spurs and smoking a pipe, calmly concludes that he is the object of the pending attack, he and his wife assemble canons from household articles and point them at the fence. When the three chiefs see the faux canons, the scene is ripe for parody: "Wie der Blitz verschwanden die Indianer!" (Like a flash of lightning, the Indians disappeared).[79] The barking of Bello and the "hearty laughter" of the farmer and his wife accompany the fearful, fleeing Indians. Bello takes it upon himself to bite Limping Rattlesnake. Tellingly, the illustrator has cropped the war bonnets of the retreating and defeated chiefs. The new sign reads: "Kriegspfad nach den Dörfern der 'hinkenden Klapperschlange.' Das unbefugte Betreten dieses Weges wird am Marterpfahle bestraft. Der Gemeinde-Vorstand" (Warpath to the villages of the "Limping Rattlesnake." Unauthorized entry of this path is punishable by torture. The Community Board). The "rhetoric of German tribalism,"[80] as Penny formulates the affinity between the presumptive warrior cultures of Germans and Indians, is depleted to suburbanize the defeated chiefs and tribalize the white settlers (fig. 29).

ETHNOGRAPHIC PLAY AND THE AMERICAN IMAGINARY   181

FIG. 29 Fritz Koch-Gotha, illustration from "Eine Indianergeschichte." The sign reads, "War path, unauthorized persons forbidden." From *Auerbach's Deutscher Kinder-Kalender auf das Jahr 1904* (Leipzig: Fernau, 1904). Photo: author.

The Koch-Gotha illustrations more closely resemble the warbonnet wearing Indian chiefs used to sell tobacco—another association mediated by commerce and addictive consumption. In the play world, the image of a doll with porcelain head, finely modeled teeth, and less ostentatious clothing provides a contrasting image. The mournful, fearful expression on the contemporary toy's face adds emotional range to the narrative portrayal of the three Sioux chiefs. This expression opens another possibility for identification; Marseille's design depicts a child, not a parody of a chief on the warpath—these objects, called "Scowling Indian Dolls," were in production around 1900.[81] The German version, "finstere Indianer," existed as well in the decorative arts. These subspecies of "character dolls" and ethnic dolls appeal both to play and display, thus meeting one criteria of the Protestant play ethic, but what do they teach? Racial paradigms do not necessarily replicate in the objects. It must be noted that "multifaced" dolls were in production, with a variety of facial expressions and racial features that could be revealed and concealed with a rotating bonnet. Additionally, folk dolls and topsy-turvy dolls[82] could represent race without history or transfer racial signifiers in a single turn.[83] Embedded in the genre of racist satire, ethnographic knowledge grounds the pedagogical moment in the story, which performs a farcical vanquishing of the easily duped chiefs. The American imaginary on this continent of the play world cedes the characteristics of the unwritten wilderness; it is settled. In the national narrative, a material object complicates the lessons of racial identification mediated by narrative entertainment and intended to interact with the images to establish white settler resourcefulness as superiority. The doll, however, reintroduces the uncanny in ways that model identification to the child, playing her way into colonial subjectivity.

CODA

Playthings, from the weightless feather and valueless wad of cotton that belie transatlantic economic and unequal exchanges to the racialized and hybrid dolls that sculpt messages about white superiority, illustrate the uncanny alchemy of signification in the materiality of the transatlantic world. The stories and objects analyzed above capture the American imaginary in the German-language reader. The feather network and hybrid dolls may be products of the imagination, but the connection to the villages of nineteenth-century Germany and to immigration stories is more than tenuous. Not accidentally, Max and Moritz meet a gruesome end, eaten by the *Federvieh*. According to Busch's biographer, Eva Weissweiler, the rambunctious boys haunt middle-class respectability but belong in the history of migration: "In the 1860s, people from poor, rural regions were massively migrating to America. There were many incredibly poor people working as day laborers, and they would leave their numerous children on their own. There were therefore thousands of children roaming around, and some of them would survive by stealing food, like Max and Moritz."[84] Published by the same press as *Knecht Ruprecht*, *Max and Moritz* inhabit the margins of the play world. Both books are displaced across the ocean to an eager audience. In the American context, migration stories invest further a presumptive superior status of European origins; in the play world, the national and transnational narratives speak German. Even though *The Katzenjammer Kids* (1897), inspired by the misbehaving Max and Mortiz, would survive in American comic-strip popularity for decades, their German antecedents would be reincarnated as Schoenhut dolls (ca. 1907). These afterlives speak in multiple registers about cultural transfers in the play world.

CHAPTER 6

The Home and the Nation

There remains the education of the home or of nature . . .
—Jean-Jacques Rousseau, *Emile* (1762)

Man vergesse nicht: die Kindheit von heute ist die Menschheit von morgen, und von der gegenwärtigen Generation hängt es ab, ob der nachfolgenden Rosen oder Dornen in ihr Leben geflochten werden!

Let us not forget: the childhood of today is the humanity of tomorrow, and it depends on the present generation whether the next generation will have roses or thorns woven into their lives!
—Frau von Marenholz-Bülow, quoted in *Der Kindergarten in Amerika*, 31

Under the influence of sociohistorical forces, relationships among the home and the nation form the nexus of childhood identities through experience, acts of reading, and the practice of play. The significant departure from Rousseau's eighteenth-century paradigm, the either/or of home and nature, ensues with the institutionalization of education for the young. The ethnographic play developed under the auspices of microcolonization for children has an impact on the acquisition of agency. Around 1900, with a progression or rather conflation of African and American imaginaries, play is reconfigured in the service of national identity. This becomes evident in migration. As we have seen, the supervisors of purposeful play morph from servants into mother, mothers into professional mothers, fathers into soldiers, explorers, and farmer/settlers—and these into teaching professionals. As the German pedagogical narrative networks across the Atlantic, it collects the domestic and political spheres into the play world, encompassing rebelling slaves as allies, domestic servants and indigenous interlocutors, and bellicose natives and cannibals, as mocked and vanquished victims— or in the satirical case of the Knecht Ruprecht debacle, victors—of play. This sphere contrasts sharply with the tameness of the domestic configuration of supervised children in the play room. In this transformation, the center of pedagogical gravity shifts.

Throughout the nineteenth century, the association between female caretakers increasingly shifted away from the intimate involvement of domestic servants and onto mothers. Concurrently, a professionalization of motherhood, demonstrated by manuals and pedagogical strategies, posited a closer relationship between good mothering and regulating childhood play. A strong endorsement of maternal modeling is legible in the reception of Friedrich Fröbel's kindergarten project. Bertha von Marenholtz-Bülow (1810–1893) emphasizes his inspiration in her memoirs: "He repeated again and again: 'The destiny of nations lies far more in the hands of women— the mothers—than in the possessors of power, or of those innovators who for the most part do not understand themselves. We must cultivate women, who are the educators of the human race, else the new generation cannot accomplish its task.'"[1] Ann Taylor Allen's illuminating study of the women in Germany and America who endorsed and celebrated Fröbel's kindergarten as an educational and civic institution and philosophy foregrounds the public role of teaching and professionalization processes that enabled female teachers, channeling political engagement and giving caregivers an entry point into the public sphere.[2] Her analysis alights frequently on the ideas of educational play, but in this chapter, the professionalization of maternal roles, decades in advance of popularized versions of Fröbel's practices, anticipates the vocation of teaching children as part of a national and institutional project.

Concurrent with dramatic geopolitical change, the islanding of childhood and alleged preservation of the domestic sphere as intimate space in need of protection strengthen their conceptual foundations. Parallel to this development, female influence expands through educational advocacy. The rhetoric of female educational activism echoes the elevation of domestic life already present in the eighteenth century: that domestic practices shape national identity. Yet the spread of German-specific pedagogical practices empowers women, and the ostensibly progressive impulses result in the spread of racialized thinking. To elaborate, I focus in this chapter on visual representations of domestic play space, the transatlantic dissemination of Fröbel's practices, and the subtext of German-ness in national, imperial, and racial rhetoric and material objects of play.

The *Kinderstube* or *Kinderkammer* (children's room) established a place in the domicile, the metonymic for a private sphere, in early modern Europe, though the playroom as a separate, dedicated space emerged only at the end of the eighteenth and beginning of the nineteenth centuries. Prior to the separation of children's space as play areas, domestic interiors and where children fit into them do organize much contemporary thought about the family, education, and play world. The family exists in a relationship of contiguity to the house. This metonymic relationship in turn arranges the subjects into generations, household hierarchies, and performances of both work and leisure activities. For children, their domestic domain contained them as preadults; play was structured as pedagogy.[3]

In one celebrated genre painting, Fritz Uhde (1848–1911) depicts the space and occupants of the Wilhelminian *Kinderstube* (1889) (fig. 30). This image recapitulates visually the interaction on canvas between interiors of play and the perspective on the exterior spaces of the world, between play agents and their objects, and between the material objects and the viewers. The painting consists of portraiture: Uhde's three daughters compose a triangle of activity in a comfortable and well-lit space for play and female "work," the hobby or profession of sewing. Multiple claims distinguish Sarah Hoke's analysis of this work; this one painting is a snapshot of daily life. With close attention to the furnishing, Hoke focuses on the clothing, the context for play and sewing, and association with domestic space. The subtle supervision of the *Kindermädchen*, outside the triangle and off to the side, models a domestic adult, also engaged in handiwork.[4] In this painting, feminine space informs the pedagogy of play. This aspect of education informs other toys (the younger girls play with dolls, the older sews). In numerous contemporary examples, books, sewing kits, dolls on wash day, and aprons breach the boundary between the imaginative realm of play and the reality of domestic chores.

The gendering of play, space, and activities—note the replication of needlework—comes as no surprise; however, the painting, when compared

FIG. 30 Fritz von Uhde, *Die Kinderstube* (Children's nursery), 1889. Oil on canvas, 110.7 × 135.5. cm. Hamburger Kunsthalle. Geschenk Alfred Beit, 1901. Photo: Wikimedia / ArishG CC BY-SA 4.0.

with roughly contemporary commercial representations of domestic children's space, yields evidence about the transatlantic intervention of German pedagogical models into the domestic sphere. Curiously, though implicitly gendered, the acts of play and coincident scenes of instruction proffer a gender-fluid paradigm for acquiring life skills.

In the German grammar of portraying the nature of the child, the "conversation" genre of painting serves best. According to the composition, the hierarchy of adult supervision stays low-key. The vitality of that supervision becomes increasingly professionalized alongside the popularization of educational practices that insist on a conjoined sphere of play and pedagogy.

The concept and institution of education as a "garden of children" traverses the transatlantic world through the advocates of Fröbel's model. The metaphor of the natural education available to any child traces its lineage to popularized philosophies drawn from Rousseau's writing. The export of the German-language model, primarily through adherents to the kindergarten as an institution, owes its success in part to a network of educated women whose work takes root on both sides of the Atlantic. It is important to mark the influence of Fröbelian models as the natural aligns with the national.

It is my intention neither to write an analysis of Friedrich Fröbel's methods nor to rewrite his biography to lend greater relevance in contemporary pedagogy. Rather, I wish to examine his legacy in ways that are specific to the practice of play as a mediator in a multifaceted discourse about childhood in transatlantic modernity.[5] The Protestant play ethic is the product of his interventions in theories and philosophies of pleasure, play, and intersectional identities. In the post-Enlightenment era, questions about childhood, play, and the purpose of life permeated the philosophical realm and seeped into the practical life world. The philosophical father of all things edifying and play-oriented in the German cultural tradition is undeniably Fröbel and his foundational practice of educating young children. Throughout the nineteenth century and industrialization in Europe and the United States, multiple factors—among them demographic shifts, increasing polarization between agrarian and urban landscapes, and intensified mechanisms of capitalism, accompanied by political and philosophical responses to widening gaps in income—exerted considerable force on the lives and representations of families and children. With varying degrees of commitment, governments joined charitable organizations in identifying social needs and institutionalizing labor and care that formerly fell into the jurisdiction of the family. Child labor was regulated, along with education and, not least, the spaces of play. In transatlantic modernity, German pedagogical models, informed by the Protestant play ethic, influenced the formation of institutions of model childhood. At the nexus of this thought lies Fröbel's commitment to the cultivation of childhood. His advocacy of play as learning has a transnational, transatlantic reach. Progressive politics of female ascendancy and the cultivation of children as citizens, however, tends to assume a patina of racialized rhetoric.

In addition to providing the point of convergence between German and American play practices, Fröbel's work defines the parameters of the changing debate about early childhood education, children's rights, and demographic shifts. The key question in the discussion and reception of Fröbel's work and of play in general—why do children play?—translates into moral, ethical, and pedagogical idioms. Huizinga bristles at all the reasons that researchers contrive to explicate play: "All these hypotheses have one thing in common: they all start from the assumption that play must serve something which is not play, that it must have some kind of biological purpose."[6] Admittedly, my argument would warrant a scolding from Huizinga as well, but the purpose of play, I think, exceeds biological parameters; instead, play, at the nexus of model childhoods and constructs of youthful innocence, serves multiple purposes, a historicization of which opens apertures into greater understanding about the human condition in the modern, transatlantic world—and that region's astonishing and appalling dominance over culturally, racially, and ethnically constructed others and corroborating images of "otherness." The ideal of self-improvement and advancement, mediated by education—a stalwart staple in the menu of Western, European American progress—colludes with an unsavory defense of hierarchies, spanning intersectionally multiple categories of differences, as the individual child becomes a specimen of the national collective. The International Kindergarten Union (IKU), established in 1892, forms a locus of controversy about "Fröbelian" and progressive kindergarteners,[7] and the publications at the center of this chapter attest to the defense of Fröbel's principles. Tensions imbricate the debate, launched in 1895, which in distilled form pits play against science. What begins as a defense of play—understood as the signifier of childhood and as the innocent imaginary—aligns with theories of improvement through eugenics around 1900. The pedagogical discourse about play, in transatlantic modernity, prepares the ground for a pedagogy of race.

Also around the turn of the century, cultural critics and aficionados detected a symmetrical relationship between the experience of art and the activity of child's play. In 1904, Paul Hildebrandt (1862–1937), once an apothecary apprentice who became a book dealer, then the editor of the Berlin *Kunstsalon* and the *Wochenbericht für Kunst* (1892), published an important book about toys and play, with general observations, sweeping histories, and biographical details from artists.[8] Hildebrandt seamlessly integrates the progression in materials and markets for toys into a trajectory of improvement and progress. Using the example of a child's desire, channeled by browsing and touching in a toy story, he notes that the wooden toy quickly yields the right-of-way to one with real wool: "Daraus können wir die Lehre ziehen, ein Kind ist vollkommen glücklich bei dem einfachsten Spielzeug, solange es noch kein besseres kennt, sobald es ein vollkommeneres kennen lernt, wird es dies meist bevorzugen" (From this we can learn the lesson: a child is perfectly happy with the simplest toy, as long as he does not know a better one; as soon as he becomes acquainted with a more perfect one, he will prefer it).[9] Particularly with toys of war, realism of the soldiers and weapons intersect with historical nationalisms.[10] Foremost, however, Hildebrandt equates play with the aesthetic experience. In the age of industrial urbanization, any garden of childhood is inscribed as both a natural and national space of public and intergenerational recreation.

Fröbel's great intervention into the childhood educational experience culminates in his commitment to the value of structured games and play. His innovation, generally known by much of Europe and North America, is the *Kindergarten*. The assumption that children should be involved in creative, imaginative play has become so widespread that we can easily forget its controversial beginnings, development, and international dissemination. While Fröbel inspired many proponents during his life, his work was to experience a revival, especially outside German-speaking Europe, in the late nineteenth century; international educators secured Fröbel's position at the forefront of play theory at a time when they were in search of a model to reform public education. As noted in the catalogue for the exhibit on the century of the child at the Museum of Modern Art in New York, Pestalozzi and Fröbel inspired a paradigm shift: "A new way of thinking about the child was taking hold, one that questioned rigid discipline in the classroom and the mind-numbing traditional methods of learning by rote. In progressive educational circles a general consensus was emerging that children were active, rather than passive, learners, and that they were best educated by women, using kindness and encouragement rather than rebuke and corporal punishment."[11]

Particularly in the English-speaking contexts of the United States and England, which were not accidentally facing challenges presented by urbanization, demographic shifts, and accelerated industrialization, theorists and educators took recourse to the past practices of enlightened play as postulated by Fröbel. Two books exemplify this type of policy-making Fröbel reception—though the "progressive" quality described above is nuanced by the comparison. The first, published by Ernst Steiger (1832–1917), represents an effort to introduce Fröbel's tools into a larger discourse about the education system in the United States around 1900. The German American author weighs in about the role of German theory in American institutions but also provides ample commentary on the efficacy of one national theory in another context. The second text, by Emily (Anne Eliza) Shirreff (1814–1897), appeared a bit later; the British educator and activist takes up Fröbel's cause in England. Together, both historical documents make a case for the national signatures of play in transnational institutions.

Each example highlights the peculiarly national traits in the international movement to legitimize play. The discourse about play in America invokes pedagogical necessity in order to articulate a defense of play. To support play as a learning activity, advocates turn with a nearly missionary zeal to Fröbel's pedagogy.[12] His insistence on structured and supervised play created a legacy that accompanied many German immigrants to their destinations in the United States but also inspired a cohort of activists and teachers in transatlantic modernity.

> Namentlich sind es die Spiele der Jugend, in denen die verborgensten Anlagen, das ganze innere Sein des Kindes zur Erscheinung gelangt. Es ist eben das Spiel diejenige Tätigkeit, die zu dem specifisch Eigenthümlichen des Kindes gehört. Ein Kind, welches z.B. ausdauernd und bis zur Ermüdung spielt, wird gewiss auch ein ausdauernder, tüchtiger und aufopfernder Mensch. Durch planmäßige Beschäftigung kann also das Kind frühzeitig zur Lebens–aufgabe des Menschen, zur Arbeit, erzogen werden; denn es wird damit nicht nur die physische Kraft, sondern auch Aufmerksamkeit, Beharrlichkeit, Hingabe und Freude an der Arbeit gefördert.

> Specifically, it is the games of youth in which the innermost aptitudes, the entire inner being of the child make an appearance. The game is also that activity that belongs to the specific characteristics of the child. A child, who, for example, plays persistently and to the point of fatigue, will certainly become a diligent, efficient, and self-sacrificing human being. Thus through regular occupation the child can be raised from the beginning to the mission in life, to work; then not only the physical skill, but also the attention, the persistence, dedication, and joy in work will be encouraged.[13]

Here, Fröbel draws a line between children at play and adults at work. Steiger, a German American publisher and writer, presents an unattributed brochure to advocate Fröbel's method of education. The pamphlet's title alerts the audience to the need for a German model in America: an asterisk alerts the reader to the mixed sources. Contents of this publication, which include an abbreviated theory of kindergarten instruction and a catalogue of available supplementals, are adapted from two German-language sources: the Lucerne teacher Joseph Bühlmann's *Friedrich Fröbel und der Kindertarten* and the director of the Gotha Teacher Seminar (for females) August Köhler's *Der Kindergarten in seinem Wesen dargestellt* (The kindergarten presented in its essence). From the former, the pamphlet adapts the short biography of Fröbel and the teaching methology; from the latter, structured as answers to questions from supporters and detractors, Steiger's booklet anticipates counterarguments (4).[14] Overall, the tone of the pamphlet is activist, with the goal of bringing the best of German education to the United States in an industrial era. Additionally, Steiger published a wide range of German and English texts devoted to education and language. His 1878 *Educational Directory* lists the brochure amid an extensive inventory of books, guides, and treatises devoted in multiple languages to education through play.[15] The close transatlantic connections among the authors, advocates, activists, and translators indicate the fervor with which Fröbel's disciples found common cause,[16] and indeed to such an extent that Steiger freely circulated the brochure *Der Kindergarten in Amerika: Entstehung, Wesen, Bedeutung und Erziehungsmittel des Fröbel'schen Systems und seine Anwendung auf hiesige Verhältnisse* (The kindergarten in America: Origin, essence, meaning and instructional methods of the Fröbel system and its application to local relationships). The images (figs. 31–36) illustrate the purpose—beyond commercial advantage—of guiding learning with play and play with pedagogy. A section of the treatise is devoted to kindergarten objects, with emphasis on the dual purpose of house and school (fig. 31). The "gifts" (figs. 32–34) elicit certain behaviors and skills, cultivated for both boys and girls (fig. 35), from building to embroidery. Compared to the Uhde painting—albeit a personal and genre-based portrait of the family—the illustrations have the cumulative effect of professionalizing the home for learning. The activities implicate the entire family (fig. 36). Whether the catalogue reaches an administrator, a teacher, or parent, the objects of home learning can be acquired by all—and the brochure sent free of charge.

Steiger himself is an intermedial figure. A bibliographer born in Saxony, he trained as a bookseller and emigrated to New York in 1855. During his publishing career, he placed great emphasis on the kindergarten as an institution. He was also the author of "Der Nachdruck in Nordamerika" (1860) (The reprint in North America), "Das Copyright-Law in den Vereinigten Staaten" (1869) (Copyright law in the United States), and the bibliography "Periodical Literature" (1873),[17] and Steiger's target audience consisted of parents, teachers, and *Kinderfreunde* (friends of children). His target language is consciously German; Steiger's commitment to German

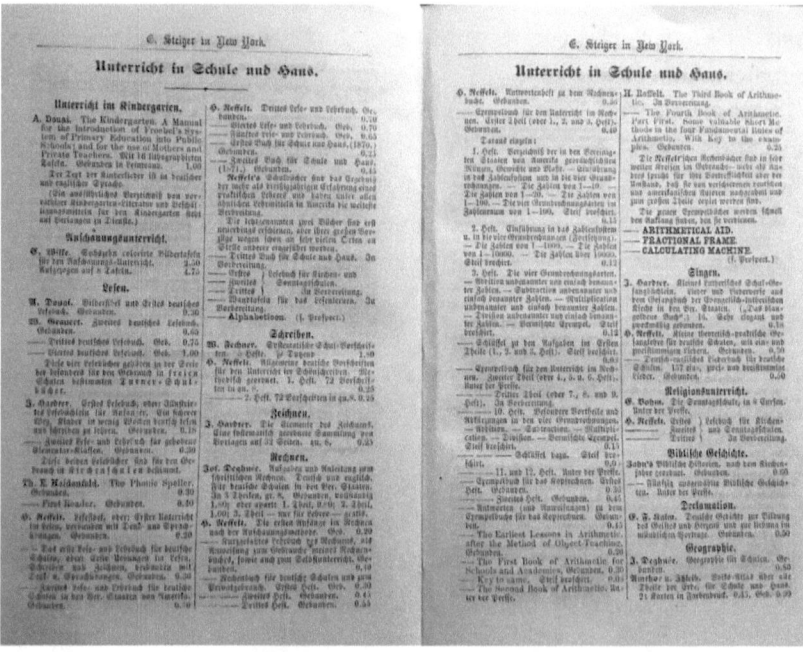

FIG. 31 "Unterricht in Schule und Haus." From *E. Steiger in New York*, June 1883, 45–46. Joseph P. Horner Memorial Library, The German Society of Pennsylvania. Photo: author.

FIG. 32 "The First Gift. The Balls." From *Catalogue of Steiger's Kindergarten Material*, June 1883. Joseph P. Horner Memorial Library, The German Society of Pennsylvania. Photo: author.

principles of education coincides with a belief in the preservation of a national language and culture, especially in cultures of immigration.

This project involves making Fröbel's work relevant in America. In his lifetime, Fröbel enjoyed a significant level of success and recognition. After his death, his kindergarten project continued to thrive. One of the strongest proponents of his work in the United States was Margarete Schurz, who founded a kindergarten in Wisconsin, and variations on the theme of that institution flourished elsewhere.[18] Most significantly, Fröbel connected play

FIG. 33 "The Third Gift. Froebel's First Building Box. Aim: to illustrate form and number, and also to give the first idea of fractions, symmetry, etc." From *Catalogue of Steiger's Kindergarten Material*, June 1883, 59. Joseph P. Horner Memorial Library, The German Society of Pennsylvania. Photo: author.

FIG. 34 "The Fourth Gift. Froebel's Second Building Box. The aim of the Fourth Gift is similar to that of the Third; but it gives rise to the observation of similarity and dissimilarity, and allows a very varied and interesting application in the production of forms of knowledge (or mathematical forms), of beauty (or symmetry), and of life." From *Catalogue of Steiger's Kindergarten Material*, June 1883, 3. Joseph P. Horner Memorial Library, The German Society of Pennsylvania. Photo: author.

with posterity and prosperity. That play is not all fun and games is clear; Fröbel's children play with purpose, with the play-filled education leading to the learning outcome of the well-oiled and contented hard working adult who does not view labor as onerous but rather as his mission. While this model touts moral content, Fröbel refrains from religious instruction in the play world. Nonetheless, his proponents identify and elaborate the moral subtext of Fröbel's theories in different national contexts.

On the inside cover page of the pro-Fröbel text, we find the following endorsement: "The Kindergarten system with its instructive plays, games, and amusements, will attach the children to schools, engender a love for books and studies, for regularity and order, and for freedom and justice. This plan of teaching is in harmony with nature; it takes up the work where the mother leaves off, and therefore prevents that sudden transition which so frequently shocks the child." Thomas Hunter, the president of Normal College, New York, authored the text, which is cited from the 1871 annual report. This book, and others like it, appeared at the cusp of

FIG. 35 "For Boys and Girls." "For Girls and Boys." From *Catalogue of Steiger's Kindergarten Material*, June 1883, 60. Joseph P. Horner Memorial Library, The German Society of Pennsylvania. Photo: author.

FIG. 36 "Embroidering." From *Catalogue of Steiger's Kindergarten Material*, June 1883, 21. Joseph P. Horner Memorial Library, The German Society of Pennsylvania. Photo: author.

institutionalizing early childhood play, especially with the shifting demographics caused by immigration, industrialization, and an evolving idea about nuclear and extended families. Not least, code switching between English validations and the German text overtly argue for polylingual identities in pedagogies of childhood play.

The collective author/editor argues that the need for Fröbel in America is more acute than in Europe. His reasons include observations about the lack of child-rearing skills and the general urgency of school reform this side of the Atlantic. The brochure identifies five main causes for needing Fröbel's practices more in America: lack of discipline, the weak results of Anglo-American schools (he mentions illiteracy), the need to be bilingual, opposition from doctors or teachers to the beginning of elementary education before the seventh year, and the need to address the practical nature of American youth, especially through an appeal to and preparation for the mission of life, the thrust of which is work. As the editor enumerates the reasons for reform, the list touches on parenting at home, inadequacies in educational practices, communication challenges, recalcitrant medical infrastructure, and national and moral citizenship in a work force. The treatment for these wide-ranging malaises lies in the spatial identity framed by play.

Steiger's pamphlet advocates a system for play based on Fröbel's plan, but other agendas are revealed. The authorial voice foregrounds the greater need in America for children to have a supervised space between the home and the street: "Im Kindergarten wird gerade diese Entwicklung der Geisteskräfte durch das Spiel in einer solchen Weise betrieben, dass dabei die Gesundheit befördert wird" (In kindergarten, precisely this development of the intellectual abilities is practiced so that health is also encouraged in this way) (7).[19] The author/editor views kindergarten as an intermediary territory between the home and public school. Some children, the author implies, fall through the cracks of private and public space, the home and the school, and into the street: the preparation for grammar schooling is thus completely lacking. This argument justifies the interpretation of the kindergarten period as a compensatory institution designed to fill a particular need:

> Somit mußte eine Bildungsanstalt geschaffen werden, welche nicht Unterricht im gewöhnlichen Sinne, sondern Spiel darböte, das in mannigfachster Weise alle Anlagen erweckt und entwickelt, und Neigung zur ernsten Arbeit des Lebens hervorruft. (8)
>
> Therefore, an educational institution must be created that would offer not teaching in the usual sense, but rather play that in many ways can awaken and develop all abilities and evoke a propensity for the serious work of life.

Again, the writer stresses the seriousness of Fröbel's enterprise, noting the timeliness of introducing the Fröbelian kindergarten in the United States, in part because the pedagogical strategies are fundamentally democratic; they appeal to every child and encourage their talents:

> Ja, was selbst manche erfahrene Lehrer nicht eher glauben wollen, bis sie es mit eigenen Augen gesehen haben, es lernt *jedes* Kind, ohne Ausnahme, die Anfänge der Künste, also zeichnen, singen, ohne Blödigkeit und mit richtiger Betonung declamiren, überhaupt sprechen; ferner turnen, die Anfänge der Mathematik, insofern sie

auf Anschauung beruhen, modelliren und mannigfache Geschicklichkeiten der Hand, des Auges und Ohres; jedes lernt Liebe zum Gesetz, zur Ordnung, zur Schönheit, zum Guten, und doch ohne alle Kopfhängerei, und indem jedes *in seiner Individualität und in seiner besonderen Eigenthümlichkeit* ausgebildet und gestärkt wird. (3)

Yes, and what even experienced teachers may not believe until they witness it with their own eyes: *every* child, without exception, learns the basics of art, therefore drawing, singing, recitation without silliness and with correct emphasis, overall they learn to speak; further, they learn basic gymnastics, early math, to the extent that it is based on observation, modeling and many motor skills of the hand, of the eye, and of the ear; each one learns love of the law, of order, of beauty, of goodness, and all of this without miserable driveling, and in that each and every one of them, *in their individuality and in their special unique traits*, are taught and encouraged.

This stance is highly invested in the inclusionary politics of Fröbel's program. The description of basic skills, the cornerstones of a lifetime of learning, conveys the continuum between the domestic and the institutional; it speaks to the issue of the home-school relationship.

The real model for learning is the home, and many of the nineteenth-century proponents of play under Fröbel's influence segue into a critique of parenting but also heighten public awareness about poverty. Some develop a compensatory relationship between the home and kindergarten, which makes mothering and teaching virtually synonymous. This author, for example, defers to Fröbel's need for a strong maternal presence in the early childhood years: "Es müssen daher, folgerte Fröbel, diese Anstalten ihre Muster nicht in der Schule bei Lehrern, sondern in der Wohnstube bei sinnigen und musterhaften Müttern suchen" (Therefore, Fröbel continued, these institutions must seek their models not in the schools with teachers, but rather in the living room with practical and exemplary mothers) (9). The fundamentals of Fröbel's system will seem familiar, but they were innovations unheard of in the late eighteenth century.[20] Though overseen by the female gaze, the inspiration for the inventory of supervised play invokes the German cultural canon, a point I return to below. The use of the "practical and exemplary" mother as a model for education confers considerable status on the maternal role, one that derives not from beauty, virtue, or sacrifice but from knowledge and practice. Fröbel's regime makes maternal skills visible but adds a professional dimension to them. The recognition granted to the role of maternity is startling.

Other aspects of the argument may also strike us as progressive. Among them is a belief in bilingual education. Children in the large German American community in the late nineteenth century attended English-speaking schools but spoke German at home and in church. The writer acknowledges the advantage of bilingualism and puts a national spin on it by praising the rich literature and culture in both languages: "—es bleibt ein unersetzlicher, überwiegender Verlust, wenn beide Sprachen eine so weltbewegende Literatur besitzen, wie die englische und deutsche" (—it would be such an irreplaceable and overwhelming loss, as both languages have such a world-moving literature, as do the English and the German) (24).

The argument goes even further and invokes German national identity in the adopted country to inspire all countrymen to spread the word and the language, described as a duty of the American citizen of German heritage. Toward this end, all are exhorted to support bilingual kindergarten instruction.[21]

Another important aspect of the teacher's role involves inspiring a love of nature through the actual gardening and planting activities. Again, the point is sharpest when it comes to play, insisting that children should, to the extent possible, be able to decide

> was sie jetzt spielen wollen, oder es soll wenigstens ihren billigen Wünschen soweit als möglich nachgegeben werden. Dafür, daß dadurch kein unberechtigter Eigensinn sich ausbilde, sorgt ohnehin die kleine Schar selber, indem jeder Einzelne sich leicht darein fügt, abwechselnd sich den Wünschen der Mehrheit unterzuordnen. (25)
>
> what they want to play now, or at least they should be able to have their modest wishes fulfilled. But, to avoid the formation of any unjustified selfishness, the little group sees to it, because each individual easily abides by the wishes of all and alternately complies with those of the majority.[22]

This last point is important, for through group play, the children learn social skills that are the basis of life in a democracy.

TEACHERS' PLAY

More than play is taught in Fröbel's kindergarten. Contemporary and subsequent advocates of incorporating play into pedagogy focus considerable energy on the recruitment and training of the teachers. In the kindergarten classroom, the crucial contribution of the teacher is the skill of facilitating play. It is her responsibility to ensure

> dass jedes Spiel zugleich eine Erholung vom andern sei, wirklich unausgessetzte Freude gewähre, und doch nie seinem ernsteren Zwecke, zur wahren, genussreichen, selbstthätigen Arbeit vorzubereiten, entfremdet werde; dass die Kindergärtnerin wirklich, so lange sie die Kinder beaufsichtigt, Mutterstelle vertrete und mit dem Muttersinne zugleich die Befähigung des Pädagogen verbinde, sich immer in die Seele der Kinder und ihre Bedürfnisse hineinzudenken und das augenblicklich Ansprechendste und zugleich Nützlichste sofort herauszufinden. (25–26)

> that every game is also a recovery from the other, genuinely preserving precious joy and still never becoming alienated from its true purpose, the preparation for true, pleasurable, individual work; and that the kindergarten teacher who is engaged in overseeing the children, insofar as she represents the maternal figure and connects a mother's sense with the ability of a pedagogue, is always able to imagine herself into the souls of the children and to discover the most appropriate and simultaneously most useful enterprise at any given time.

The teacher's role is determined by her ability to think like her pupils and direct play accordingly. Just as with female instruction, play-related activity establishes the continuum between the home and the school. Steiger's catalogue locates the two realms in the same category. Those persons endowed with aptitude must be recruited, their abilities developed, and the skills eventually implemented. The potential teacher is a woman with a good education, an independent mind, a facility for working with children, but also a healthy constitution, some musical ability and a decent singing voice, at least one year of practical experience, and the desire to gain theoretical knowledge through professional development through establishing *Vereine* or organizations (26–27).

Home-based and institutional play, under the auspices of a professionalized maternal pedagogue, collaborate in the construction of a society in which kindergarten lays the foundation for the architecture of labor. Socioeconomic arguments are introduced, noting that many children are deprived of parental supervision, either because these need to work, or because mothers die too soon. Too much freedom leads kids to the streets and to juvenile detention centers. Similar arguments are mobilized in the crusade to build playgrounds as well; there is a motivated relationship between the playroom and the playground. Finally, the author argues that even for wealthy families the social dimension of kindergarten learning—labeled *"die Erziehung zur Gemeinschaft"* (the training for community)—makes it indispensable (29).

PLAY AND THE GARDEN OF CHILDREN

The international impact of Fröbel's kindergarten is evident in England at the same time Steiger was writing and publishing books about the German experience in American immigration contexts. In 1883, Emily (Anne Eliza) Shirreff, president of the London Froebel Society, published *Essays and Lectures on the Kindergarten: Principles of Froebel's System and Their Bearing on the Higher Education of Women, Schools, Family and Industrial Life*, not coincidentally with Steiger functioning here as the publisher.[23] Shirreff, considered a pioneer in women's education, could be described as an activist for Fröbelian practices in England. She additionally deals more explicitly with the role of women as both mothers and teachers. Noting developments in Germany, she includes a dedication to the presidents of Vassar, Smith, and Wellesley Colleges, linking the education of women to the importance of enabling mothers and teachers to implement the practices and attain the goals of the kindergarten.

Shirreff's enterprise in this publication, with a more focused section on industrial workers and their families, furthers the cause of play but responds to a more pressing need to justify it within a school setting. Though she has one foot in America, Shirreff aims her justification of play at her English readership. Her goal is education reform:

> To the English public generally the Kindergarten system, so far as it is known at all, is represented by the games which, being sold in inviting-looking boxes, have been purchased for

> nursery amusement, or perhaps as an introduction to the ordinary object-lessons. These games, however, while they are doubtless a source of some amusement to the children in school, are also the tools, so to speak, to aid the teacher in her labors. Accuracy, observation, the first principles of reasoning, are taught by means of these simple toys, while nicety and dexterity of handling, and pleasure in active exertion, are trained by every exercise. (6)[24]

With the lofty yet practical goals of education reform, educating women, and leveling class difference, Shirreff has to sell the regime of play for the greater social good. Shirreff's mission is to forge toys into tools.

To achieve this end, Shirreff emphasizes that the toys used are more than they may appear to be. Her strategy involves persuading the presumed skeptics in the audience and among her readers that play has purpose beyond childhood, that toys represent tools in a toolbox of nurturing nature into socialization processes. She opens her treatise with a description of "Froebel's Gifts": "They are not toys merely, because they are intended for instruction; they are not for lessons only, since they are meant as games; they combine both characters and are designed to stimulate and guide the natural activity of the child in both directions. To fuse into one lesson work and play is the purpose of the Kindergarten, and this fusion 'becomes possible only when the objects with which the child plays allow room for mental and bodily activity'" (8). In part to overcome an implied resistance to the idea that play is frivolous or optional, she stresses that Fröbel's is a system, and that it is insufficient to turn the games over to a governess or someone unfamiliar with the system as a whole without forfeiting its pedagogical benefits.

Children do not learn by play alone. Shirreff also highlights Fröbel's inclusion of physical movement, dance, and rhythmic exercises. Sedentary games alternate with ball play, for example, to achieve the type of balanced activities Steiger also publicizes. The series of "gifts" fosters an appreciation for symmetry and design, cultivating an aesthetic template along with encouraging knowledge of structure and balance. The gifts are essentially shapes: there is a sphere, a cube, and a cylinder. Others include a cube composed of eight smaller cubes; another cube of the same dimensions is subdivided into eight oblong pieces; the fifth and sixth gifts are also cubes, subdivided differently. There are also small sticks or thin laths. Shirreff lists these items, interspersing instructions for their implementation. Here she emphasizes the proximity of the teacher, especially while the children are engaged in cutting out and folding paper. Supervision is required, justified by the fact that words are often "void of meaning" and "vague" (21–22). In contemporary jargon, the teacher is both the "sage on the stage" and the "guide on the side" when it comes to the hands-on play of kindergarten children. And the materials appeal to multiple senses for optimal learning.

In explicating Fröbel's principles, Shirreff reveals her purpose, which is "merely to supply illustrations of a method so deeply philosophical in its principle, yet so simple in its outer aspect, that its greatest danger is that of being treated as a plaything" (27). The disparaging rhetoric about play weaves through her own prose because it is implicit in Fröbel's program. He recognized in play "the germ of man's activity, and hence through games he devised the means of drawing out that active instinct into conscious exercise. He sought to guide and direct the childish impulse, and that direction gives the playthings their education value" (28). The teacher is responsible for the method and the appropriate use of the objects; lapses destroy the entire value of the system.

The same template for advocacy that informs Steiger's work is present in Shirreff's, though each element is more pronounced in the latter's. Steiger calls attention to the importance of play, but his tone is not as defensive. He conceives of kindergarten education as part of a civic mission, and he also commits to women teachers as maternal surrogates; he values the feminine contribution to education. In each category, Shirreff exceeds the limits of Steiger's appeal to the reader and policy maker. As discussed above, she feels compelled to explicate the system of toys and games. I now turn to two of the other elements—the education of women, and the civic role of kindergarten education—to make a point about the national differences in Fröbel's international influence.

Shirreff emphasizes the crucial role of Fröbel's system with regard to industrial training and the working class as part of the collective contribution to "the life of the nation" (45). Even though she posits the universal appeal of Fröbel's approach, she argues that it is "doubly essential to the poor child" (45). About the allegorical child of the working class, she writes, "*His working life would begin from an altogether different level of intelligence*" (45 [my emphasis]). In focusing her attention on the education of all, including the poor and working class, Shirreff necessarily crosses swords with the institutions that govern family life: the church and the state, intervening in the conflict with the proposed solution of higher education for women. She unveils her own interest in the primacy of women's education through the justifiable interest in the welfare of the young, but she views the agency of all concerned within the larger context of the welfare of the nation. Her arguments, though morally upright and implicitly Christian, remain secular. Boys and girls both must attend kindergarten, the former to prepare for professional life, the latter to train for "their office as mothers" (51). The language leaves a contemporary reader feeling uncomfortable, but it reveals much about arguments to justify the importance of motherhood across class in late nineteenth-century Europe and North America: these girls are to be "the spiritual mothers of the race" (54). Here Shirreff cites Fröbel and echoes his appeal to women: "The effect was thrilling. Young mothers came for counsel and direction, childless widows and unmarried women devoted themselves unselfishly to the cause which he preached, as that of the nation, that of humanity" (54). Fröbel's own dedication and charisma attracted the teacher trainees. Shirreff takes this opportunity to include a larger discussion of the family.

With the increasing recognition of women as mothers and teachers and the concomitant acknowledgment of their social contribution, the assignment of paternal roles in the domicile tingles with ambiguity. If the mother figure becomes so central both at home and in early childhood education—that is, in public institutions—what happens to men? Shirreff takes this opportunity to reassert the division of gendered labor: "To men seems to fall naturally all important labor in the State, to women only household care and the rearing of children. But when the care of children shall be recognized in its true light, it will be seen that no labor for the State exceeds, if any equals in importance, that which women have thus laid upon them" (60). As the kindergarten movement progresses, however, Shirreff envisions an enhanced parenting role for fathers but critiques those interested only in the later stages of education. Later in her text, she belittles the father who cannot take an interest in his sons until they begin the Latin grammar. She concludes the thought: "Where the limit of his interest in his girls, if he has any, may be placed, I do not know" (165).

Shirreff uses the ambiguity emerging from her call to the classroom to contextualize the importance of educating women: "In the history of that long struggle between Church and State for the control of Education, women may learn to measure the power that is theirs, independent alike of Church or State decrees, and which their own feebleness or ignorance can alone curtail or pervert" (60–61). Conferring agency on women through education, a heightened awareness of early childhood needs, and elevating motherhood—all the above lay the groundwork for a female public sphere that is neither church nor state. The Fröbelian insurrection in kindergarten informs the female revolution that locates women at the vanguard of civil society. The political potential of child's play cannot be confined to the playroom.

The solution to the imbalance in parenting also can be found in the kindergarten, with its implicit awareness of early childhood education and nurturing. The importance of teaching very young children leverages the ability to persuade fathers that they should assume more active roles in the home:

> Were it once so considered it would rise in importance, it would no longer be left to nurses, but would become the mother's first care, it would no longer be left to mothers alone, but would grow in importance with fathers also. They have been accustomed . . . to consider the school they would choose . . . , but of that first growth of habits and associations, of notions and capabilities which springs up in the early home years, and will be carried by the child to school, to affect his whole career there, the father has seldom thought at all, and this is what acquaintance with Fröbel's system will make him think of; one of the greatest benefits that system can confer upon us is this, of turning the serious attention of parents to the importance of that early training, and through it to a new sense of their own responsibility, since with them alone it must rest. (156–57)

By extension, education reform will reshape home life and restructure the gendered duties within the family. These changes, Shirreff hopes, cross class boundaries. At one point, she writes about the derision some wealthy children display at "simple" toys and games: "It is there that caprice is most likely to reign, it is there that children are supposed often to need change of air, to be wanted for some visit, to be so loaded with toys and books, and surrounded with slaves to their pleasure, that the simple toys and amusements of the Kindergarten have less charm" (159–60). In this example, the status conferred by wealth is no advantage but rather a liability. The danger in the worker's home is "neglect through ignorance," and in the wealthy home it is "corruption through luxury and servility" (161). She locates middle-class women as torn between upward aspirations and fulfilling all household duties herself. The kindergarten equalizes, educating both upwardly mobile and morally uppity children in the same space, with the same methods. As is clear from the above quotation, Fröbel's legacy has the potential to inspire the paternal commitment to children in the playroom as well as in the public school. Play becomes a panacea.

In closing this section, I return to the centrality of play. In her discourse, Shirreff stresses the literal meaning of the "garden of children" (139). Play in itself recapitulates both the literal and figurative meaning of the phrase: "Physical activity, which first manifests itself in the pleasure the infant takes in moving its limbs, becomes *play* with the growing child, and as physical exercise lay is generally much and rightly valued, but the mental activity drawn out in play, and forming a great part of true delight, is too commonly overlooked. Fröbel recognized and saw character, imagination—the first dawning of the creative faculty—manifested in play. Having thus observed all the child's natural tendencies, he devised a system by means of which they should be healthily developed—and the system is Kindergarten training" (138). The system, inspired by Fröbel's observations of children, found its physical and philosophical location in "*a garden of children*" (139 [emphasis in the original]). There was to be no catechism, as Fröbel thought the children would learn to love God through nature (142), which effectively sidesteps religious instruction—one of the thornier issues about who should teach what to whom.

The secular, modern institution that carries the flag for social change is the kindergarten, with its shapes and songs and games. Not the frivolous party many contemporaries accused it of being, instead it lays the firm foundation for national identity. The garden of children, according to Fröbel's nineteenth-century disciples, has the potential to transform all into citizens of the cultivated nation: "And thus here a little and there a little, by slow and often halting steps, our small *Society* will become one of the most powerful instruments of a reform, which, beginning at the core of national life, will gradually affect the most powerful currents of national thought and feeling" (174). Shirreff's advocacy closely connects play with citizenship of a particular nation. In other words, she is participating in the metanarrative about the nation-state as the organizing principle of identity in the late nineteenth century. This approach marks play's modernity.

TRANSATLANTIC CHILDHOODS: THE DANGERS OF PLAY

The discourse and projects privileging play were by no means univocal, but around 1900, they share a commitment to advancing the role of women as mothers and educators. While a transnational endorsement of a female hand in the shaping of the child could enroll in a progressive political program, its attendant commitments to nationalizing natural attributes invite scrutiny. Ellen Key's *The Century of the Child* inspired a generation of parents and educators on an international scale. Her positive and progressive message tends, however, to mask racial politics as feminist causes. The Swedish teacher, suffragist, and writer, discussed in chapter 3 in conjunction with Goethe's genius, advocates state support in raising children, instilling moral uprightness through equality in the household, and approaching children as creative and intelligent beings who benefit from disease-free homes and balanced outlooks. In other words, she rejects the practice of raising children in a childhood that is separate, or in more recent critical terms, "islanded" from the adult world. On the contrary, she attacks the idea. Homes that produce the best "men and women with the strongest morality" treat children as human beings. Key also espouses education that includes professional teachers and parental support but eschews any Fröbelian attention to play. Again, on the contrary, while she acknowledges the importance and popularity of the Pestalozzi-Fröbel model of kindergarten, she labels it insufficient. Throughout her treatise, Key refers liberally to works of literature and philosophy that dominated the German-European tradition, from Goethe to Nietzsche. Her rhetoric is suffused in the canonical teachings of Protestantism, while nuanced when it comes to feminism.

Like many of her contemporaries, she holds views about hygiene, euthanasia, and race that leave readers today in a profound state of moral ambiguity. For many reasons, these among them, she does not figure prominently in my study. More pertinently, however, she rejects play as a pedagogical principle. Key advises storytelling and narrative but disparages playthings that smack of luxury of caprice.[25] While taking the position that playing the right way with children amounts to "a great art," she also affirms that "games constantly accompanied by a teacher make play a parody."[26] In this strong voice, a variation on the theme of sound and healthy upbringings for the world's children in their century, play represents the worst modernity has to offer.

Though differing in their conclusions and points on a moral compass, advocates of an independence cultivated in children through play amplify an argument about character and the fate of the nation. One aspect of the discourse, mediated by in some ways progressive ideas about women's professional roles in caregiving and child-rearing, nonetheless strengthens connections between childhood and citizenship, a neutral formulation for a more sinister form of pedagogy and play that teaches and replicates national identity in the service of empire and imperial expansion.

In the appendix to Shirreff's work, Elizabeth P. Peabody intervenes to emphasize the crucial importance not only of the national and natural but of the racial achievements implicit in enhancing the role of women in kindergarten education. While these categories continue to inspire debate about their present and historical significance, Peabody differentiates among them. Quoting Shirreff from the preface to the second edition of her work in England, Peabody writes of the need "to bring home to women their paramount moral obligation 'to fit themselves to be the Educators of the race.'"[27] Peabody's closing remarks, while largely citational, emphasize the universalizing project of kindergarten advocacy and the persistent issue of institutional agency. She writes, "Some persons, however, contend that the Kindergarten can only be universalized, without losing its spontaneous character, by Philanthropy and Religion acting independently of the State."[28] The elevation of childhood education to an issue of state supervision locates it at the nexus of the home and nation. When Peabody praises Shirreff's platform of women educating "the race," the universalizing project suggests she intends all of humanity. Yet historicizing these arguments draws toward other, less inclusive ideologies.

Repeatedly, advocates of play as a pedagogy cite German cultural icons to corroborate their activism. In one chapter from the volume about the kindergarten in America, "Erziehungsmittel des Kindergartens," the epigraph reads: "'Gebt ihm zu thun! / Das sind reiche Gaben, / Das Kind kann nicht ruhn, / Will zu schaffen habe.'"[29] By contrast, Key attacks the idea. Homes that produce the best "men and women with the strongest morality" treat children as human beings. She writes, "In a home like this nothing is especially arranged for children; they are regarded not as belonging to one kind of being while parents represent another, but parents gain the respect of their children by being true and natural; they live and conduct themselves in such a way that the children gain an insight into their work, their efforts and, as far as possible into their joys and pains, their mistakes and failures."[30] In the decade following Key's millennial work, the transnational accents on iconic players, such as Goethe, as discussed previously, respond to the changing demographics of the transatlantic world, including the rise of mass-produced toys and the spread of acquisitiveness of cheaper toys to the working class. The politics of toys and play further reflect patterns of consumption.

In particular, German play and toys, disseminated in the Americas, transition into a marketing nexus of German and American. In my introduction, marketing copy from the 1912 catalogue of toy manufacturer A. Schoenhut and Sons opens my view of the play world as a cognitive and commercial construct produced by German early modern philosophy and religion and broadcast transatlantically through the production of texts, toys, and migration stories. The company leaders, comprised largely of Schoenhut sons, capitalized on their German heritage, signifying high-quality craftsmanship, materials, and technical prowess, all enhanced by their American ingenuity. Their trademark signals quality, catering to local loyalty and global markets. Originally known for the high-quality toy piano, the company was made famous by their production of successful sets of figures, such as the Humpty Dumpty Circus. Schoenhut, who emigrated to the United States during a period of German economic recession (1873–1879),[31] initially repaired pianos for a department store, struck out on his own, and in addition to the circus figures eventually produced an array of popular dolls, also beloved for their durability and mobility. The paterfamilias designed some in the image of his own children.[32] I follow the Schoenhut legacy in toy production across the Atlantic to extend the arc of my argument about the agency of objects in movement.

Integral to mapping the experience of migration and transatlantic manufacturing via the toy market is the further exploration of imaginative imperialism. The play world accommodates the home and the nation. Beyond the critique of mass production implicit in the migration story of the young jungle girl, and exceeding the function of cognitive toys from the Fröbel play paradigm, the "imaginary citizens" of the German-speaking play world evolve with and respond to the existence of real German expansionism and its production of texts and toys. While Hamlin focuses on toys in cultivating the individual, the theorists of democratic play march into the territory of racial pedagogy. The storied legacy of German toy manufacturers collides with the geopolitical impact of migration, war, and cultural conflicts between the old and new play worlds in the empire of toys.

CHAPTER 7

Empire of Toys

Toys, as agents of historically transmitted national identity, participate in the narration and dissemination of immigration stories as well. The cross continental connections between European and American production and consumption tell a particularly German story. Historian David Hamlin observes that toy makers function as "almost cultural mediators."[1] Going beyond his focus on Germany, I would omit the "almost." In his cogent coverage of three toy-producing centers in the nineteenth century, Hamlin describes Nuremberg as home of "the metal toy," Sonneberg as the "land of dolls," and the *Erzgebirge* reputation for wooden toy production as "the essence of Germanness."[2] In transatlantic modernity, while the "Made in Germany" cache for toys and games broadcasts quality, centers dispersed. In the conscious mobilizing of German technical skills and quality material, grafted onto the American market, the Schoenhuts do play the role of cultural mediators. In migration, the national traits of toys underwent a process of internationalization in transatlantic modernity that left legible traces in the annals of economic as well as cultural history. The colonial imaginary, for those citizens of the nation and empire who never ventured beyond their borders, was nonetheless constructed through cultural artifacts and, not least, youth culture. Ethnographic play engaged imaginary citizenship for the young through texts and toys that allowed for identification with the imperial subject in relation to both human subjects and material objects.

In his superb study of imperial ideology and a young audience, Jeff Bowersox articulates the relationship among products and their ability to naturalize colonial power hierarchies: "Clarifying the dynamics at work thus requires us to understand the relationships between parents and children, teachers and students, and producers and consumers."[3] With his focus on the contiguous German-speaking states of the newly established nation and their impressionable citizens, Bowersox illuminates the role played by toys, games, curricula, and texts in inculcating the young with the attitudes appropriate to children of empire. This multistranded narrative forms a reticulated identity with the New World, connecting the imperial homeland with the experience of immigration. Bowersox, in paying his work forward, invokes the need for extending the discussion beyond the imperial age and locating German colonial culture in a transnational context, recognizing that "Germany's colonial culture was intertwined with those across Europe and North America before 1914."[4] In following toy makers themselves in crossing the Atlantic, my argument traces the intricate network surrounding the production and consumption of these childhood accessories that capitalize on German origins combined with American legacies with a focus on a family of toy producers. The Schoenhut enterprise epitomizes the play world.

The transition from national to imperial epistemologies of the toy, in narrative, is exemplified by the dynastic rhetoric of a company founded by Albert Friedrich Schoenhut (1849–1912), who began as a wood lather in Württemberg.[5] In 1866, he immigrated to the United States to work at John Wanamaker's Philadelphia department store, where he was responsible for repairing the glass sounding pieces of toy pianos imported from Germany. An entrepreneurial immigrant, he set out on his own in 1872 and founded the Schoenhut Piano Company. His family background as a third-generation German toy maker and his early training as a manufacturer of toys and toy pianos in Württemberg played a significant role in the early success of his American enterprise. After all, the toy piano, the product on which his company was originally based, was a German creation whose roots extend back to Dessau in 1792.[6] His legacy reveals the imperial impulses articulated in the making and marketing of toys.

The Philadelphia-based toy firm initially focused on the manufacture of toy pianos and other musical instruments, quickly establishing a reputation for quality that was based largely on German handicraft traditions. Over time, the company expanded and began manufacturing other products, such as the aforementioned Humpty Dumpty Circus, which was introduced around 1900. In addition, the Schoenhut family business began producing dolls, games, play sets, and a variety of figures, all of which enjoyed immense popularity. In the process, the A. Schoenhut Company became the largest toy manufacturer in America. Schoenhut himself became known as the "King of Toy Makers" and the "Santa Claus of Kensington."[7] Despite the air of legend that surrounded him, Schoenhut always kept a careful eye on his business, which continued to grow through his emphasis on innovation, his pursuit of transatlantic markets, and his implementation of broad advertising strategies. Hamlin points out that in the late nineteenth century, German toy producers thought of New York as their market.[8] Lower transportation costs and wider distribution networks contributed to growth in exports. The Schoenhut marketing strategies expanded their appeal. By the time that Albert Schoenhut died in 1912, the "House of Schoenhut" included a plant and offices in Philadelphia, a sales office in New York, and a thriving catalogue business. His six sons inherited and grew the company until 1935.[9] Though the company underwent numerous incarnations and changes in ownership since then, it still exists today as Schoenhut Toy Piano.

Schoenhut's toy production and marketing strategies bridge the Atlantic, representing the confluence of material cultures, German philosophies about play, and American production and consumption of products. A third-generation toy maker, Albert Schoenhut was trained from an early age by his father, Frederick, and his grandfather, Anton, both of whom passed on their technical and artisanal skills as well as their passion for the business. The family's trade was far from uncommon in Göppingen, which has a long history of toy production and has been home to firms such as Märklin since the middle of the nineteenth century. The reasons for Schoenhut's emigration are described in various—and likely apocryphal—accounts.[10] According to one narrative, Albert Schoenhut's toy making skills captured sufficient attention to land him a job across the pond: "In 1866," as one source explained, "John Dahl, a buyer for Wanamaker's department store, heard of young Albert's talent and brought the seventeen-year-old to Philadelphia where he worked as a repairman on glass sounding pieces in German toy pianos that had been damaged in shipping."[11] At the time, virtually all of the toy pianos available in the United States had been manufactured in Germany and imported. Unfortunately, the instruments' glass sounding pieces were very delicate and often broke during the ocean voyage. For firms like Wanamaker's, it made sense to have a German-trained craftsman on staff. The training Schoenhut had received at home in Göppingen served him well in the United States, where he became a naturalized citizen in 1868.¹² Literally and figuratively, national and "imagined" citizenship and its acquisition interweave the production and consumption of childhood play world identities.

German heritage figures prominently in the creation of mass-market toys and their distribution. In particular, Schoenhut's business drew on two longstanding German traditions: toy making and the production of musical instruments, in which German and German American firms had long excelled (e.g., Wurlitzer and Steinway). Indeed, Schoenhut toy pianos soon developed a reputation for quality workmanship and excellent sound. Schoenhut's emphasis on technical innovation is evidenced by the numerous patents that he acquired for improvements to the toy piano and other musical instruments such as the trumpet (1892).¹³ In the 1880s, toy manufacturing in the United States was on the cusp of a major transformation.¹⁴ The industry was not only expanding but changing as well. Historian Gary Cross describes Schoenhut as one of the "leaders in the transition from the conventional production of European-style toys sold like dry goods to the mass production of distinctly American playthings advertised as novelties and appealing to the new ideas of childrearing."¹⁵ Citizenship, national-ethnic work ethics, and commerce establish a reciprocal relationship, an immigrant feedback loop that structures and organizes the play world through mimesis.

Mimetic play and material culture inevitably, sometimes subliminally, interact with contemporary trends in popular and political cultures. In the late 1890s, business was flourishing, and the following decade saw even greater growth. The success of the company at that particular time was largely attributable to Schoenhut's prescient decision to purchase, in 1902, the rights to a newly patented jointed toy clown developed by fellow German immigrant Fritz Meinecke.¹⁶ As the story goes, Meinecke "walked into Schoenhut's office with the invention, for which he wanted one hundred dollars outright. Schoenhut assured him [that] royalties would pay him far more in time, but the man refused."¹⁷ Schoenhut paid Meinecke the $100 that he requested for the transfer of the toy and the patent rights.¹⁸ The circus was officially in town.

At the time of Schoenhut's meeting with Meinecke, big top circuses, such as those run by the Ringling Brothers and P. T. Barnum, were enjoying immense popularity with American audiences. In 1903, Schoenhut decided to capitalize on the contemporary circus mania by selling Meinecke's jointed clown, along with a chair and a ladder, as part of a three-piece set called the Humpty Dumpty Circus. Schoenhut's circus sold well and additional pieces—a donkey, an elephant, a white horse, and the like—were quickly added to the set. Soon, the standard version of the Humpty Dumpty Circus included ten core performers, over thirty different animals, and a variety of accessories ranging from simple props to a three-dimensional canvas tent.[19]

If the toy piano built Schoenhut's reputation, then the Humpty Dumpty Circus catapulted it to financial success. A local, national, and even international sensation, the Humpty Dumpty Circus was one of the few early American toys to be exported in quantity. In addition to tapping into the widespread public interest in circuses, the Humpty Dumpty Circus satisfied children's desire for open-ended play. Play sets of the sort encouraged unrestricted play by providing children with a context—in this case, a circus—in which their imaginations could be granted free rein. This kind of imaginative play, it was felt, had great educational value; it schooled children not only in fantasy, but also in role-playing as a form of preparation for the adult world. Recoded through circus play, the hegemonic practices of fantasy, the adult world, and role-play underwrite citizenship of the play world, for the middle class as well as the wealthy.

MARVELOUS, MIDDLEBROW, AND MIDDLE CLASS

The circus crosses boundaries of social stratification and class; it also breaches borders between adult and childhood play and pedagogy, a justification for entertainment enterprises. Phineas T. Barnum (1810–1891) became the American poster boy for the popularization of spectacle, his name synonymous with the culture industry. In a cogent and lively introduction to a 2005 volume on Barnum's life and impact, editor James W. Cook writes about the significant contributions of P. T. Barnum to the "culture industry" of the nineteenth century.[20] Cook notes the origin of that phrase (Horkheimer and Adorno's 1947 *Dialectic of Enlightenment*) but also elaborates on his reasons for applying the term—essentially a rather bleak and often disparaging Frankfurt School commentary on the production and consumption of "mass culture" in the twentieth century. His reasoning, however, is persuasive, given the incomparable fame P. T. Barnum, perhaps the first American "spin doctor," achieved in his lifetime through self-proclaimed "humbugs." The writings by and about the Barnum phenomenon, from the intimate hoaxes to the large-scale spectacles of the traveling circus, raise any number of questions about the social and economic factors in nineteenth-century America and Europe that contribute to the stunning success, both qualitatively and quantitatively measured, of Barnum's culture industry, particularly as the audience shifted from the general adult population to the appeal to children. The popularization of spectacle, the "exoticized" otherness of bodies that vary from the presumed hegemony of whiteness, wholeness, and sovereigty, and prurient optics of miniaturization all constitute, as I contend, articulated desires of the middle class that toys recapitulate.

Barnum's ability to manipulate displays to match "taste" and please crowds, from Joice Heth to General Tom Thumb's meeting Queen Victoria's children, indicate a malleability and adaptability that was not only shrewd but genius. He managed to target the growing European American middle class, through an appeal not only to rational judgment by combining science and humbugs, but also through a political and moral stance (situationally antislavery, protemperance/Universalist doctrines, family values, etc.); at the same time, he shifted his focus from "freaks" and curiosities (the "What Is It?" exhibits, and the Feejee mermaid, for example) to more legitimate and cultured spectacles, from the giant sea lion (in warm Havana) to the high-priced Jenny Lind, as she was critiqued in the *Times* of London review. In this way, Barnum bridged "low" and "high" culture by putting examples of it on display in the same types of venue, but also through the use of image and spectacle (the Currier and Ives lithographs), and narrative and spectacle. Toys mediate this shift in the domestic sphere, instantiated by the production and consumption of play sets, such as the Humpty Dumpty Circus.

More specific to the Schoenhut inspiration, the play and enactments of George Washington Lafayette Fox (1825–1877) project the combined influence of European comedy and American performance. Writing about theater history, Theresa Saxon observes: "America's most famous *commedia* white-faced clown was George Washington Lafayette Fox, whose incarnations in *Humpty Dumpty* travelled the length and breadth of America. *Humpty Dumpty*, premiering in 1867, was performed over 1,000 times during Fox's lifetime."[21] Though the origins of the gleefully macabre nursery rhyme are disputed, the popularity of the pantomime is not.

In her analysis of nineteenth-century theater spaces, Saxon draws important connections between performance and the political arena. She writes, "Throughout the nineteenth century a whole range of divisions between 'types' emerged in theatres; in addition to class, concepts of race, gender and political ideologies as boundary markers were taking to the stage. What emerged, therefore, across American centres as well as within those individual centres, was an ideological division in the body politic between cultural forms, social structures and economic groups."[22] In particular, she identifies stage performances as explorations of anxieties "about Manifest Destiny, about slavery and slave insurrections, about the working classes, about gender and social behaviours, and about the condition of the nation."[23] Toys, again, are not "products of nature," as Hamlin reminds us.[24] They function instead as lenses that refract the projection of anxieties about the nation. Hamlin's analysis of toys in the emerging mass market around 1900 in Germany notes attention to "the little man on the income scale" amid the growing number of consumers.[25] In the United States, German quality was marketed widely, with a range of price points. The replication of class-based politics in play, the oscillation between lowbrow and highbrow, between entertainment and edification, enfolds political anxieties and desires as well, including the politics of race.

One factor to consider is the European cognate of *commedia*'s whiteface clown and the performativity of race—in this case, of whiteness. More specifically, Schoenhut transforms the performance, a two-act pantomime, and the attendant references to popular songs and rhymes into the constitutive objects of the play world with only oblique reference to the literary and theatrical antecedent, focusing instead on the persona of the white-faced clown at the center. The reciprocity among the theater, the circus, and the toy factory reinforces the hegemonic relationship between racialized identities and the play world. Here, Eric Ames's work on Carl Hagenbeck's theme spaces as corporate spaces provides a model for my own interpretation. Hagenbeck (1844–1913) is known as an animal dealer and ethnographic showman. He changed the way animals in captivity were displayed (*Tierpark*) and put living beings on display in his models of the "theme space," which Ames defines as "one that choreographed the use of material objects and living bodies as integral components of the display, while at the same time developing a full-bodied approach to the immersive experience of spectatorship."[26] Hagenbeck's habitats, consonant with the *Völkerschau* of the time, conveyed a "racial logic," but Ames's analysis emphasizes the opportunity for participants and spectators to engage in a reciprocal relationship during the live performance.[27] This line of argumentation, increasingly made about the "freak" shows in the United States and Show Indians employed by William F. Cody's Wild West Show, prompts Ames to see the causal relationship between the shows and German colonialists who protested the display of colonial subjects. He writes, "What arises from this historical controversy is not only the connective dynamic of mass culture, but also the capacity of theme space to accommodate rival forms of racism."[28] Another disciplinary perspective reinforces the conclusion. The staged encounters between whites and American Indians, depicted as savage warriors and as a docile race under "civilizing" influences of westward expansion, gained purchase for decades in the United States and Europe. In his work on American Indians who performed in Wild West Shows, L. G. Moses characterizes controversies about the consequences of performances for the performers in terms of a "struggle to see whose image would prevail."[29] Such a struggle omits the agency of the historical subjects themselves. Though the exhibition of human beings predates the circus and Wild West Shows, the spectacle forges links between the science of seeing as knowing and racialized assuptions about what constitutes humanity. As his analysis unfolds, Ames connects theme spaces to branding and defines them as well as "corporate spaces, where entertainment and merchandise were creatively linked and grouped around a certain theme, where mass spectators were directly addressed as consumers, and vice versa."[30] The figures designed, produced, and sold in the Schoenhut Humpty Dumpty Circus instantiate the confluences of racialized, corporate, and play spaces in the contemporary United States. The theatrical inspiration, the selection of characters, and the marketing of the circus set resonate with Hagenbeck's ethnographic displays but go beyond spectatorship by populating the play world and its pedagogy of race. Popularity is the origin of the term "bandwagon" (fig. 37). Schoenhut borrowed figures that include the Ringmaster, Lion Tamer, Gent Acrobat, Lady Acrobat, Negro Dude, Hobo, and the Clown.[31]

Over time, the company placed greater emphasis on the educational value of the Humpty Dumpty Circus and began marketing it to parents and teachers. In one promotional publication, for instance, the company wrote: "In the home and also in the kindergarten the educational training of eye and hand are more and more appreciated the longer these toys are used, especially when the children are encouraged to work out their own ideas by means of the figures."[32] The copy, which dates from 1928, even posits a connection between play and performance later in life: "Boys that started to play with the Humpty Dumpty Circus Toys in the early years of 1903–4–5 are men now, some of great prominence, Doctors, Lawers [sic], Judges, Manufacturers, Merchants, etc., etc. and many of them refer to the Happy Days they spent with Schoenhut's Humpty Dumpty Circus Toys."[33] Schoenhut's play sets, it seems, were not only fun but also edifying: in company

FIG. 37 The A. Schoenhut Company's circus bandwagon, 1910–30. Courtesy of The Strong, Rochester, New York.

parlance, they were "The Most Popular and Most Instructive Toys in the World." Children—or more often, their parents—could acquire figures on a piecemeal basis, as their budget allowed, with the goal being the acquisition of the entire set. According to the company, there were "thousands of children boasting of having our complete Circus."[34] While circus figures appeal across gender, other toys encompass sex roles and gender performativity.

GENDERED PLAY

Toys regulate gendered play, and children "perform" gender when they use toys, especially certain toys, such as dolls and guns. Toys appeal to historically specific gendered categories, and Schoenhut products were no exception: their manufacture and marketing aligned with the division of gendered labor in the private and public spheres. This performative play begs the question of whether the gendering of play fluctuates historically—that is, if toys and their manufacture and marketing align with the division of gendered labor in the private and public spheres. To claim that play is socially constructed echoes and extends the argument that gender is socially constructed as well. Play in modernity would logically replicate the experiences of the adult world. The instrumentalization of play, however, can be historicized in productive ways. In the following analysis of the toy piano image, the performing child is female, playing to and for a maternal audience.

As a result, play in modernity replicated the experiences of the adult world: girls recreated bourgeois households and rehearsed their future roles as wives and mothers, and boys were schooled in citizenship and prepared to become policemen, soldiers, and leaders. In the anniversary catalogue, the Schoenhut sons credited their father with creating real and imaginative toys for boys that responded to their lust for adulthood: "He made it possible for the youngsters to play at soldier, policeman, etc., in costumes that looked the part."[35] The toys helped boys "try on" the identity of male authority figures and, at the same time, strengthened their bond with their fathers. According to the catalogue, "Toy Shooting Galleries, with guns shooting hollow rubber balls or corks, make as much fun for the father as for the boys. They satisfy the innate desire to shoot without the risk attendant upon bullet-shooting guns."[36] Here, the Schoenhuts' claim naturalized the masculine "desire to shoot" but introduced a safety feature, or minimal risk; this add-on enabled a shared experience between fathers and sons. This subtle but crucial point remained ancillary to the marketing strategy, which was to promote sales.

Generally speaking, Schoenhut toys relegated female play to the household and left the building of models and the wearing of uniforms to boys. Still, while reflecting the mores of the time, some Schoenhut products, such as the "Build a village" series, also crossed gender in their appeal. Although the Schoenhut Company viewed boys as the primary consumers of toy airplanes, it made marketing overtures to girls as well. A 1928 company trade catalogue asked: "Where Is There a Boy Not Interested in Aeroplanes?" and then announced: "EVERY BOY WANTS TO BUILD AN AEROPLANE."[37] Predictably, the prose was accompanied by an illustration of two boys building a plane. The boys face each other and occupy the center of the scene. The image, however, also includes a little girl who plays with an airplane as well. She appears in the margins, and her role is clearly secondary, but she is featured nonetheless. Thus, the play world included both boys and girls. As a result, the Schoenhuts were able to market their airplanes to all children, thus expanding their customer base.

To maximize their audience, the Schoenhuts marketed not only to boys and girls, but to parents as well. Ultimately, Schoenhut toys centered the family, and advertising copy throughout decades emphasized the ways in which parents benefitted from purchasing toys for their children's play and education. In the 1928 catalogue, the company laid out their view of retail success: "To have a Mother or Father come into their Toy Store, and say they want to buy a Set of Schoenhut's Humpty Dumpty Circus Toys for their children."[38]

When Albert Schoenhut died on 3 February 1912, just two days short of his sixty-third birthday, his company was profiting handsomely from the newly introduced "All Wood Perfection Art Doll." His sons took over the family business; they were well prepared, having worked and trained at the firm for years.[39] The year of Schoenhut's death coincided with the fortieth anniversary of the founding of the firm, an occasion that was duly celebrated by his sons. In the anniversary catalogue, the second generation of Schoenhuts announced proudly, "The largest toy factory in the world is in the city of Philadelphia—**The House of Schoenhut**. Not only is it the largest, but also the one which has set a new record for the world in originality and quality of product." This continued until the outbreak of the First World War.[40] But unlike the countless German American firms that suffered from anti-German discrimination during the war years (especially after the United States joined the war effort in 1917), the Schoenhut company fared relatively well between 1914 and 1919. In 1914, two years after celebrating its fortieth anniversary, the A. Schoenhut Company reached peak production. Cross attributes the firm's success and reputation to an ethnically driven marketing strategy: "Schoenhut drew on the snob appeal of its German lineage while also bragging of its American inventiveness."[41] Cross's assessment is certainly borne out by the tone of the anniversary catalogue, which presented the company as the embodiment of the best of two national traditions. But in the following years, particularly the war years, the company tailored its message and portrayed itself as more American than German. In 1918, a year after America entered the war against Germany, the Schoenhuts ran an advertisement that stated "Schoenhut Toys. Made in the U.S.A. since 1872."[42] A similar advertisement from 1919 read "Schoenhut Toys. American Ingenuity and Invention."[43] In some respects, the company may have even benefitted from the war insofar as it limited European imports, and I return to the point below and in the conclusion. The legacy of the German American toy connection warrants closer examination.

THE CIRCUS AND RACIALIZED TOYS

The circus in Schoenhut's manufacturing participated not only in a discourse but a practice of constructing racial identities through racialized toys. Between 1908 and 1910, an American toy manufacturer capitalized on the intersection of two major factors in constructing racial and gendered identities in the first decade of the new century: the appeal of the American circus and the politicized masculinity of Theodore Roosevelt. A. Schoenhut and Sons, successful entrepreneurs of play and creators of the patented Humpty Dumpty Circus, created an accessory, Negro Dude, which represented a departure from the performance of racial identities under the big top in which white clowns appeared in blackface. The reciprocity between the stage and the play world, demonstrated elsewhere, also borrows from the first American popular entertainment, blackface minstrelsy. In his article "Blackface Minstrelsy and Jacksonian Ideology," Alexander Saxton unpacks the ideological implications of the genre that "became the most popular form of entertainment in the United States."[44] Saxton focuses on the American context preceding the Civil War (1861–65). That the social and political content of the performances underwrote Jacksonian democracy is a crucial element in Saxton's argument, but more significant is the conclusion: "Blackface minstrelsy's dominance of popular entertainment amounted to half a century of inurement to the uses of white supremacy."[45] The Humpty Dumpty theatrical performances of Fox peaked in popularity in the postwar era of the 1870s. Racialized toys instantiate the tools of "inurement" that Saxton identifies. The transition in the character "Negro Dude" from a clown inspired by white performers in blackface to a phenotype inspired by an African servant and commercial expediency reveals the play world accessory not only as a conduit of racial hierarchy but also as a miniature projection of competing forms of racism and racialized play.

For Negro Dude, the toy company in fact used caricatured facial construction. Saxton's eloquent description of the ideological impact involved in blackface minstrelsy penetrates any exoskeleton of denial: "Blackface performers were like puppets operated by a white puppetmaster. Their physical appearance proclaimed their non-humanity; yet they could be manipulated not only to mock themselves, but also to act like human beings."[46] In his closing discussion of "Swanee River," he quotes the dialect: "The black puppets are striving to be white, singing in white voice, while the white audience in the new city or the new West lingers through a moment of self-pity and regret for things past, before the rattle of tambourine and bones calls up the clowns again."[47] In this performance, nostalgic regionalism, and white longing for the lost homeland, resonates not only in the context of westward expansion and urbanization but also for the recommitment to the myth of American exceptionalism sustained by waves of European immigration. Each generation experienced the need to reinvent itself as hybrid; the business model of Schoenhut and Sons recapitulates this national narrative in its self-identification as the best of German skill and American know-how. Embedded within that immigrant DNA is the genetic marker of racialized play; toys inherit the racial signifiers of the American fantasy. The design and production of the toy "Negro Dude" embodies this nationalizing narrative.

After the production and promotion of Teddy's Adventures in Africa (fig. 38), Negro Dude (fig. 39) underwent a transformation, from an incarnation of blackface minstrelsy to a reincarnation as a racially marked American circus doll. The decision could have been inspired by the popularization of ethnographic shows and world's fares that emerged toward the end of the nineteenth century. In fact, the decision had everything to do with supply-and-demand issues and commercial acumen and very little to do with any concern about racial identities around 1900. Still, the decision raises compelling questions about how politics, commercial enterprises, and the production of circus-inspired toys all contribute to the construction of racial and racist identities. As Janet M. Davis writes, "Schoenhut's 'Negro Dude' looked effectively identical to an antebellum minstrel show performer."[48] Toy design responds selectively to historical events.

In Teddy's Adventures in Africa, another playset produced by the same toy company, African natives were produced and sold along with the repurposed toy tigers, lions, and rhinos from the Humpty Dumpty Circus. In his postpresidential capacity, Theodore Roosevelt embarked on an adventure that is known as the Smithsonian-Roosevelt African Expedition. The postpolitical expedition shifts the focus from the political to the natural arena, accompanied by a photographer (also featured as a toy), Smithsonian zoologists, Smithsonian representatives, a field naturalist, and other supporting staff. The press lavished attention on the expedition; Roosevelt himself wrote articles about it for *Scribner's*, but the lasting star of the show is the collection amassed for the museum: "The result was that the United States National Museum acquired approximately 1,000 skins of large mammals, 4,000 of small mammals, and other specimens totaling approximately 11,400 items. About 10,000 plant

FIG. 38 The A. Schoenhut Company's "Teddy's Adventures in Africa." Courtesy of The Strong, Rochester, New York.

FIG. 39 The A. Schoenhut Company's "Negro Dude," ca. 1907–18. Courtesy of The Strong, Rochester, New York.

specimens were also obtained, as well as a small collection of ethnological objects."[49] Perhaps with Frederick Jackson Turner's 1893 pronouncement of the Western frontier's closing, American national identity shifted from the acquisition of contiguous land to pushing other boundaries.[50] The "imagined community" that forms the foundation of the nation coincides with dominance of the natural world, and these jointly enter the exhibition space of the museum. In the early twentieth century, the exhibition of human subjects, as seen in the world's fairs and exhibitions, provided a space for spectacle, science, and entertainment. Certainly there are prominent figures, such as the merchant and entrepreneur Hagenbeck, for whom the circus, the museum, and the "human zoo" constituted a single enterprise. But by the founding of the National Museum of Natural History in 1910, science, display, and nature also played a prominent role in education. There was, I suggest, a differentiation between work and play.

In the play world of the circus and playsets, the miniature Roosevelts carried a rifle, dressed in safari garb, and wore a pith helmet. The "toy" was marketed as a collection, and part of Schoenhut and Company's acumen involved accessorizing the long-lasting figures with add-ons that enhanced the reality of the miniature world the child could recreate. The set came with an original inventory of twenty-five pieces.

From the production perspective, leftover heads from the African Natives toys were repurposed in the later production of Negro Dude, meant for the circus (fig. 39). In the world of the museum, the display of African peoples in dioramas—a practice that persisted in South Africa until the 1990s—was not the purpose. Rather, the "natural" habitats of animals not native to North America were the feature of the Smithsonian-Roosevelt Expedition. Nevertheless, the toy industry observed no such distinctions, lagging behind the reality of racial displays.

DYNASTY: SCHOENHUT AND COMPANY AND GENDERED CITIZENSHIP

> The largest toy factory in the world is in the city of Philadelphia—
> **The House of Schoenhut**. Not only is it the largest, but also the one which has set a new record for the world in originality and quality of product.

This Philadelphia factory is making and selling toys and dolls to the children of Germany, who seek high class playthings just as eagerly as those of our own country. The old idea that all toys are originated in Germany has long been refuted.[51]

Prowess in toy production is linked more closely with historical issues of German American immigration narratives than we may think. The source of the prose quoted above stems from catalogue copy of the A. Schoenhut Company's celebration on the occasion of its fortieth anniversary—just after the publication of Julie Hirschmann's volume of games and stories discussed previously. The expansive tone of the toy catalogue's writing, attributed to the six sons of the late Albert Schoenhut Senior (1849–1912), challenges the presumption that Germany might still hold dominion over the world of toys. While denying German toy hegemony, the text still contains an acknowledgment of that country's belated supremacy in the empire of play. The Schoenhut enterprise, itself a commercial and familial dynasty, has overtaken the prime competitor, represented as both a nation and as an agonistic industry rival: "The House of Schoenhut is not only shipping toys to Germany," the catalogue essay continues, "but to all parts of Great Britain, Continental Europe, Australia, South America and other parts of the world where German toys were once supreme. American ingenuity and resourcefulness have joined with the German hereditary instinct of toy making to produce the most wonderful toys the world has ever known" (5–6).[52]

Two aspects of this assertion are crucial. First, the authors stake an economic claim to the export market once dominated by Germany; they do so in language that echoes colonization strategies. Second, and perhaps more significant, is the reference to a nearly genetic ability to produce the famous and iconic toys and musical instruments on which Schoenhut's reputation and achievement are based. At the same time, the voice of collective authorship (The House of Schoenhut) makes explicit that the intercultural identity of the family, its German heritage combined with American know-how, are contributing factors to the trajectory of success.

The catalogue I discuss here appeared in the year of Schoenhut's death; written by his sons, it commemorates the company's contributions to toy making but also serves as a kind of eulogy for the man who lent his name to the manufacture of quality toys and instruments. Embedded in the family romance between toys and the German American House of Schoenhut is a fundamental identity among play, technological innovation, and pedagogy.

The emphasis on this relationship varies in interesting ways, depending on the gendered nature of the toys and of play. As the catalogue explains, Mr. Arthur Schoenhut started with the Toy Piano ("Sing Mama, I Play"), the success of which is explained by its innovative steel plates "that are accurately tuned so that a child's ear for music is improved, instead of being spoiled by discordant sounds." The spacing of the keys, we learn, is designed in proportion to that of a "real piano, so that the child unconsciously learns to properly spread the fingers" (9). The "play world" implicitly rehearses the child for life as an adult. In other words, the combination of ingenuity, commercial strategy, and practice contributes to the shaping of children into experts, in this case, proficient pianists. Key to the intention of toy design is the presumption that the learning curve will involve a steep but enjoyably unconscious process.

The relationship between the play world and the life world is complex and always in need of historicization. We associate modernity with the "islanding" of childhood, to invoke historian John R. Gillis's argument that many child studies scholars elaborate and expand on fruitfully.[53] Nick Lee writes that "the Enlightenment view of the child, as 'becoming' an adult, rather than simply 'being' a child, remains a dominant conception of children."[54] This position is contested by the notion that contemporary ideas of childhood involve the historical concept of "islanding," inspired by Gillis's work. Through an examination of toy catalogues and sales strategies from mid-nineteenth- to early twentieth-century Philadelphia, I hope to demonstrate that the "islanding" or integrating of childhood play can be further historicized by concentrating on the representation of gender roles. This argument in some ways expands on the chapters about maternity in the playroom and paternity in the play world. The feminization of the play world for girls as fanciful and imagined preserves the "islanding" of girls in play; it is an extension of female epistemology of the domestic. By contrast, a historical look at the shifting representation of the play world for boys allows us to identify the traits of their play that posit a continuity between their childhood activities and adult male enterprises. By further extension, men play more, but their play is valorized as the work of the nation. The naturalized masculine project of play posits a metonymy between the play world and the real world.

In the prose of Schoenhut's catalogue, delicate differences in the rhetorical strategies employed to describe and sell the toys reveal gender differences that in turn disclose a deeper relationship between the presumably ahistorical nature of girls' work and the public presence of masculine

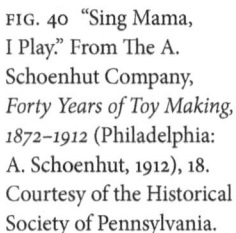

FIG. 40 "Sing Mama, I Play." From The A. Schoenhut Company, *Forty Years of Toy Making, 1872–1912* (Philadelphia: A. Schoenhut, 1912), 18. Courtesy of the Historical Society of Pennsylvania.

desires. A closer reading of the image "Sing Mama, I Play" (fig. 40), for example, alerts us to a complex interaction between the child "expert" and the accompanying adult—a role reversal in itself.

The scenes of family play and instruction, from Zoffany's conversation painting through the home desks and profitable diversions of the Fröbel "gifts" to Uhde's genre piece, are effectively transformed by the Schoenhut miniature. In this ad, the piano perfectly accommodates the daughter's size. The mother occupies the foreground; her high collar and long skirt provide contrast to her daughter's exposed knees and loosely tied apron. The brand "Schoenhut" is clearly legible, with some reference to Gothic typeface, across the front of the piano, and the correspondence between the daughter and mother is reinforced by their musical cooperation; the difference between them strikes the viewer and consumer chiefly as a matter of scale. They are engaged in a joint venture: producing music. But the toy piano empowers the child to issue an imperative: "Sing Mama." The piano confers agency onto the child in the family setting. In this process, play becomes performative beyond a means of rehearsing adult behavior and laying the foundation for future expertise; it allows the child to deliver commands to the maternal parent.

The trope of the real, however we choose to define it—and it is a choice—informs the analysis of Schoenhut's empire of toys. Defined as "true-to-life," the toy piano is said to characterize a new era: "Before that time, toys were fanciful creations, obeying no law other than the mind of the toy maker. But deep down in the heart of every child is the passion for *real* life, for *true* stories" (9; emphasis original) In an examination of Schoenhut's play world, the question arises: How does imaginative play with circus figures, dolls, and other objects contribute to the construction of a model childhood?

Realism motivates sales in the marketing of material objects. In the minds of children, Schoenhut dolls could do everything but eat and talk, and this zeal for the real, so to speak, was largely responsible for the dolls' phenomenal success. Indeed, in the celebratory fortieth-anniversary catalogue, Schoenhut's sons attributed the success of their products, including their dolls, to "the era of realism" (9).[55] Back in 1872, Schoenhut's first product, the toy piano, had been lauded as "true to life," and for this reason, it ushered in a new era in American toy manufacturing. Realism expiates the imagination—objects of commerce replace the objects of Nature in generating the appeal of the play world. In the case of dolls, they allow for play as a rehearsal of reality, as an unconscious process of preparation for adult life. Schoenhut's toys function on the principle of mimetic model, but that model acquired new attributes in transatlantic modernity.

Does this zeal for play as a rehearsal of reality reconcile with the unconscious process of playing as preparation for adult life? The assertion that toys made prior to this time were "fanciful creations" seems a clear overstatement. The verisimilitude of Nuremberg dollhouses, the details of eighteenth-century mechanical toys, such as the guillotine, and the nineteenth-century kitchens, complete with tableware, expose the assertion as inflated marketing. The lust for the real may reside in every child, but, I would suggest, it would be prudent to consider that the desire is regulated by gender. In the Schoenhut play world, the toys make the man. Thus toys and play enact the citizen-building qualities of much contemporary pedagogy while continuing to relegate female play to the household.

The subsequent pages of the 1912 anniversary catalogue present male-specific play in a framework that privileges the local production of toys over European (specifically German) imports. The authors highlight the contrast between the homegrown and the ostensibly foreign: "When a youngster dressed himself in a foreign-made soldier suit, he didn't look like an American boy in blue. Likely the suit wasn't blue, but red. Mr. Schoenhut changed all this. He made it possible for the youngsters to play at soldier, policeman, etc., in costumes that looked the part" (10). In this example, the element of advertised realism is painted in true colors, blue denoting the dress uniform of the American army, red presumably a reference to the import of British military uniforms. The now available local color (blue) of the soldier suit corroborates a process of identification among the child, the act of dressing up, and the American national context; Mr. Schoenhut's color and design decision facilitates the clear correlation.

The filial authors of the catalogue credit Mr. Schoenhut with Americanizing the real and imaginative toys for boys with a lust for adulthood. Not only do the children occupy or "try on" the identity of male authority figures, but they also strengthen the bond with their fathers. The correspondences between "Sing Mama, I Play" and catalogue copy about masculinizing play attests to the ability of toys and intergenerational play to forge and strengthen bonds between same-sex children and parents. Play acts with same-gender parents become reciprocal. The differences, though, are worth noting as well. In music, both daughter and mother are practicing an acquired skill with child's hands and a mother's voice; by contrast, the authors attribute the genetically programmed impulse to shoot projectiles to both father and son. Gendered toys construct childhood through their citizenship in the play world: childhood, just as gender, is performed, as is parenthood.

Another source corroborates the use of the male-specific toys to engage boys in identifying with real authority figures, men in uniform, beyond their relationship to fathers. In this way, playing with guns becomes a constitutive element in the construction of private as well as public subjectivities for boys; they flourish through fun, bonding first with fathers, then with collective masculinity. An article from the *Philadelphia Record*, though it falls beyond my time frame, reports on a baseball game between the local police force and the Germantown Boys Club team. The photo op depicts a boy with a baseball cap checking an officer's weapon, with two other adult police officers looking on with different degrees of amusement and seriousness in their facial expressions. The handwritten sign in the photo reads: "CHECK 'GUNS' HERE FOR COPS and BOYS' PARTY." The caption varies this message: "A few of the 30 policemen who attended the Cops and Boys Party at the club check their guns with Martin Joyce before entering the grounds on W. Penn St. A couple of junior G-men left their toy weapons there, too."[56] The good-natured tone of the short news story is completely appropriate in the context of community involvement of the police with a Philadelphia organization for boys. Other images depict the uniformed boys from both parochial and public schools engaged in drills for Safety Day (5 May 1941) exercises. But the intergenerational baseball event seems to rely on the shared experience of bonding through the "innate desire to shoot," however laudatory the intent may be.[57]

To return to the booklet about Schoenhut products, the catalogue acknowledges only indirectly that toys appeal to boys and girls separately, but it does posit a stronger connection between technology, toys, and male customers. Scattered throughout the prose are references to the attractiveness of display areas in stores and the colorful marketability of certain items. In the section on sailboats, the authors emphasize the high quality and low price of the vessels, but especially the fact that they actually sail. In this line, technical innovation serves the goal of realism. The text mentions the installation of "a new line of machinery" to produce the toys, with the patent extended keel, at a reasonable price (12–13). The booklet overall, the target audience for which is toy-store proprietors and buyers, also notes that the boy who owns a toy sailboat represents a satisfied customer: "There is a large measure of satisfaction to the average boy in possessing a sailboat that really sails, the sails of which he can lower, raise and reef just as the real sailor does. This is the kind of satisfaction that the dealer in Schoenhut sailboats sells. There is no disappointment in Schoenhut boats to reflect on the toy store's other stocks" (13). The image that accompanies the discussion of the boats illustrates two boys playing; another documents the patent extending keel from 1911.

Again, the realism of the toy, enabling the child to mimic the adult sailor, is the index of customer satisfaction. This pleasure to be gained is not meant exclusively for boys; this would be bad business for a toy producer. Still, within this framework of gendered toys, "the average boy" is empowered as a customer.

The gendering of toys confers agency on girls as well, as evidenced in the discussion about the toy piano. Yet a different type of empowerment occurs in the discussion of dolls, one that borders on disturbing. The development and improvement of the **"Schoenhut All-wood Perfection Art Doll"** are described as the most significant contribution of the company to the history of toy production (18). We learn that a famous sculptor designed the model for the doll head, forging an association between the plastic arts and the art doll. The child's need for and appreciation of realism in play assume uncanny aspects in the discussion of dolls: "They are the sort of dolls that children love—real little playmates" (19). The description intentionally blurs the distinction between reality and fantasy in play: "You know how the little girls love their *old* dolls; the doll with the chipped nose and one arm. She loves this doll [Perfection Art Doll], not because of its imperfections, but because it's her *old friend*—she has lived with it the longest" (19). In asserting the unbreakable nature of this particular plaything, clearly aimed at girls, the doll morphs into a friend, one designed to age gracefully, which means not at all, and it "never loses an arm or a leg, nor does that fatal catastrophe—a broken head—ever occur" (20). This category of gendered toys allows girls constant companions that, unlike the girls themselves, demonstrate no signs of aging, nor the wear and tear of everyday life. Moments in the prose recall the Coppelia story of the automaton that wins the love of the hapless hero through her mechanical perfection.

While boys connect with the reality of real authority figures, girls bond with their toys as a means of replicating family life. The catalogue points out that the illustrations of the dolls are "from life. But live *dolls*; not live children" (20). The emphasis is intended to fall on the flexibility of the dolls, their movable limbs, the swivel joints, the fashionable wardrobe, "so that they look like up-to-date little girls and boys" (21). The catalogue shines a light on the lifelike qualities toys embody. This said, there is a distinction between the real and the doll: "It is alive to the delicate fancy of the child or the imagination of the child's father or mother" (20). Finally, the single toy inspires a need for the entire doll family, complete with butler and maid and a dining room set. The replication of a bourgeois household is the goal, but unlike the boy toys that are designed to reinforce connections to the real, the toys for girls are designed realistically to appeal to fantasy and the imagination—and to inform their content. The difference is subtle but crucial.

The success of Schoenhuts' toys is predicated on reputation, but also on the loosening of economic ties to Europe in the later nineteenth-century context. The German American connection is crucial, and I turn now to the strategies of an earlier competitor to illustrate this point. In Charles Dummig's advertisement dating from the middle of the nineteenth century, the author, who is described as an importer, also a wholesale and retail dealer, stresses his buying trips to Europe as the means to his success and the quality of his products. In the announcement "To the Public," he writes, "Charles Dummig, having lately returned from Europe, where he made his purchases and selection of NEW GOODS himself, begs leave to inform his friends and the public generally, that his stock of goods comprises now the greatest variety of Fancy Articles, Toys, and Musical Instruments."[58] Further, Dummig insists that his prices are the lowest, and he identifies the market as the city in which he lives and conducts business: "Our Stores offer inducements in variety of articles and cheapness of prices, unsurpassed in Philadelphia."[59] The booklet is undated, but Dummig's store is listed in directories from 1852; his wares are also advertised in a book dated 1864, so his business slightly predates the founding of Schoenhut, which seems to have cornered the toy market quite quickly. The center of the toy storm is Philadelphia.

The Schoenhut claims, perhaps more moderate than mine, do not stake out an empire, but they modestly imply a place of importance in the national infrastructure. The Schoenhuts set up a context in which the nation organizes the play world. They are the artisans of play, custodians of pleasure and pedagogy, and the technicians of citizenship. On the whole, the geopolitical trade conflict produced ambivalence; while German Americans were the target of suspicion during World War I, the bellicosity shored up the attempts of the second generation of Schoenhuts to distance themselves from their European origins and brand the company as American. Their efforts, it would appear, were supported by the local press, which published flattering articles about the company. A 1914 news item from the Philadelphia *Evening Ledger*, for instance, introduced Schoenhut dolls under the subheading "Fine American-made dolls." The author wrote: "Perhaps the finest American-made dolls on the market are made by A. Schoenhut Company, of Philadelphia. They are made of all wood and can do most everything but talk. They can stand, sit, assume the poses of the most modern dances, play football and at least talk with their hands."[60] The journalist added further context by referencing the war and the former prominence of German toy makers and exporters.

After the Schoenhut sons took over, they sought to expand markets, and one strategy was creating closer ties to educational institutions. With the help of teachers and school administrators, the Schoenhut Company introduced a line of "Concentration and Manipulative Toys for the Nursery and Kindergarten." The "concentration" toys were designed and tested by E. Jensen of Merrill Palmer School, Detroit, and the Oak Lane County Day School, Philadelphia, while the "manipulative" toys were designed by E. Armstrong of the Merrill Palmer School, Detroit. A company advertisement for the toys featured an endorsement from Murza Mann Lauder, who announced: "These toys were introduced, tested, and approved by 'TESTED TOYS,' Detroit, Michigan."[61] Among the edifying playthings featured in the advertisement were objects resembling building blocks and games from Friedrich Fröbel's original kindergarten practice: peg boards, nested trays and nested boxes, design matchers, and other objects specifically designed to enhance motor skills and aesthetic sensibility. The Schoenhut catalogue from 1930 featured an endorsement from a teacher and introduced the company factory as "The Largest Plant in the World Devoted Exclusively to the Manufacture of Toys and Articles for the Education and Happiness of Children."[62]

Over the years, the Schoenhuts had built their reputation on workmanship and innovation. In the end, as Cross concludes, "The company may well have been a victim of its quality."[63] The remarkable durability of Schoenhut products—from toy pianos to dolls—meant that they lasted for years and rarely needed to be replaced. In terms of quality and longevity, these products certainly lived up to Schoenhut company advertisements, and while this surely benefitted the firm's reputation, it may have also damaged its bottom line by effectively eliminating the need for repeat purchases. High quality toys also entailed relatively high production and purchase prices, and this, too, became problematic as the American economy slowed. To cut production costs and make their products more affordable to consumers in the increasingly difficult 1920s, the company was forced to replace the steel springs in its "All Wood Perfection Art Doll" with elastic bands; likewise, it had to replace the glass eyes in its Humpty Dumpty Circus figures with painted ones.[64]

In concluding this chapter, I hope to have demonstrated the links between European American identity and the pedagogical purpose of teaching race in the production and consumption of racialized toys. Displaying and performing race in American Progressive-era politics became part of the economic project in manufacturing toys, but also in corroborating and endorsing American immigrant whiteness. The ability of popular and material cultures to replicate, reinforce, and disseminate racialized models of identity, based on the binary opposition posited between civilization and barbarism, is a constitutive element in the persistence of American hegemony.

In the fortieth-anniversary catalogue of 1912, Albert Schoenhut's sons described the firm's contributions to American national posterity: "Other men create the national policies, build the railroads, revise the currency and carry on enterprises that make for the health and comfort of the people, but it remains for the craftsmen of playthings to furnish the world in which the children live, move and have their being. In this work we have tried to do our part and we take pleasure in saying that our friends of the trade likewise have done their part in helping us."[65] While their claims did not quite stake out an empire, they modestly implied a place of importance in the national infrastructure. The Schoenhut family, with Albert at the helm, created a context in which the American nation, and its children, organized the play world. In the process, the Schoenhuts emerged as artisans of play, custodians of pedagogy, and technicians of citizenship.

Conclusion
"A Very Brilliant House"

Shades of Goethe, Gounod and Great Guns! Was there ever such a soldiers' chorus?

Give me an army of musical Devils, Crazy Girls, Courtiers, Carmens, Fausts . . . and Marguerites and I'll conquer the world quicker than Puck could throw a girdle around it, and without a brass band, too.
—"A Very Brilliant House," unsigned review of Metropolitan Opera House Gala Night Performance, *New York Herald*, 24 April 1896

The imperial play space conveyed in the phrase "Empire of Toys," a hybrid geography of German pasts and American presents and futures, expands transnational connectivity in the Gilded Age, the Belle Époque, but was effectively ended by the age of bellicosity that commenced in 1914. At the turn of the century, German-language influences still resonated with exemplarity and eccentricity attributed to Goethe and his reception as a player and cultural icon in the transatlantic world. By the time Ellen Key inducts Goethe into her pantheon of pedagogical models, both for his biography and his texts, the Faust material was a fixture in the opera repertoire. The "brilliant house" seems to burst with mythical and human figures of the devil, ghosts, and lovers driven to distraction, alongside the singing soldiers and courtiers. Thus the zenith of German cultural and aesthetic play is performed in a gala evening. If we recall that Goethe cautions the New World poet against fantastic specters that haunt the basalt edifice of European literature, we might imagine his disdain at the portrayal above of his work—which ultimately refuses to decide on the redemption of the eternally striving male principle, except through the divine intervention of the feminine. This ambivalence does not translate well.

Let us return to the gala! The anonymous author proclaims: "This afternoon 'Faust' will be given to one of the largest audiences ever seen in the Opera House. At 9 o'clock last night no less than 290 applications for seats had been refused at the box office for the good reason that every seat in the house had been sold."[1] Goethe's legacy persisted throughout the nineteenth century; not least, Gounod's opera and a retinue of Harvard students and transcendentalist intellectuals celebrated him as a poet, a genius, and a humanist. All the while, Goethe inhabits a play world that his heterodoxy shaped. Around 1900, with German immigration still enhancing a cultural and political profile of the immigrant communities across the United States, his iconic status is a matter of celebration—in the elaborate world of the opera stage. The iconic Goethe is poised between the highbrow and folkloric: the discourse revolves around the pressures of Protestant play and his play ethic.

This study began with the argument that texts and toys in transatlantic modernity, particularly their manifestations within German-speaking Europe and the Americas, have constructed and accessorized the play world and the imaginations and identities of the young citizens who inhabit it. From the seventeenth-century child-rearing treatises and dollhouse interiors—encoded and erected to teach both boys and girls their roles in the bourgeois household, a metonymy for the family and society—to the Humpty Dumpty Circus figures and jointed dolls produced by the empire-building "craftsmen of playthings,"[2] the material objects featured in my analysis instantiate the pedagogically motivated artifacts of emulative play. Though the arc of my argument is casually chronological, it is not causally historical. However, the attributes of pedagogical play become more volatile when economic mobility is itself in play. Stories of empathetic children who recognize the historical and parental failings of their downwardly mobile peers abound, imparting a moral message of understanding and gratitude to young (male) readers. Parallel to these class negotiations, intersectional elements of gendered, ethnic, and racial identities enter the discourse of imaginative texts and performativity of actual toys. The model childhood of modernity that Connick and others describe,[3] one experienced as separate and discrete, may seem distant from the images interacting with texts that bring the child into the world while confined to the playroom. The more modern the toy, the more manufactured. Yet in migration stories, the single doll is precious, cherished, hybridized—a reward for lessons learned and work accomplished through acquiring adaptability. In modernity, the play ethic becomes a corollary of the work ethic. Material objects, in migration and global economic circulation, are the coin of the childhood realm; the agents of history educate historical actors. Those objects, in turn, are encoded in a transatlantic network about national identity, cultural patronage, and consumer practices.

The legacy of German exemplarity coexists with eccentricity. We see this in Goethe's approaches to play and the acquisition of toys. The legacy of his mother's lament about his desire to purchase a toy guillotine for his son August echoes across history and geography to San Francisco at the time of the Teddy Bear fashion. In the *San Francisco Call*, published on 7 February 1910, one headline reads: "Guillotine As Toy For Children In 1793: Goethe's Mother Refused to Buy Machine for Youth." The article recapitulates a discussion of Goethe, his mother's disapproval, and the appetite for toy trends:

> There is a long interval between New Year's day 1793 and that of 1910; both in time and in the character of children's toys, observes the London Globe. Today it is the Teddy bear which delights the small boy. In 1793 the German child was humored with the present on the New Year of a toy guillotine. In 1793 we find Goethe writing to his mother at Frankfort asking her to send to little Augustus this sanguinary machine in miniature. Mme. Goethe was indignant, and wrote to her famous son as follows: "Dear Son—I have only one desire, and that is to give you pleasure. I will execute any command, but to buy so infamous a machine of slaughter I will not in any circumstances. If I could I would arrest the makers and burn such toys by the executioner. Why should children be encouraged to amuse themselves with things so repugnant by putting into their hands this instrument of murder and blood? No, it must not be." Goethe did not dispute the maternal admonition.[4]

The unattributed article I quote above deserves close attention, not only because the author identifies Goethe as a fashionista of toys but also because the piece draws attention to the political, historical, and ethnic-national economic factors in toy production and consumption—some more legible than others. The national culture of German play takes on religion, dysfunctional families, work, wars, colonialism, slavery, and poverty. With literary beacons as their guides, German Americans invest in their own status by advancing a German cultural paradigm through importing Weimar's heroes as icons. In the process, as I have demonstrated, economic factors infiltrate the innocent imaginary of the children's play world. The materiality of texts, toys, and games transmits eugenics, racial pedagogy, and social injustice. From porcelain and leather to cotton, wood, and feathers, global markets are inscribed into the DNA of play. One final story collects the threads of my argument.

SUGAR

The *San Francisco Call*, the newspaper that published the article about Goethe's dispute with his mother, established a connection between the San Francisco publisher John Dietrich Spreckels (1853–1926) and the complex history of sugar production and consumption in the transatlantic world. German influence migrated across the expanse of the United States, from the toy manufacturing center of Philadelphia and German Town of New York to the Midwestern homesteaders and synods to the rush toward prosperity in California. The Spreckels's family history participated in a genealogy of cross-cultural influences. Weimar's cultural presence in San Francisco is more than contingent; it is enabled by sugar.

In *Sugar: A Bittersweet History*, Elizabeth Abbott follows the economy and brutality of sugar plantations from the Caribbean to Hawaii. It was Mark Twain who called Hawaii "the king of the sugar world."[5] Abbott highlights the use of indentured labor, the imperious assumption that plantations bring "civilization," and, by virtue of an 1876 reciprocity treaty, the effective status of Hawaii as "an American economic colony."[6] Dietrich Spreckels's father, Claus Spreckels (1828–1908), was among the German Americans in San Francisco who collaborated in efforts to erect the Goethe-Schiller monument in Golden Gate Park. Known as the "'sugar king' of Hawaii and the West," Uwe Spiekermann counts him among the top ten wealthiest Americans of his time.[7] Like many of his compatriots, he left Germany in

1848, began with a brewery, learned about sugar production, and eventually, with an eye toward the growing sugar market, planted on the Sandwich Islands and purchased significant lands on the island of Maui. In his expansion, he established a refinery in Philadelphia. Amassing a fortune, he diversified. Spiekermann writes that the entrepreneur's empire consisted of "building and breaking monopolies in sugar, transport, gas and electricity, real estate, newspapers, banks and breweries."[8] The robber baron's children feuded among themselves; some with the patriarch.

One son, who was trained in Hannover, inherited the fortune of his sugar magnate progenitor. He and his cultural patriots in the Goethe-Schiller Denkmal Gesellschaft of San Francisco began raising money in 1894 for the monument and pedestal; they eventually celebrated its unveiling in 1901.[9] Other monuments followed in immigrant communities across the United States. In this context, familiarity with the vaunted tradition of Goethe's national stature—and statue—as exemplary, interacts with a readership, a comingling of toy traditions, and a call for responsible grandparenting in the face of parental lapses. Transatlantic readers in the early twentieth century were sufficiently acquainted with Goethe's name to cite him as an authority on diversion: on play, education, and the human condition.[10] The economic shift to transpacific exchange, labor, and play was well underway.

The elusive W. Helmar, Maria Hellemeyer, published a collection of short fairy tales in 1893. In the first, "Die Zuckerfee" (The sugar fairy), little Trudchen begs her mother for a piece of sugar. Her prudent mother refuses, warns about the harmful effects, and consoles the crying child with a wheat *Brötchen* smeared with golden butter. To lend imaginative force to her substitution, Trudchen's mother tells a story about evil dwarves who invade the teeth of sugar-consuming children. They harvest the ivory and fashion tables, chairs, beds, plates, even cutlery for their little houses. Their hammering causes children excessive pain.[11] Predictably, Trudchen raids the sugar in her mother's absence and suffers the consequences. From the distancing of slavery in stories about the islands to the carving of ivory houses from decaying teeth in didactic fantasies to the monumentalizing of Goethe and Schiller in San Francisco, the play world connects the domestic sphere with the politics and economics of migration. This realm of reference suggests a homology between German and American cultural constructions of material objects along with pedagogies of play. At the same time, philanthropically minded activists turn to poverty and public play. One example of this advocacy is the Playground Movement, a philanthropic endeavor initiated to provide poor urban children with safe public space. One advocate, Stoyan Vasil Tsanoff, is credited with the first book published in America devoted exclusively to playgrounds. Tsanoff, the author and also the general secretary of the Culture Extension League, advocates passionately for the building of playgrounds in his *Educational Value of the Children's Playground* of 1897. Here he justifies the claim that "playgrounds are most important educational factors," and that "a child's moral culture depends upon his play."[12] Though Tsanoff is ambivalent about much of Friedrich Fröbel's kindergarten theory, his work on the value of play effectively bridges the divide between child-rearing practices at home and those enacted in the public sphere, connecting the dots between education and responsible citizenship. As early as 1897, he forces us to consider and focus on the rights of the child as more than a ploy in his rhetorical strategy. First, he establishes that childhood is a separate phase of life.[13] He goes beyond any articulation of play inherited from German-speaking Europe when he writes:

> No abuse of human rights, for which revolutions and bloody wars have been waged and kingdoms overthrown, has ever surpassed the horror of trampling upon the child's rights, and for whom no voice is raised! The unfortunate little ones have had simply to bear their misery in silence, though it has resulted in shortening lives, ruining health, perversion of their souls, stunting of their minds! I feel as if humanity should be covered in rags of shame and disgrace for committing such a horrid sin of depriving the pure and angelic child of his "soul's nourishment," and thus turning him into paths of misery and degradation. It seems as if man has in no other way expressed his cruel injustice towards the weak, as he has done towards the helpless child.[14]

Decades in advance of an international discussion of humanity (as a political category), human rights, and crimes against humanity, Tsanoff, through his efforts to establish and expand the perimeters of play, asserts the human rights of the child—and the right of every child to be a citizen of the play world.

Play becomes a human right. The goals of play are still predicated on building the foundations of moral character and good citizenship, however subsumed they may be into a paradigm of childhood as an island—with a fence around it. German models of play after World War I would highlight the instrumentalization of play in the service of national identity. These, too, will have a profound impact on the American models of play in the interwar period. World war disrupts the narrative about German and American cultural cross-pollination, technical know-how, and artistic heights when nations and national narratives confront each other and must choose sides. In closing the previous chapter, I pointed out that the Schoenhut advertisement to celebrate the joys and markets of the season intentionally edged away from the German heritage. Tellingly, the article "Toys, Yes, Plenty of Them, To Make Merry Christmas," appeared adjacent to a headline that read, "Pittsburgh Steel Expert Trailed by German Spies."[15] The "Christmas Bustle Wherever the Eye Looks"[16] is juxtaposed with the news about the enemy within, with spies in the heart of American industry. The First World War does drastic damage to the reputation of the label "Made in Germany," an association among quality materials, technical sophistication, and lasting value. Collateral damage extended to American toy manufacturers.

After the Armistice, the Schoenhuts continued to emphasize their national and even local allegiance. During the company's forty-eighth anniversary celebration in 1920, the Schoenhuts led with location: "Made in Philadelphia." The German American background that had figured so importantly in the 1912 anniversary catalogue was nowhere to be found; instead, emphasis was placed on the Schoenhuts' Philadelphia home turf. Marketing materials for that year unfolded under the banner of the local. The shift in strategy was no doubt prompted by an intervening world war in which Germany fought on the opposite side of the United States. At the conclusion of the war, at the onset of which German language publications were prohibited, the Schoenhut ad emphasizes that the toys are made in America. Marketing toys for the holiday takes on a patriotic imperative, one that reasserts the particulars of national identity into the universality of the childhood expectations of Christmas. In the *Ladies' Home Journal* for December 1918 (fig. 41), the copy reads: "Upon the happiness of little children the shadow of war should not fall. The Christmas days of childhood are all too few. We must not let even one of them be saddened."[17] The nineteenth-century association between the German and the hegemony of the Christmas holiday practices in the United States, effectively severed by war, persists in the marketing strategy of the Schoenhut company. The language appeals to the grammar of childhood innocence and the imperative to sequester play space from the trauma of war. Even the childless can demonstrate authentic feeling with the gifting of a quality toy to a child

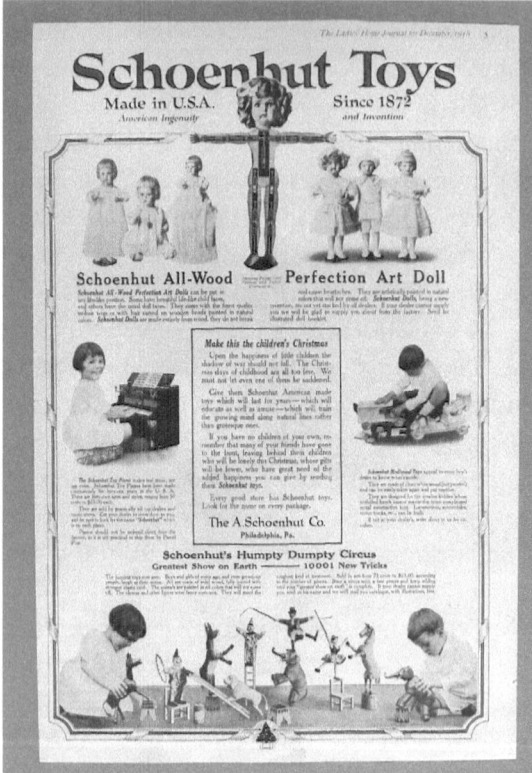

FIG. 41 Christmas advertisement, "Schoenhut Toys, Made in U.S.A. Since 1872," 1918. Courtesy of The Strong, Rochester, New York.

whose family life the war has disrupted. Toy giving can be a form of sacrifice and an expression of genuine patriotism.

When the war ended in 1919, the trade competition between Europe and the United States in toy production resumed. The following year, a Schoenhut advertisement boasted that the Humpty Dumpty Circus was "acknowledged in all parts of the World as the greatest PLAYTHING ever invented."[18] A company that had once celebrated its German roots now took pride in its status as the largest American exporter of toys to Germany.

Though historical wars informed the mechanical guillotine, the yoyo, uniformed toy soldiers and national costumes, cautionary tales of exemplary goodness and dignified poverty, and a range of references to revolutionary politics, world war, after the emergence of mass markets and mass production around 1900 established transatlantic economic exchanges, relegated toys to the status of superfluity and luxury. Imports dropped; American companies shuttered. German cultural legacies underwent a process of national revision. In 1937, Lebert H. Weir (1878–1949), director of the National Recreation Association, published his study *Europe at Play: A Study of Recreation and Leisure Time Activities*, suspended between the Olympics hosted in Berlin and Nazi Germany's *Anschluss* or annexation of Austria.[19] A sociological study, Weir's book focused on leisure and recreation from the interwar period as evidence of growing identification between "play" and adult activities that require their own "playgrounds," with an emphasis on the homology between child and adult leisure. Weir, also the editor of *Parks: A Manual on Municipal and County Parks*, rehearsed the history of designing and dedicating public space in most European countries; he traced this development from large leisure parks of the past through trends intended to counter the deleterious effects of industrialization to the need for intergenerational spaces of collective (outdoor) play. Weir's study, while maintaining a tone of objectivity and ostensible neutrality, interpreted certain types of European masculine play through their openness to instrumentalization by fascist and communist ideological agendas. Ultimately, though he identified public play, recreation, and community activities as sites of potential resistance toward collectivizing politics; he valorized the German model of reconnecting man and nature through "gardens" of play. Even though play is autonomous, and as such ideally unavailable to capture by political parties, he reset the perimeters of play around freedom in nature and society.

The catastrophic consequences wrought by National Socialism, consequences for Germany and the world, occluded the brief moment in 1937 when an American social scientist and parks bureaucrat might have looked favorably on the progress of play in a country that triggered two world wars. The German construction of the play world in the Americas prior to 1914, however, allows us to recuperate a sense of the human in play. When we consider Tsanoff and his inspiration, underwriting the insistence on play as a human right, we witness a concept of humanity that derives from primarily European worldviews and the conviction that these need to be extended to include multiple manifestations of otherness within an American play world.

Notes

INTRODUCTION

1 See, for example, Schwartz, *Roll the Bones*.
2. Webster, *Johan Zoffany*, 141.
3. Ibid., 164.
4. Ibid., 165.
5. See, for example, the interview of Jaak Panksepp, "Science of the Brain." Panksepp discusses biases on the part of grant reviewers against terms such as "*crying, psychological pain, playfulness,* and *laughter*" (261, italics original).
6. Weber-Kellermann, *Die Kinderstube*, 25.
7. Gehrke-Riedlin, "Das Kinderzimmer im deutschsprachigen Raum," 40.
8. Weber-Kellermann, *Die Kindheit: Kleidung und Wohnen*, 14.
9. Kant, *Critique of Judgement*, 165.
10. Marcuse, *Eros and Civilization*, 188.
11. Ibid., 173.
12. Ibid., 174.
13. Ibid., 195.
14. Ariès, *Centuries of Childhood*, 33.
15. Ibid., 68.
16. Huizinga, *Homo Ludens*, iv.
17. Caillois, *Man, Play and Games*, 12. See also Cross, *Kid's Stuff*, 12–13.
18. Caillois, *Man, Play and Games*, 13.
19. Ibid., 19.
20. Brookshaw, "Material Culture," 367. By considering the effect of adult agency, Brookshaw in this article reprises the research on childhood studies and the reliance on material culture to understand the varying social and economic contexts that inform childhood interactions with material culture.
21. Gillis, "Epilogue."
22. Lefebvre, *Production of Space*, 11–12.
23. DeMause, *History of Childhood*, 1. This volume, ambitious in its scope to write the history of childhood in the West, originated as a research project under the auspices of the Association for Applied Psychoanalysis. See the editor's preface on page iii.
24. Zornado, *Inventing the Child*, 3.
25. Coffman, Leonard, and O'Reilly, *Atlantic World*, 1.
26. Stievermann and Scheiding, *Peculiar Mixture*, 2.
27. Sassen, *Expulsions*, 15.
28. Cross, *Kid's Stuff*, 5.
29. Zantop, *Colonial Fantasies*; Berman, *Enlightenment or Empire*; Israel, *Radical Enlightenment*.
30. Buck-Morss, *Hegel, Haiti, and Universal History*, 111 and 113.
31. See the discussion of worlding in Tautz, *Translating the World*, 16–17. I use the term in a circumscribed sense,

avoiding, for this study, any analysis of Edmund Husserl (1859–1938) and the *Lebenswelt* or Martin Heidegger (1889–1976) and *Dasein*.

32. Most prominent are the voices of Gayatri Spivak (*Critique of Postcolonial Reason*) and Donna Haraway (*Staying with the Trouble*). My interrogation of the play world critiques the formation of childhood agency from within the model each indicts.

33. See Trumpener, "Picture-Book Worlds."

34. Tautz, *Translating the World*, 117.

35. Marenholtz-Bülow, *How Kindergarten Came to America*, 3. See Allen, *Transatlantic Kindergarten*, esp. 41, on Marenholtz-Bülow's encounter with Fröbel.

36. Wyness, *Childhood and Society*, 11.

37. Friedrich Froebel, cited in Marenholtz-Bülow, *How Kindergarten Came to America*, 54. Throughout this study, I spell this as "Fröbel" while at the same time preserving alternative spellings that occur in quoted original texts.

38. Campe is perhaps best known for his tutoring of Alexander and Wilhelm von Humboldt. He gained prominence for pioneering children's and young adult literature. His adventure story *Robinson der Jüngere* (Robinson the younger) adapts Daniel Defoe's novel for a younger audience; it was followed by *Die Entdeckung von Amerikas* (the discovery of America).

39. In the German tradition beginning in the eighteenth century, there is a sustained and philosophical debate about play that revolves around its purpose or, to use the Kantian term, *Zweck*. Play is situated in the modern European, enlightenment enterprise of reason (*Vernunft*) and assumes philosophical features. In the popularization of Kant's philosophy, Friedrich Schiller departs from Kant's definition of play as "purposefulness without purpose," replacing the formula with an innate impulse, the *Spieltrieb* (play drive). Although the wrangling over play occurs in the realm of aesthetic education and art, it does not necessarily incorporate attributes of children or childhood. Much has been written about adult play, focused on gambling, card playing, billiards, the hunt, theater, festival, tableau vivant, and the visual and verbal arts in general. By contrast, eighteenth-century theories and practices of children at play present themselves in pedagogy and material culture. On Fröbel's institutionalization of play, see Hamlin, *Work and Play*, 136–39.

40. Cohen, *Sentimental Education of the Novel*.

41. Moretti, "Slaughterhouse of Literature."

42. Weber, *Protestant Ethic and the Spirit of Capitalism*, 32.

43. Brookshaw, "Material Culture," 381.

44. Grenby, "Origins of Children's Literature," 3.

45. Hamlin, *Work and Play*, 222.

46. The term "intersectionality" was coined by Kimberle Crenshaw in her study of race and gender as factors in employment discrimination; it has become a widely used and indispensable conceptual and practical tool for analyzing the varying and competing components of human identity and their social perception. See her "Mapping the Margins." For a critical reading of the American "classics," see MacCann, *White Supremacy in Children's Literature*.

47. Colomer, Kümmerling-Meibauer, and Silva-Díaz, *New Directions in Picturebook Research*, 1.

48. Chakkalakal, *Die Welt in Bildern*, 7.

49. Scholars of visual cultures mine images for other purposes related to the exploration of childhood. See Averett, *Early Modern Child in Art and History*.

50. Brookshaw, "Material Culture," 381.

51. Appadurai, *Social Life of Things*, 4.

52. Heesen, *World in a Box*, 9.

53. Appadurai, *Social Life of Things*, 4.

54. Purdy, *Tyranny of Elegance*, ix and 2.

55. Auslander, "Beyond Words," 1017.

56. O'Brien, *Story of American Toys*, 11.

57. Rountree, *Dollhouses, Miniature Kitchens, and Shops*.

58. Cross, *Kid's Stuff*, 14.

59. Gutman and de Coninck-Smith, *Designing Modern Childhoods*, 2.

60. Ibid., 2–3.

61. Stewart, *On Longing*, 37–38.

62. Stauss, *Frühe Spielwelten*, 344–45.

63. Beyond my explication of the theoretical influences on my title, I also consider the way space, encompassing both built and natural environments, participates in the construction of childhood identity. Though a detailed consideration of physical space is not forthcoming, I take under advisement Dorothy Massey's work on space and gender, which also informs my work, especially as the activity of play metonymizes the playroom into a contiguous relationship with the playground as a space of entitlement, with both as gendered territories. See Massey, *Space, Place, and Gender*. While I draw on historical sources from textual and material cultures, I refer liberally to contemporary theory. To formulate my argument more generally, for example, I rely on the work of Tracey Skelton and Gill Valentine, who highlight the absence of the young from public spaces; see Skelton and Valentine, *Cool Places*, 1–2. Their conclusion, that public space is defined as adult space, prompts me to apply this insight retrospectively, asking about the relationship between children and space in transatlantic modernity.

64. Nel and Paul, *Keywords for Children's Literature*, 1.

65. Moretti, "Slaughterhouse of Literature," 207.

66. Davis, *Women on the Margins*, 2.

67. Langer, *Pallas und ihre Waffen*, 37. Langer recaps Gersdorff's entry into the early modern *Frauenlexika*.

68. See http://www.kochbuch sammler.de/geschichte.htm.

69. Susanne Barth, "Jacobs, (Christian) Friedrich (Wilhelm)," in Killy, *Killy Literaturlexikon*, 60.

70. *Deutsches Literatur-Lexikon*, 33: 83–91.

71. See Deleuze and Guattari, *Anti-Oedipus*.

72. *Ladies Home Journal*, December 2018, no page.

73. Schoenhut, *Forty Years of Toy Making*.

CHAPTER 1

1. Locke, "Some Thoughts Concerning Education." Cited here from the Sophia Project (1999), 3. http://www.sophia-project.org/uploads/1/3/9/5/13955288/locke_education.pdf.

2. Heesen, *World in a Box*, 48–49.

3. Reinhart, *Early-Modern German Literature*.

4. See, for example, Laura Lunger Knoppers's introduction to her

Cambridge Guide to Early Modern Women's Writing, 1–17.

5. Knape, "Poetics and Rhetorics," 251.

6. Hinds, "Prophecy and Religious Polemic," 236.

7. See the entry in the *Deutsches Literatur-Lexikon*, 6: 754–55.

8. Ibid., 656–57.

9. Trotta, *Die bleierne Zeit*.

10. Allen, *Transatlantic Kindergarten*, 35.

11. Weber, *Protestant Ethic and the Spirit of Capitalism*, 32.

12. Langer, *Pallas und ihre Waffen*, 37. Langer recaps Gersdorff's entry into the early modern *Frauenlexika*.

13. Maché, "Gersdorf, Henriette Catharina Freifrau von." Maché refers to an entry in the standard literary lexicon (Goedecke) as well.

14. Langer, *Pallas und ihre Waffen*, 123.

15. Ibid., 151.

16. Ibid., 43. Gersdorff supported, among other institutions, August Hermann Francke's Halle orphanage, founded on the belief that human betterment depended on the education of the young (75). Gersdorff additionally supported female education, with differing results and degrees of sustainability. The Gynäceum foundered, in part owing to insufficient attention to class expectations (111–13). The Magdalenenstift in Altenburg enjoyed both her support and benefitted from her persistent relevance (117–21).

17. *Grimms Wörterbuch*, gabe (Bd. 4, Sp. 1111) http://woerterbuchnetz.de/cgi-bin/WBNetz/wbgui_py?sigle=DWB&lemid=GG00005#XGG00005.

18. Appadurai, *Social Life of Things*, 11.

19. Ibid., 11–12.

20. Allen, *Transatlantic Kindergarten*, 27.

21. Langer, *Pallas und ihre Waffen*, 205.

22. Teigeler, *Zinzendorf als Schüler*, 8. Teigeler's focus on the school experiences of Zinzendorf intersects on occasion with the influence of his grandmother.

23. Heywood, *History of Childhood*, 9.

24. Arnold, "Familie—Kindheit—Jugend," 145.

25. O'Malley, *Making of the Modern Child*, 124.

26. Stewart, *On Longing*, 61.

27. Ibid., 37.

28. Gröber, *Children's Toys of Bygone Days*, 23.

29. Großmann, "Vorwort," 7.

30. Müller, *Ein Idealhaushalt*, 24.

31. Ibid., 15.

32. Ibid., 20. See also Gröber, *Children's Toys*, 21–22.

33. Gröber, *Children's Toys*, 21.

34. Gröber's description indicates the opposite, indicating the front wall, modeled on the façade of the house, protecting the decorations and furnishing from "curious fingers." Ibid., 23.

35. The contemporary "Haus-Halterin," cited by Müller, makes this point.

36. Müller, *Ein Idealhaushalt*, 30.

37. Mezerers, *Herrnhuterian Pietism*, 19. I thank the librarians in Special Collections at Love Library for assistance with this research.

38. Ibid., 72.

39. Kidd, *Great Awakening*, 39. On controversies surrounding Zinzendorf and the Moravians, see 147.

40. On the songs, see Allen, *Transatlantic Kindergarten*, 27–29. The songs, "Mutter- und Koselieder," were translated into English. Allen analyzes the

work of Ida Seele, who in Blankenburg used two rooms, "one devoted to games based on the *Mother and Nursery Songs*, and the other to structured play with educational toys" (30–31).

41. Biographical details are summarized from information in the *Deutsches Literatur-Lexikon*, 35: 656–58; and the preface to the American edition thereof.

42. Meyer, *Child Nature and Nurture*.

43. Ibid., 7.

44. Ibid.

45. See https://www.wdl.org/en/item/15126.

46. Campe, *Robinson der Jüngere*, 47–48.

47. For biographical details, see Erdmann, "Woltersdorf, Ernst Gottlieb," in *Allgemeine Deutsche Biographie* (1898), [online version]; http://www.deutsche-biographie.de/pnd120948125.html.

48. Woltersdorf, *Kinder-Lieder*, 5–6. Accessed at https://books.google.com/books/about/Kinder_lieder.html?id=ktOZxgEACAAJ.

49. Ibid., 6.

50. See also ibid., 57. The hymnal includes an image of three children on the floor praying together, to illustrate a poem. See also "Vereinigtes Geschrei betender Kinder" (United cries of praying children) (59), which carries the note: "Die Unbeständigkeit ist eine Pest oder Hauptkrankheit geistlicher und leiblicher Kinder" (Inconstancy is a plague or main illness of spiritual and corporeal children). The interaction between the images and texts reinforces the meaning of the hymns. Further images include one depicting "Das Vorbild des zwölfjährigen Jesu im Tempel" (The model of the twelve-year-old Jesus in the Temple) (57) and one of a male child in bed, surrounded by five boys and called "Gebet für die Knaben" (Prayer for the boys) (69). Gender equality is also represented. See the image of two praying girls, "Gebet für die Mägdlein und Jungfrauen" (Prayer for the girls and young women) (72). Another image emphasizes the intergenerational importance of prayer. It represents an adult Christ figure with children, two adults, and a woman with a baby; it is entitled "Der kindliche Sinn der Kinder" (The childlike meaning of children) (75).

51. See Schutt, "What Will Become of Our Young People?"

52. Parenthetical citations in this chapter refer to Meyer, *Child Nature and Nurture*.

53. See ibid., 110. "Nowhere in these writings does he deliberately contradict or frankly disavow the orthodox Lutheran position regarding either doctrine. But he does frequently contradict them in fact either by his way of interpreting them and explaining them away, or by the emphatic announcement of his views of the nature and religious status of the child which in themselves cannot be reconciled with the theories of original sin and baptismal regeneration."

54. See Peucker, "Inspired by Flames of Love." On Christian Renatus and the 1748 choir festival, an intense and highly eroticized celebration of Christ's sidehole, see 46–49.

55. Ibid., 30.

56. Ibid., 34–36.

57. Zinzendorf, "In den ersten Gnadentagen," 117.

58. From an address to the Choir of Married People, 8 August 1744.

59. Elsewhere, for example, in the English-German prayer book, "Sünder"

(sinners) is frequently rhymed with "Kinder" (children).

60. Meyer notes that the Countess von Gersdorff, his subject's grandmother, encouraged the move to found a school for poor children in Bertelsdorf. Meyer recognizes the supporting role of the countess, whom I cast in a leading one, at least on this and three other occasions in his study. See Meyer, *Child Nature and Nurture*, 56, 132, and 146.

CHAPTER 2

1. Gehre-Riedlin, "Das Kinderzimmer im deutschsprachigen Raum," 36.
2. See Engelstein, *Anxious Anatomy*, 32.
3. Müller, *Ein Idealhaushalt*, 55.
4. Cadogan, "An Essay upon Nursing."
5. See Zwicker, "Heroism of the Mother."
6. *Deutsches Wörterbuch von Jacob und Wilhelm Grimm*. 16 Bde. in 32 Teilbänden. Leipzig 154–961. Quellenverzeichnis Leipzig 1971.
7. D. Friedrich Benedict Weber, *Handbuch der ökonomischen Literatur*, 286–89.
8. Petschauer, "Eighteenth-Century German Opinions."
9. Ibid., 268.
10. Parenthetical citations in this section refer to Löffler et al., *Oekonomisches Handbuch*.
11. Germershausen and Gericke, *Die Hausmutter*, 10.
12. Ibid., 10.
13. Parenthetical citations in this section refer to Löffler et al., *Oekonomisches Handbuch*.
14. Germershausen, "Regierung des männlichen Gesindes," in *Der Hausvater*, 251.
15. Ibid., 251.
16. Ibid., 257.
17. Campe, *Kleine Kinderbibliothek*, 63.
18. Susanne Barth, "Jacobs, (Christian) Friedrich (Wilhelm)," in Killy, *Killy Literaturlexikon*, 60.
19. Parenthetical citations in this section refer to Jacobs, *Allwin und Theodor*.
20. Simpson, "Recoding the Ethics of War."
21. See Krimmer, *Representation of War in German Literature*, esp. 47–55. Krimmer characterizes the play's events in highly relevant terms, as a superpower in conflict with terrorists, yet observes that it is "actually a testimony to Kleist's intellectual engagement with contemporary military challenges and reform movements" (48).
22. *Völkerschlacht*, 125. See illustration SML Inv.-Nr: W/K 8.
23. See Simpson, *Erotics of War*, especially the introduction. The toy soldier collection in the Sonneberg Museum, along with numerous examples from the Bestelmeier catalogue, corroborate the relationship between war toys and direct historical antecedents. See, for example, the riding Hussar (ca. 1785, 1803, 1830) in Stauss, *Frühe Spielwelten*, 297.
24. *Völkerschlacht*, 104. See illustration SML Inv.-Nr: W/K 21.
25. Hildebrandt, *Das Spielzeug im Leben des Kindes*, 285.
26. Ibid., 286.
27. See, for example, Gustafson, *Absent Mother and Orphaned Fathers*.
28. *Deutscher Literatur-Lexikon*, 33: 83–91.

29. Parenthetical citations in this section refer to Wilmsen, *Der deutsche Kinderfreund*.

CHAPTER 3

1. For a sustained reading, see Saure, "Agamemnon on the Battle Field of Leipzig."
2. Saul, "Goethe and Colonisation," 85.
3. There is an imperial logic from the *Lehrjahre* to the *Wanderjahre* (1821), as Nicholas Saul observes, in which America can be read as indicative of "Goethe's utopian thought." He notes the Turmgesellschaft "is joined by the patriarchal Enlightenment demesne of the Oheim, the Pädagogische Provinz, Lenardo's Emigrants League, and Odoard's inner European colonisers" (Saul, "Goethe and Colonisation," 85).
4. See Boyle, "Introduction."
5. See, for example, Lieder, "Goethe in England and America."
6. For comments that helped shape the argument of this chapter, I owe thanks to Eva Geulen, Simon Richter, and Dr. Christof Wingertszahn.
7. See Wilson, *Das Goethe-Tabu*, for a sustained consideration of this topic.
8. Stauss, *Frühe Spielwelten*, 384–85.
9. Ibid., 370–71.
10. Schiller, "*Schillers Sämmtliche Werke*, chapter 3, 14th Letter. Translation from Schiller, *On the Aesthetic Education of Man*, 74–75. My modification.
11. Schiller, "*Schillers Sämmtliche Werke*, chapter 3, 15th Letter. Translation from Schiller, *On the Aesthetic Education of Man*, 79.
12. See, for example, Chapman, "A Case Study of Gendered Play." In national print media, see, for example, Perri Klass, M.D., "Breaking Gender Stereotypes in the Toy Box," *New York Times*, 5 February 2018, no page. https://www.nytimes.com/2018/02/05/well/family/gender-stereotypes-children-toys.html.
13. Goethe, *Tagebücher 1775–1804*, 151. My translation.
14. Lloyd, *Arts and Crafts*, 165.
16. According to Lloyd, some prisoners of war in England held at depots fared better than others; they had work and some direct access to markets.
15. Benjamin, "Toy Exhibition at the Märkisches Museum," 100.
16. Gersdorff, *Goethes Enkel*, 69.
17. See my *Erotics of War*, 192, on Goethe's willingness to risk his own safety in order to experience heavy artillery in a way that intersects with an almost Kantian notion of the sublime.
18. See Gersdorff, *Goethes Enkel*, 69. Alma was not left out; she received a doll.
19. Gröber, *Children's Toys of Bygone Days*, 3.
20. See, for example, Becker-Cantorino, "Witch and Infanticide." Diverging opinions about Goethe's own stance on human rights issues and political decisions funnel around, among other events, the publication of his official writings. See Wilson, *Das Goethe-Tabu*, and his review essay, "Goethe's Writings as Minister of State."
21. See, for example, Rehwinkel, "Kopflos, aber lebendig?"
22. Sutton-Smith, "Play and Ambiguity," 299.
23. Goethe, *Erotic Poems*, 15.
24. Ibid., with my insertions to emphasize repetition of the word "hand."
25. Benjamin, "Randbemerkungen zu einem Monumentalwerk," 131.

26. Benjamin, "Marginal Notes on a Monumental Work," 120.
27. Goethe, *Erotic Poems*, 92.
28. Ibid., 93. See my modification to the translation in parenthesis to emphasize the playfulness of the game, with its underlying seriousness.
29. Browne and Davis, "Goethe and the Yo-Yo," 101.
30. See, for example, Hexter, "Poetic Reclamation and Goethe's Venetian Epigrams," especially 534–35.
31. Böhm, "Epoche Machen." The dissertation focuses on the origin and publication history, with attention to contemporary politics briefly considered (206). Many focus on the relationship between political upheaval, erotic exploration, and the modernizing of classical form. See, for example, Scheuer, *Manier und Urphänomen*; Wild, *Goethes klassische Lyrik*, argues that Goethe's classical poetry was "Teil und Ausdruck des 'Projekts Klassik'"—that is, a process, an aesthetic reconciliation between modernity and antiquity; see also Lange, "Goethe's Strategy of Self-Censorship," and Oswald, *Früchte einer großen Stadt*.
32. Freud, *Beyond the Pleasure Principle*, 14–17.
33. Bertaux, '*Gar schöne Spiele spiel' ich mit dir!* 100.
34. Benjamin, "Kulturgeschichte des Spielzeuges," 117; translation is from Benjamin, "Cultural History of Toys," 116.
35. Goto-Jones, "Secret Life of Yo-Yos."
36. McClellan, "Hunting for Everyday History."
37. Oliver, "History of the Yo-Yo."
38. Benjamin, "Randbemerkungen zu einem Monumentalwerk," 131; translation is from Benjamin, "Marginal Notes on a Monumental Work," 120.
39. Gillis, "Epilogue."
40. Key, *Century of the Child*, 198. On eugenics and Key's consideration of Francis Galton's *Hereditary Genius*, see 20–24.
41. See, for example, her discussion of the perennial challenges involved in balancing the soul and the body (Key, *Century of the Child*, 6); she refers here to Goethe's call for boldness. On Nietzsche's "superman," see 25–26; Nietzsche on fidelity, see 35–36.
42. Ibid., 106.
43. Ibid., 107. Key is relying on popularized European models of natural education for her interpretation of Goethe and childhood.
44. Ibid., 184. Later, she advocates teaching history through great works of literature, among them Goethe's *Egmont* (220).
45. Marenholtz-Bülow, *How Kindergarten Came to America*, 95.
46. Kohlmeyer, *Die Pädagogische Provinz*, 4.
47. Quoted in Fröbel, *Student's Froebel*, ix.
48. Goethe, *Dichtung und Wahrheit*, 75. My translation, supplemented by Heitner's translation in Goethe, *From My Life*, 61.
49. Goethe, *Dichtung und Wahrheit*, 75; translation by Heitner in Goethe, *From My Life*, 61.
50. Key, *Century of the Child*, 249.
51. Goethe, *Dichtung und Wahrheit*, 14–15; translation by Heitner in Goethe, *From My Life*, 22.
52. Hamlin, *Work and Play*, 63.
53. Quoted in Michel, *Goethe*, 281.
54. Gersdorff, *Goethes Enkel*, 40.
55. Ibid., 41.

56. Goethe, *Dichtung und Wahrheit*, 35; translation by Heitner in Goethe, *From My Life*, 48.
57. Catharina Elisabeth Goethe, *Die Briefe der Frau Rath Goethe*, 321.
58. Ibid.
59. Ibid., 322.
60. See Geiger, *Goethe und die Seinen*, 139.
61. Melz, "Goethe and America," 428.
62. Saul, "Goethe and Colonisation."

CHAPTER 4

1. See, for example, Niekerk, *Radical Enlightenment*, a response to Jonathan Israel's work.
2. Emmerling, *Johann Conrad Seekatz*, 169.
3. Heywood, *History of Childhood*, 34.
4. See Deleuze and Guattari, *Anti-Oedipus*.
5. Gallagher, "Women and Girls in German Colonial Fiction." Gallagher summarizes the theoretical framework that informs her argument about the intersection of race and gender during the German imperial era, foremost among them Wildenthal's *German Women for Empire*, whose extensive original research and analysis of gender models in colonial literature highlight different cohorts of colonialist women. See also Walgenbach, *"Die weiße Frau."* While each contributes to an understanding of race and gender in colonial discourse, national identity and citizenship rights, and realities in the colonies, the pedagogical purpose of colonial literature directed at children and young adult readers is not a primary consideration.
6. Bowersox, *Raising Germans*, 56.
7. Ibid., 122.
8. Insa Fooken, *Puppen*, 101–5.
9. Bowersox, *Raising Germans*, 123.
10. Ibid., 126–27.
11. Stauss, *Frühe Spielwelten*, 138.
12. Ibid., 137–38.
13. Ibid., 213.
14. Ibid., 214–15 and 336–37.
15. Ibid., 348–49.
16. See digitized game, "Deutschland's Kolonien-Spiel," ca. 1890, https://primo.getty.edu/primo-explore/fulldisplay?vid=GRI&docid=GETTY_ROSETAIE1540602&context=L&lang=en_US.
17. *Deutscher Dichter-Lexikon*, 8: 128–30.
18. See http://www.abenteuerroman.info/autor/horn/horn.htm.
19. *Deutscher Dichter-Lexikon*, 8: 1.
20. On the historical stereotype of colonialist absenteeism, see Abbott, *Sugar*, 157–66.
21. Horn, *Ein Kongo-Neger*, 56.
22. Bowersox, *Raising Germans*, 140.
23. Auslander, "Beyond Words," 1015.
24. Wolgast, *Das Elend unserer Jugendliteratur*, 112.
25. Dyhrenfurth-Graebsch, *Geschichte des deutschen Jugendbuches*.
26. Parenthetical citations in this section refer to Horn, *Ein Kongo-Neger*.
27. Bitterli, *Die "Wilden" und die "Zivilisierten,"* 155–56.
28. See http://www.detlef-heinsohn.de/ki-jahrb-auerbach.htm.
29. See Ruth Geede, "Beliebtes Jahrbuch. Vor 120 Jahren wurde Auerbachs Kinderkalender gegründet," with a focus on the later editor Adolf Holst. In *Das Ostpreußenblatt/Landesmannschaft Ostpreußen* e.V. / 13 October 2001. Please note: the use of "Preußen" in the title can be indicative of a regional perspective. Geede's article deals mostly with Holst (1867–1945), without political

commentary. I cite it for the reputed popularity and persistence of the "Kalendermann" in collective memory. http://www.webarchiv-server.de/pin/archivo1/41010b18.htm.

30. Chakkalakal, *Die Welt in Bildern*, 162.

31. Bowersox, *Raising Germans* 65.

32. Ciarlo, *Advertising Empire*, 3.

33. Ibid., 11.

34. Ibid., 225.

35. Ibid., 225–26.

36. Ibid., 226.

37. Ciarlo observes the use of caricature in both American and German advertising and in mass-produced books directed at children: it is "one bridge between transgressive minstrelsy and colonialist child's play. More broadly, caricature thus came to be marketed to multiple audiences, from sophisticated readers of the educated middle classes to marginally literate groups, such as children" (ibid., 249).

38. Stafford, "*Journeys through Bookland*'s Imaginative Geography," 149.

39. Bowersox, *Raising Germans*, 120.

40. Oloukpona-Yinnon, *Unter Deutschen Palmen*, 27.

41. Sembritzki, *Kolonial-Gedicht und -liederbuch*, 22. From *Kolonie und Heimat*.

42. Ibid., 3.

43. Klotz, "Introduction," xii.

44. O'Donnell, Bridenthal, and Reagin, *Heimat Abroad*, 15.

45. See https://www.malerwinkelhaus.de/index.php?id=single-aktuelles-archiv&tx_ttnews%5Btt_news%5D=79&cHash=18b4f4061675165e4b595acb86ac9ab0.

46. Chakkalakal, *Die Welt in Bildern*, 73. See also Bitterli, *Die "Wilden" und die "Zivilisierten,"* for his discussion of oppositional language to differentiate between indigenous peoples and Europeans. He further identifies paradigmatic shifts in thinking about *Naturkinder* (children of nature) in the realms of literature and art. Influenced in part by Robinson adventure tales, the ennobling of the "savage" occurs "fast immer als reine Ausgeburten der Einbildungskraft" (almost always as pure products of the imagination) (236).

47. Buck-Morss, *Hegel, Haiti, and Universal History*, 111.

48. Ziemann, *Mola Koko!*, 179.

49. Bowersox, *Raising Germans*, 20.

50. Th. von Kramer, "Toys," *International Exposition St. Louis 1904. Official Catalogue of the Exhibition of the German Empire*, trans. G. E. Maberly-Oppler (Berlin: Imperial Commissioner, 1904), 218.

51. See Blakely, *Blacks in the Dutch World*, 145.

52. Nissenbaum, *Battle for Christmas*, 96.

53. Ibid., 99.

CHAPTER 5

1. Agamben, *Homo Sacer*, 36.

2. Truettner, *West as America*.

3. Zantop, *Colonial Fantasies*, 2.

4. See Ganaway, *Toys, Consumption, and Middle-Class*; Hamlin, *Work and Play*; and Bowersox, *Raising Germans*.

5. Penny, *Objects of Culture*, 17.

6. Hamlin, *Work and Play*, 5.

7. Ibid., 8.

8. Weikle-Mills, *Imaginary Citizens*, 1.

9. Ibid., 6.

10. Quoted in Hirschmann, *Guckkasten Bilder*.

11. The brief entry in the *Deutsches Literatur-Lexikon* (7: 1249) does not include the year of her death.

12. Busch, *Max und Moritz*, 4–18.

13. See Pataky, *Lexikon deutscher Frauen*, 359–60. Accessed online at http://www.zeno.org/nid/20009048812.
14. Parenthetical citations in this section refer to Hirschmann, *Guckkasten Bilder*.
15. Barthes, "Plastic," 97.
16. Beckert, *Empire of Cotton*, xx.
17. Ibid., 23–25.
18. Ibid., 135.
19. Ibid., 138–39.
20. Buck-Morss, *Hegel, Haiti, and Universal History*, 102.
21. Beckert, *Empire of Cotton*, 243.
22. Ibid., 248.
23. Ibid., 355–56.
24. Bruck, "Cotton Industry in Germany," 99.
25. Hirschmann, *Guckkasten Bilder*, 14.
26. Bowersox, *Raising Germans*, 2.
27. Hirschmann, *Guckkasten Bilder*, 367.
28. Thomas More, quoted in Tucker, "Child as Beginning and End," 251–52.
29. Austin, *How to Do Things with Words*.
30. Butler, *Gender Trouble*.
31. Chakkalakal, *Die Welt in Bildern*.
32. Julius Lohmeyer was editor from 1899–1900; Georg Bötticher edited from 1901–1918. Despite the personnel shifts, the content adhered to the popular format, though, as I argue, contemporary events exerted influence on the narratives and images.
33. Tenberg, "Bötticher, Georg."
34. Helmar, *Vom Urwald zur Kultur*, 1:70.
35. Helmar, "Die kleine Urwälderin," 69.
36. Ibid., 70.
37. Bowersox, *Raising Germans*, 124.
38. Schäffer, *Brasilien als unabhängiges Reich*, especially 304–6.
39. Penny, *Objects of Culture*, 1.
40. Bowersox, *Raising Germans*, 49.
41. Ibid., 132.
42. Helmar, "Die kleine Urwälderin," 69.
43. Ibid.
44. Ibid., 70.
45. Cassidy, "Germanness, Civilization, and Slavery," 28.
46. Obermeier, *Brasilien*, 7.
47. Ibid., 37.
48. Ibid., 132.
49. Ibid.
50. Wildenthal, *German Women for Empire*, 1–2.
51. Ciarlo, *Advertising Empire*, 4.
52. Obermeier, *Brasilien*, 70.
53. Helmar, "Die kleine Urwälderin," 70.
54. Ibid., 71.
55. Helmar, "Die Giraffe."
56. Helmar, "Die kleine Urwälderin," 71.
57. *Deutscher Pionier am Río de la Plata*, Sonntag, den 30. November, 1879, Nr. 143, 2 Jahrgang, 2.
58. Benjamin, "Cultural History of Toys," 115.
59. Helmar, "Die kleine Urwälderin," 73.
60. Ibid.
61. See Auslander, "Beyond Words," 1017.
62. Helmar, "Die kleine Urwälderin," 73.
63. Ibid., 74.
64. In *Vom Urwald zur Kultur*, Anni and Caschumka journey to Germany with Herr Villinger and Anni's husband.
65. Françozo, "Beyond the Kunstkammer," 121.
66. Ibid., 113.
67. See Fiorentino, "Those Red-Brick Faces."
68. Ibid., 404.

69. Bowersox focuses on the contrasts between two periodicals, the specifics of the Brazil story are not rehearsed. See *Raising Germans* 136.

70. Helmar, "Die kleine Urwälderin," 74.

71. All translations from German, unless otherwise indicated, are my own.

72. Löher, *Land und*, 3:174–75.

73. Löher, "Ein Besuch bei den Indianern," 574.

74. Penny, *Kindred by Choice*, 20.

75. Florentino, "Those Red-Brick," 403.

76. Stetler, "Buffalo Bill's Wild West in Germany," 145.

77. On racial classification and images, see Chakkalakal, *Die Welt in Bildern*, 71. Though she focuses on the racial hierarchies of Blumenach and others in images from the long eighteenth century, these continue to exert considerable control over the optics of race in literature directed at children beyond that time period in intractable ways.

78. "Eine Indianergeschichte," 90.

79. Ibid., 93.

80. Penny, *Kindred by Choice*, 32.

81. At this site, two experts identify an Indian doll ca. 1900 as the work of Armand Marseile, Sonneberg. http://www.br.de/fernsehen/bayer isches-fernsehen/sendungen/kunstund krempel/schatzkammer/spielzeug /kunst-krempel-indianer-puppe-100 .html.

82. The scholarship on the function of these dolls is significant but beyond the scope of my study. See Wallace-Sanders, *Mammy*, 34–35.

83. On multifaced dolls, which also changed facial expressions, not only color and race, see Herlocher, *200 Years of Dolls*, 254–55; on ethnic (character) dolls and their awakening of "interest for the exotic," see 144; on vintage folk dolls and the "Topsy" doll, see 91. This volume is a catalogue of prices and traits for the collector, and as such is extremely informative about the history of individual manufacturers, but not a source for the context of play or the social implications of the objects.

84. Quoted in Petra Lambeck, "Max and Moritz: How Germany's Naughtiest Boys Rose to Global Fame." *DW Online*, 27 October 2015. https://p.dw.com/p /1GuyG.

CHAPTER 6

1. Marenholtz-Bülow, *How Kindergarten Came to America*, 3.

2. Allen, *Transatlantic Kindergarten*, especially 85–86 on women and public culture.

3. Gehrke-Riedlin, "Das Kinderzimmer im deutschsprachigen Raum," 40.

4. Hoke, *Fritz Uhdes "Die Kinderstube"*; on furnishing, see 197; on girls' clothing, see 234–38; on the governess, see 197. For material and architectural structures of the "Kinderstube" from an historical perspective, see Weber-Kellermann, *Die Kindheit: Eine Kulturgeschichte*.

5. On Fröbel's work, see Liebschner, *Child's Work*.

6. Huizinga, *Homo Ludens*, 2.

7. Wortham, *Childhood*, 22–23.

8. For a brief summary of Hildebrandt's life, see https://www.museum -digital.de/hu/portal/index.php?t=ob jekt&oges=185429&navlang=en.

9. Hildebrandt, *Das Spielzeug im Leben des Kindes*, 4.

10. See my discussion in the previous chapter.

11. Kinchin and O'Connor, *Century of the Child*, 30.

12. Steiger's focus on the mechanics of the pedagogy and play practices sets his project outside of Allen's; though Steiger notes the professionalization of women, he eschews the topic of political emancipation.

13. Friedrich Fröbel, quoted in Steiger, *Der Kindergarten in Amerika*, 11.

14. Parenthetical citations in this section refer to Steiger, *Der Kindergarten in Amerika*, 4. For the source material contained in the note, see Bühlmann, *Friedrich Fröbel und der Kindergarten*; also Köhler, *Der Kindergarten in seinem Wesen dargestellt*. In the discussion of this composite text, I refer to a singular author/editor.

15. *Steiger's Educational Directory for 1878* (New York: E. Steiger, 1878), 131.

16. For an incisive article, see Richards-Wilson, "German Social Entrepreneurs."

17. See a brief biography at https://mki.wisc.edu/library/catalog/deutsch-englisches-liederbuch-fuer-deutsche-schulen-den-vereinigten-staaten-von.

18. On Margarete Schurz, and her introduction to Elizabeth Peabody, see Allen, *Transatlantic Kindergarten*, 49–50.

19. Ernst Steiger published this text but did not claim authorship. The text itself, which relies heavily on references to other proponents of the kindergarten, appears to have been written by Steiger, but that remains speculation.

20. Steiger's brochure rehearses the entire list of activities and skills encouraged and exercised in the kindergarten curriculum:
   1. Übungen des Körpers durch Bewegungs- und Ballspiele (physical exercises through movement and ball play)
   2. Das Bauen (building)
   3. Das Legen verschiedenfarbiger Täfelchen, welche geometrische Flächen darstellen (assembling different tablets with geometric shapes)
   4. Das Verschränken von Spänen (interlacing shavings)
   5. Das Stäbchenlegen (laying sticks)
   6. Das Kreislegespiel (circular placement game)
   7. Die Erbsenarbeiten (work with peas)
   8. Das Zeichnen (drawing)
   9. Das Falten (folding)
   10. Das Ausstechen und Ausnähen (cutting out and sewing)
   11. Das Verschnüren (lacing)
   12. Das Flechten (braiding)
   13. Das Modelliren (modeling)
   14. Das Ausschneiden (cutting out)

The text notes that activities thought of as "play" with objects should in general be varied with song and discussion. Steiger, *Der Kindergarten in Amerika*, 14–22.

21. Ibid., 24:

Man braucht nicht einmal an das deutsche Nationalgefühl Berufung einzulegen, um diesen unnöthigen Verlust, wenn er der deutschen Sprache droht, abzuwenden; als amerikanische Bürger haben wir die Pflicht, unsere deutsche Literatur zum Gemeingute der Nation machen zu helfen, um deren Geist zu bereichern, ihre weltbürgerliche Bestimmung jedem Bürger dieses Landes zugänglich zu machen.

One does not even have to appeal to German national feeling in order to avert this unnesnary loss if it threatens the German language; as American citizens we have the duty to help make our German literature the public good of the nation, to enrich its spirit, to make its cosmopolitan destiny accessible to every citizen of this country.

22. Parenthetical citations in this section refer to Steiger, *Der Kindergarten in Amerika*.

23. Shirreff's work does not fall into the purview of Allen's study, though the involvement of Peabody, who becomes a champion of the kindergarten, demonstrates the strength of the core group of kindergarten activists in the United States (*Essays and Lectures on the Kindergarten*, 50–55; 137–40).

24. Parenthetical citations in this section refer to Shirreff, *Essays and Lectures on the Kindergarten*.

25. Key, *Century of the Child*, 220 and 181.

26. Ibid., 168–70 and 263.

27. Elizabeth P. Peabody, in Shirreff, *Essays and Lectures on the Kindergarten*, 177.

28. Ibid., 187.

29. Steiger, *Der Kindergarten in Amerika*, 14.

30. Key, *Century of the Child*, 198. On eugenics and Key's consideration of Francis Galton's *Hereditary Genius*, see 20–24.

31. Hamlin, *Work and Play*, 64.

32. The development and gradual refinement of the "All Wood Perfection Art Doll" is generally regarded as the Schoenhut Company's most significant contribution to the history of toy production. Schoenhut et al., *Forty Years of Toy Making*, 18.

CHAPTER 7

1. Hamlin, *Work and Play*, 64.
2. Ibid., 78, 86, and 92.
3. Bowersox, *Raising Germans*, 3.
4. Ibid., 17.
5. Some inaccuracies persist in records of Schoenhut's life. The Germany Emigration Index lists an A. Schoenhut birthdate as 2 May 1848, whereas US passport application records suggest 5 February 1849. According to an authoritative (as yet unpublished) genealogy, Albert Schoenhut was born 5 February 1849 in Göppingen; he died 12 May 1912 in Philadelphia. I thank Dr. Karl-Heinz Ruess for the reference and for sharing an unpublished copy of his genealogy of Schoenhut.

6. Eriksson, "Joy Is in the Playing," 21.

7. A reference to Schoenhut's Philadelphia neighborhood. See Julia M. Klein, "A Look at Intricate Old Toys and a Venerable Phila. Firm," *The Philadelphia Inquirer*, 18 April 1995.

8. Hamlin, *Work and Play*, 99.

9. Manos, *Schoenhut Dolls and Toys*, 11–13.

10. See "Early 19th Century Schoenhut Toy Piano—For Sale," http://www.antiques.com/classified/Music---Instruments/AntiqueMusical-Instruments/Antique-Early-19th-Century-Schoenhut-Toy-Piano. For instance, according to one legend, after a young Albert Schoenhut fashioned a toy piano for his landlord's daughter, word spread of the beautiful little instrument, requests poured in, and the Schoenhut Piano Company came into being." Another version of the Schoenhut story suggests that he was "erfolglos" (unsuccessful) at home as a woodworker and decided to seek a fresh start abroad. See "Göppingens Aufstieg zum Spielzeug-Zentrum."

11. See https://www.findagrave.com/memorial/87164468. See also Manos, *Schoenhut Dolls and Toys*,

9, and "Upright Piano, c. 1900," Strong National Museum of Play, https://artsandculture.google.com/asset/pianoupright-piano/qAHbyOioiLjhRw. Another account places his first job at John Deiser & Sons in Philadelphia. See O'Brien, *Story of American Toys*, 73.

12. One document from the Superior Court of New York County lists 1 October 1868 as the date of naturalization, whereas another source, from the Quarter Session Court of Philadelphia, records the date 25 September 1873. Ancestry.com, http://trees.ancestry.com/tree/61938151/person/32077568202/print.

13. U.S. Commissioner of Patents, Annual Report, 1 January 1893, vol. 3066, 422.

14. The 1880 census, for example, listed 173 toy manufacturers; twenty years later, as Richard O'Brien has observed, that number had jumped to 500. O'Brien provides further evidence of the toy industry's growth by referencing the publication of the monthly magazine *Playthings* (1903). Schoenhut ran advertisements in the second edition. See O'Brien, *Story of American Toys*, 53.

15. Cross, *Kids' Stuff*, 37.

16. Ackerman, *Under the Big Top*, 3.

17. See O'Brien, *Story of American Toys*, 74. The $100 sum is equivalent to approximately $2,990 in 2020. All current values (in 2020 USD) are based on Samuel H. Williamson, "Seven Ways to Compute the Relative Value of a U.S. Dollar Amount, 1774 to present," MeasuringWorth.com, using the Consumer Price Index.

18. Ackerman, *Under the Big Top*, 3.

19. "Humpty Dumpty Circus, play set, c. 1920," Strong National Museum of Play, https://artsandculture.google.com/asset/play-set-humpty-dumpty-circus/KQHe64ClfuF-Tg.

20. Cook, *Colossal P. T. Barnum Reader*, 1.

21. Saxon, *American Theatre*, 114. Saxon also explores the emerging boundaries involving race, class, and gender in the theater more generally.

22. Ibid., 115.

23. Ibid., 115.

24. Hamlin, *Work and Play*, 68.

25. Ibid., 73.

26. Ames, *Carl Hagenbeck's Empire of Entertainments*, 4.

27. Ibid., 15.

28. Ibid.

29. Moses, *Wild West Shows*, 5.

30. Ames, *Carl Hagenbeck's Empire of Entertainments*, 4.

31. "Schoenhut's Humpty Dumpty Circus and the Great American Circus," http://www.oldwoodtoys.com/schoenhut.htm.

32. Schoenhut, "At Schoenhut's Toy Humpty Dumpty Circus," under the title "Schoenhut's Humpty Dumpty Circus Toys," Schoenhut Company Catalogue, 1928, 3. https://s90001.eos-intl.net/S90001/OPAC/Details/Record.aspx?BibCode=432736.

33. Ibid.

34. Ibid.

35. Ibid., 10.

36. Ibid., 11.

37. Ibid. 31. This image is reproduced in other catalogues and trade sheets as well.

38. Ibid., 2.

39. See Manos, *Schoenhut Dolls and Toys*, for commentary on this transition. "Albert Schoenhut left a Germany that was feudal by demand and nature in its outlook and discipline. Because of his early training and background, he too demanded respect and no questions

from his children. His organization was run as tightly as a smoothly operated military machine and each son entered the business at posts designated by their father. He was the patriarch, the ruler, the head of the family and business" (9).

40. During the war, the Schoenhuts presented themselves not only as an American firm but as one that supported the US war effort. In the 4 June 1918 issue of the *Evening Public Ledger* (Philadelphia), A. Schoenhut & Sons was listed in the War Chest Honor Role announcement in the 90 percent category. The laudatory prose read: "Every giver who has done his or her utmost should be on the War Chest Honor Role. Space will not permit the publication of the full list, and therefore the Committee has decided to confine the record in the public press to the industries whose employes [sic] have reached the splendid standard of 90% or more." *Evening Public Ledger* (Philadelphia), 4 June 1918, 9.

41. Ibid.

42. Schoenhut advertisement in the *Ladies' Home Journal* (December 1918), 5; see fig. 41 in this volume.

43. Schoenhut advertisement in the *Ladies' Home Journal* (November 1919), 48. https://artsandculture.google.com/asset/advertisement-schoenhut-toys-american-ingenuity-and-invention/fwG-8RdvbHtokw.

44. Saxton, "Blackface Minstrelsy and Jacksonian Ideology," 114–15.

45. Ibid., 138. See also Lott, "Commentary," 141, where Lott highlights this resonant quotation.

46. Saxton, "Blackface Minstrelsy and Jacksonian Ideology," 138.

47. Ibid., 139.

48. Davis, "Moral, Purposeful, and Healthful," 55.

49. "Smithsonian Roosevelt African Expedition (1909)," https://www.si.edu/object/auth_exp_fbr_EACE0006.

50. Frederick Jackson Turner, "The Significance of the Frontier in American History," A paper read at the meeting of the American Historical Association in Chicago, 12 July 1893, during the World Columbian Expedition. http://nationalhumanitiescenter.org/pds/gilded/empire/text1/turner.pdf.

51. From Schoenhut et al., *Forty Years of Toy Making*. The document, located in the collection of the Historical Society of Pennsylvania, is marked as a gift of George W. Schoenhut to the Historical Society of Pennsylvania. The date typed in indicates 15 October 1969.

52. Parenthetical citations in this section refer to Schoenhut et al., *Forty Years of Toy Making*.

53. See Gutman and de Coninck-Smith, *Designing Modern Childhoods*, especially their introductory section on "The Islanding of Contemporary Childhood," 5–7. John R. Gillis contributes the illuminating epilogue to this volume, on "The Islanding of Children—Reshaping the Mythical Landscapes of Childhood," 316–30.

54. In McGlynn, *Families and the European Union*, 27, quoting Lee's 2001 *Childhood and Society: Growing Up In an Age of Uncertainty*.

55. Realism, both as a literary and artistic mode of representation, dominated the nineteenth-century aesthetic. The novels of Charles Dickens, Leo Tolstoy, and Theodor Fontane segued into the technical advances in photography and film. Theorists from Georg Lukács, Walter Benjamin, and, more recently, Fredric Jameson and Jean Baudrillard have alerted us to the truth and fiction of realism as an articulation of objectivity.

56. The article and image are located in the Historical Society of Pennsylvania's archive. They are catalogued in a folio with the general dates 1937–46. Though the record is undated, the placement in the folder indicates that this piece was published in 1937.

57. The events I refer to here, the ball game and the Safety Day exercises, are only two examples of Germantown Boys Club activities. At least one other article (undated) in the same folder indicates that girls sometimes were invited to participate. It recounts the events of the "Little Sister Contest" sponsored by the club. Other reported activities include a Tom Thumb Wedding and images of boys with their pets.

58. Dummig, "Fancy Articles, Toys, and Musical Instruments," document in the Historical Society of Pennsylvania archives.

59. Ibid., 1.

60. "Toys, Yes, Plenty of Them, To Make Merry Christmas," *Evening Ledger* (Philadelphia), 23 November 1914, 3. It is worth noting that an adjacent article appeared under the headline "Pittsburgh Steel Expert Trailed by German Spies."

61. A. Schoenhut, "Schoenhut's Illustrated Catalogue, "Schoenhut's Concentration and Manipulative Toys for the Nursery and Kindergarten," cover copy, 1930. The Strong National Museum of Play. The author of the statement, Murza Mann Lauder, was born in 1899, and, according to the *Michigan Alumnus* (1984), died in 1983.

62. A. Schoenhut Company, "Schoenhut's Illustrated Catalogue" (1930), 42. The Strong National Museum of Play.

63. See Cross, *Kids' Stuff*, 42.

64. "Schoenhut Sales-Sample Doll, doll, 1911," Strong National Museum of Play, https://artsandculture.google.com/asset/sales-sample-doll-schoenhut-sales-sample-doll-the-a-schoenhut-co/WAFLnUycs8sFKA.

65. Schoenhut et al., *Forty Years of Toy Making*, 23–24.

CONCLUSION

1. "A Very Brilliant House," unsigned review of Metropolitan Opera House Gala Night Performance, *New York Herald*, 24 April 1896.

2. Schoenhut et al., *Forty Years of Toy Making*.

3. Gutman and de Coninck-Smith, *Designing Modern Childhood*.

4. *San Francisco Call*, 7 February 1910, 8.

5. Abbott, *Sugar*, 336.

6. Ibid., 336.

7. Spiekermann, "Claus Spreckels," 2011.

8. Ibid.

9. *Das Goethe-Schiller Denkmal in San Francisco*. An image of Claus Spreckels is included (13).

10. Wulf, *Invention of Nature*, 38.

11. "Die Zuckerfee," in Helmar, *Märchenschatz*, 3–4.

12. Tsanoff, *Educational Value of the Children's Playgrounds*.

13. Ibid., 65–66.

14. Ibid., 42–43.

15. *Evening Ledger* (Philadelphia), 23 November 1914, 3.

16. This is the title of Hamlin's third chapter in *Work and Play*, 103.

17. *Ladies Home Journal*, December 2018, no page.

18. Historical Society of Pennsylvania, Advertisement in the Campbell Collection, v. 26: 197.

19. For a sustained and brilliant reading of the Olympic event in Berlin from the perspective of history and sports, see Large, *Nazi Games*.

Bibliography

Abbott, Elizabeth. *Sugar: A Bittersweet History*. New York: Overlook, 2010.

Ackerman, Evelyn. *Under the Big Top with Schoenhut's Humpty Dumpty Circus*. Annapolis, MD: Gold Horse, 1996.

Agamben, Giorgio. *Homo Sacer: Sovereign Power and Bare Life*. Translated by Daniel Heller-Roazen. Stanford: Stanford University Press, 1998.

Allen, Ann Taylor. *The Transatlantic Kindergarten: Education and Women's Movements in Germany and the United States*. New York: Oxford University Press, 2017.

Ames, Eric. *Carl Hagenbeck's Empire of Entertainments*. Seattle: University of Washington Press, 2008.

Appadurai, Arjun, ed. *The Social Life of Things: Commodities in Cultural Perspective*. Cambridge: Cambridge University Press, 1988.

Ariès, Philippe. *Centuries of Childhood: A Social History of Family Life*. Translated by Robert Baldick. New York: Vintage Books, 1962.

Arnold, Klaus. "Familie—Kindheit—Jugend." In *Handbuch der deutschen Bildungsgeschichte*. Vol. 1, 15. Bis 17. Jahrhundert: Von der Renaissance und der Reformation bis zum Ende der Glaubenskämpfe, edited by Notker Hammerstein with August Buck, 135–52. Munich: Beck, 1996.

Auerbach, Aug. Berth, ed. *Auerbach's Deutscher Kinder-Kalender auf das Jahr 1889*. Leipzig: Fernau Verlag, 1889.

Auslander, Leora. "Beyond Words." *American Historical Review* 110, no. 4 (October 2005): 1015–45.

Austin, J. L. *How to Do Things with Words*. Cambridge, MA: Harvard University Press, 1962.

Averett, Matthew Knox, ed. *The Early Modern Child in Art and History*. London: Routledge, 2015.

Barth, Susanne. "Jacobs, (Christian) Friedrich (Wilhelm)." In *Literaturlexikon: Autoren und Werke deutscher Sprache*, ed. by Walther Killy et al., vol. 6, 60. Munich: Bertelsmann, 1990.

Barthes, Roland. "Plastic." In *Mythologies*, 97–99. Translated by Annette Lavers. New York: Farrar, Straus and Giroux, 1972.

Becker-Cantorino, Barbara. "Witch and Infanticide: Imaging the Female in Faust I." *Goethe Yearbook* 7 (1994): 1–22.

Beckert, Sven. *Empire of Cotton: A Global History*. New York: Knopf, 2014.

Benjamin, Walter. "Altes Spielzeug: Zur Spielzeugausstellung des Märkischen Museums." In *Gesammelte Schriften*, edited by Rolf Tiedemann and Hermann Schweppenhäuser, 4.1:511–15. Frankfurt am Main: Suhrkamp, 1991.

———. "The Cultural History of Toys." In *Selected Writings*, vol. 2, *1927–1934*, edited by Michael W. Jennings, Howard Eiland, and Gary Smith, translated by Rodney Livingstone et al., 113–16. Cambridge, MA: Harvard University Press, 1999.

———. "Kulturgeschichte des Spielzeuges." In *Gesammelte Schriften*, edited by Rolf Tiedemann and Hermann Schweppenhäuser, 3:113–17. Frankfurt am Main: Suhrkamp, 1991.

———. "Marginal Notes on a Monumental Work." In *Selected Writings*, vol. 2, *1927–1934*, edited by Michael W. Jennings, Howard Eiland, and Gary Smith, translated by Rodney Livingstone et al., 117–21. Cambridge, MA: Harvard University Press, 1999.

———. "Randbemerkungen zu einem Monumentalwerk." In *Gesammelte Schriften*, edited by Rolf Tiedemann and Hermann Schweppenhäuser, 3:127–32. Frankfurt am Main: Suhrkamp, 1991.

———. "The Toy Exhibition at the Märkisches Museum." In *Selected Writings*, vol. 2, *1927–1934*, edited by Michael W. Jennings, Howard Eiland, and Gary Smith, translated by Rodney Livingstone et al., 98–102. Cambridge, MA: Harvard University Press, 1999.

Berman, Russell A. *Enlightenment or Empire: Colonial Discourse in German Culture*. Lincoln: University of Nebraska Press, 1998.

Bertaux, Pierre. "'Gar schöne Spiele spiel' ich mit dir!" In *Zu Goethes Spieltrieb*. Frankfurt am Main: Insel, 1986.

Biesanz, John, and Mavis Biseanz. "The School and the Youth Hostel." *Journal of Educational Sociology* 15, no. 1 (September 1944): 55–60.

Bitterli, Urs. *Cultures in Conflict: Encounters Between European and Non-European Cultures, 1492–1800*. Translated by Ritchie Robertson. Stanford: Stanford University Press, 1989. First published in German 1986; translation Polity Press, 1989.

———. *Die "Wilden" und die "Zivilisierten": Grundzüge einer Geistes- und Kulturgeschichte der europäisch-überseeischen Begegnung*. 3rd ed. Munich: C. H. Beck, 2004.

Blakely, Allison. *Blacks in the Dutch World: The Evolution of Racial Imagery in a Modern Society*. Bloomington: Indiana University Press, 1993.

Böhm, Elisabeth. "Epoche Machen. Goethes Konstruktion der Weimarer Klassik zwischen 1786 und 1796." PhD diss., University of Bayreuth, 2010.

Bötticher, Georg, ed. *Auerbach's Deutscher Kinder-Kalender auf das Jahr 1902: Eine Festgabe für Knaben und Mädchen jeden Alters*. Leipzig: Fernau, 1902.

———. *Auerbach's Deutscher Kinder-Kalender auf das Jahr 1904: Eine Festgabe für Knaben und Mädchen jeden Alters*. Leipzig: Fernau, 1904.

———. *Auerbach's Deutscher Kinder-Kalender auf das Jahr 1905: Eine Festgabe für Knaben und Mädchen jeden Alters*. Leipzig: Fernau, 1905.

Bowersox, Jeff. *Raising Germans in the Age of Empire: Youth and Colonial Culture, 1871–1914*. Oxford: Oxford University Press, 2013.

Boyle, Nicholas, and John Guthrie, eds. *Goethe and the English-Speaking World: Essays from the Cambridge Symposium for His*

250th Anniversary. Rochester, NY: Camden House, 2002.

———. "Introduction: Goethe and England; England and Goethe." In Goethe and the English-Speaking World: Essays from the Cambridge Symposium for His 250th Anniversary, 1–17. Rochester, NY: Camden House, 2002.

Brookshaw, Sharon. "The Material Culture of Children and Childhood: Understanding Childhood Objects in the Museum Context." Journal of Material Culture 14, no. 3 (2009): 365–83.

Browne, Richard J., and M. C. Davis. "Goethe and the Yo-Yo." Modern Language Quarterly (March 1953): 98–101.

Bruck, W. F. "The Cotton Industry in Germany." Translated by George F. Cole. Annals of the American Academy of Political and Social Science 92, no. 1 (November 1920): 99–105.

Buck-Morss, Susan. Hegel, Haiti, and University History. Pittsburgh: University of Pittsburgh Press, 2009.

Bühlmann, Joseph. Friedrich Fröbel und der Kindergarten. Frauenfeld: J. Huber Verlag, 1871.

Busch, Wilhelm. Max und Moritz. Eine Bubengeschichte in sieben Streichen. Munich: Verlag von Braun und Schneider, 1925.

Butler, Judith. Gender Trouble: Feminism and the Subversion of Identity. London: Routledge, 1990.

Cadogan, William. "An Essay upon Nursing and the Management of Children, from Their Birth to Three Years of Age." London. 1772.

Caillois, Roger. Man, Play and Games. Translated by Meyer Barash. Urbana: University of Illinois Press, 2001. Les jeux et les hommes. Paris: Gallimard, 1958. English translation The Free Press, a division of Simon and Schuster, 1961.

Campe, Johann Heinrich, ed. Kleine Kinderbibliothek. Volume 1. 15th ed. Braunschweig: 1815.

———. Robinson der Jüngere: Ein Lesebuch für Kinder. 28th ed. Braunschweig: Verlag der Schulbuchhandlung, 1837.

Cassidy, Eugene S. "Germanness, Civilization, and Slavery: Southern Brazil as German Colonial Space." PhD diss., University of Michigan, 2015.

Chakkalakal, Silvy. Die Welt in Bildern: Erfahrung und Evidenz in Friedrich J. Bertuchs "Bilderbuch für Kinder" (1790–1830). Göttingen: Wallstein, 2014.

Chapman, Rachel. "A Case Study of Gendered Play in Preschools: How Early Childhood Educators' Perceptions of Gender Influence Children's Play." Early Childhood Development and Care 186, no. 8 (2016): 1271–84.

Charles, Victoria, and Klaus H. Carl. Rococo. New York: Parkstone International, 2010. eBook Collection (EBSCOhost), EBSCOhost.

Ciarlo, David. Advertising Empire: Race and Visual Culture in Imperial Germany. Cambridge, MA: Harvard University Press, 2011.

Clifford, Bridget, and Karen Watts. An Introduction to Princely Armours and Weapons of Childhood. Leeds: Royal Armouries Museum, 2003.

Coffman, D'Maris, Adrian Leonard, and William O'Reilly. The Atlantic World. London: Routledge, 2015.

Cohen, Margaret. Sentimental Education of the Novel. Princeton: Princeton University Press, 1999.

Colomer, Teresa, Bettina Kümmerling-Meibauer, and Cecilia Silva-Díaz, eds. New Directions in

Picturebook Research. New York: Routledge, 2010.

Cook, James W., ed. *The Colossal P. T. Barnum Reader: Nothing Else Like It in the Universe*. Urbana: University of Illinois Press, 2005.

Crenshaw, Kimberle. "Mapping the Margins: Intersectionality, Identity Politics, and Violence against Women of Color." In *Violence Against Women: Classic Papers*, edited by Raquel Kennedy Bergen, Jeffrey L. Edleson, and Claire M. Renzetti, 93–118. Boston: Pearson, 2005 (1989).

Cross, Gary. *Kid's Stuff: Toys and the Changing World of American Childhood*. Cambridge, MA: Harvard University Press, 1997.

Davis, Janet M. "Moral, Purposeful, and Healthful: The World of Child's Play, Bodybuilding, and Nation Building at the American Circus." In *Body and Nation: The Global Realm of U.S. Body Politics*, edited by Emily S. Rosenberg and Shanon Fitzpatrick, 42-60. Durham: Duke University Press, 2014.

Davis, Natalie Zemon. *Women on the Margins: Three Seventeenth-Century Lives*. Cambridge, MA: Harvard University Press, 1991.

Deleuze, Giles, and Felix Guattari. *Anti-Oedipus: Capitalism and Schizophrenia*. Translated by Robert Hurley, Mark Seem, and Helen R. Lane. Minneapolis: University of Minnesota Press, 1983.

DeMause, Lloyd, ed. *The History of Childhood*. New York: Psychohistory Press, 1974.

Deutscher Literatur-Lexikon: Biographisch-Bibliographisches Handbuch. Vol. 8, HOHBERG-BER. Edited by Heinz Rupp and Carl Ludwig Lang. 38 volumes. Bern: Francke Verlag, 1981.

Deutsches Literatur-Lexikon: Biographisch-Bibliographisches Handbuch. Edited by Bruno Berger and Heinz Zimmermann. 38 volumes. Berlin: De Gruyter, 1968.

Dickason, Jerry G. "Playground Movement." In *Encyclopedia of Children and Childhood: In History and Society*. http://www.faqs.org/childhood/Pa-Re/Playground-Movement.html.

Dummig, Charles. "Fancy Articles, Toys, and Musical Instruments." Historical Society of Pennsylvania, 1864.

Dyhrenfurth-Graebsch, Irene. *Geschichte des deutschen Jugendbuches*. Hamburg: Verlag Eberhard Stichnote, 1951.

Emmerling, Ernst. *Johann Conrad Seekatz 1719–1768: Ein Maler aus der Zeit des jungen Goethe. Leben und Werk*. Revised by Brigitte Rechberg and Horst Wilhelm. Landau/Pfalz: Edition PVA, 1991.

Engelstein, Stepanie. *Anxious Anatomy: The Conception of the Human Form in Literary and Naturalist Discourse*. Albany: State University of New York Press, 2008.

Eriksson, Eric Zwang. "The Joy Is in the Playing: Die Erfolgsstory des Toy Piano." *Neue Zeitschrift für Musik* 160, no. 2 (March/April 1999): 20–23.

Fiorentino, Daniele. "'Those Red-Brick Faces': European Press Reactions to the Indians of Buffalo Bill's Wild West Shows." In *Indians and Europe: An Interdisciplinary Collection of Essays*, edited by Christian F. Feest, 403–14. Lincoln: University of Nebraska Press, 1989.

Fooken, Insa, with Robin Lohmann. *Puppen—heimliche Menschenflüsterer: Ihre Wiederentdeckung als Spielzeug und Kulturgut*. Göttingen: Vandenhoeck & Ruprecht, 2012.

Françozo, Mariana. "Beyond the Kunstkammer: Brazilian Featherwork in Early Modern Europe." In *The Global Lives of Things: The Material Culture of Connections in the Early Modern World*, edited by Anne Gerritsen and Giorgio Riello, 105–27. London: Routledge, 2016.

Freud, Sigmund. *Beyond the Pleasure Principle*. Vol. 18 of *The Complete Psychological Works of Sigmund Freud*. New York: Norton, 1976.

Friedrichsmeyer, Sara, Sara Lennox, and Susanne Zantop. Introduction to *The Imperialist Imagination: German Colonialism and Its Legacy*, edited by Friedrichsmeyer et al. 1–29. Ann Arbor: University of Michigan Press, 1998.

Fröbel, Friedrich. *The Student's Froebel*. Adapted by William H. Herford. Introduced by Professor M. E. Sadler. London: Sir Isaac Pitman & Sons, 1916.

Frost, Joe L., and Barry L. Klein. *Children's Play and Playgrounds*. Boston: Allyn and Bacon, 1979.

———. *A History of Children's Play and Play Environments: Toward a Contemporary Child-Saving Movement*. New York: Routledge, 2010.

Gallagher, Maureen O. "Women and Girls in German Colonial Fiction, 1900–1913." *Women in German Yearbook: Feminist Studies in German Literature and Culture* 32 (2016): 111–37.

Ganaway, Brian. *Toys, Consumption, and Middle-Class Childhood in Imperial Germany, 1871–1918*. Oxford: Peter Lang, 2009.

Gehrke-Riedlin, Renate. "Das Kinderzimmer im deutschsprachigen Raum." PhD diss., University of Göttingen, 2002.

Geiger, Ludwig. *Goethe und die Seinen. Quellenmäßige Darstellungen über Goethes Haus*. Leipzig: R. Voigtlanders Verlag, 1908.

Germershausen, Friedrich Christian. *Der Hausvater in systematischer Ordnung*. Leipzig: Johann Friedrich Junius, 1784.

Germershausen, Friedrich Christian, and Friedrich C. Gericke. *Die Hausmutter in allen ihren Geschäften*. Vol. 1. 4th ed. Hannover: Hahn, 1812.

Gersdorff, Dagmar von. *Goethes Enkel: Walther, Wolfgang und Alma*. Frankfurt am Main: Insel, 2008.

Gillis, John R. "Epilogue: The Islanding of Children—Reshaping the Mythical Landscapes of Childhood." In *Designing Modern Childhood: History, Space and the Material Culture of Children*, edited by Marta Gutman and Ning de Coninck-Smith, 316–30. New Brunswick: Rutgers University Press, 2008.

Goethe, Catharina Elisabeth. *Die Briefe der Frau Rath Goethe*. Edited by Albert Köster. Frankfurt am Main: Insel, 1969.

Goethe, Johann Wolfgang. *Dichtung und Wahrheit, I/II*. Vol. 8 of *Werkausgabe in zehn Bänden*. Cologne: Könemann, 1998.

———. *Erotic Poems*. Translated by David Luke. Introduction by Hans Rudolf Vaget. Oxford: Oxford University Press, 1988.

———. *From My Life: Poetry and Truth*. Parts 1–3. Translated by Robert Heitner and edited by Thomas P. Saine and Jeffrey L. Sammons. Vol. 4 of *Goethe's Collected Works*, edited by Victor Lange, Eric A. Blackall, and Cyrus Hamlin. New York: Suhrkamp, 1983.

———. *Goethes Ehe in Briefen*. Edited by Hans Gerhard Gräf. 2nd ed.

Frankfurt am Main: Rütten & Loening, 1922.

———. *Tagebücher 1775–1804*. Altenmünster: Beck, no date.

Goethe-Schiller Denkmal in San Francisco, California. Erinnerungen an den "Deutschen Tag" der California Midwinter International Exposition 1894, an das "Goethe Schiller Fest" 1895 und an die "Enthüllung des Denkmals in Golden Gate Park 1901." San Francisco: C. Leidecker, 1901.

Goto-Jones, Chris. "The Secret Life of Yo-Yos." *Atlantic*, 9 April 2015. https://www.theatlantic.com/technology/archive/2015/04/the-yo-yo-effect/389868.

Grenby, M. O. "The Origins of Children's Literature." In *The Cambridge Companion to Children's Literature*, edited by M. O. Grenby and Andrea Immel, 3–18. Cambridge : Cambridge University Press, 2009.

Grenby, M. O., and Andrea Immel, eds. *The Cambridge Companion to Children's Literature*. Cambridge: Cambridge University Press, 2009.

Gröber, Karl. *Children's Toys of Bygone Days: A History of Playthings of All Peoples from Prehistoric Times to the XIXth Century*. Translated by Philip Hereford. New York: Frederick A. Stokes, 1928.

Großmann, G. Ulrich. "Vorwort." In Heidi A. Müller, *Ein Idealhaushalt im Miniaturformat: Die Nürnberger Puppenhäuser des 17. Jahrhunderts*, 7–8. Nuremberg: Verlag des Germanischen Nationalmuseums, 2006.

Gustafson, Susan E. *Absent Mother and Orphaned Fathers: Narcissism and Abjection in Lessing's Dramatic Production*. Detroit: Wayne State University Press, 1995.

Gutman, Marta, and Ning de Coninck-Smith, eds. *Designing Modern Childhoods: History, Space, and the Material Culture of Children*. New Brunswick: Rutgers University Press, 2008.

Habermas, Jürgen. *The Structural Transformation of the Public Sphere*. Cambridge, MA: MIT Press, 1989.

Hamlin, David D. *Work and Play: The Production and Consumption of Toys in Germany, 1870–1914*. Ann Arbor: University of Michigan Press, 2007.

Hansen, Volkmar. "Homo ludens—der spielende Mensch. Goethe und das Spiel." In *Homo ludens: Der spielende Mensch*, edited by Volkmar Hansen and Sabine Jung, 32–49. Bonn: Goethe-Museum Düsseldorf, 2003.

Harvey, David. *Spaces of Hope*. Berkeley: University of California Press, 2000.

Heesen, Anke te. *The World in a Box*. Translated by Ann M. Hentschel. Chicago: University of Chicago Press, 2002. Originally published as *Der Weltkasten* (Göttingen: Wallstein Verlag, 1997).

Helmar, W. (Maria Hellemeyer). "Die Giraffe." In *Auerbach's Deutscher Kinder-Kalender auf das Jahr 1902*, edited by Georg Bötticher, 138–40. Leipzig: L. Fernau Verlag, 1902.

———. "Die kleine Urwälderin." Illustrated by Max Loose. In *Auerbachs Deutscher Kinder-kalender auf das Jahr 1902*, edited by Georg Bötticher, 69–74. Leipzig: L. Fernau Verlag, 1902.

———. *Märchenschatz: Neue Märchen*. With five color illustrations by W. Schäfer. Wesel: Verlag von W. Düms, 1893.

———. *Vom Urwald zur Kultur: Erlebnisse eines Mädchens*. 2 vols. Berlin: Verlag von Otto Janke, 1898.
Henricks, Thomas. *Play and the Human Condition*. Urbana: University of Illinois Press, 2015. Ebook collection. EBSCOhost. Accessed 22 January 2018.
Herlocher, Dawn. *200 Years of Dolls*. 2nd ed. Iola, WI: Krause, 2002.
Hexter, Ralph. "Poetic Reclamation and Goethe's Venetian Epigrams." *Modern Language Notes* 96, no. 3 (1981): 526–55.
Heywood, Colin. *A History of Childhood: Children and Childhood in the West from Medieval to Modern Times*. 1st ed. Cambridge: Polity, 2001.
Hildebrandt, Paul. *Das Spielzeug im Leben des Kindes*. Berlin: G. Söhlke Nachf. H. Mehlis, 1904.
Hinds, Hilary. "Prophecy and Religious Polemic." In *The Cambridge Guide to Early Modern Women's Writing*, edited by Laura Lunger Knoppers, 235–46. Cambridge: Cambridge University Press, 2009.
Hirschmann, Julie. *Guckkasten–Bilder: Erzählungen für Kinder 8–16 Jahre*. Berlin: Winckelmann & Söhne, 1862.
Hoke, Sarah. *Fritz Uhdes "Die Kinderstube": Die Darstellung des Kindes in seinem Spiel- und Wohnmilieu*. Göttingen: Universitätsverlag Göttingen, 2011.
Horn, W. O. von. *Ein Kongo-Neger: Eine Geschichte aus Sankt Domingo, der deutschen Jugend und dem Volke erzählt*. Stuttgart: Bardtenschlager, ca. 1900.
Huizinga, Johan. *Homo Ludens: A Study of the Play-Element in Culture*. Boston: Beacon, 1955.
Hüther, Gerald, and Christoph Quarch. *Rettet das Spiel! Weil Leben mehr als Funktionieren ist*. Munich: Carl Hanser Verlag, 2016.
Israel, Jonathan. *Radical Enlightenment: Philosophy and the Making of Modernity 1650–1750*. Oxford: Oxford University Press, 2001.
Jacobs, Friedrich Christian Wilhelm. *Allwin und Theodors: Ein Lesebuch für Kinder*. Part 1. Dritte verbesserte Auflage. 3 vols. Leipzig: Dyk'schen Buchhandlung, 1817.
Jameson, Frederic. *The Political Unconscious: Narrative As a Socially Symbolic Act*. Ithaca: Cornell University Press, 1981.
Kant, Immanuel. *Critique of Judgement*. Translated and analytical indexes by James Creed Meredith. 13th impression. Oxford: Oxford University Press, 2009.
Key, Ellen. *The Century of the Child*. Translated based on German version by Frances Maro. Revised by Ellen Key. New York: G. P. Putnam's Sons / The Knickerbocker Press, 1909.
Kidd, Thomas S. *The Great Awakening: The Roots of Evangelical Christianity in Colonial America*. New Haven: Yale University Press, 2007.
Kinchin, Juliet, and Aidan O'Connor, eds. *Century of the Child: Growing by Design 1900–2000*. New York: Museum of Modern Art, 2012.
Klotz, Marcia. "Introduction." In *Germany's Colonial Pasts*, edited by Eric Ames, Lora Wildenthal, and Marcia Klotz, xi–xxi. Lincoln: University of Nebraska Press, 2005.
Knape, Joachim. "Poetics and Rhetorics in Early Modern Germany." In *Early-Modern German Literature, 1350–1700*, edited by Max Reinhart, 247–80. Rochester, NY: Camden House, 2009.
Knoppers, Laura Lunger, ed. *The Cambridge Guide to Early Modern*

Women's Writing. Cambridge: Cambridge University Press, 2009.

Köhler, August. *Der Kindergarten in seinem Wesen dargestellt: 28 Fragen für Freunde und Gegner desselben*. Weimar: Hermann Böhlau Verlag, 1868.

Kohlmeyer, Otto. *Die Pädagogische Provinz in Wilhelm Meisters Wanderjahren: Ein Beitrag zur Pädagogik Goethes*. Langensalza: Julius Beltz, 1923.

Krimmer, Elisabeth. *The Representation of War in German Literature: From 1800 to the Present*. Cambridge: Cambridge University Press, 2010.

Krimmer, Elisabeth, and Patricia Anne Simpson, eds. *Enlightened War: German Theories and Cultures of Warfare from Frederick the Great to Clausewitz*. Rochester, NY: Camden House, 2011.

Kühme, Dorothea. *Bürger und Spiel: Gesellschaftsspiele im deutschen Bürgertum, 1750–1850*. Frankfurt am Main: Campus Verlag, 1997.

Landrum, Ney C. *The State Park Movement in America: A Critical Review*. Columbia: University of Missouri Press, 2004.

Lange, Horst. "Goethe's Strategy of Self-Censorship: The Case of the Venezianische Epigramme." *Monatshefte* 91, no. 2 (1999): 224–40.

Langer, Robert. *Pallas und ihre Waffen: Wirkungskreise der Henriette Catharina von Gersdorff*. Dresden: Neisse Verlag, 2008.

Large, David Clay. *Nazi Games: The Olympics of 1936*. New York: Norton, 2007.

Lefebvre, Henri. *The Production of Space*. Translated by Donald Nicholson-Smith. Oxford: Blackwell, 1991.

———. *State, Space, World: Selected Essays*. Edited by Neil Brenner and Stuart Elden. Translated by Gerald Moore, Neil Brener, and Stuart Elder. Minneapolis: University of Minnesota Press, 2009.

Levine, Robert A. "Ethnographic Studies of Childhood: A Historical Overview." *American Anthropologist* 109, no. 2 (2007): 247–60.

Liebschner, Joachim. *A Child's Work: Freedom and Guidance in Froebel's Educational Theory and Practice*. Cambridge: Lutterworth, 2006.

Lieder, Frederick W. C. "Goethe in England and America." *Journal of English and Germanic Philology* 10, no. 4 (October 1911): 535–56.

Lloyd, Clive L. *The Arts and Crafts of Napoleonic and American Prisoners of War, 1756–1816*. Woodbridge, UK: Antique Collectors Club, 2007.

Locke, John. "Some Thoughts Concerning Education." In *The Works of John Locke*. Vol. 8. London: Rivington, 1824. 12th ed. https://oll.liberty fund.org/titles/1725.

Löffler, Friederike Luise, et al. *Oekonomisches Handbuch fuer Frauenzimmer: Anweisung zu Frauenzimmer-Arbeiten zur Behandlung von Haushaltungs-Sachen und zur Körper-Schönheitspflege. Nebst einer Anleitung zur Bereitung von Speisen und Getränken für Kränke, und zur Anwendung von Haus-Mitteln*. Vol. 2. 4th ed. Stuttgart: Steinkopf, 1826.

Löher, Franz. "Ein Besuch bei den Indianern in Nordamerika." *Deutsches Museum: Zeitschrift für Kunst, Literatur und öffentliches Leben* 8. Jahrgang. Edited by Robert Pruß, 570–78. Leipzig: Brockhaus, 1858.

———. *Land und Leute in der alten und neuen Welt*. 3 vols. Göttingen: Georg H. Wigand, 1857–1858, 1860.

Lott, Eric. "Commentary." In *Locating American Studies: The Evolution of a Discipline, edited by Lucy Maddox, 140–42. Baltimore: The Johns Hopkins University Press, 1999.

MacCann, Donnarae. *White Supremacy in Children's Literature: Characterizations of African Americans, 1830–1900*. New York: Garland, 1998.

Maché, Ulrich. "Gersdorf, Henriette Catharina Freifrau von." In *Literaturlexikon: Autoren und Werke deutscher Sprache*, edited by Walther Killy et al., vol. 4, 139–40. Munich: Bertelsmann, 1989.

Maisak, Petra. *Johann Wolfgang Goethe Zeichnungen*. Stuttgart: Reclam, 1996.

Man, Paul de. "The Epistemology of Metaphor." *Critical Inquiry* 5, no. 1, special issue on metaphor (Autumn 1978): 13–30.

Manos, Susan. *Schoenhut Dolls and Toys: A Loving Legacy*. Paducah, KY: Collector Books, 1976.

Marcuse, Herbert. *Eros and Civilization: A Philosophical Inquiry into Freud*. Boston: Beacon, 1955.

Marenholtz-Bülow, Bertha von. *How Kindergarten Came to America: Friedrich Froebel's Radical Vision of Early Childhood Education*. Translated by Mrs. Horace Mann. New York: The New Press, 2007. First published 1895.

Massey, Doreen. *Space, Place, and Gender*. Minneapolis: University of Minnesota Press, 1994.

Mazlish, Bruce. *The Idea of Humanity in a Global Era*. New York: Palgrave Macmillan, 2008.

McClellan, Marjorie L. "Hunting for Everyday History Theme 1: Toys and Games." In *Hunting for Everyday History: Local and Regional Organizations*. Wright State University CORE Scholar, 2003. https://corescholar.libraries.wright.edu/hunting/3.

McGlynn, Clare. *Families and the European Union*. Cambridge: Cambridge University Press, 2008.

Melz, Christian F. "Goethe and America." *College English* 10, no. 8 (May 1949): 425–31.

Meyer, Henry H. *Child Nature and Nurture According to Nicolaus Ludwig von Zinzendorf*. New York: The Abingdon Press, 1928.

Mezerers, Valdis. *The Herrnhuterian Pietism in the Baltic and Its Outreach into America and Elsewhere in the World*. North Quincy, MA: The Christopher Publishing House, 1975.

Michel, Christoph, ed. *Goethe: Sein Leben in Bildern und Texten*. Preface by Adolf Muschg. Frankfurt am Main: Insel, 1982.

Mikula, Maja, "Games, Toys and Pastimes." In *Greenwood Encyclopedia of World Popular Culture*, edited by Gary Hoppenstand and Gerd Bayer, 173–95. Westport, CT: Greenwood Press, 2007.

Moretti, Franco. "The Slaughterhouse of Literature." *Modern Language Quarterly* 61, no. 1 (2000): 207–27.

Morton, Timothy. *Ecology Without Nature: Rethinking Environmental Aesthetics*. Cambridge, MA: Harvard University Press, 2007.

Müller, Heidi A. *Ein Idealhaushalt im Miniaturformat: Die Nürnberger Puppenhäuser des 17. Jahrhunderts*. Nuremberg: Verlag des Germanischen Nationalmuseums, 2006.

Nel, Philip, and Lissa Paul, eds. *Keywords for Children's Literature*. New York: New York University Press, 2014.

Niekerk, Carl, ed. *The Radical Enlightenment in Germany: A Cultural Perspective*. Amsterdam: Brill, 2018.

Nissenbaum, Stephen. *The Battle for Christmas: A Cultural History of America's Most Cherished Holiday*. New York: Vintage, 1996.

Obermeier, Franz. *Brasilien "für die Jugend und das Volk." Kinder- und Jugendliteratur aus und über Brasilien vom 18. Jahrhundert bis in die Mitte des 20. Jahrhunderts*. 2016. https://www.academia.edu/28756263.

O'Brien, Richard. *The Story of American Toys: From the Puritans to the Present*. New York: Abbeville Press, 1990.

O'Donnell, Krista, Renate Bridenthal, and Nancy Reagin, eds. *The Heimat Abroad: The Boundaries of Germanness*. Ann Arbor: University of Michigan Press, 2005.

Oliver, Valerie. "History of the Yo-Yo." Museum of Yo-Yo History, http://www.yoyomuseum.com/museum_view.php?action=profiles&subaction=yoyo.

Oloukpona-Yinnon, Adjaï Paulin. *Unter deutschen Palmen: Die "Musterkolonie" Togo im Spiegel deutscher Kolonialliteratur (1884–1944)*. Frankfurt am Main: IKO—Verlag für Interkulturelle Kommunikation, 1998.

O'Malley, Andrew. *The Making of the Modern Child: Children's Literature and Childhood in the Late Eighteenth Century*. New York: Garland, 2003.

Oswald, Stephan. *Früchte einer großen Stadt: Goethes Venezianische Epigramme*. Heidelberg: Universitätsverlag Winter, 2014.

Panksepp, Jaak. "Science of the Brain as a Gateway to Understanding Play: An Interview with Jaak Panksepp." *American Journal of Play* (Winter 2010): 245–77.

Pataky, Sophie. *Lexikon deutscher Frauen der Feder*. Vol. 1. Berlin, 1898.

Penny, H. Glenn. *Kindred by Choice: Germans and American Indians Since 1800*. Chapel Hill: University of North Carolina Press, 2013.

———. *Objects of Culture: Ethnology and Ethnographic Museums in Imperial Germany*. Chapel Hill: University of North Carolina Press, 2002.

Petschauer, Peter. "Eighteenth-Century German Opinions about Education for Women." *Central European History* 3 (1986): 262–92.

Peucker, Paul. "'Inspired by Flames of Love': Homosexuality, Mysticism and Moravian Brothers around 1750." *Journal of the History of Sexuality* 15, no. 1 (2006): 30–64.

Planefors, Per-Inge, ed. *Ellen Key: Creating a European Identity*. Ödeshög, Sweden: Alvastra förlag, 2013.

Pratt, Mary Louise. *Imperial Eyes: Travel Writing and Transculturation*. London: Routledge, 1992; 2008.

Purdy, Daniel L. *The Tyranny of Elegance: Consumer Cosmopolitanism in the Era of Goethe*. Baltimore: Johns Hopkins University Press, 1998.

Rehwinkel, Kerstin. "Kopflos, aber lebendig? Konkurrierende Körperkonzepte in der Debatte um den Tod durch Enthauptung im ausgehenden 18. Jahrhundert." In *Körper mit Geschichte: Der menschliche Körper als Ort der Selbst- und Weltdeutung*, edited by Clemens Wischermann und Stefan Haas, 151–71. Stuttgart: Franz Steiner Verlag, 2000.

Reinhart, Max, ed. *Early-Modern German Literature, 1350–1700*. Rochester, NY: Camden House, 2009.

Richards-Wilson, Stephani. "German Social Entrepreneurs and the First Kindergartens in Nineteenth Century America." In *Immigrant Entrepreneurship: German-American Business Biographies, 1720 to the Present*, vol. 2, edited by William J. Hausman. German Historical Institute, 2016. http://www.immigrant entrepreneurship.org/entry.php?rec =277.

Rountree, Susan H. *Dollhouses, Miniature Kitchens, and Shops from the Abby Aldrich Rockefeller Folk Art Center*. Williamsburg, VA: Colonial Williamsburg Foundation, 1996.

Rydell, Robert W. "Buffalo Bill's 'Wild West': The Racialisation of the Cosmopolitan Imagination." In *Colonial Advertising & Commodity Racism*, edited by Wulf D. Hund, Michael Pickering, and Anandi Ramamurthy, 97–118. Racism Analysis, edited by Wulf D. Hund, Series B: Yearbook Vol. 4. Münster: LIT Verlag, 2013.

Salen, Katie, and Eric Zimmermann, eds. *The Game Design Reader: A Rules of Play Anthology*. Cambridge, MA: MIT Press, 2006.

Sassen, Saskia. *Expulsions: Brutality and Complexity in the Global Economy*. Cambridge, MA: Harvard University Press, 2014.

Saul, Nicholas. "Goethe and Colonisation: The *Wanderjahre* and Cooper." In *Goethe and the English-Speaking World: Essays from the Cambridge Symposium for His 250th Anniversary*, edited by Nicholas Boyle and John Guthrie, 85–98. Rochester, NY: Camden House, 2002.

Saure, Felix. "Agamemnon on the Battle Field of Leipzig: Wilhelm von Humboldt on Ancient Warriors, Modern Heroes, and *Bildung* through War." In *Enlightened War: German Theories and Cultures of Warfare from Frederick the Great to Clausewitz*, edited by Elisabeth Krimmer and Patricia Anne Simpson, 75–102. Rochester, NY: Camden House, 2011.

Saxon, Theresa. *American Theatre: History, Context, Form*. Edinburgh: Edinburgh University Press, 2011.

Saxton, Alexander. "Blackface Minstrelsy and Jacksonian Ideology." In *Locating American Studies: The Evolution of a Discipline*, edited by Lucy Maddox, 114–39. Baltimore: The Johns Hopkins University Press, 1999.

Schäffer, Ritter von. *Brasilien als unabhängiges Reich in historischer, mercantilischer und politischer Beziehung*. Altona: J. F. Hammerich, 1824.

Scheuer, Hans Jürgen. *Manier und Urphänomen: Lektüren zur Relation von Erkenntnis und Darstellung in Goethes Poetologie der "geprägten Form."* Würzburg: Königshausen & Neumann, 1996.

Schiller, Friedrich. *On the Aesthetic Education of Man in a Series of Letters*. Translated and introduced by Reginald Snell. New Haven: Yale University Press, 1954.

———. *Schillers Sämmtliche Werke*. Vol. 4. Stuttgart: J. G. Cotta'sche Buchhandlung, 1879. http://gutenberg .spiegel.de/buch/-3355/3.

Schoenhut, A. F., Theodore C. Schoenhut, Harry E. Schoenhut, Otto F. Schoenhut, William G. Schoenhut, and Gustav A. Schoenhut. *Forty Years of Toy Making, 1872–1912*. Philadelphia: A. Schoenhut, 1912.

Schutt, Amy C. "'What Will Become of Our Young People?' Goals for Indian Children in Moravian Missions." *History of Education*

Quarterly 38, no. 3 (Autumn 1998): 268–86.

Schwartz, David G. *Roll the Bones: The History of Gambling*. New York: Gotham, 2007.

Sedgwick, Eve Kosofsky. *Epistemology of the Closet*. Los Angeles: University of California Press, 1990.

Sembritzki, Emil, ed. *Kolonial-Gedicht und -liederbuch*. Berlin: Deutscher Kolonial-Verlag (G. Meinecke), 1911.

Shirreff, Emily. *Essays and Lectures on the Kindergarten: Principles of Froebel's System and Their Bearing on the Higher Education of Women, Schools, Family and Industrial Life*. Appendix by Elizabeth P. Peabody. New York: E. Steiger, 1883.

Simpson, Patricia Anne. *The Erotics of War in German Romanticism*. Lewisburg: Bucknell University Press, 2006.

———. "Recoding the Ethics of War in Grimms' Fairy Tales." In *Enlightened War: German Theories and Cultures of Warfare from Frederick the Great to Clausewitz*, edited by Elisabeth Krimmer and Patricia Anne Simpson, 151–72. Rochester, NY: Camden House, 2011.

Skelton, Tracey, and Gill Valentine, eds. *Cool Places: Geographies of Youth Cultures*. London: Routledge, 1997.

Spiekermann, Uwe. "Claus Spreckels: Robber Baron and Sugar King." In *Immigrant Entrepreneurship: German-American Business Biographies, 1720 to the Present*, vol. 2, edited by William J. Hausman. German Historical Institute. http://www.immigrantentrepre neurship.org/entry.php?rec=5.

Stafford, Margot. "*Journeys through Bookland*'s Imaginative Geography: Pleasure, Pedagogy, and the Child Reader." In *Space and Place in Children's Literature: 1789 to the Present*, edited by Maria Sachiko Cecire, Hannah Field, Kavita Mudan Finn, and Malini Roy, 147–61. Surrey, UK: Ashgate, 2015.

Stauss, Thomas. *Frühe Spielwelten: Zur Belehrung und Unterhaltung; Die Spielwarenkataloge von Peter Friedrich Catel (1747–1791) und Georg Hieronimus Bestelmeier (1764–1829)*. Hochwald, Switzerland: Librum, 2015.

Steiger, E. *Der Kindergarten in Amerika: Entstehung, Wesen, Bedeutung und Erziehungsmittel des Froebel'schen Systems und seine Anwendung auf hiesige Verhaeltnisse*. New York: E. Steiger, 1872.

Stetler, Julia Simone, "Buffalo Bill's Wild West in Germany: A Transnational History." PhD diss., University of Nevada, 2012.

Stewart, Susan. *On Longing: Narratives of the Miniature, the Gigantic, the Souvenir, the Collection*. 8th paperback ed. Durham: Duke University Press, 2003.

Stievermann, Jan, and Oliver Scheiding, eds. *A Peculiar Mixture: German-Language Cultures and Identities in Eighteenth-Century North America*. University Park: The Pennsylvania State University Press, 2013.

Sutton-Smith, Brian. "Play and Ambiguity." In *The Game Design Reader: A Rules of Play Anthology*, edited by Katie Salen and Eric Zimmermann, 296–313. Cambridge, MA: MIT Press, 2006.

Tautz, Birgit. *Translating the World: Toward a New History of German Literature Around 1800*. University Park: Pennsylvania State University Press, 2018.

Teigeler, Otto. *Zinzendorf als Schüler in Halle 1710–1716*. Halle: Verlag der Franckeschen Stiftungen, 2017.

Tenberg, Reinhard. "Bötticher, Georg." In *Literaturlexikon: Autoren und Werke deutscher Sprache*, edited by Walther Killy et al., vol. 2, 88. Munich: Bertelsmann, 1989.

Trotta, Margarete von, dir. *Die bleierne Zeit* (*The German Sisters*, also *Marianne und Juliane*). Performed by Jutta Lampe, Barbara Sukowa. Bioskop and Sender Freies Berlin, 1981.

Truettner, William H. *The West as America: Reinterpreting Images of the Frontier, 1820–1920*. Washington, DC: Smithsonian, 1991.

Trumpener, Katie. "Picture-Book Worlds and Ways of Seeing." In *The Cambridge Companion to Children's Literature*, edited by M. O. Grenby and Andrea Immel, 55–75. Cambridge: Cambridge University Press, 2009.

Tsanoff, Stoyan Vasil. *Educational Value of the Children's Playground: A Novel Plan of Character Building*. Philadelphia: Self-published, 1897.

Tucker, M. J. "The Child as Beginning and End: Fifteenth and Sixteenth Century English Childhood." In *The History of Childhood*, edited by Lloyd deMause, 229–57. New York: Psychohistory Press, 1974.

Ulm-Sanford, Gerlinde, ed. *Goethes Briefwechsel mit seinem Sohn August*. 2 vols. Weimar: Verlag Hermann Böhlaus Nachfolger, 2005.

Valentine, Deborah Shine. "Playing at Learning and Learning at Play: A History of Race, Play and Early Education in Philadelphia, 1857–1912." PhD diss., Rutgers University, 2013.

Veerman, Philip E. *The Rights of the Child and the Changing Image of Childhood*. Dordrecht: Martinus Nijhoff, 1992.

Walgenbach, Katharina. *"Die weiße Frau als Trägerin deutscher Kultur" Koloniale Diskurse über Geschlecht, "Rasse" und Klasse im Kaiserreich*. Frankfurt am Main: Campus Verlag, 2005.

Wallace-Sanders, Kimberly. *Mammy: A Century of Race, Gender, and Southern Memory*. Ann Arbor: University of Michigan Press, 2008.

Warren, Louis S. *Buffalo Bill's America: William Cody and the Wild West Show*. New York: Vintage, 2005.

Wassong, Stephan. "The German Influence on the Development of the US Playground Movement." *Sport in History* 28, no. 2 (2008): 313–28.

Weber, D. Friedrich Benedict. *Handbuch der ökonomischen Literatur oder Systematische Anleitung zur Kenntnis der deutschen ökonomischen Schriften die sowohl die gesammte Land- und Hauswirtschaft als die mit derselben verbundenen Hülfs- und Nebenwissenschaften angehen; mit Angabe ihres Ladenpreises und Bemerkung ihres Werthes*. Berlin: Duncker und Humblot, 1809.

Weber, Max. *The Protestant Ethic and the Spirit of Capitalism*. Translated by Talcott Parsons. Introduction by Anthony Giddens. London: Routledge, 1992. First published 1930 by Allen and Unwin.

Weber-Kellermann, Ingeborg. *Die Kinderstube*. Frankfurt am Main: Insel, 1991.

———. *Die Kindheit: Eine Kulturgeschichte*. Frankfurt am Main: Insel, 1997.

———. *Die Kindheit: Kleidung und Wohnen, Arbeit und Spiel: Eine Kulturgeschichte*. Frankfurt am Main: Insel, 1979.

Webster, Mary. *Johan Zoffany, 1733–1810*. New Haven: Yale University Press, for the Paul Mellon Centre for Studies in British Art, 2011.

Weikle-Mills, Courtney. *Imaginary Citizens: Child Readers and the Limits* of American Independence, 1640–1868. Baltimore: The Johns Hopkins University Press, 2013.

Weinkauff, Gina, Ute Dettmar, Thomas Möbius, and Ingrid Tomkowiak, eds. *Kinder- und Jugendliteratur in Medienkontexten: Adaption—Hybridisierung—Intermedialität—Konvergenz*. Frankfurt am Main: Peter Lang, 2014.

Weir, L. H., *Europe at Play: A Study of Recreation and Leisure Time Activities*. New York: A. S. Barnes, 1937.

Wild, Reiner. *Goethes klassische Lyrik*. Stuttgart: Metzler, 1999.

———. "Goethe's Writings as Minister of State in Saxe-Weimar and Eisenach." *Goethe Yearbook* 22 (2015): 261–66.

Wildenthal, Lora. *German Women for Empire, 1884–1945*. Durham: Duke University Press, 2001.

Wilmsen, F. P. *Der deutsche Kinderfreund: Ein Lesebuch für Volksschulen; Erste amerikanische Auflage, von der sechzigsten europäischen, vermehrt mit geographischen Zusätzen und einer kurzen deutschen Sprachlehre für amerikanisch deutsche Volksschulen*. Philadelphia: Gedruckt auf Veranstaltung der Schulverbesserungs-Committee und Korporation der deustch Lutherischen St. Michaelis, 1830.

Wilson, W. Daniel. "Goethe's Writings as Minister of State in Saxe-Weimar and Eisenach." *Goethe Yearbook* 22 (2015): 261–66.

———. *Das Goethe-Tabu: Protest und Menschenrechte im klassischen Weimar*. Munich: Deutscher Taschenbuchverlag, 1999.

Wischermann, Clemens, and Stefan Haas, eds. *Körper mit Geschichte: Der menschliche Körper als Ort der Selbst- und Weltdeutung*. Stuttgart: Franz Steiner Verlag, 2000.

Wolgast, Heinrich. *Das Elend unserer Jugendliteratur*. 6th ed. Leipzig: Verlag Ernst Wunderlich, 1922.

Woltersdorf, Ernst Gottlieb. *Kinder-Lieder*. New York: American Traktat-Gesellschaft, 1823.

Wortham, Sue C. *Childhood, 1892–1992*. Wheaton, MD: Association for Childhood Education International, 1992.

Wulf, Andrea. *The Invention of Nature: Alexander von Humboldt's New World*. New York: Knopf, 2015.

Wyness, Michael. *Childhood and Society*, 2nd ed. New York: Palgrave Macmillan, 2012.

Zantop, Susanne. *Colonial Fantasies: Conquest, Family, and Nation in Precolonial Germany, 1770–1870*. Durham: Duke University Press, 1997.

Ziemann, Grete. *Mola Koko! Grüße aus Kamerun. Tagebuchblätter*. Berlin: Wilhelm Süssrott, 1907.

Zinzendorf, Christian Renatus von. "In den ersten Gnadentagen." Hymn 307. In *Gesangbuch der Evangelischen Brüdergemeinde in Nordamerika. Neue vermehrte Auflage*, 116–17. Bethlehem, PA: Moravian Publication Office, 1891.

Zornado, Joseph L. *Inventing the Child: Culture, Ideology, and the Story of Childhood*. New York: Garland, 2001.

Zwicker, Lisa Featheringill. "'Heroism of the Mother': Women's Rights Pioneer Jeannette Schwerin, Motherlove, and Women's Leadership in German-Speaking Central Europe, 1899–1914." In *Realities and Fantasies of Female Leadership from Maria Antonia of Saxony to Angela Merkel*, edited by Elisabeth Krimmer and Patricia Anne Simpson, 165–83. Rochester, NY: Camden House, 2019.

Index

Italicized page references indicate illustrations. Endnotes are referred with "n" followed by the endnote number.

Abbott, Elizabeth, 236–37
absent parents, 80–83
adult play and experience, 1
   Goethe's fascination with the yoyo, 103–5
   Goethe's militarized masculinity, 114–15
   play drive, 4
   play in modernity replicating, 217–18
   play shaping the character of the adult, 190–91
   play world as rehearsal for, 224–27
   public space as adult space, 245n63
   toys as material objects, 17–18
   war games, 96–97
adventure play
   colonial objects of play, 120–21
   Dorfgeschichten romanticizing and reiterating racial hierarchies, 122–31
   mapping a cognitive landscape onto racial identity, 119
advertising. *See* marketing and advertising
Advertising Empire: Race and Visual Culture in Imperial Germany (Ciarlo), 134–36
aesthetic play, 97–98
African imaginary
   in *Auerbach's Kinder-Kalender*, 131–40, 179
   German claim to a moral high ground, 140–43
   "Knecht Ruprecht in Kamarun," 143–45
   portrayal of flora and fauna, 135–37
   zodiacal activities to alleviate boredom, 131–40
African Natives toys, 222
Agamben, Giorgio, 149
agency and empowerment, 8
   consumerism through toys, 150–51
   gendering and marketing toys and dolls, 228–29
   through ethnographic play, 183–84
   through worlding, 10–11
Alice's Adventures (Carroll), 14
Allen, Ann Taylor, 184
Allwin und Theodor (Jacobs), 23, 74–79, 84–88
almanacs, 25, 131–40, *135*, 169–70
American imaginary
   conflating Africa and America, 149–50
   formation of, 150
   in the German colonial play world, 151
   the history of cotton and feathers, 156
   jungle stories, 163–64
   Koch-Gotha's caricatures of American Indians, 181–82
American Indians. *See* Native Americans
Ames, Eric, 214
animals
   display of captive animals, 214
   Helmar's jungle stories, 169–70
   Oekonomisches Handbuch recommendations for children's space, 67
   play associated with, 3
   portrayal of African flora and fauna as a threat, 135–37

INDEX 275

racially marked dolls and toys, 220, 222
teaching and learning paternal love, 79–80
Arendt, Hannah, 141
Ariès, Philippe, 5, 38–39
Arnim, Achim von, 80–81
art and play, 188–89
ästhetische Erziehung der Menschen, in einer Reihe von Briefen, Die (The Aesthetic Education of Man in a Series of Letters) (Schiller), 97–98
astrological cycle, 117–19, 131–40
Auerbach, August Bertold, 121, 131–40, 160–61
Auerbach's Deutscher Kinder-Kalender, 131–40, 160–61, 179
Aunt Jemima, 134
authority
  cautionary tales, 88–89
  gendered play, 227–29
  love inspiring, 53
  paternal authority in colonial literature, 165
  play replicating adult behavior, 217, 227–29

balance
  balanced approach to parenting, 92, 203–5
  cautionary stories advocating, 88–89
  in Fröbel's kindergarten model, 200–201
  Oekonomisches Handbuch für Frauenzimmer recommendations, 63–64
Barnum, Phineas T., 212–13
Barth, Susanne, 74–75
Barthes, Roland, 156
baseball, 227–28
Battle for Christmas, The (Nissenbaum), 144
Baumwollkulturkampf (cotton-growing struggle), 157
Beckert, Sven, 156–57
Behaim, Martin, 120, 137
Benjamin, Walter, 16–17, 104, 106, 172
Bergman, Ingmar, 33
Bertuch, Friedrich Justin, 15–16

Beschäftigung (play drive), 68–71, 77, 97–99
Bestelmeier, Georg Hieronimus, 96
Bilderbogen (sheet pictures), 143–44, 146
Bilderbuch für Kinder (Picturebook for Children) (Bertuch), 15–16
bilingual education, 197, 255n21
biological facets and purpose of play, 4, 187–88
birthday celebrations, 25, 112, 154
blackface minstrels, 219–20
Bookland series, 138
boredom, alleviating, 131–40
Bötticher, Georg, 162–63
Bowersox, Jeff, 119–20, 124, 137, 143, 159, 165, 209
Braun & Schneider publishers, 144
Brazil, 164, 166
Brentano, Clemens, 80–81
brilliant house, 233–34
Britain
  children's training and management, 37
  exporting Fröbel's theories to, 27
  the impact of Fröbel's kindergarten, 199
  Schoenhut exports to, 223
  Seven Years' War, 94
Brockhaus-Konversationslexicon, 179
broken toys, 229
Bühlmann, Joseph, 190–91
Burucker, Wilhelm, 96–97
Busch, Wilhelm, 153, 182
Butler, Judith, 161

Cadogan, William, 60
Caillois, Roger, 5
Cameroon, 141–48
Campaign in France (Goethe), 102
Campe, Joachim Heinrich, 12, 23, 76, 244n38
  masculine fathers and ideal sons, 71–74
  the nature of Nature, 116–17
  pedagogy through the canonical and the secular, 44–45
cannons, 102
capitalism, 8
  change in the lives of families and children, 27, 187

capitalism (*continued*)
   the institutionalization of play, 31–32
   textile production, 157
   Weber's consideration of work, 13–14
caricature, 180
Carroll, Lewis, 14
Catalog von E. Steiger, 122, *122*
cautionary tales, 71, 88–91, 115, 135–37
Centuries of Childhood (Ariès), 5, 38–39
Century of the Child, The (Key), 108, 205
Chakkalakal, Sylvy, 15–16, 132, 141, 162
Channing, William Ellery, 33
character dolls, 181
child development
   the importance of free play, 56–57
   Zinzendorf's migration narrative, 43–44
"Childhood" (More), 161
childhood development, 31
childhood of modernity, 235
Child Nature and Nurture According to Nicolaus Ludwig von Zinzendorf (Meyer), 22, 43
children's rights
   citizenship in the play world, 238–39
   Fröbel's work defining the parameters of, 187–88
Children's Toys of Bygone Days (Gröber), *101, 102*
Chodowiecki, Daniel Nikolaus, 60
Christmas
   Goethe's celebration, 101–2
   hymn narratives, 50–51
   Knecht Ruprecht stories, 25, 141, 143–45
   postwar emphasis on patriotism and national identity, 239–40
Ciarlo, David, 134–35, 252n37
circuses
   blackface minstrels, 219–20
   Schoenhut's Humpty Dumpty Circus, 209–13, 215, *216,* 218–20, 231, 234, 240
   targeting the middle class, 212–13
citizenship, 18
   imaginary citizenship of young adult readers, 151–52
   Jacobs's writings as teaching for, 76–78
   kindergarten education as civic mission, 201
   Schoenhut Toys gendering, 222–31
   the value of playgrounds, 238
   women's child-rearing, 205–6
civic institution, kindergarten as, 184–85
class divisions
   adult-child relationship, 61–62
   Barnum's circus targeting the middle class, 213
   circus industry, 213
   colonial imaginary, 164
   education reform balancing inequities, 203–4
   Humpty Dumpty Circus reflecting hegemonic practices, 212
   identity construction through play, 37–38
   maternal and paternal roles in home and family, 203–4
   Playground Movement, 237–38
   regulatory purpose of games, 156–58
   sympathies in the French Revolution, 122–23
   toys and child-rearing treatises teaching, 234–35
   toys as tools, 199–200
   toys' role in dialogue with the nation, 106
clowns, 213–14, 219–20
Cody, William F. "Buffalo Bill," 177–78
colonial America, 42
Colonial Fantasies (Zantop), 140
colonialism, 24
   adventure play superimposing a racial identity, 119–20
   colonial expansion of the play world, 140–43
   dolls in colonial landscapes, 162–63
   fantasy landscapes in stories, 163–65
   "freak" shows, 214–15
   intertwining of European and North American cultures, 209
   jungle stories, 163–64
   marketing European toys and housewares, 170–71
   objects of nature, 117
   pedagogical objects and the justification of, 120–21

postcolonial examination of childhood and the domestic, 9–10
racial motifs in visual imagery, 134–36
Schoenhut Toys gendering citizenship, 222–31
the significance of cotton and feathers, 156–58
worlding, 10–11
colonial literature
German claim to a moral high ground, 140–43
the global scope of Horn's *Dorfgeschichten*, 121–22
Ein Kongo-Neger embedding racial hierarchies in adventure narratives, 122–31
"Knecht Ruprecht in Kamarun," 144–48
racialized tales targeting youth, 124–25
for young readers, 137–38
Comenius, Johann Amos, 11–12
commedia, 214
commodities, toys as, 17, 35
concentration toys, Schoenhut's, 230–31
consumer culture
cautionary tales warning against, 87
Germany's pre-industrial consumerism, 17
metaphor of cotton, 157
toys as access to, 150–51
conversation painting, 186–87
Cook, James W., 212
costumes, 226–27
cotton, 25, 155–58
Critique of Judgment (Kant), 3–4
Cross, Gary, 211, 231
crossover play, 6
culture, 240–41
bilingual education, 197, 255n21
German perceived superiority over American Indians, 178–79
preserving German education, language and, 192–93
revolution shaping German identity, 94–95
toy makers as cultural mediators, 208
See also identity

death of a parent, 78–79
Defoe, Daniel, 44–45
deMause, Lloyd, 7
democracy
inclusionary politics of Fröbel's systems, 195–96
the kindergarten model, 197
demographic shifts
changing the dynamics of families and children, 187–89
transition in German self-identity, 140–41
destructive play, 146
deutsche Kinderfreund: Ein Lesebuch fuer Volksschulen, Der (Wilmsen), 23–24, 88–89
Deutscher Pionier am Río de la Plata, 170
"Deutschland's Kolonien-Spiel" game, 121
Dichtung und Wahrheit (From My Life: Poetry and Truth) (Goethe), 110–11, 146
dollhouses, 22
as elaboration of the miniature, 38
realism of, 226
the study of play, 39–41
dolls
cannibals roasting, 146–47, *147*
conferring agency, 228–29
German manufacture and materials, 172
girls modeling maternal behavior, 73–74
Helmar's tale of a European doll in the wild, 162–75
human animation of an object, 143
Knecht Ruprecht's beneficent giving, 145
parody of American Indians, 181
postwar shift in national identity of manufacturers, 240
racially marked dolls, 220, 222
Schoenhut Perfection Art Doll, 218, 228–29, 231, 256n32
the stoic Indian, 175–78
symbolism of the single treasured toy, 235
toy-producing centers, 208

domestic life
    children's treatment of servants,
        71–73
    effect of games of war, 97
    the importance of educating women,
        199
    Jacobs's faith in the value of, 78
    kindergarten as intermediary
        between home and public school,
        195
    metonymic relationship of children's
        space, 185–87
    as model for learning, 196–97
    paternal role in the home, 202–4
    professionalization of motherhood,
        184–85
    Schoenhut toys teaching gender,
        217–18
    Uhde's *Die Kinderstube* illustrating,
        185–86
Dorfgeschichten (Village Stories) (Horn),
    121–25
Dummig, Charles, 229–30

economics of migration, 237–38
economies of play, 152–62
economies of possession, 26–27
education
    developmental qualities, 18
    as fundamental for religious prac-
        tice, 34–35
    hymns as pedagogical agents, 43–47
    institutionalization of, 183–84
    the need for unsupervised self-reflec-
        tion, 76–78
    play as outcome of religious educa-
        tion, 42–43
    professionalization of motherhood,
        184–85
    Schoenhut's ties to educational insti-
        tutions, 230–31
    Steiger's commitment to German
        educational ideals, 191–96
    See also Fröbel, Friedrich; pedagogy;
        play as
Educational Directory (Steiger), 191
*Educational Value of the Children's Play-
    ground: A Novel Plan of Character
    Building* (Tsanoff), 29

education of women, 201–4
education reform
    geography from a colonial world-
        view, 119–20
    the need for Fröbel's practices in the
        US, 193–94
    restructuring gendered home duties,
        203–4
    Shirreff's justification of play,
        199–200
Emile (Rousseau), 116
Empire of Cotton (Beckert), 156–57
emulative play
    national and transnational explora-
        tion through, 117–18
    purpose of material objects in,
        234–35
    thinking colonially through, 24
Enchiridion (Zinzendorf), 53–54
enlightened play
    mother love and, 61–62
    paternal roles in play, 71–79
    progressive education theory in the
        United States, 189–90
Enlightenment educational principles,
    116, 244n39
Eros and Civilization (Marcuse), 4
erotic games and experiences
    Goethe's fascination with the yoyo,
        103–5
    Goethe's militarized masculinity, 114–15
    homoerotic nature of Zinzendorf the
        younger's hymns, 55
Essays and Lectures on the Kindergarten
    (Shirreff), 199–200
ethnic dolls, 181
ethnographic displays
    Humpty Dumpty Circus, 209–10,
        211–12, 215, *216*, 234, 240
    racially marked dolls and toys, 220,
        222
    relentless collecting of museums,
        164–65
ethnographic literature
    Helmar's story of a European doll in
        the wild, 162–75
    imaginary citizenship of readers, 25
    myth of the stoic Indian, 175–78
    racialization of toy production, 27

ethnographic play, 25
  acquisition of agency through,
    183–84
  colonizing world supplanting indigenous knowledge, 150–52
  ethnographic toys, 153
  imperial identification through, 208
  the origins of feathers and cotton,
    155–58
eugenics, 188
evangelical narratives, 45–48, 57
evil, toys as, 59
exploration: the global scope of Horn's *Dorfgeschichten*, 121–22

fairy tales, 81–84, 237
family life and roles
  correlation with religious community, 56–58
  dollhouses portraying, 39–41
  Schoenhut Toys emphasizing intercultural identity, 223–26
  toys and child-rearing treatises teaching, 234
  Weber's consideration of work, 14
  Zinzendorf's understanding of child development, 43–44
Fanny and Alexander (film), 33
fantasy
  African colonial literature, 25,
    122–26, 129–31, 139–40, 164
  Goethe's dedication to, 112–13
  in the natural world, 118–20
  portrayal of imagined foreign lands,
    164–75
fatherhood, 23
  fathers at play, 71–79
  Goethe's darker side of play, 100–101
  the importance of nature to contentment, 78–79
  learning paternal love, 79–88
  masculinity and paternity in the late eighteenth century, 31–32
  Oekonomisches Handbuch für Frauenzimmer recommendations for, 63
  paternal role in the home, 202–4
  Protestant paternal influence over the child, 32–34

Faust (Goethe), 112–13, 233–34
feathers, 25, 155–58, 162–63, 173–74, 182
Fellenberg, Immanuel von, 110
feminism, racism disguised as, 205–6
Feuer, Wasser, Kohle (fire, water, coal) game, 154
Florentino, Daniele, 178
Fooken, Insa, 120
Fox, George Washington Lafayette, 213
Francke, August, 42
"freak" shows, 214–15
free development principle, 56–57
free play, 56–57, 65
French Revolution, 24, 96–97, 103, 106, 107–8, 122–23, 124, 131
Freud, Sigmund, 16–17, 105
Friedrich Fröbel under der Kindergarten (Bühlmann), 190–91
"Fritzchens Herzenswunsch" (Sembritzki), 138
Fröbel, Friedrich, 238
  activities and skills in the kindergarten curriculum, 255n20
  bringing the German model of play to America, 26–27, 190–96
  building boxes, 193
  education as a garden of children,
    186–87
  education of women as a civic mission, 202–4
  the function and role of the "gifts,"
    200–201
  Gaben as playthings, 35
  on Goethe's theories of education,
    109–10
  influence on the Protestant play ethic, 187–88
  Jacobs's narratives, 76–78
  Schoenhut's concentration and manipulative toys, 230–31
  shifting away from regulated play,
    12–13
  success and relevance of his work in America, 192–93
  See also kindergarten

Gaben (gifts), 35
games: group play at modeled parties,
    153–55

gender
    colonial play in stories, 165
    effect of war and violence, 100–101
    islanding of girls in play, 224–26
    masculinity and paternity in the late eighteenth century, 31–32
    racism disguised as feminism, 205–6
    theater performance, 213–14
gendered play
    at a coed party, 155
    group play at a textually modeled party, 154–55
    Jacobs's stories, 75
    paternal thoughts and play, 71–79
    play space as gendered territory, 245n63
    Schoenhut advertising gendering toys, 224–27
    Schoenhut Perfection Art Doll, 228
    Schoenhut Toys gendering citizenship, 222–31
    Schoenhut toys performing gender, 216–18
    Uhde's *Die Kinderstube* illustrating, 185–86
    war stories and games, 83–88
gender roles
    children's treatment of servants, 72
    maternal and paternal roles in the home, 202–4
    play as rehearsal for reality, 226
    professionalization of motherhood, 184–85
    Schoenhut toys teaching, 217–18
    stories modeling gendered parenting, 73–74
    story cycles modeling, 153–54
    toys teaching, 234
Gender Trouble (Butler), 161
genocide, 179–80
geography, 17, 119–21, 137–38, 167
Gerhard, Paul, 61
German Colonial Society, 138
Germantown Boys Club, 259n57
Germershausen, Christian Friedrich, 71–72
Gersdorff, Dagmar von, 101–2

Gersdorff, Henriette Catharina Freifrau von, 30–31, 34–36, 42, 246n16, 248n60
Gersdorff, Nikolaus Ludwig Count von, 51
"Geschichte vom braven Kasperl und dem schönen Annerl, Die" (Brentano), 80–81
gifts, 191, *192*
    exchange of literal and figurative objects, 35
    function and role of Fröbel's, 200–201
Gillis, John R., 224
"Giraffe, Die" (Helmar), 169–70
globes, 120–21, 138
Goethe, August, 28, 112–15, 235–36
Goethe, Johann Wolfgang von, 21, 24, 93
    aesthetic play, 98–99
    bridging folklore and high culture, 233–34
    the child as individual, 109–10
    cultural legacy of warfare, 94–96
    eccentricity in parenting, 111–15
    Faust, 233–34
    the guillotine, 99–103
    international and transatlantic reception, 108–11
    the nature of play and the acquisition of toys, 235–36
    relationship to toys, 94–95
    war toys, 97
Goethe, Katharina Elisabeth "Frau Rath," 28, 112, 113
Goethe-Schiller monument, San Francisco, 236–37
Goto-Jones, Chris, 106
governesses, 73–74
Grimm Brothers, 81
Gröber, Karl, 39, 102, 172
Guckkasten-Bilder (Hirschmann), 25, 153–55, 158
guillotine, 28, 96, 97, 99–103, *101*, 107, 113, 114, 235–36
guns, playing with, 227–28

Habermas, Jürgen, 5
Hagedorn, Friedrich von, 61
Hagenbeck, Carl, 214, 215, 222
Haitian Revolution, 123, 131

INDEX

Hamlin, David, 208, 210, 214
Hampelmann (jumping jack), 145, 147
hands-on parenting, 113
hands-on play: dollhouses, 40–41
Hausmutter in allen ihren Geschäften, Die, 67
Hausvater, 23
Hausvater in systematischer Ordnung, Der, 71
Hausväterliteratur genre, 71–79
Hawaii, 236–37
Haywood, Collin, 119
Heesen, Anke te, 17
Hegel, G.W.F., 9
Heimat Abroad, 140
Hellemeyer, Maria, 162–75, 237
Helmar, W., 162–75
Herrnhut settlement, 35, 41–42, 51–53
Herrnhuterian Brotherhood, 42
Hessian figurines, 93
Hildebrandt, Paul, 83–85, 188–89
Hilpert, Johann Gottfried, 84
Hirschmann, Julie, 25, 153, 158, 159–61
historicization of play, 6–7
Hoffman, Heinrich, 115
Hoffmann, E.T.A., 143
Hoke, Sarah, 185
holistic education, Goethe's, 110–11
home-nation nexus
   gendering of space and play, 185–86
   German education theory in American education institutions, 189–96
   institutionalization of labor and care, 186–88
   kindergarten filling domestic deficits, 196–97
   the purpose of play, 187–88
   responsibility for children's education, 204–8
   shifting gender and domestic roles, 183–85
   the social value of play, 199–204
   teacher training for play in the kindergarten, 198–99
Homo Ludens: A Study of the Play Element in Culture (Huizinga), 5
Horn, W.O. von, 25–26, 121–25, 129–31, 148
Huizinga, Johann, 5, 187–88

human being, emergence of the child as, 38–39, 108–10
human rights
   colonial entitlement conflicting with, 128–29
   play as, 28–29, 238–39
Humpty Dumpty Circus, 209–13, 215, 216, 218–20, 231, 234, 240
Hunter, Thomas, 193
Huttenlocher, Henriette, 23
hybrid dolls, 162–75
hymns and hymnody, 22, 32–33, 59
   Herrnhuterian Brotherhood, 42–43
   homoerotic nature of Zinzendorf the younger's hymns, 55
   images and texts supporting the meaning, 247n50
   Kinder-Lieder, 45–48
   modeling Christ's life, 46
   modeling Pietism, 34–35
   as pedagogical agent, 43–47, 53–55

identity
   agency through worlding, 10–11
   bilingual education, 197
   children's literature contributing to, 15
   in the context of war, 113
   cotton as signifier of cultural identity, 157
   domestic practices shaping, 184–85
   effect of war and violence, 100–101
   establishing a white identity in a colonial geography, 120–21
   forming the American imaginary, 150
   Fröbel's kindergarten model, 186–87
   Herrnhuterian Brotherhood, 42
   international legitimization of play, 189–90
   intersectional elements in texts and toys, 235
   mapping a cognitive landscape onto racial identity, 119
   Native Americans and masculine identity, 178
   postwar models of play, 239–40
   racialized toys and European-American identity, 231–32

identity (*continued*)
  responsibility for children's education, 206
  revolution shaping, 94–95
  Schoenhut's ambivalence over, 230
  Schoenhut's circus constructing racial identity, 219–20
  Schoenhut's combination of play, technology and pedagogy, 223–24
  space and the construction of childhood identity, 245n63
  toys creating a racialized imperial identity, 150–51
  transmutable gender identities, 161
  of white settlers, 175
  See also imperial identity and culture
imaginative play, 3–4
  Goethe's ambivalence to, 95–96
  Humpty Dumpty Circus fostering, 212
  lifelike qualities of dolls, 229
  masculinized play, 76
  puppet theater and plays, 112–13
imagined play, dollhouses representing, 39–40
immersive play: colonizing world supplanting indigenous knowledge, 150–51
immigration. *See* migration
immigration narratives, 208–9, 223
imperial identity and culture, 25, 223
  play space, 233–34
  self-image of citizenship in play and storytelling, 151–52
  toy making and marketing reflecting, 209–10
  toys as preparation for adult behavior, 225–26
  See also colonialism; Schoenhut Toys
independence, children's, 205–6
"Indianergeschischte, Eine" (An Indian story), 25
indigenous peoples, 24, 25, 121–31, 215, 252n46
individuality: inclusionary politics of Fröbel's systems, 195–96
industrialization, 27
  bringing the German model of play to America, 190–96

nature as counter to, 117
  the significance of cotton and feathers in games, 156–58
industrial workers, 199–200
infantilization of Africans, 141–42
innateness of play, 6
innocence
  the myth of childhood, 6–7
  mythologizing nature, 119
  postwar shift in national identity, 239–40
  Winnebago rituals, 176–77
interiority, fathers teaching, 87
International Kindergarten Union (IKU), 188
intersectionality, 244n46
  in *Allwin und Theodor* narratives, 76
  children's literature, 15
Irving, Washington, 115
islanding in childhood, 6, 28–29, 108, 184–85, 205, 224
Italienische Reise (Goethe), 99–100

Jacobs, Christian Friedrich Wilhelm, 23, 53, 74–79, 84–88, 153
jeux et les hommes, Les (Caillois), 5
John, Fourteenth Lord Willoughby de Broke, and His Family (Zoffany), 1–2, *2*
jungle stories, 163–64

Kabale und Liebe (Schiller), 93, 94–95
Kant, Immanuel, 3–4, 244n39
Katzenjammer Kids, The, 182
Key, Ellen, 108, 110–11, 205, 233–34
kindergarten
  activities and skills in the curriculum, 255n20
  American endorsement, 192–94
  bilingual education, 197
  as intermediary between home and public school, 195
  international expansion and impact of, 189, 199–200
  materials, *193*, *194*
  maternal and paternal roles in home and family, 203–4
  maternal modeling, 184–85

moral, ethical, and pedagogical explications of play, 187–88
philosophical and physical location, 204
teacher training, 198–99
theory and philosophy, 238
transatlantic movement of, 186–87
See also Fröbel, Friedrich
Kindergarten in seinem Wesen dargestellt, Der (The kindergarten presented in its essence) (Köhler), 190–91
Kinder-Kalender, 131–40, 160–61, 179
Kinderkammer (children's room), 185
Kinder-Lieder (Woltersdorf), 45, 45–48, 51
Kinder Reden (Zinzendorf), 56
"Kinderspiel, Das" (Overbeck), 153
Kinderstube, Die (Uhde), 185–86, *186*, 191
Kinderstube (play space), 22–23
  combining sleeping space with, 60–61
  as primary locus of instruction, 3
  as representation of domestic space, 185
  See also play space
Kinderzimmer, 3
Kindred by Choice (Penny), 175
"Kind und die Hofmeisterin, Das" (The child and the governess) (Campe), 73–74
Kleine Kinderbibliothek (Campe), 23, 73–74
"kleine Urwälderin, Die" ("The little jungle girl"), 25, 162–75, *168*
Kleist, Heinrich von, 125
Klotz, Marcia, 140
"Knecht Ruprecht in Kamarun," 141, 144–48, 184
Koch-Gotha, Fritz, 179–81
Köferlin, Anna, 40, *41*
Köhler, August, 190–91
Kolonie und Heimat periodical, 138
Kongo-Neger, Ein: Eine Geschichte aus Sankt Domingo (A Congo-Negro: A Story from Santo Domingo) (Horn), 122–31, *123*, 149
Kopfloser Reiter, 115
"Krankenbett, Das" (Jacobs), 86–87
"Krieg, Der" (Jacobs), 80–85
"Kulturgeschichte des Spielzeuges, Die" ("The Cultural History of Toys") (Benjamin), 1–6

labor, 43
  German pedagogical models, 187–88
  importance to the paternalized personality, 32–34
  play as a path to a productive life, 152–53
  the purpose of Fröbel's education, 193
  sugar plantations, 236–37
  toys as tools for socialization and, 199–201
Ladies' Home Journal magazine, 239
land ownership, 150
Land und Leute in der alten und neuen Welt (Lands and people of the old and new worlds) (Löher), 175
language
  bilingual education, 197, 255n21
  discourse about colonial lands, 127
  jungle stories, 163–64
  kindergarten models of play and pedagogy, 193–94
  performative, 161
Lauder, Murza Mann, 230, 259n61
Lautere Milch (pure milk) discipline, 52–53
Lee, Nick, 224
Lefebvre, Henri, 6, 117
Lehrjahre (Goethe), 94–95
letter and word games, 18–19, *20*
Letters on the Aesthetic Education of Man (Schiller), 4
literary theory, 161
literature, children's
  Auerbach's Deutscher Kinder-Kalender, 131–40, 179
  cautionary tales, 71, 88–91, 115, 135–37
  colonial literature for young readers, 137–38, 162–66
  diverse functions of texts, 14–15
  the materiality of, 19
  modeling social behavior, 153–54
  pedagogical influence of hymns, 44–45
  See also colonial literature

literature, women's, 32
Locke, John, 30–31, 149–50
Löffler, Friederike Luise, 22–23
Löher, Franz, 175–78
Loose, Max, 162, *168*, 168–70

magic and magic shows, 112–13
Manifest Destiny, 148, 175, 180, 214
manipulative toys, 230–31
manufactured toys, 226–27, 235
    See also Schoenhut Toys
mapping the world in the playroom, 137
Marcuse, Herbert, 4–5
Marenholtz-Bülow, Bertha von, 109–10, 184
marketing and advertising, 257n14
    Barnum circus, 213
    class- and race-based, 214
    European toys in South America, 170–71
    marketing colonial themes to youth, 120
    the pedagogical value of Humpty Dumpty Circus, 215–16
    postwar shift in national identity, 239–40, *240*
    racial motifs in visual imagery, 134–36
    racialized tales targeting youth, 124–25
    Schoenhut connecting cultural identities, 229–30
    Schoenhut gendering toys, 217–18, 224–27
    Schoenhut's technological innovation and realism, 228
    tobacco, 181
"Marsch nach Paris, Der" (The battle of Paris) game, 96–97
masculinity, 23
    in *Allwin and Theodor*, 75–77
    Americanization of masculine play, 227
    dominating the late eighteenth century, 31–32
    German fascination with Indians, 175–78
    hands-on parenting, 113
    modeling paternal love, 81–84

Schoenhut islanding girls in play, 224–27
mass culture, 212
mass markets, 240–41
mass production, 240–41
material culture, 236
    aesthetic play, 97–99
    contribution to a happy childhood, 18
    ideology and morality in dollhouse use, 38
    imaginary citizenship and, 150–52
    imperial identity formation, 25
    Playground Movement, 237–38
    postcolonial examination of childhood and the domestic, 10–11
    racialized toys, 231–32
    reiterating racializing hierarchies, 124
    Schoenhut's production and marketing, 210–11
materialities of the play world, 16–18, 172
Max and Moritz, 153, 182
May, Karl, 142–43, 164, 175, 178
Meinecke, Fritz, 211
Metropolitan Opera House Gala, 233–34
Meyer, Henry H., 22, 43, 52–53, 54, 55
migration
    bringing the German model of play to America, 190–96
    colonizing world supplanting indigenous knowledge, 150–52
    etymology of the yoyo, 107–8
    German emigration to Brazil, 166
    Helmar's jungle stories, 162–64
    Locke's view of exploration, 149–50
    national identity reconfiguring play, 183–84
    preserving German education, language and, 192–93
    of the Schoenhut family and business, 210–11
    symbolism of the single treasured toy, 235
    the transatlantic world, 8–10
    of war cultures, 94–96
militarization of play: Goethe's parenting style, 114–15
militarized masculinity in *Allwin and Theodor*, 75–76
mimetic play, 211

dollhouses representing, 39–40
Helmar's jungle stories, 170
importance of toys in, 17
as rehearsal for reality, 226
See also dollhouses
mimicry, 5
miniatures, 38, 93, *93*, 120–21
minstrelsy, 219–20, 252n37
missionaries, 52
mobility, economic and social, 234–35
model childhood, 17–18
Mola Koko! Grüße aus Kamerun (Ziemann), 141–42
monuments, 236–37
moral behavior
   children's treatment of servants, 71–73
   circus and theater, 213
   colonial literature for young readers, 137–38
   Jacobs's narratives challenging consumerism, 87
   Locke and Gersdorff's theories of, 31
   teaching and learning paternal love, 79–80, 87–88
   through performative play, 37
   the white characters in *Ein Kongo-Neger*, 128
   women's moral obligations to educate a race, 205–6
Moravian Brethren, 11–12, 21–22, 34, 43, 51–53, 54, 55–56
Moravian Pentecost, 52
More, Thomas, 161
Moretti, Franco, 13
Moses, L.G., 215
motherhood
   dollhouses mimicking the life world, 40
   female teacher training to emulate, 198–99
   Fröbel's model and the maternal role, 196–97
   Gersdorff's Pietism, 34–35
   merging play space with sleeping space, 60–61
   Oekonomisches Handbuch für Frauenzimmer, 61–67
   professionalization of, 184–85

wild children, 35–36
Wilmsen's criticism of weak mothers, 89–90
women teachers as surrogate mothers, 201
Zinzendorf's migration narrative, 43–44
See also parenting
mother's heart, 61–62
music, 209–10, 211, 224, 225, 256n10
See also hymns and hymnody

narcotics, 176–77
nation, the role of women's education in, 201–3
Native Americans, 25, 121, 175–82, 215
natural science, 17, 117–21, 137, 167
nature
   in *Auerbach's Kinder-Kalender*, 131–40
   cotton and feathers, 155–58
   education through conversation with, 116–17
   formation of imaginary spaces, 117
   German fascination with the natural world, 175–78
   Key's naturalization of education, 109–10
   kindergarten teachers instilling the love of, 197
   Locke's view of exploration, 149–50
   as a source of inspiration and contentment, 78–79
   teaching and learning paternal love, 79–80, 85–88
Naturvölker (primitive indigenous peoples), 24
Nazi ideology, 132
Negro Dude, 219, 220, *221*, 222
networks, 9
nihilistic play, Goethe's, 111
Nissenbaum, Stephen, 144
nonmaterial possessions, 36
Nuremberg dollhouses, 38, 39–41, 226
nursing mothers, 63–64
nutcrackers, 145–47, *146*

Obermeier, Franz, 166, 167–68
Objects of Culture (Penny), 150
O'Brien, Richard, 257n14

Oekonomisches Handbuch für Frauenzimmer, 22–23, 61–67, 64, 68–71
Oertel, Friedrich Wilhelm Philipp, 25, 121
Oktoberkind (Negerkind), 25, 179
Oliver, Valerie, 107
Oloukpona-Yinnon, Adjaï Paulin, 138–39
O'Malley, Andrew, 37–38
open-ended play, 212
opera, 233–34
otherness, 24, 188, 213, 241
Overbeck, Christian Adolph, 153
ownership, 36–38

Pädagogische Provinzen (School regions) (Goethe), 109–10
Pan-American imaginary, 165–66
parenting, 23–24
    the balanced approach, 92–93
    cautionary tales, 88–91
    child-servant relations, 73–74
    fathers at play, 71–79
    gendered play at a coed party, 153–55
    Goethe's complex relationship to toys, 95–99
    Goethe's eccentricity, 111–15
    Locke advocating play, 30–31
    Oekonomisches Handbuch für Frauenzimmer recommendations for, 62–67
    patriotism and, 113
    performing parenthood through gendered play, 224–27
    professionalization of, 44
    Schoenhut as head of family and business, 257n39
    Schoenhut Toys' marketing strategy, 218
    through cautionary tales, 88–91
    See also fatherhood; motherhood
Parry, William Edward, 120–21
party games, 153–55
patriotism, 113, 218
Peabody, Elizabeth P., 206
pedagogy, play as
    analysis of Goethe's model, 109–11
    education through conversation with, 116–17
    the educational value of playgrounds, 238
    function of the Nuremberg dollhouses, 39–40
    gendered play, 216–18
    Goethe's *Faust*, 233–34
    Key rejecting the pedagogical value of play, 205
    marketing Schoenhut's Humpty Dumpty Circus, 215–16
    pedagogical value of toys, 16–18
    play shaping the character of the adult, 190–91
    Schoenhut's combination of play, technology and pedagogy, 223–24
    training teachers to facilitate play, 198
    the value of theater and imaginary play, 112–13
    Zinzendorf's innovations, 51–53
    See also education; Fröbel, Friedrich
Pennsylvania Germans, 8
Penny, Glenn, 150, 164, 175, 178, 180
Perfection Art Doll, 218, 228–29, 231, 256n32
performative language, 161
performative play
    learning moral behavior through, 37
    physically constructing racial hierarchies, 136–37
    rehearsing adult behavior, 225–26
    worlding, 10–11
Pestalozzi, Johann Heinrich, 12
Petschauer, Peter, 62
Philanthropists, 12, 116
philanthropy: Playground Movement, 237–38
philosophies of play, 3–4
physical activity
    child development and, 204
    the importance of balancing play with, 200–201
    Oekonomisches Handbuch recommendations, 64–65
    regulating play space and activities, 68–71
    teaching and learning paternal love, 79–80
    Wilmsen's parenting through cautionary tales, 88–91

physical play world, 3–4
pianos, 209–10, 224, 225, 256n10
picture puzzles, 19
Pietism, 31, 34–35, 41–42, 45–47, 51
plantation economy, 122–31, 156–58, 164, 237
play drive
 in aesthetic play, 97–99
 biological nature of, 3
 as expression of freedom, 4
 Goethe's fascination with the yoyo, 103–5
 Jacobs gendering play, 77
 Kantian situation of play, 244n39
 naturalizing the drive for activity, 68–71
play ethic. *See* Protestant play ethic
Playground Movement, 29, 199, 237–38
play space
 the construction of childhood identity, 245n63
 merging sleeping space with, 60–61
 Oekonomisches Handbuch für Frauenzimmer recommendations for, 62–67
 regulating the space and activities, 68–71
 as women's jurisdiction, 32
 Zinzendorf on the role of education and play, 56
play world, 31
political culture
 blackface minstrelsy, 219–20
 circus and theater, 213
 politics of migration, 237–38
 revolution influencing the politics of play, 94
 theater performance emulating, 213–14
popular culture, 211
Portugal, 164
postcolonial theory and scholarship, 9–10, 24, 119
poverty
 Fröbel heightening public awareness of, 196
 in the *Guckkasten-Bilder*, 156–59
 Playground Movement, 237–38

prayer. *See* hymns and hymnody; religious education and practice
prisoners of war, 100, 249n14
private-public spaces, 5, 10
privileging play, 204–5
professionalization of parenthood, 31, 44, 102–3, 197
 See also parenting
Protestantism: moral issues in Key's rhetoric, 108–9
Protestant play ethic, 22, 235
 activities for alleviating boredom, 133–40
 forming the American imaginary, 150
 influence of Fröbel on, 187–88
 Locke and Gersdorff's theories of play, 31
 paternalistic influences on the child, 32–34
 the path to a productive life, 152–53
 play shaping the character of the adult, 190–91
 preaching piety and teaching play, 34–36
Protestant work ethic, 13, 138, 235
public education
 kindergarten as intermediary between home and, 195
 as state responsibility, 205–6
public play: Playground Movement, 29, 199, 237–38
public space as adult space, 245n63
puppet theater, 111–13
purpose, play with, 244n39

race and racism
 adult-child relationship, 61–62
 in *Auerbach's Kinder-Kalender*, 131–40, 160–61, 179
 blackface minstrels, 219–20
 circus industry, 213
 eugenics and the biological aspects of play, 187–88
 in fantasy landscapes, 164
 "freak" shows, 214–15
 images in word and letter games, 19, 20
 mapping a cognitive landscape onto racial identity, 119

race and racism (*continued*)
   metaphors of freedom with the reality of subjugation, 141–42
   physically constructing racial hierarchies through performative play, 136–37
   racial differences portrayed in *Kinder-Lieder*, 50–51, *51*
   racialization of toy production, 27
   racialization through storytelling, 161–62
   racialized toys and European-American identity, 231–32
   racism disguised as feminism, 205–6
   the significance of cotton and feathers in games, 156–58
   themes of race in Horn's *Dorfgeschichten*, 121–24
   toys creating an imperial identity, 150–52
   Weltmeer and the play world, 165–66
   white-face performers, 213–14
   See also slavery
racial identity, 24–25
reading
   colonizing world supplanting indigenous knowledge, 150–52
   pedagogical value of letter and word games, 18–19
   racial images in word and letter games, 20
   See also literature, children's
realism, 258n55
   lifelike dolls, 229
   marketing toys and dolls, 226–27
   Schoenhut Perfection Art Doll, 228–29
   technical innovation, 228
regimes of value, 16–17
regulatory literature, 74–75
regulatory purpose of play, 156
religious community
   teaching and learning paternal love, 80–81
   Zinzendorf's teachings forming the core of, 57
religious education and practice, 21–22
   Fröbel's model, 193
   inspiration for Schoenhut toys, 27
   Jacobs's stories, 75
   Kinder-Lieder's evangelical narratives, 45–48
   pedagogy as, 11–12
   Pietism and the transatlantic play ethic, 41–42
   the role of women's education in the church, 201–3
   soldier stories, 82
   transformative and reformative qualities, 50–51
   Weber's consideration of work, 13–14
   Wilmsen's cautionary tales, 88–91
   Zinzendorf shifting away from heterodoxy, 12–13
   Zinzendorf's *Enchiridion*, 53–55
   Zinzendorf's life and pedagogical innovations, 51–53
   See also hymns and hymnody; Protestant play ethic
revolution: representation of toys, 94–99
"Revolutions - oder Dreieck-Spiel, Ein" (A revolution or triangle game), 96–97
Ringlein (little ring) game, 154
Robinson Crusoe (Defoe), 44–45
Robinson der Jüngere (Campe), 44–45, 116
Roman Elegies (Goethe), 103–4
Roosevelt, Theodore, 220
Rough Riders, 178
Rousseau, Jean-Jacques, 116, 183–84, 186–87

Sachs, Hans, 61
Safety Day, 227–28, 259n57
sailboats, 228
San Francisco Call newspaper, 28, 236–37
Santo Domingo, 122–23
Sassen, Saskia, 8
Saxton, Alexander, 219
Schäffer, Georg Anton von, 164
Schiller, Friedrich, 4, 93, 94, 95, 97, 244n39
Schlafraum (sleeping space), 3
Schmitt, Carl, 149
Schoenhut, Albert, 27, 256n5, 256n10, 257n39
   death of, 218

history, 209–11, 256n5
Schoenhut advertising gendering toys, 227
US war effort, 258n40
Schoenhut, Albert Friedrich, 209
Schoenhut, Anton, 219
Schoenhut, Frederick, 219
Schoenhut Piano Company, 27, 209, 256n10
Schoenhut Toys, 240, 256n5
  Americanization of masculine play, 227
  gendering citizenship, 222–31
  growth and expansion, 209–10
  Humpty Dumpty Circus, 209–13, 215, 216, 218–20, 231, 234, 240
  Max and Moritz, 182
  Negro Dude, 219, 220, 221, 222
  performativity of whiteness, 214
  performing gender with manufactured toys, 216–18
  pianos, 209–10, 224, 225, 256n10
  racialized toys and dolls, 220, 221, 222, 231–32
  shifting national allegiance, 239–40
  technological innovation and realism, 228
  Teddy's Adventures in Africa, 220, 221
  war effort, 258n40
Schurz, Margarete, 192–93
Second Treatise of Civil Government (Locke), 149–50
Seekatz, Johann Conrad, 117–19
Seele, Ida, 246n40
self-reflection, 76–78
Sembritzki, Emil, 138
servants, children's treatment of, 71–73
Seven Years' War (1756–63), 80–81, 84, 94
Shirreff, Emily (Anne Eliza), 27
  education of women, 201–2
  education reform through kindergarten practices, 199–200
  maternal and paternal roles in the home, 202–4
  national signatures in transnational institutions, 189–90
  philosophical and physical location of the kindergarten, 204
  play and physical exercise, 204

"Simon: Die Lebensgeschichte eines Negersklaven in Brasilien" (Horn), 121–24
"Sing Mama, I Play," 224–25, 225, 227
slavery
  colonized Brazil, 163–64, 166, 173
  Helmar's narratives, 166
  inspiring Zinzendorf's missionary work, 52
  Moravian Brethren, 11–12
  postcolonial examination of childhood and the domestic, 9–10
  the significance of cotton and feathers, 156–58
  space in the American imaginary, 149
  stage performances exploring, 214
  themes of race in Horn's *Dorfgeschichten*, 121–24, 126–30
sleeping space, 63–65
Smithsonian-Roosevelt African Expedition, 220
social class. *See* class divisions
social construct
  childhood as, 36
  gender and play, 216–17
  Schoenhut's circus constructing racial identity, 219–20
socialization
  story cycles modeling, 153–54
  the value of kindergarten for, 199
social life of things, 16–17
social stratification, 31
society roles, toys and child-rearing treatises teaching, 234
socioeconomic status
  in the *Guckkasten-Bilder*, 156–59
  rhetoric of ownership, 36–37
  social dimensions of kindergarten, 199
  See also class divisions
sodomy, 55–56
soldier stories, 80–84
Sonneberg, Germany, 208, 248n23
Spener, Philipp Jakob, 34, 36
Spiekermann, Uwe, 236–37
Spieltrieb (play drive), 4
Spielwelt (play world), 3, 9
spiritual space, 42
Spreckels, Claus, 236–37

Spreckels, John Dietrich, 28, 236–37
Stafford, Margaret, 138
state support: responsibility for education, 205–6
Stauss, Thomas, 96, 120
Steiger, Ernst, 26–27, *122*, *192*, *194*
    activities and skills in the kindergarten curriculum, 255n20
    bringing the German model of play to America, 190–96
    national signatures in transnational institutions, 189–92
    Shirreff's education reform, 199–201
Stetler, Julia, 178
Stewart, Susan, 38
stoicism, 175–78
Storm, Theodor, 141
storytelling
    epistolary nature of Hirschmann's narratives, 159–61
    modeling social behavior, 153–54
    racial differences portrayed in the village story genre, 122–24
    racialization through, 161–62
    white masculinity and indigenous people, 179–80
    See also colonial literature; literature, children's
storytelling uncle, 160–61
Stromer house, 39, 40
Structural Transformation of the Public Sphere (Habermas), 5
Struwwelpeter (Hoffmann), 115
subliminal pedagogy, 12–13
Sugar: A Bittersweet History (Abbott), 236–37
sugar production and consumption, 236–37
Sutton-Smith, Brian, 103–4
"Swanee River," 219–20

Tales of Sleepy Hollow (Irving), 115
teachers
    desirable qualities for kindergarten, 198–99
    learning the use of Fröbel's "gifts," 200–201
Teddy bears, 235
Teddy's Adventures in Africa, 220, *221*

Tenberg, Reinhard, 162
territorialization, 119
textile production, 157
theater
    circuses, 213–14
    puppet theater, 111–13
tobacco, 181
tolle Invalide auf dem Fort Ratonneau, Der (Arnim), 80–81
toy makers, 257n14
    as cultural mediators, 208
    German consumerism, 150–51
    German manufacture of dolls, 172
    industry growth, 257n14
    See also Schoenhut Toys
toy soldiers, 83–84, *93*, *94*, 248n23
transatlantic childhood, 161–62, 204–7
transatlantic play ethic, 41–51
travel narratives, 99–100, 150, 166
Tsanoff, Stoyan Vasil, 29, 238
Turner, Frederick Jackson, 222

Uhde, Fritz von, 185–86, *186*, 191
universal play world, 11
universality of play, 2–3, 4
unsupervised play, 76–78
Unter Deutschen Palmen (Oloukpona-Yinnon), 138–39
upward mobility: regulatory purpose of games, 156–58

Venetian Epigrams (Goethe), 103–5
village story genre, 121–25
Vom Urwald zur Kultur: Erlebniss eines Mädchens (Helmar), 162–63
Vulpius, Christiane, 103–5

Wanamaker, John, 209
warrior culture, 178
war stories, 80–85
war toys and games, *93*, *94*
    the cannon, 102
    the French Revolution inspiring, 96–97
    the guillotine, 99–103, 114
    guns, 227–28
"Watte pusten " (cotton blowing) game, 155–57
Weber, D. Friedrich Benedict, 62

Weber, Max, 13, 16–17, 33
Webster, Mary, 1
Weikle-Mills, Courtney, 151–52
Weir, Lebert H., 240–41
Weissweiler, Eva, 182
Welt in Bildern, Die (Chakkalakal), 132
Weltmeer (world sea), 165–66
Werther (Goethe), 109–10
westward expansion, 117, 215, 222
white-faced clowns, 213–14
whiteness, German
    comparing white masculinity with Indian culture, 178
    construction a new racial identity abroad, 165–67, 174
    cotton and feathers as metaphors, 156
    exotic nature of circus shows, 213–14
    the German transnational childhood and white identity, 161–62
    justification of slavery, 11–12
    Protestant depiction of, 51
    racialized colonial stories defining, 25, 124, 131, 138, 140, 152
    reinventing and reimagining, 9–10
    white supremacy in Knecht Ruprecht, 144–48
wild children
    children's treatment of servants, 72–73
    dire outcomes, 115, 182
    Gersdorff's son, 36
    Max and Moritz, 153, 182
    parenting through cautionary tales, 23–24, 88–92
Wild West Shows, 174, 177–78, 215
Wilmsen, Friedrich Philip, 23–24, 88–91
Winnebago people, 175–77
"Wochenstube, Die" (Chodowiecki), *60*

Woltersdorf, Ernst Gottlieb, 22, 42–43, *45*, 45–48, *51*
women
    admiration for American Indians, 177–78
    education of, 201–4, 246n16
    play spaces as women's jurisdiction, 32
    See also gender; motherhood
wooden toys, 188–89, 208
word games, 18–19, *20*
work ethic. *See* Protestant work ethic
worlding, 10–11
world's fairs and exhibitions, 222
World War I, 230
    postwar models of play, 239–40
    Schoenhut's role in the war effort, 258n40

yoyos, 96, *97*, 103–8, 114

Zantop, Susanne, 140
Ziemann, Grete, 141–42
Zinzendorf, Christian Renatus von, 55–56, 247n53
Zinzendorf, Nikolaus Ludwig Count von, 21–22, 48
    Herrnhut settlement, 51–53
    the importance of free play, 56–57
    Moravian Brethren, 41–44
    moving education away from religious instruction, 11–12
    tying authority to emotion, 53–54
zodiacal representations, 117–19, 131–40
Zoffany, Johann, 1, *2*, 22, 225
Zornado, Joseph, 7
"Zuckerfee, Die" (The Sugar Fairy), 237
zwölf Monatsbilder: Januar, Die (Seekatz), 117–19, *118*

www.ingramcontent.com/pod-product-compliance
Lightning Source LLC
Chambersburg PA
CBHW022037290426
44109CB00014B/885